Secure from Rash Assault

Secure from Rash Assault

Sustaining the Victorian Environment

James Winter

UNIVERSITY OF CALIFORNIA PRESS

Berkeley · Los Angeles · London

University of California Press
Berkeley and Los Angeles, California

University of California Press, Ltd.
London, England

©1999 by
The Regents of the University of California

Library of Congress Cataloging-in-Publication Data

Winter, James H., 1925–

    Secure from Rash Assault : Sustaining the
Victorian environment / James Winter.
      p. cm.
    Includes bibliographic references (p.   ) and
index.
    ISBN 0-520-21609-1 (alk. paper)
    1. Human ecology—Great Britain—History—
19th century. 2. Nature—effect of human
beings on—Great Britain.   I. Title.
GF551.W56 1999
333.7′13′094109034—dc21   98-43970

Printed in the United States of America
9 8 7 6 5 4 3 2 1

Contents

List of Illustrations   vii

Preface   ix

Introduction   1

1. Innovation and Continuity   7
2. The Cultural Landscape   19
3. Lowland Fields   40
4. Upland Moors   62
5. Woods and Trees   83
6. Cutting New Channels   104
7. Holes   124
8. Heaps   143
9. The City in the Country   166
10. Greening the City   189
11. The Environment of Leisure   209
12. The Hungry Ocean   231

Conclusion   249

List of Abbreviations   259

Notes   261

Bibliography   309

Index   333

Illustrations

1. Portable Petroleum Motor   14
2. George Perkins Marsh   30
3. Combined Thresher and Finisher   46
4. Steam Cultivation in Sutherland   75
5. Tree Felling by Machinery   92
6. Excavating Scoop   116
7. The Great Subsidence   128
8. Manchester from Kersall Moor   154
9. Lake Thirlmere Becoming a Reservoir   185
10. Poor Woman's Roof Garden   201
11. Ladies' Golf Championship at Portrush, Ireland   226
12. Bucket-and-Ladder Dredging Machine   239

Preface

Our ship reached Southampton late in the day. Numbed and disoriented, foliage scratching against the canvas overhead, we twisted down country lanes until the convoy of trucks came to a halt. The tailgate dropped, and we jumped down stiffly into blackness, stumbled to a Nissen hut, and shivered under mounds of blankets until the first pale light and the sergeant's whistle. In a white mist, we were counted, given a breakfast of sorts, lined up two by two, and sent off on a long hike to improve our morale and muscle tone. The line of march led down deep-cut lanes hedged with yew to Middle Wallop, its houses thatched and gathered cozily together, and, a bit further on, to Over Wallop with its ancient parish church. Then we turned north and west into Wiltshire and the eastern edge of the Salisbury Plain. In that one morning we passed from village clusters and bounded fields following along a calmly moving stream out to the edges of an unbounded world of open, rolling, gently sculpted downs and wolds—the images I had brought with me across the Atlantic made so completely, so immediately, manifest!

How I perceived those landscapes had little to do with experience. There was no "landscape" in the flat land where I grew up—or so my culture told me. There might, perhaps, be "countryside," but only in the most literal sense: large rectangular cornfields, isolated barns and sober farmhouses, roads pointing straight to the horizon. No footpaths led walkers across fields from one settled place to another. Travel between towns would most likely be by private car. Motorists left town gradually, entering the surrounding country past ragged roadside developments. A steady accumulation of billboards, Burma-Shave signs, gas stations, taverns, and scruffy fringe enterprises then guided travelers toward the next town and its center. As students of the region have noted, that center would seldom be a communal green or an imposing building, whether sacred or profane, but Main Street—lined with red brick shops at ground level with a floor or two of offices above. Towns like mine seemed to have been built by and for people who were always prepared to move on. If I close my eyes, I can summon up individual houses: large, wooden ones with deep front porches, expanses of green—the whole framed by huge elms and oaks—but I have difficulty picturing the community and its surrounding countryside as a distinct place, in finding mental images that enable me to set my hometown apart from any other in that level and, to my eyes, undifferentiated expanse of geography.

Thus I was led or conditioned to look elsewhere for landscape, to New England, but especially to old England. Home and school provided a compact cultural amalgam: Wordsworth's *Tintern Abbey* and *Michael*, Gray's *Elegy*, a cluster of novels and stories: *Tess, The Mayor of Casterbridge, Wuthering Heights, Silas Marner, The Railway Children*. But the image that returns to me with particular force is a paperweight on a study bookshelf. Fastened to the bottom of this half-sphere was a section from Samuel Palmer's *The Sleeping Shepherd*. If one narrowed one's eyes and peered long enough through the thick glass, the figure of the shepherd in the foreground sunshine would take on an extra dimension. His head resting on his hand, a yellow straw hat on his head, he reclines, his feet and one of his legs disappearing into loose, golden hay. Lulled by warmth and quiet, he dozes. Close by his flock stands grazing, the flow of their fleeces and bodies anticipating and blending with the undulating russet grassland above and beyond. The young tender of sheep is part of this finished land: hills and valleys shaped by nature but cultivated over the centuries by a long partnership between animals and their keepers. Rest, fruitful harmony, coherence, continuity—these were what I had been prepared, consciously and unconsciously, to look for. And those virtues were, not surprisingly, what I found and, at that troubled moment in world history, responded to with all my heart.

Since that icy November morning, so many years ago, when "actual" and symbolic landscapes seemed to converge, I have learned to approach British landscapes with more circumspection. William Hoskins's *The Making of the English Landscape* suggested to me, as it has to so many others, that in order to read a landscape in any depth, the reader must isolate and examine the many themes, notice how and when they were introduced, and observe the intricate way they were woven into harmonious compositions. An afternoon spent on a New Hampshire hillside with an ecologist, Herbert Bormann, tracing root grafts in a grove of hemlocks, gave that metaphor of the intricately fashioned web a new dimension and did so only a few years before Rachel Carson's *Silent Spring* shocked almost everyone of my generation with its revelations about the way modern technology can work below the surface to corrupt these harmonies. Further study taught me to treat even the concept of harmony with caution and to recognize what escaped me so completely on that first encounter with the British countryside: that every landscape is an ambiguous and layered text whose meaning will alter with the culture as well as the political and social circumstance of the reader. Thus surface tensions will be apparent, in the author as well as the subject, between an awareness that a countryside must be a living and therefore a changing entity and a desire to preserve that image of beauty, order, and community, formed so early in my imagination.

Two geographers, John Robinson and Graeme Wynn, gave me an idea of what it means to be an environmental historian. Other friends and associates made criticisms, spotted errors, suggested refinements, offered encouragement: Dianne Newell, Thomas Blom, Robert Kubicek, Anne Gorsuch, Robert Allen, James Huzell, Ruth Richardson, Peter Bailey, Beryl Morphet, Jean and Roderick Barman, Allen Sinel, Peter Ward, Christopher Friedrichs, Michela Sorrentino, Matteo Hermani, Robert Winter. To all of these worthies and especially to my wife and confederate, Pierrette, I am greatly in debt and offer thanks.

Introduction

While workmen, entrepreneurs, inventors, and engineers were discovering new ways to apply the power of steam, a number of individuals began, at the beginning of the Victorian era, to voice alarm about the consequences of releasing so potent a force upon fragile nature. In 1848, when the second paroxysm of railway speculation was just beginning to subside, the noted geographer Mary Somerville confessed to having been astonished by the "successive convulsions" the "application of the powers of nature to locomotion" had caused. In her *Physical Geography*, she predicted that the new communication technology would radically shift the power balance toward man and away from nature, a shift that would force people to reconsider "the relationship between man and animate beings."[1]

This new relationship was the subject of Thomas Carlyle's "Signs of the Times," published some two decades earlier. Armed not only with steam but also with all manner of artifice, engineer mountain movers were, he announced, emerging everywhere victorious from their "war with rude nature." He announced that a new "Age of Machinery" had arrived and was consolidating its gains: "Nothing is now done directly, or by hand; all is by rule and calculated contrivance. For the simplest operation, some helps and accompaniments, some cunning abbreviating process is in readiness. Our old modes of exertion are all discredited and thrown aside." Increasingly calculated contrivances would, he thought, make sure that "nothing follows its spontaneous course."[2]

As we near the end of a millennium, pundits among us are similarly inclined toward prophecy; some of it hopeful, some angst-ridden. Either way, one notices that these predictions usually assume, as did those of Somerville and Carlyle, that technology, and the cast of mind that causes people to embrace it or at least accept it as inevitable, must transform society and its mechanisms as well as the material environment.

One example will suffice: an academic task force at one large North American university recently advised colleagues to recognize that "technological innovation is transforming education and exercising a significant influence on almost every aspect of daily life, including our leisure and cultural activities." This memorandum then expands on how computers are making jobs less office-centered; how they are reversing the long migration from the country to the city; how they, along with the use of automation, are undermining expectations of long-term employment and placing a premium on those skills that allow for occupational mobility; how they are rapidly constructing an electronic global village, a multicultural environment that will require that more attention be paid to cross-cultural studies and to foreign language training. Even in these post-Marxist times, it would seem, the proposition that the superstructure must eventually reflect changes in the material base can still be taken as a given.

The usual objections to this simplistic theory of causation will be raised in what follows. However, the focus will not be on a generalized future but on a particular past. Central to the enterprise will be a search for an answer to a question William Wordsworth posed in 1844 on hearing that engineers intended to build a railway line from Kendal to Windermere—into the heart of his beloved Lake District. Two lines of the sonnet he wrote on that occasion ask, "Is then no nook of English ground secure / From rash assault?"

Retrospect permits an answer but assures that it cannot be a straightforward yes or no. The sudden advent of new tools and methods for transforming and controlling nature, most of them worked out and applied first in Britain, did provide, directly or indirectly, the means and incentive to make large alterations and to do so almost everywhere. These mechanisms did not, of course, operate in a social, economic, or demographic vacuum. Intrusions into the fabric of landscapes and land surfaces happened when human beings were replicating at a dramatic pace relative to almost every other form of animate life, when the population scale shifted from rural to urban, when British entrepreneurs and manufacturers were leading the world in the process of industrialization, and when British farmers were providing a model for those who wished to exploit land intensively. Under those circumstances, few nooks were likely to remain completely secure. There can also be no doubt that areas of English, Welsh, Scottish, and Irish ground were indeed rashly assaulted and left in ruins during the age of steam.

The forces of change were formidable enough. Almost everywhere in the island kingdom formerly self-contained ecological systems needed to react to the pull of urban centers and to those distant markets around the globe that had been opened by a revolution in communications technology. Localities responded by specializing their land uses, exporting water, minerals, and energy and adapting to the influx of artificial products from the outside world.

Nevertheless, what strikes us is the degree of continuity in the Victorian land and landscape—the continually shifting balances that were worked out—not the amount of change. As subsequent chapters will attempt to show, Victorian and Edwardian arable agriculture remained "ecologically benign," as did woodlands, which resisted large-scale coniferization and, as a consequence, retained much of their ecological complexity. Concentrations of industrial blight were confined and closely hemmed in with natural scenery, and experiments were made in restoring derelict sites. Popular tourism transformed areas of the seacoast without inflicting serious damage on the hinterland. The process of greening cityscapes advanced at the same time as the country was leaving the city. Overall, a distinctive and celebrated landscape retained its health and unique beauty.

No single, overarching, theoretical strategy will be employed to explain why these tensions could be balanced during a time when "steam" became a metaphor for artifice and innovation of every kind—cultural as well as technological. Offered instead will be a complex of factors that, coming together and interacting, created in Britain (to borrow a rotund phrase from Oliver MacDonagh) "a peculiar concatenation of circumstances in the nineteenth century." [3]

One of these circumstances was the capacity to lead the rest of Europe in draining resources from less industrially developed parts of the world. The fact of empire, "the empire of free trade," also allowed Britain to use steamships and steam locomotives to export at least some of its environmental damage. In that sense, the new technology acted as a domestic conservator. We see this clearly in the agricultural and forestry sectors. Yet, paradoxically, this technology also assisted in developing a sheep-grazing monoculture on rough upland pastures, thus adding to the forces that were depleting a meager stock of soil nutrients on upland hillsides.

By way of balance, these new forms of transport helped to promote highly intensive and, at the same time, sustainable arable farming. This achievement, surely one of early and mid-Victorian Britain's most impressive, was brought about, not primarily by mechanization (steam or otherwise) or specialization, but by sophisticated crop rotation and a mixed-farming regime that relied heavily on the use of animal fertilizers and on skilled labor to increase productivity. This labor gave polish to the fields. Hedgerows in such a farming regime retained their utility and remained arguably the single most distinguishing feature of the "traditional" British (especially English) visual landscape—a landscape that had actually been remade in the seventeenth and eighteenth centuries.

As the first chapter will argue, some of the inherent limitations of steam machinery must be added to the factors that caused this landscape to retain much of its variety and characteristic pattern. To a certain extent because of these limitations, agriculture, forestry, mining, and quarrying never were as fully rationalized as enthusiasts for applying the model of advanced industry to those sectors would have wished. Furthermore the inflexibility of rail transport, the prime mover of popular tourism (itself the product of rapid urban growth and some relaxation of work discipline), directed the flow of day trippers and vacationers along narrow channels to resorts and recreation grounds built purposely for leisure.

Yet it would be difficult to find a single instance in which technological advances alone are sufficient to explain either change or continuity. Mechanisms worked inside cultural contexts that, more often than not, valued customary ways and familiar vistas. Because, for example, so few owned so much of the land surface and rented or leased it out to capitalist employers of labor, an elite could remain at some distance from day-to-day encounters with the exploitation process. Being interested in using their estates to sustain their social and political privileges as well as to line their pockets, squires and aristocrats often promoted efficiency, yet resisted making that value into an obsession. "Improvement" and amateurism remained restlessly companionate. Most landowners responded in ambivalent ways to the idea that the soil they had responsibility for arranging or the products their tenants produced from it were simply commodities. When opportunities opened, landowners were quick to accept offers from mining or quarrying interests who wanted to dig up parts of their properties, even though all parties to such agreements knew that, when leases expired, the land to be repossessed would be seriously ravaged. But sometimes estate owners did go to considerable lengths to repair the visual and ecological damage left behind.

Landlords could afford to behave this way because, in many cases, their income sources were diversified. Their investments would probably include resource-exploiting ventures located in one or another part of the direct and indirect empire. Given these circumstances, it is hardly surprising that they were more inclined to listen attentively to the estate gamekeeper than to the estate forester, especially when cheap, easily available foreign softwood made heavy investment in the latest silviculture methods problematic.

Paternalistic attitudes toward the estate and its surroundings, including the animate and inanimate inhabitants, were perfectly compatible with a sentimental attitude toward nature—a sense that particular trees, woods, streams, and valleys had intrinsic value, that they were infused, as Wordsworth perceived them, with a "deep power of joy." Preservationists—those who wanted to protect nature from exploitation—were the lifeblood of the opposition to what they usually described as ruthless utilitarianism, by which they meant the impulse to systematize, rationalize, standardize, innovate, and develop. Conservationists—those who would control exploitation, limit waste, and increase productivity in sustainable ways—had a part to play but tended not to stand at the barricades or supply the rhetoric. Surface tensions could be contained or counteracted as well as they were because sense and sensibility so often interacted. It seems evident then that consideration of one aspect of the changing face of Britain must lead, although seldom in a straightforward way, to a consideration of all the others.

The argument that follows will have a topography that conforms to the folds and undulations found in so much of the British countryside. Straight lines will not converge to a clearly discernible, distant horizon as they might in Kansas or Saskatchewan. At the outset, we approach a complex of pathways, and as we stride along, we note that we are moving forward through familiar countryside, never losing sight of where we have been. We ask ourselves why there seems to be so much continuity and for a while follow one of the many lines of explanation: the social, cultural, and geographic limitations on the use of new machinery and the intrinsic limitations of steam power itself. But then we remind ourselves that reciprocal relationships always exist between culture and technological innovation. Farther on, we pause to ask about the attitudes Victorians held about the environment and wonder why British subjects should have been alert and concerned about the role of humans in geo-morphology when posted abroad but relatively complacent about such matters when safe at home.

Around the next corner lie lowland fields, beyond them highland moors, and then woods and trees. In these places the themes of ecological balance and imbalance come directly into view. Machinery, its potential and its limitations, provides the pathway and directs us to a discussion of projects where railway and canal builders experimented with the use of mechanical power to dig into the earth and pile up the leavings. We notice how rail transportation affected travelers' perceptions of the countryside as it flashed by. Leaving behind cuttings and embankments, we discover other, more toxic, heaps—and some of the holes they arose from. We perceive the effects on the earth's surface of the methods miners and quarrymen used to extract salt, slate, and granite. Then we enter into the Black Country and the Lower Swansea Valley to observe how reformers attempted to deal with the blemishes, scars, and poisons mines and smelters inflicted on the land. We look for balance there between dereliction and reclamation but are able to locate only a few uncoordinated attempts to bring about such a difficult reconciliation.

We will need to look closely at the next turn to discover the connections between railway building, the concentration of industry in cities, urban density and urban expansion, the need for cities to reach out into the country to dispose of wastes and tap new supplies of water, the consequent birth of the organized countryside protection movement, and the campaign by reformers to return green nature to ever more congested urban centers.

After that, the track leads, as it must in an island kingdom, to the seashore. We will note how steam transport concentrated at spots along the coast much of the rapidly developing popular recreation industry. A brief digression will allow us to factor in advances in the making of concrete and show how recreation and construction interests raised the level of concern about ocean defenses and stimulated a search for ways to prevent coastal erosion. These destination resorts and their defenses will remind us of what we have noticed before only in passing: that tourists and tourism were beginning to enter into serious competition with farmers, foresters, grazers, diggers, and developers for the use of the land. In each case, we will measure the tensions these developments and innovations created against the forces of containment and balance. Finally, at journey's end, we will reflect on the direction our chosen path has taken.

1
Innovation and Continuity

Yet, how late in the world's history was ushered in the era
when mind, by the aid of the steam-engine, commenced its
most glorious triumph over matter.

Thomas Craddock,
The Chemistry of the Steam Engine, *1847*

In a poem he wrote in 1873, called "Old Ruralities," Alfred Tennyson's
brother, Charles (Tennyson) Turner, acknowledged technology's recent
triumph over material nature but, not inclined to celebrate, chose "Regrets" for his subtitle. He asked his readers to recall the "busy sound of
the slip-shouldered flail," "[h]eath-bells," the spinning-wheel's hum "far
down in yon valley," the "unshorn hedgerow," and invited them to reflect
that these once-familiar aspects of country life had now become "relics"
from a time before the "boom of science" shook the countryside apart:

> Ah! sweet old world! thou speedest fast away!
> My boyhood world! but all last looks are dear;
> More touching is the death-bed than the bier![1]

We tend to smile: the amiable poet-squire may have shared the valley with
the "poor man" who threshed his grain by hand, with "old Alice" and
her "hatch and house-leek," and with the spinner at her wheel, but he
did not share their poverty or the monotony of their work. Still, it is only
the most hard-eyed among us who cannot be touched by evocations of
a more natural world somewhere long ago.

Jacquetta Hawkes, who wrote with feeling about Britain's material
past, thought there was substance beneath this kind of nostalgia. In *A
Land,* written in the wake of the Second World War, she claimed that

the relationship between land and people reached its greatest moment of intimacy in the century before the steam era fully arrived.

> By the middle of the eighteenth century men had triumphed, the land was theirs, but had not yet been subjected and outraged. Wildness had been pushed back to the mountains, where now for the first time it could safely be admired. Communications were good enough to bind the country in unity lacking since it was a Roman province, but were not yet so easy as to have destroyed locality and the natural freedom of the individual that remoteness freely gives. Rich men and poor men knew how to use the stuff of their countryside to raise comely buildings and to group them with instinctive grace. Town and country having grown up together to serve one another's needs now enjoyed a moment of balance.[2]

The first to accept responsibility for having destroyed this "achievement—the unfaltering fitness and beauty of everything"—were the Victorians themselves, and particularly the intelligentsia: the novelists, poets, painters, philosophers, social theorists, and socially conscious journalists. During the period of early industrialization, their predecessors had composed a counterpoint between pride at the growing capacity to change the face of the land and alarm at the disappearance of familiar contours and features. Tensions between these two emotions intensified when, in the 1820s and 1830s, engineers found ways to apply steam power to transport. Some residents of the countryside, particularly in the Raveloes and Helstones of the rural south, might go on enjoying for many years the gentle harmonies of village life; yet even in those quiet places people were becoming aware that what Lewis Mumford called a "widespread perversion and destruction of the environment" was underway in parts of the homeland, particularly in the Midlands and north.[3] By the 1840s, when mine developers and railway navvies began invading previously unblemished regions, only those on the fringes could remain oblivious to the changes being imposed on the landscape. George Eliot concludes *Middlemarch* with the arrival of a railway survey team at the town's outskirts, a harbinger of the new order.

About the time of the 1851 Crystal Palace Exhibition (Mumford called it paleotechnic industry's "cock-crow of triumph"[4]), there seems to have been a noticeable shift in the mood of artists and other recorders of change. Fewer paintings and poems celebrated the transforming power of steam and speed. Some midcentury artists and writers joined Charles Turner in expressing their regret at the loss of landscape beauty, their indignation at the pollution of the air, the lakes, the rivers.[5] Those whose perceptions were influenced by the writings of Ruskin and Carlyle assumed that a steam-driven juggernaut of great destructive power was rolling through the cultural and psychic landscapes as rapidly as through the physical. For most writers, the prospect of a mechanized landscape was a nightmare, not something to be welcomed as a visual sign of the achievement of world peace and domestic harmony. They predicted that mobile machinery, given volcanic strength by steam, would sap nature of its vitality and convert the countryside into a dull, uniform, monotonous, rationalized, geometrically apportioned, polluted wasteland.[6]

Critics of laissez-faire capitalism, ranging in degrees of radicalism from left to right, deplored the unrestrained workings of the cash nexus or the need of industrial capitalism to turn nature into merchandise. A Manchester cotton manufacturer, Friedrich Engels, argued that this kind of arrogance was to be expected so long as the prevailing ideology embraced "energetic self-assertiveness, unembarrassed by too many moral or aesthetic sentiments."[7] William Morris also reacted to the ugliness at the heart of industrial society, as did Dickens, Gaskell, Ruskin, Carlyle, Pugin, and, at least when writing *Sibyl,* Disraeli. Society had, they charged, ravaged and defiled the countryside in a fit of greed.

Optimists granted that this degradation was real but asserted their faith that the advance of science and technology would repair the damage once the progress of rationalization had educated entrepreneurs to see that wasting resources worked against their own interests. Pessimists, on the other hand, questioned this deeply entrenched assumption that human beings could continue to advance material civilization while remaining faithful stewards of God's providence. Both persuasions did agree, however, that manipulating the landscape could have, at least in the short run, appalling consequences: whole regions denuded, pitted, and blackened; green countryside paved with brick and stone; the air of industrial cities laden with noxious chemicals and fermenting putrefaction. One young Oxford undergraduate recalled how John Ruskin, Slade Professor of the History of Art in 1870, had, during a lecture, held up a picture by J. M. W. Turner of a charming rural landscape. It depicted an ancient stone bridge over a sparkling stream. Picking up a palette and a brush, Ruskin painted over the drawing's covering glass. He gave the old bridge hideous iron girders and diverted the stream into a power source for a monstrous mill, its stack billowing smoke and obscuring the sun. Then, turning the picture to his listeners and pausing for them to consider the transformation, he pronounced in a dramatic voice: "That is what you are doing with your scenery."[8]

More than a century later, we still occasionally blame Victorian cap-

italists for having been "litter louts on the grand scale" and for having
made the proposition that "muck equals money" the "unquestioned
equation" of the age.[9] However, our tone of superiority seems to have
moderated as we began to note the effects of our more sophisticated technology on land surfaces and the earth's biosphere—more destructive by
far than anything even imagined before.[10] When bulldozers dug into the
hedgerows to prepare the terrain for the great machines of later twentieth century industrial agriculture, when government incentives encouraged the conversion of upland pasture and lowland meadow to arable
farming, and when government agencies and faceless insurance company landlords established "gloomy timber factories"[11] on hill and dale,
it became obvious that the technology of food and fiber production since
the Second World War was recasting a traditional countryside that had
evolved over two centuries.[12]

Sir John Clapham was struck by the contrast between the disruptive
effect of twentieth century technology on the shape of the land and the
comparatively mild effect of technological advances during the previous
century. Writing in 1926, he remarked on the high degree of continuity
in the nineteenth century landscape. He imagined how the British Isles
would have appeared to someone given the power to soar above the land
at the beginning of Victoria's reign, again at midcentury, and finally at
the time of the Jubilee in 1887. Clearly visible on the first two flights
would have been the fresh gashes and raw brick embankments and
viaducts made by the railway. By the last one, this line of damage would
have "sunk into the landscape, like the road and the canal before it."
Evidence of the continuing encroachment of the town into the surrounding countryside would have been clearly visible in 1887, as would
the dark stains left behind here and there when mines and factories became derelict. If the flight pattern were high enough over the Pennines
or the Scottish Highlands to make railway lines into tiny threads, the observer would still have had the feeling, over that open, upland country,
that "solitude could be found without much seeking." "The broad visual impression," Clapham concluded, would have been of a landscape
that had changed surprisingly little over the fifty years "since Cobbett
rode about baying at tax-eaters and Scotchmen and pitying the fortunes
of the poor."[13]

Continuity was certainly not what earthbound Victorians perceived.
At least the articulate among them were impressed instead by how much
the environment of their childhood had altered. Britain, it was often

said, had entered a new age, the age of steam and nothing would ever again be the same.

There was, of course, much more to the steam age than steam energy, steam machinery, and steam locomotion. In a few deft paragraphs of *The Unbound Prometheus,* David Landes traced the fuguelike relationship between a complex of technological advances.[14] Discovery of how to use coal and coke to make high-quality iron and steel led collieries to follow seams deeper into the earth. To do this, they needed to purchase steam pumping engines, which required the precisely tooled cylinders the metal-working industry was learning to manufacture. Entrepreneurs then grouped increasingly efficient condensing engines together in factories. In doing so, they worked out techniques for coordinating production and exploiting labor more efficiently. Meanwhile, others were discovering how to make artificial alkali, acids, dyes, cement, and fertilizers—in the process, using immense quantities of coal directly or indirectly. Chemicals, stone, clay, and metal products, machines, and textiles then reached ever-expanding world markets, carried, part way at least, by steam, but directed by telegraph and expedited by increasingly professional accounting procedures, financial services, and marketing and exchange mechanisms, each one of these technologies shaping and stimulating the other—with significant and often unanticipated effects on the land and landscape. Thus when commentators spoke about the anticipated revolutionary effects of steam locomotion, they usually had in mind not just one but a cluster of technologies.

A pamphleteer predicted in 1833 that the nation stood on the eve of a "total revolution in the domestic relations of society." He thought that existing barriers to change, being challenged by the "Restless Spirit of Discontent" then abroad in the land, would be swept aside by the unprecedented breakthrough in communications technology: steam transport was about to bring a tide of foreign food to Britain's shores; landlords and tenants would be forced to respond by substituting steam engines for horses on their farms, releasing enough grain to feed 4,800,000 people; ancient inequalities would disappear incrementally as, for the first time in history, production adjusted itself to consumption in an economy of plenty.[15]

What actually happened did not, as Asa Briggs has noted, fulfill the prophecies of future peace and plenty or of widespread ugliness and ruin.[16] An imperfect, constantly shifting balance was maintained between contending land uses. That meant that a considerable degree of

continuity in the landscape could be maintained throughout a period
when an industrial civilization became established, when steam and cognate technologies became diffused throughout the economy, when the
population expanded rapidly and became preponderately urban, and
when governments exercised so little control.

Although not put forward as anything like a complete explanation,
the point keeps emerging that the steam engine had intrinsic limitations.
It was by no means the only mover and shaper in the age of steam; but,
if there was such a thing as a "prime mover" during Victorian and Edwardian times, then the steam engine was surely it. In spite of the rapid
development of new energy sources in the last quarter of the century,
steam machinery supplied ninety-two percent of Great Britain's primary
power in 1911.[17] Therefore an assessment of the steam engine's limitations must be included among the complex of factors preventing what
Mumford called "carboniferous capitalism" from fully mechanizing and
rationalizing agriculture and the extractive industries. Also, as we will
see later, these limitations help to explain why a popular recreation industry could expand without seriously corroding the rural environment.

The possibilities, not the limitations, of steam locomotion were what
impressed the great railway pioneer George Stephenson. He gave the
name "Rocket" to the engine he entered in the famous contest at Rain-
hill to convey the idea that the steam engine on rails promised speed of an
extraterrestrial kind. Later, when prototypes developed into the working
locomotives and traction engines of midcentury, there was a tendency to
choose names that expressed godlike might and power rather than swift-
ness. Charles Turner used that image in these lines from his "Greatness of
England," composed in 1864:

> Full long ere Europe knew the iron road,
> The 'Railway' thunder'd on our English soil;
> There was a trembling in the sea-girt isle,
> Where 'Hercules' or mighty 'Samson' trod,
> Heavy and swift; for Nature bore our yoke
> Far earlier than elsewhere.[18]

Hindsight suggests a more prosaic reading. Only with difficulty could
Goliath, who caused the whole isle to tremble when he moved, be asked
to perform delicate tasks. Engineers managed to reduce inefficiencies:
they lightened steam engines and vehicles, decreased their bulk, adapted
them to new tasks, improved their fuel economy, made them quicker to
start and easier to operate and maintain. Impressive though these inno-

vations were, engineers never managed to make the steam engine flexible enough to displace animal and human skills or to move cheaply and easily into every corner of the workshop, quarry, mine, forest, field, home, and landscape.[19]

Stationary alternating steam engines were costly to construct, service, and house; heavy power users like textiles and other enterprises whose operations allowed for a concentration of machinery around the power source were the first to employ them. Steamboats were immediately successful because the weight, hunger, and thirst of their engines were not a serious inhibition. Where the manufacturing process called for a disbursal of power sources and intermittent use, as in iron and engineering trades, the smaller engines, designed to meet that need, proved to be inefficient and labor hungry.[20] Heaviness and lack of flexibility were even more of an impediment in agriculture. In 1908, only about one in ten farms of fifty acres or more had a wide enough range of uses for power to afford to install a fixed engine. Such an engine could not easily be turned on and off, needed frequent cleaning and lubrication, and was most economical when harnessed to perform many functions simultaneously.[21]

Locomotives and traction engines needed ready and inexpensive access to large supplies of coal and water and also needed expensive tracks or surfaces to bear their weight. Because, compared to other movers, they had a low ratio of power production to size and weight, they were most efficient when run at a steady pace and not required to start, speed up, slow down, or stop often.[22] Thus the failure to develop steam road vehicles to rival railways cannot be attributed entirely to a conspiracy on the part of turnpike, coaching, canal, or railway interests. Inventors sometimes succeeded in scaling down steam engines to a size suitable for agricultural tractors, lawn mowers, portable timber saws, delivery vehicles, toys, even aircraft engines; but most of these items were insufficiently light and adaptable to meet the demand from smaller operators for versatility and low maintenance costs.[23] (See Figure 1.)

This is not to claim that the peculiar characteristics of a technical apparatus determine how and when it will be used. Cultural preferences, social and political considerations, as well as consumer demand or the search for profit supply the context and always affect decisions about which power source should be chosen.[24] Jeremy Adelman notes how differently wheat growers on the Argentine pampas and on the Canadian prairies—regions with so many environmental similarities—responded to mechanization. He concludes that property relationship was the decisive factor; that technology, far from being an exogenous

Figure 1. Portable petroleum motor (1889). Promoters of this coal oil (kero-
sene) engine noted these advantages over a steam equivalent: lightweight fuel,
no boiler, no hot ashes, sparkless, activates in moments, needs little attention.
(*Engineering* 47, 1889)

force, was only a dependent variable.[25] Nathan Rosenberg has also reminded us that improvements in technique, even spectacular ones, seldom translate into "the texture of the economy" immediately or in an
uncomplicated, direct, or predictable way.[26] As we will see, steam enthusiasts often ignored costs in their desire to innovate or in their compulsion simply to test a machine's limits. Some hirers of labor clung to
traditional technologies out of habit, concern for the social consequences of abandoning them, or respect for the skills they had called
into being.

Custom and aesthetic considerations often restrained innovation. For
example, cheap barbed wire for fencing came on the market in America
around 1880 but did not appear in European landscapes to any extent
until decades later.[27] Sentiment and social conscience might delay the
diffusion of technological innovations or cause innovations to be applied
inappropriately. But decisions to cling to older ways might be, in certain

circumstances, "rational" in the sense of being based on the careful calculation of economic advantage—hence, for example, the continued importance throughout the century of the waterwheel and the sailing vessel.[28] After commenting on the love affair that blossomed early in the twentieth century between the American public and the automobile, Eugene Ferguson warns against rushing to the conclusion "that our use of technology is somehow rational, guided by objective assessment of advantages and disadvantages and of good and evil."[29]

Leo Marx found at the heart of American culture tension between an ideal of the garden (either primitive and unspoiled or cultivated and pastoral) and an almost visceral attraction to the machine. According to his formulation, as the nation industrialized, the real and the ideal tended to lose points of contact, the pastoral being increasingly consigned to nature "reservations."[30] The tension, which kept building between the ideal and the real, was eventually resolved by "compartmentalizing" treasured garden spaces into parks, protected deserts and forests, front lawns, back gardens, golf courses, gardenesque suburbs, and the exurban countryside. The rest of the landscape was left to technology, blatantly expressed after the arrival of automobilism, by the proliferation of parking lots, strip developments, shopping malls, industrial estates, superhighways, and the countryside of monoculture—littered with power lines, telephone poles, communication dishes, and tourist attractions, its former calm punctured by the roar of diesel trucks and jet aircraft.[31]

It is possible to think of the British landscape of the nineteenth century as the mirror opposite of what America and much of the industrialized world have become. Held in check by the steam engine's intrinsic limitations and restrained by hostile forces in the British culture (stronger in the south than in the north), the new technologies failed to transform agriculture and the extractive industries.[32] The state did not stand in the way of mechanization, steam or otherwise. On the contrary, it repressed Luddism and placed few restrictions on innovation or technology transfer. Nevertheless, it saw no need to force the pace of agricultural mechanization and was far slower than France or Germany to support research or advanced training in agricultural science and silviculture.

Generally speaking, the improving initiative was left to tenant farmers and landed proprietors who concentrated their effort on increasing the productivity of their soil through crop rotation systems and careful use of animal wastes rather than concentrating it on mechanization. Thus the method of landholding served to check industrialization throughout the century.

Despite franchise reforms, the landlord interest was able to deflect most of the pressures to reorganize the structure of agriculture. The Liberal victory of 1906, Lloyd George's budget of 1909, the demotion of the House of Lords in 1911, rising labor costs, and, most important, the slump and then the stagnation of rents did eventually upset the status quo; but until then, the government left control over the countryside to landowners and tenant farmers, who were (with numerous exceptions and often at a considerable human cost) faithful stewards of the land and of traditional landscape values. This meant that the disparity between the real world of advancing industrialism and urbanization and the ideal, fixed in the national psyche by romantic literature and art,[33] was not as dramatic as Ruskin and like-minded artists and intellectuals portrayed it.

Steam and the technologies associated with it were disturbing agents, but they were healers and protectors as well. It is a fairly easy task to list the credits and losses to land surfaces and amenities. The difficulty comes when it is time to assign values and to draw up accounts. The intensive, highly capitalized, sustainable agriculture of early and mid-Victorian times, called high farming, depended on access to markets that railways and steamships, to a large but indeterminate extent, made possible. High farming depended on the rotation-with-stock system, and this system tended to preserve many of the hedgerows inherited from the past and thus preserve the distinctive patchwork of lowland Britain. Therefore, steam transportation can, in an indirect way, be placed on the credit side.

Steam railways, in combination with steamships and sailing vessels, also acted indirectly to maintain the open highland landscape. In a framework of free trade, their carrying capacity meant that the forest resources of Asia, Scandinavia, eastern Europe, and North America could be used to answer most of the demand for softwoods—a demand created by an expanding population and its need for housing and an expanding coal industry and its need for pit props. Consequently, British landlords had no compelling economic incentive to go against their inclinations and cover high, open slopes with alien conifers. Rapid train travel brought rich city dwellers to the deer forests of the Scottish Highlands, thus adding strength to the claim that steam was an ally of landscape richness and diversity.

On the other side of the ledger were the steam plows and their need for large, flat, unencumbered fields. Furthermore, rail freight made it possible to roof urban industry and housing with slate. This meant that lovely Welsh hillsides were cut into and left covered with piles of gray detritus. More important, steam locomotion joined with other factors to expand city margins into the surrounding countryside and to help cities reach out to remote places and tap water and other resources.

The creation of organized support for many late Victorian and Edwardian conservation causes was one by-product of the colonization of the country by the city. Railways increased urban congestion long before they did much to relieve it and thus helped to provoke a determination to preserve and construct urban green spaces. When connected by rail, seaside resorts flourished and expanded. When their promoters tried to protect their investments by erecting sea walls, these defenses interfered with natural erosive processes along the shoreline. Wherever steam engines were at work pumping water to allow mines and quarries to be worked at lower levels, holes deepened and broadened, and heaps piled ever higher.

Yet in all these events, cause and effect were confused. Technology was the means to ends often circumscribed by the means. And the ends achieved were never quite the ends anticipated. As George Perkins Marsh took great pains in 1864 to emphasize in his challenging book, *Man and Nature,* "the collateral and unsought consequences of human action [are] often more momentous than the direct and desired results." [34] In his *Autonomous Technology,* Langdon Winner stated the point succinctly: "Technology always does more than we intend." [35]

To some extent Britain's nineteenth century offers us cautionary lessons about the unfortunate effects of initiating actions without thought of consequence. That past also contains sermons on the evils of unchecked selfishness and political irresponsibility. How we think and speak about environmental neglect and decay has been, to a large extent, shaped by the reaction to, as Sir Stafford Cripps once put it, "the grip of the Beast of industrialism, with all its foul habits of spoliation." [36] In *The Making of the English Landscape,* W. G. Hoskins chose the chemical manufacturing town of St. Helens as the best illustration of what Victorian industry at its worst could do to the land: "The atmosphere was being poisoned, every green thing blighted, and every stream fouled with the chemical fumes and waste. Here, and in the Potteries and the Black Country especially, the landscape of Hell was foreshadowed." He acknowledged that the despoiling began with the industrial revolution, "but until steam-power became generally used," he added, "these landscapes did not achieve their final horrific form." [37]

It cannot be denied that horrific injuries were inflicted on the face of the land during the years when Britain's engineers and entrepreneurs were the world's leading innovators. Yet it should also be borne in mind that the society that treated the environment as if it were a "boundless cornucopia, to be enjoyed, plundered, and re-arranged for profit" [38] also created an agriculture that gave heart to the soil and did so with little or no use of pesticides and herbicides and with far less expenditure of energy than modern industrialized agriculture and forestry. The result was, writes Colin Duncan, "perhaps the most ecologically benign among all the highly productive farming systems the world has seen." [39]

Blight and beauty also advanced together. While some Victorians and Edwardians were ruthlessly pillaging their environment, others were helping to make and sustain the "world's most celebrated landscape." [40] The result was a dynamic balance that owed more to culture and custom; the structure of agriculture; the ability to exploit the soil, mineral, and forests resources of the rest of the world; and the intrinsic limitations on the diffusion of steam machinery than it did to foresight.

Few technical limitations remain today. Our machinery can go anywhere, do almost anything: the plowman need no longer contend directly with the earth he plows. Now, more easily and rapidly than ever before, landscapes can be made to order. Thoughtful Victorians sensed that their space was shrinking and losing substance; we have managed to collapse time as well. In the last fifty years, anxiety aroused by those physical and perceptual shifts has been democratized. Meanwhile, the gulf between our conceptual world and that of the nineteenth century has conspicuously widened, so much so that many among us assume that "the environment" is a recent discovery. A step back into the past should correct that error.

2

The Cultural Landscape

Will the earth save her face in the years before us, and, if she
saves her face, will it be taken at face value?

Sir Charles Lucus, 1914

Sir Charles's apprehensions about the future of the planet's surface were
not widely shared in Britain, even at this terminal point of the long nineteenth century. When Victorians and Edwardians used the word "environmentalism," they usually had in mind, not concern about the state of
the planet, but an interpretative framework: the proposition that crucial
aspects of human life and history are determined by distinct physical
settings. The gradual incorporation of the Darwinist and pre-Darwinist
concept of natural selection strengthened conceptual underpinnings for
the notion that physical surroundings supply the structure within which
and against which civilizations evolve. "Environmentalists" accepted
that a particular setting provided the context for a people's cultural development and that landscapes were visual signs of various acts of reci-
procity worked out between a culture and the particular soil, climate,
and topography that sustained it. Thus, when Victorians used the word
environment (and this would have been rare), they would probably not
have had in mind a general setting to which all the world's inhabitants
must adjust. Neither would they be thinking of an interacting global
system where every human intervention must have some wide-ranging
consequence. In the nineteenth century, connotations would have been
closer to the etymological roots of *environment*: the country around, the
neighborhood, the environs, the stretch of topography that gave definition to a place, one's own surroundings.

Depending on circumstance and occasion, that sense of propriety might attach to a valley, a village, a county; or, especially when traveling abroad, it might widen out to include the whole island kingdom. Even for the traveled, "home" seemed a place apart, its frontiers defined by God. How Britons exploited their own land and landscape, how they accepted or declined to accept the cornucopia of new machinery and artificial products pouring onto the market, how they set about promoting or resisting innovation, how they sought to balance change and continuity—all of these strategies and patterns of behavior were affected at every level by this sense of uniqueness, of particularity.

The fact that they were an island people was a source of pride and comfort for most Victorians, especially the English among them. That steam transport was rapidly bringing the far-off steadily nearer strengthened rather than diminished this self-perception. Few could have been unaware that a British-led revolutionary change in transport technology had occurred during their lifetimes. In two bursts of energy, one in the mid-1830s and another in the mid-1840s, engineers and navvies had put a network of rails in place. By 1850 trains carried passengers rapidly from Dover to the west coast of Scotland. At that date Londoners could board a train to all the major English cities, buy a railway ticket to Holyhead in Wales, and travel on to Ireland by steamship. Telegraph lines followed the tracks, and in 1851 an undersea cable carried messages to Paris. Enthusiasts spoke about a transformation in the way space was perceived. Wrote the architect and engineer George Godwin as early as 1837: "If the true criterion of distance be *time* . . . and who can doubt it?—the port of Liverpool and the manufacturing town of Manchester are now hardly other than one place." [1] Yet like so many others, he eventually came to regard that shrinking process with ambivalence—to think of the island homeland as a bastion against the approaching other—a refuge, a retreat, a place of gentleness, familiarity, security—a place apart.

Paradoxically, insularity (thought of in a descriptive rather than a pejorative sense) advanced along with consciousness of Britain's leading role in international trade. Adults living in the 1860s were aware that British engineers and entrepreneurs had created a global environment where the results of building a new railway, digging a new mine, or cutting an old forest in some remote region would be quickly felt at home. In that decade, investors, shippers, import and export companies, international railway engineers, politicians, and military strategists were forming a world trade, insurance, banking, information, and communications network centered in London. Demand from that center for primary goods to feed Britain's urban population, supply her factories, and build her houses prompted the people of the colonies, former colonies, or economic dependencies to clear land for export commodity production—which usually meant specialized monoculture. Intensive growing, especially of cotton, cereals, tobacco, and timber, inevitably depleted the soil and created what Eric Jones calls "hyper-developed" ecosystems out of what had been, in some cases, natural forest and grasslands. Britain took the lead, Jones writes, in making Europe into "a sink for global protein, raw materials, fertiliser, and energy." As a result, he notes, Europe's economy became "progressively detached from its native ecological base."[2]

Nevertheless, consciences seem not to have been deeply troubled. There were occasional expressions of guilt and outrage at reports about inhumanities inflicted by insensitivity and greed on conquered peoples and their ways of life. Occasionally warnings were heard about the long-term economic effects of the wasteful gathering of resources in the formal and informal empire. But few seemed to have been anxious about the global effects of erosion and pollution their enterprises were causing in remote places. There was always the comforting thought that constantly expanding markets, so many of them opened by British entrepreneurs and investors and served by British ships and British-built railways, were necessarily creating common interests and increasing the total stock of riches. That this leadership in the march of progress might entail accepting a large measure of responsibility for degrading the global environment was a proposition few, domiciled in their island home, would have been prepared seriously to entertain.

Demonstrations of a connection between tree cutting, soil erosion, and river and stream sedimentation could be set aside, even by conscientious and generous-minded people, as someone else's problem. Alexander von Humboldt's accounts of his explorations and his writings about the webs connecting organic and inorganic environmental elements, published over the first three decades of the nineteenth century, had prepared the scientifically inclined in Europe and many of the European colonies to recognize the wide-ranging results of deforestation. But the consequences of Britain's having lost most of its forest cover was hardly a national preoccupation. Most of the damage had been done so long ago. Nor had the thorough and protracted denuding of the British landscape brought about serious erosion, or so it seemed to the untrained eye. Of all the geomorphological agents Victorian geographers concerned themselves with, erosion (other than coastal erosion) seems to have troubled them the least. Especially in England, nature was moist, genial, Anglican. There were no towering mountain ranges and thus little threat of destructive landslides. No Mississippi demonstrated what could happen when a mighty river decided to revert to the wild. There were no vast spreads of dry prairie to blow away in searing winds. As the modern geographer David Jones remarks, "the United Kingdom is not an environment prone to natural hazard impacts." [3]

When posted as colonial administrators to places in Africa and Asia, Britons were, of course, inclined to take natural hazards far more seriously. Specialists on the environmental effects of colonialism call attention to a number of paradoxes: Empire and land transformation were, in most places, synonymous. Colonial land managers were under pressure from distant investors to exploit resources for maximum short-term gain. Until the middle years of the nineteenth century they were subject to few restraints. A "civilizing ideology" led colonial administrators to restructure existing traditional practices in order to make land use "rational"—as Europeans understood that term. On the other hand, these same officials found themselves resisting excessive exploitation.

This impulse to conserve stemmed from a variety of sources, not all of them compatible. The paternalist noticed how Western technology dislocated village ways and tried to protect vulnerable people; the politician concerned himself with the possible hostilities such disruptions might cause and sometimes urged caution; the physician saw the connection between environmental damage and public health and sounded warnings; the scientist measured the effects of deforestation and urban development on climate and water runoff and communicated his assessment of consequences; the civil servant calculated the adverse effects of resource depletion on the tax revenue and converted to the cause of conservation and restoration. [4] Turned in different directions by a wish to modernize what they believed to be backward economies and a wish to heed these conservationist promptings, colonial policy makers often tried to repair with one hand the damage they had inflicted with the other. They promoted the destruction of traditional agricultural practices, sometimes including sophisticated strategies for curbing erosion, and expedited the substitution of a monoculture that mined the resources of the land. Yet they also tried to control the degradation that "rationalization" inflicted on soil and landscape. [5]

There was one consistency, however: colonial officials chose to conserve, plant, or destroy forests depending on which activity seemed at the time to serve the interests of empire. Rather than replace the previ-

ously existing mixed forests, servants of the Raj set out specialized plantings of conifer, teak, and sal, regardless of local needs, because they believed these species to be better commercial investments. While they were
ordering this planting, they were also expediting the sale of forest land
to European tea and coffee planters and building roads and railways to
service them, thereby giving loggers access to forest resources in remote
areas.[6] Villagers were forbidden to burn, engage in shifting cultivation,
lop branches, or graze animals in the protected and commercialized
forests. As a consequence, they had little choice but to overuse what was
left to them.[7]

From these tensions between aims and policies in mountainous, tropical, or dry colonial regions came early stirrings of what we now identify
as "environmental consciousness." Therefore a case can be made for
moving the search for the beginnings of the mid-nineteenth century conservationist awakening away from Europe and out to the colonial peripheries. Richard Grove does this in his *Green Imperialism* in which he
examines the emergence of state conservation in the West Indies, Bengal,
and especially Mauritius, South Africa, and Madras. He shows that a
number of Scottish surgeons in the employ of the East India Company,
most prominent among them Alexander Gibson, Andrew Balfour, and
Hugh Cleghorn, had begun as early as the 1840s to call attention to the
close connections between deforestation, the erosion of the soil, and the
subcontinent's health, economy, and social welfare.[8]

In response to the influence and pressure of these men, Lord Dalhousie appointed the German-born-and-educated forester Dietrich Brandis to the position of superintendent of the forests of Pegu. Brandis managed to save large areas of this and other Burmese teak forests from
rapacious timber merchants, and Dalhousie made him the first inspector general of forests to the government of India when a forestry service
was established there in 1860. The aim of that service was to protect the
greatly enlarged area of state forests from ruinous exploitation by private contractors and villagers.[9] Under Brandis and his successor, William Schlich, the Indian Forestry Service became a school where British
foresters could learn the most advanced silviculture and conservation
practices from German or French experts.[10] But there was little demand
for their talents back home—Schlich (who eventually administered a
school of forestry at Oxford) being, as he recognized, an exception. The
awakening in remote reaches of empire seems to have made little impression on environmental attitudes back in the mother country.

What stirred passions and consciences at home was the perception that the spirit of "improvement" was threatening to obliterate everything in the natural or built environment that visibly connected past, present, and future. The reaction was as old as the innovative impulse. Well-rooted in the culture was a desire to resist unchecked capitalist enterprise with its callous disregard for holy places. For several centuries, resentment had been building against landlords who, ignoring communal claims, used their influence in Parliament to enclose common lands. The seventeenth and eighteenth century expropriation of the land by the aristocracy, the rearranging of the landscape in walled and hedged parcels, the huge draining and planting projects had stirred some conservative-minded people to protest and moved them to express their anger at the changes forced on the countryside. During the eighteenth century, a philosophical and theological case had been made against the "improvers," those who would refashion waste and wildwood to serve their own self-interest and their own notions of taste. Early in the next century, Romantic poets, especially Coleridge and Wordsworth, had, by opening eyes and hearts to impulses from vernal woods, educated sensibilities to admire solitudes, ancient buildings, and harmonious places.

From the middle of the nineteenth century onward, there was a perceptible widening of unease about the effects of technological advances and population growth on the natural and built environment. When in 1854 John Ruskin called for a society to protect the integrity of medieval buildings, few had responded. Twenty-three years later William Morris's plea for the same kind of pressure group was enthusiastically received and resulted in the Society for the Protection of Ancient Buildings. During this interval, a number of influential people, most of them members of what Harold Perkin has called the emerging professional society,[11] came to realize that concerted action needed to be taken and joined together in this and other societies to preserve natural sites and conserve endangered species.

First in the field was the Commons Preservation Society, formed in 1865 by a group of urban reformers, most prominently, George John Shaw-Lefevre, Robert Hunter, and Octavia Hill. This organization went on to win a series of court battles against enclosing lords of manors and pressured Parliament to pass an act in 1866 to forbid enclosure of commons in the Metropolitan Police District.[12] Three years later, Henry Fawcett persuaded his fellow CPS members to extend their battles for the rights of commoners to the whole of England. He took the lead in convincing Parliament to delay enclosures on rural commons and to pass legislation in 1876 that virtually put an end to further appropriation by private interests by acknowledging that the general public as well as the commoner and the manor lord had an interest in these green spaces.

This campaign spawned other preservationist causes and societies. In the mid-1860s, moves to protect certain species of birds threatened with extinction encouraged drives to protect other vulnerable creatures.[13] Octavia and Miranda Hill formed their Kyrle Society in 1876 to bring flowers and the experience of nature to slum dwellers. At the same time, John Lubbock and his fellow anthropologists were saving the prehistoric stone ring at Avebury from its development-minded owner and agitating for state protection of ancient monuments. Interest in folklore expanded and in 1878 found expression in a society and in a journal. Intrusions into the Lake District, first by railways and then by the Manchester Water Commission, produced, in the 1870s, a prototype for organizations to protect what was perceived to be a vanishing natural countryside.

Looking back on these events from the perspective of the 1880s, Shaw-Lefevre concluded that a significant shift in awareness had taken place in the 1860s and 1870s, a change of consciousness that his Commons Preservation Society had both profited by and contributed to. He believed that people began to look on land and its uses in new ways once fears over the repeal of the Corn Laws calmed. By the middle years of the century the interested public could no longer see the point of adding a few more acres to Britain's cultivated area: free trade and communication improvements were making cheap imported food and fiber easily available. He thought that as a consequence the public had awakened to the idea that "open spaces in their natural state, adding so much to the beauty of their districts and to the general enjoyment of the public, had a value."[14] The ability to exploit outside resources so easily and cheaply seemed to have permitted people at home to look upon their own remaining sites of natural beauty as national treasures to be enjoyed—not fenced, mined, cut down, plowed up, or built over.

Shaw-Lefevre and his associates counted on this new awareness to back them in their efforts to find antidotes to what a late Victorian physician called "urbomorbis"—the physical and moral evils supposedly arising from the crowded conditions of mid-Victorian cities.[15] Only rarely, and then late in the century, did these reformers turn to precedents from remote places to support their agendas at home. As we will see later, John Ruskin could endorse the construction of reservoirs in Italy yet, apparently with no sense of contradiction, rage against attempts to do the same in his beloved Lake District.

Of course, there were many sides to Ruskin. As several commentators have noted, one side sought to redirect Victorian conservation from its obsession with preserving particular buildings or places to a more active program that would conserve "old things," maintain them "as pillars, not as pinnacles—as aids, but not as idols." He tried to promote, writes Gill Chitty, "the conservation of context rather than of individual places and landscapes." Rather than "an artificially closed past of curated artifacts," he wished for "a present that interacted sympathetically within an inherited environment." [16] However, the inheritance he seemed to have had in mind was largely a family matter between fellow nationals, at its furthest stretch between western Europeans—not something all earthlings could expect to share. The map of the nineteenth century world may have been painted red, but nineteenth century "natural piety" was far from ecumenical.

An invitation to think more broadly, more "scientifically," appeared in 1864: George Perkins Marsh's extraordinary book, *Man and Nature*. It began with this dramatic assertion: "Man is everywhere a disturbing agent. Wherever he plants his foot, the harmonies of nature are turned to discords." [17] What followed was a bringing together of the latest findings of European and American scholarship, all pointing toward what was to become recognized in later years as the science of ecology.

Marsh's thesis challenged accepted wisdom. How his message was received can give insights into how people in the nineteenth century thought about their relationship to the natural world and how they rationalized their growing perception that technology was giving humans increasing mastery over natural processes. Closer to our purpose, it provides us with a device for appreciating how thoughtful but conventionally minded mid-Victorians understood their relationship to and responsibilities toward land and landscape. Therefore some attention must be paid to the shape of Marsh's argument.

At one level, *Man and Nature* could be taken as a call to action—the need to respond to a clear and present danger by exercising prudence when exploiting or controlling natural forces. At another level, the warning could be interpreted as an attempt to change a way of perceiving. Of all the powers man seeks to acquire, Marsh wrote in his "Introductory," the most difficult "is that of seeing what is before him. Sight is a faculty; seeing is an art." Changing the aim of vision would, he believed, open up an entirely new field of inquiry into the natural sciences and bring about a revolution in the way "every traveller, every lover of rural scenery, every agriculturalist" experiences the natural world.[18] Europeans had become accustomed to appreciate landscape values, for the most part, visually. Marsh wanted to impress on his readers the fact that more fundamental alterations proceed underneath these surfaces, usually out of sight. His landscape contained much that was difficult or impossible for the untrained eye to detect: the "ducts and fluids of vegetable and animal life," the rivers and streams, trees and grasses, the air surrounding them, "peopled by the minute organisms which perform most important functions in both the living and the inanimate kingdoms of nature." [19]

Marsh recognized that to understand the natural landscape this way— as interconnected complex relationships and not merely as a place, or a mental picture, or an artistic representation of a place—required a new kind of awareness. He believed such a redirection of sight to be of greatest urgency: "The world cannot afford to wait till the slow and sure progress of exact science has taught it a better economy," he stated, "for we are, even now, breaking up the floor and wainscotting and doors and window frames of our dwelling, for fuel to warm our bodies and seethe our pottage." [20]

For such recklessness to end, people in positions to educate the public must abandon the notion that residence in humankind's terrestrial home would become progressively easier and more abundant with every technological advance. Harmonious though Eden must have been for the lower creation, it was not well suited to the higher one. The advance of civilization was essential for the full development of human potential. Every step forward required that "brute and unconscious nature be effectually combatted and, in a great degree, vanquished by human art." [21] Yet the more human beings subjected nature and transformed it into artifice, the less restrained (Marsh would say "measured") they had become in choosing their weapons and methods of conquest. To advance, he warned, was inevitably to destroy; and the faster the rate of advance, the greater the rate of destruction: "The destructive agency of man becomes more and more energetic and unsparing as he advances in civilization, until the impoverishment, with which his exhaustion of the natural resources of the soil is threatening him, at last awakens him to the necessity of preserving what is left, if not restoring what has been wantonly wasted." [22]

If there were some way out of this dilemma, it would be discovered when the plunderers had exhausted the last reserves to the point where economic growth was no longer possible; only then would political and industrial leaders be likely to search for ways to alter nature without seriously deranging "the combinations of inorganic matter and organic life" that "through the night of aeons" nature "had been fashioning and balancing."[23] The problem was that such a last-minute awakening might come too late.

This passionate call for a new awareness was heard, or at least partly heard, everywhere that English was spoken and read, and it drew a response from continental European, North American, and British colonial conservationists and politicians.[24] The "educated and informed minority" in New Zealand, who managed to impose legislative restraints in 1874 on the reckless exploitation of the country's timber supply, used *Man and Nature* to help make their case, as did the colonial administrators who struggled to preserve forests in India.[25] Australian journalists and reformers paid Marsh the compliment of paraphrase and plagiarism.[26] American conservationists in the 1870s used Marsh as the main authority for a successful campaign to persuade Congress to establish national forest reserves.[27] Soon after Confederation in 1867, Canadians were stimulated enough by the book to think seriously about timber management.[28] The American poet James Russell Lowell advised readers of *The North American Review,* shortly after *Man and Nature* appeared in 1864, that Marsh's message and the evidence sustaining it ought to be placed in every public as well as academic library so that literate and thinking persons might be engaged in the discussion the book was bound to promote.[29] From India, Hugh Cleghorn wrote to Marsh in 1868 that he had "carried your book with me all along the slope of the northern Himalaya, and into Kashmir and Tibet."[30] Another colonial conservationist, A. J. Stuart, also found in Marsh a valuable ally and published extracts from *Man and Nature* as part of the campaign to curb careless and excessive logging in Madras.[31] Marsh's name never became a household word in his own country or any other, but, obviously, his message did manage to reach people in a position to use it.

Britain was an exception. It is true that the great English geologist Charles Lyell wrote to Marsh acknowledging that reading the book had led him to revise his view that man's influence on geomorphology had been inconsequential. Granted, a few British geographers did occasionally refer to Marsh's works during the last quarter of the century.[32] But if there was a filtering effect from the top down, it never amounted to more than a trickle. No significant public discussion followed *Man and Nature's* appearance; sales were disappointing.

Why that should be so is worth exploring. Fortunately, two of Britain's serious journals published reviews of *Man and Nature:* a substantial one in the *Athenaeum* and a longer one in the *Edinburgh Review.*[33] These do not disclose to us "public opinion," but they do help us place the issues Marsh raised in the context of Victorian Britain when it was still the world's most urbanized, industrial, and technologically advanced power.

Both reviewers agreed that Marsh had shortcomings: He claimed to draw his model from world history, but he never, in fact, escaped from the narrow confines of his American upbringing; he exaggerated the capacities of men and women to mold their surroundings and underrated the determining force of geography; he was blind to the possibility that natural processes were purposive; and finally, he failed to appreciate how science and steam technology equipped advanced civilizations eventually to repair the damage they necessarily inflicted.

It is not difficult to understand why few among Britain's educated elite would have been inclined in the mid-1860s to be lectured by an American whose country was locked in a brutish civil war and whose people were notorious for their callous, wasteful use of nature's resources. Even so, Marsh's credentials as a geographer, conservationist, and man of letters could not easily be dismissed. Although born into a pioneering family in the northern New England town of Woodstock, Vermont, he was no backwoodsman. Tutored in Greek and Latin by his landowning father, he had gone on, after graduating from nearby Dartmouth College, to become a recognized Icelandic scholar and a master of most Western languages, including his own. President Zachary Taylor appointed him minister from the United States to the Ottoman Empire. President Abraham Lincoln later named him minister plenipotentiary to the Kingdom of Italy, where he spent the rest of his life. Matthew Arnold once referred to Marsh as "that *rara avis,* a really well-bred and trained American . . . a savant . . . redeemed from Yankeeism by his European residence and culture." [34] What made him rarer still was his passionate interest, stirred not just by an astonishing breadth of reading but by direct experience, in the natural sciences of his day—geology, geography, agronomy, forestry, and climatology. He had made himself into a sophisticated ecologist before the term came into being. In every sense he was an example of Arnold's ideal of "sweetness and light," and something more, a humanist, but capable of moving easily in, as his twentieth century biographer puts it, "the borderlands linking science and the public weal." [35] (See Figure 2.)

The reviewer for the *Edinburgh Review,* Sir Henry Holland, was well-equipped to appreciate these cultural credentials but would not have been inclined to be overwhelmed by them. A great-grandson of Josiah Wedgwood, cousin of Elizabeth Gaskell, fellow of the Royal Society,

Figure 2.   George Perkins Marsh (1882). Engraving made from a photograph
taken shortly before his death, eighteen years after publication of *Man and
Nature*—a pioneering work on the consequences of human capacity to destroy
natural harmonies. (Baker Library, Dartmouth College, 1883)

physician extraordinary to Queen Victoria and Prince Albert, and amateur geologist, Holland believed himself entitled to adopt a magisterial
and condescending tone.[36] Both he and the anonymous reviewer for the
Athenaeum went to some lengths to suggest that a pessimistic message
delivered with over-heated rhetoric—"rather florid and ambitious"—
might be expected from someone coming from a part of the world, suffering from the insecurities consequent on rapid expansion and unset-
tled by the ruthless exploitation of its abundance.[37]

In making this point, the reviewers took their lead from comments

Marsh himself made when speaking about American institutions. "The natural, perhaps the necessary defect of ours," Marsh had written, "is their instability, their want of fixedness, not in form only, but even in spirit." He went on to admit that the landscape of the United States had inevitably come to be "as variable as the habits of the population."[38] Furthermore, the reviewers noted, the author himself seemed to support the theory that civilization moved in successive stages from the highly destructive pastoral one to "advanced states of culture" where resources were consumed less wastefully.[39] What relevance then did such a warning have for an ancient country with an advanced civilization whose land had long ago passed through the slash-and-burn phase? England was manifestly not America, and neither was it one of those hot, dry, mountainous former provinces of the Roman Empire that Marsh offered as proof for his contention that people were capable of transforming their physical surroundings.

Holland pointed out that advanced cultures were also less prone to regard land and landscape as a collection of commodities and were, therefore, more inclined to reverence. Had Marsh spent less energy exalting man's superiority to nature and freedom from its forces, wrote Holland in his review, his heart might have been more open to the "manifest and wonderful design in the whole"—a whole of which man is not the single object. He thought Marsh had failed to supply any higher meaning to his story. "Nature" in *Man and Nature* was not purposive: it disclosed no high destiny, no indication of God's design. In this account, human agency seemed to be entirely random and free. Not only that, such a premise implied a degree of self-determination that was entirely unjustified, considering that the debate about the origin of species and the origins of land forms was still undecided. Who knew, after all, what unfathomable forces were at work in the world, guiding human and animal life in ways unknown, toward "some higher and nobler development in the time yet to come?"[40] Perhaps there was more in heaven and earth than was contained in Marsh's philosophy.

The *Athenaeum* reviewer tended to agree: humility might have reminded Marsh of the "common belief" that the role assigned to us here on earth is to improve nature by acting, not as her master, but as her steward. It was this anonymous reviewer's opinion that a more reverent intelligence would have concentrated attention on acts that have made the "earth more beautiful and fruitful" rather than on actions that show man "defacing nature, and making earth into a hell." Perhaps, the reviewer mused, the peoples of the Mediterranean basin had been led to

denude the land, not entirely as free agents but as unconscious media-
tors in fulfilling the Creator's "grand design—part of a divine purpose—
that political and moral revolutions shall successively change the face
of nature in different countries." Places like "the Etruscan sea-coast,
the Campagna and Pontine Marshes, Calabria, Sicily and Asia Minor"
were perhaps denuded by some "compensatory force" so that other, morally robust regions, could be allowed "new and vigorous cultivation."
Clearly, a "once uncultivated Britain" had become "now more glorious
and fruitful than the olden Italy." Perhaps, the reviewer concluded, the
steep slopes of the old civilizations had been allowed to shrivel and erode
in order that the new might blossom as the rose.[41]

Neither of Marsh's critics were indifferent to the implications of his
evidence about human impact or to his warning that the exercise of human power over the physical surroundings must necessarily have consequences too remote and complex to grasp fully. What disturbed them
was the apparent rejection of teleology. Marsh's "Nature" was an abstraction; its governing principle was a mechanical equilibrium; humankind stood outside nature and inflicted damage that could be irrepara-
ble without further human intervention. The forces in his natural world
were certain to strike back, but blindly, without malevolent or benevo-
lent intent.[42] If greed and ignorance led the exploiters of the earth to
bring their house down about their ears, their hands alone would do the
deed. True, careful stewardship was a moral duty, but that duty was to
other forms of life and future generations and not to some higher power
or in obedience to some divine edict. If the floodwaters came again on
the face of the earth, they would be released by human folly, not as pun-
ishment for human folly. There could be no new covenant. Humans
must bear responsibility alone.[43] It was the loneliness implied by such a
construction of reality that troubled the reviewers most.

Clearly Marsh was out of tune with the questing spirit of the time.
His pragmatism offended not only those who clung to a faith in the forward march of civilization toward its destiny but also those who followed Wordsworth in wishing to divert that march away from remaining nooks of holy ground, still "mid the busy world kept pure."[44] Keenly
interested though Marsh was in protecting unspoiled wilderness sites, in
Man and Nature he tended to put emphasis on the need for sustainable
development. Like the utilitarian "conservation crusaders" who rallied
around Gifford Pinchot and Teddy Roosevelt in early twentieth century
America, Marsh sought not only to prevent unnecessary waste but to renew the resource base so that material civilization might advance.[45] He

agreed that a planted and managed forest lacked a sense of timelessness that so many find profoundly moving in an ancient, natural stand of trees; but plantations, he explained, had the advantage of being free of rot and senility. Unlike romantic preservationists, he wanted to manage the woods according to rational guidelines, not save trees from being harvested.[46]

Presumably, he must have believed that some method of sustained yield could ensure an adequate timber supply and at the same time maintain the fertility and stability of the forest soil. But he knew that sustainability was difficult even to define. It was his great insight that the process whereby the forest floor replenishes nutrients was highly complex, depending on a symbiotic relationship between the fungi, rodents, and insects that break down the rotting mulch and the birds and animals that form part of that chain. A mechanism so intricately balanced could not, when broken, be easily restored or replaced.

Marsh put his trust, qualified though it was, in managerial efficiency, not an outlook much favored by preservation societies during the last quarter of the century. Marsh read in past landscapes accounts of human greed and carelessness: the object of his book was to persuade future architects of the human abode to carry out their renovations in harmony with the natural site, in all its complexity and interconnectedness.[47] By contrast, later nineteenth-century preservationists in Britain seemed to turn against the renovators and remodelers, believing that harmonies had been achieved in the past that future innovations were unlikely to replicate.

Those of more optimistic persuasion, including the champions of efficiency, would likely have agreed with the two reviewers that Marsh's pessimism, his exaggerated estimate of nature's fragility, was ill-considered. According to Holland, Marsh had not listened carefully enough to the discussion then raging about Darwin's explanation of the origin of species. What a pity it was that this Yankee diplomat had failed to notice how Darwin's discoveries supported the theory that observable natural processes could, if given millions of years to work, account for alterations in plant and animal species as well as in landforms. If Marsh had read more extensively in works about the shaping effect of volcanic and tidal action, earthquakes, wind and rain erosion, and the wearing effect of frost and glacial scouring, then presumably he would have been less impressed by the comparatively puny role played by human beings.[48]

Furthermore, in asserting so forcefully "the supremacy of the mind of man over the material elements of the globe," Marsh had, Holland believed, failed to take environmentalism seriously. Apparently he had overlooked evidence recently presented by Henry Thomas Buckle showing the determining effect of climate, food, soil, and landscape on culture and history.[49] As a consequence of this failure to appreciate Buckle's point about nature's determining function, "our American Evelyn," Holland wrote, tends to exaggerate man's power as a disturber of harmonies and seems to forget that air and sea currents, the sun's radiation, the evaporation of water, the forces of gravity and magnetic attraction are, except perhaps locally and temporarily, unalterable.[50]

How, Marsh's critics asked, could someone who believed that human ingenuity had become the major determinant of geomorphology have so little faith in the power of technology to repair the damage the progress of material civilization inflicted on nature? Holland in particular took Marsh to task for having concentrated his attention on the effect of ancient tools on the earth's surface. In doing so he had virtually ignored the implications of modern steam- and science-based techniques—something perhaps to be expected from a person who had grown to manhood in a resource-based rather than an advanced manufacturing economy. The future might have looked brighter to him had he considered it from the perspective, not of a raw continent, but of a highly evolved country possessing the world's most sophisticated technology.

Already, Holland thought, there were encouraging signs in western Europe that science and engineering were beginning to join together what population growth, urban expansion, and resource exploitation had torn asunder. Had not the last fifty years introduced "a new era of human power" in which innovative technologies did "more to subjugate the earth and ocean to human purposes, than in the total period forming the prior history of mankind?" Had concern about the possibility of soon exhausting Britain's coal resources not been met by employing increasingly powerful steam pumps? Steam engineers were making steady progress in finding ways to economize on heat. The telegraph and steam transport had created a revolution in communications. Railway engineers were every day demonstrating, with their bridges, tunnels, cuttings, viaducts, and excavations, "a still stronger impress of genius and power." These relatively recent triumphs had made it possible for "one region of the globe to minister to another."[51]

Among the benefits of this integration was the possibility of moving plants around the globe in order to restore lost soil fertility. For example, bent grass could now be brought from afar to fix the shifting desert sands. Holland acknowledged there was a price to be paid for this mobility: "unwholesome and unprofitable speed . . . restless hurry and the love of change." [52] Yet there was comfort in the thought that the advance of material civilization held out the promise of increasing rationality and capacity for restraint in using the earth's riches. Besides, Holland asked, what was the point of detailing accounts of human wastefulness, what was the point of making doleful predictions, when it was obvious that no one had yet attempted, least of all Marsh, to quantify the extent of the damage that interventions of all kinds had caused?

This last point, repeated by other critics, Marsh was ready to concede. He did try to make amends by adding a few remarks on the effects of urban and industrial expansion in a revised version of his book, published in 1874.[53] Had he gone on to develop this theme further, his work might have been more immediately relevant to the British nineteenth century reform agenda. As it was, no British geographer undertook a comprehensive treatment of the subject until 1922, when a Cambridge geographer, Robert Sherlock, published his *Man as a Geological Agent*.[54] Freely acknowledging his debt to Marsh, Sherlock expanded the scope of the investigation into the human factor in geomorphological process to include the effects of steam-powered machinery on mining operations, railway and highway excavations, coastal modification, waterway management, and urban development. In addition he supplied numbers: 39,709,000,000 cubic yards of rock, for example, excavated in Britain by 1913 to make roadways, railways, and canals and furnish materials to construct foundations for buildings, harbors, and docks.[55]

Considering the voracious appetite Victorians had for statistics, the wonder is that British geographers or social historians had not attempted a comprehensive study of this kind before. Select committees, royal commissions, and reports to Parliament had built up, especially from the 1840s on, a vast repository of information about the effects of quarrying, mining, canal and railway construction, and industrial air and water pollution. In 1906 a royal commission began exhaustive inquiries into the connection between deforestation, the mining of beaches, and coastline erosion.[56] Geographers and geologists had, necessarily, been involved in all of these investigations; yet, until Sherlock, no one had attempted to draw general conclusions from all this "hard" evidence showing how rapidly industry was increasing its capacity to lay waste to nature.

Investigation of this kind would not greatly have interested Marsh. The complex, widespread, and unpredictable consequences of human intrusion was his subject. Where or when or with what instruments woods were cut down, waters diverted, sand dunes created, and canal projects carried out were not for him matters of primary importance. He was content to show that projects undertaken by the cultures and political regimes he knew about had worldwide repercussions, trusting that studies made outside the realm of his own experience and researches would lead to the same conclusions. As Lewis Mumford once remarked, "Marsh's subject was the planet itself." [57]

For Marsh, the history of the planet had, from the time that human beings acquired the means to shape it, been the history of man's perception of nature. He was convinced that the only way to prevent that story from ending in tragedy was to change consciousness. And here he was guardedly hopeful. He thought he detected signs of a reorientation, a new way of looking at the ancient question about how human beings should relate to nature. His evidence came from the work of a new school of geographers, especially Alexander von Humboldt, Karl Ritter, and Arnold Henry Guyot. By demonstrating the influence of "external physical conditions" on human society and social progress, these authorities had "given to the science of geography a more philosophical, a more imaginative character." Previously, geographers had shared the general assumption that the Creator had prepared a home for man here on earth and assigned this privileged being responsibility for fulfilling the uncompleted design. Believing this, the geographic profession had limited itself, as Marsh put it, to delineation of terrestrial surface and outline, and "to description of the relative position and magnitude of land and water." [58]

In recent times, however, this "narrow view" of geography had, he believed, widened, "so that, in its improved form, it embraces not only the globe itself, but the living things which vegetate or move upon it, the varied influences they exert upon each other, the reciprocal action and reaction between them and the earth they inhabit." [59] It was now understood that not only the configurations of the earth's surface but "every plant, every animal, is a geographical agency" and that those agencies "have influenced the social life and social progress of man." According to Marsh, this realization had "half awakened" the intellectual community of Europe to the interrelationships and mutual dependencies between man and nature and consequently to the immediate need to restore "disturbed harmonies." This new conceptual framework had led men to study the complexity of natural systems in order "to use the world as not abusing it." Marsh made clear his intention to communicate this need to "the general intelligence of educated, observing, and thinking men" in order to turn half-awakening into full awakening.[60]

We would now call the transformation he sought a paradigm shift. It is the persuasive thesis of Kenneth Robert Olwig, a historical geographer, that what makes *Man and Nature* "an enduring classic" was its success at reversing the premise that climate, natural resources, and topography of a region to a large extent determined the society, economy, and culture of its human inhabitants. Might it not be more productive, Marsh had asked, to look instead at how extensively humans, over time, had determined their own "material habitation"?[61] Olwig does not claim that Marsh alone had that insight or deserves all the credit for introducing this new "problematic" or theoretical structure within which all problems must be posed. But he does credit him with having most clearly "delineated the process of transition from a place bound to a spatially integrated society, both in terms of awareness and actuality." Marsh had, in other words, supplied a detailed exegesis for John Donne's poetic metaphor "no man is an island entire of itself." Neither, Marsh had added, can a country or even a continent stand apart in isolation— nothing of this world is "entire of itself."

Olwig draws attention to this passage in Marsh's 1860 *Christian Examiner* article:

> In proportion to man's advance in natural knowledge, and his consequent superiority over outward physical forces, is his emancipation from the influence of climatic and other local causes, and the more clearly does he manifest those attributes of his proper humanity which vindicate his claim to be called a being, not a thing,—a special creation living indeed *in* Nature, but not a product of her unconscious action, or wholly subject to her inflexible laws.[62]

It seemed, therefore, that Marsh had already answered the question he posed in the closing line of *Man and Nature* about whether man is under nature or above her. His solution was to adopt a new framework or formulation that conceived of nature as a process of interaction between inorganic and organic life, in which man, as a uniquely conscious agent, understands enough about these systems of interrelations to manipulate them and so becomes a creative, because a disruptive, force of nature—a being in nature but in dialectical conflict with nature's laws.

Marsh was unrealistically optimistic about the readiness of his readers to think of the whole earth as their home and to accept that every technological advance had global consequences, not all of them predictable or desirable. To demonstrate that larger thesis, he devoted the first section of his book to a detailed examination of what happened when forests were destroyed. But readers attended much more closely to the illustrations than they did to the deeper message. People directly involved with forest management and policy were the first to apply what was immediately useful, especially his account of how, in forest lands, one tug at nature's web would be felt on nearly every strand of the complex whole.

From Buffon and von Humboldt, Marsh took the premise that forests are the key to ecological balance, since they tend to keep moisture in equilibrium and thus act as a sponge, a "great reservoir." Cutting destroys the balance: leaves no longer filter the sun's rays, and the mold and underbrush on the forest's floor no longer protect the topsoil from freezing or drying out. Consequently, winters are colder and shorter and summers longer, hotter, and, possibly, drier. Springs, once fed regularly by the forest reservoir, dry up in hot weather and turn into torrents in seasons of rain or melting snow; water that directly reaches the parched or frozen ground either sweeps away the loosened dust or runs directly into rivers and streams; abrasive material then cuts the banks of these outlets, releasing more sand and gravel and raising the beds of the water courses. The effect is to divert channels and obstruct river outlets. Originally set in motion by conscious human action, the process progresses according to natural laws, but in a complex and often mystifying pattern of relationships.[63]

For reasons that will be explored later, few Britons were deeply concerned about the domestic consequences of deforestation. At least until the shock of the First World War, reform-minded Britons tended not to respond to warnings about the fragility of the global fabric and the widespread consequences of every heedless intervention into nature. Their attention was concentrated on finding ways to contain or eliminate hazards posed by their own urban growth and industrial pollution. These vital matters required practical remedies. At least from the 1830s on, reformers began to generate schemes for making city traffic flow more smoothly; for clearing slums and housing the poor decently; for finding pure water supplies and uses for city wastes; for developing machines, smelters, and chemical processors that could consume their own effluents. With equal enthusiasm, they searched for ways to provide pent-up city dwellers with country recreations and promoted schemes for returning green nature and open spaces to the urban core—the object being to compensate for or find antidotes to the steady advance of brick and mortar.

There was keen debate about who should guide and decree these improvements: whether voluntary agencies, ad hoc commissions, parishes, municipalities, county councils, or the central bureaucracy were best equipped to do so with the minimum loss of individual freedom. Ministries and commissioners pondered the difficulties involved in identifying who or what was causing damage to the physical surroundings. Behind this particular kind of environmentalism, one of the things that set it apart from our own, was a high degree of confidence about one day finding the answers and putting things right. And about such matters, Marsh had little to say and little comfort to give, save his trust that nature, when deranged, "sets out herself at once to restore, as nearly as practicable, the former aspect of her dominion."[64]

No search will be made in what follows for Victorian origins of present-day attitudes and anxieties. Instead, there will be an attempt to follow Donald Worster's advice and pay attention, not just to theorists, but also to the behavior of those people who interacted directly with the land and expressed their values in the landscapes they helped to make.[65] Beyond the monochromatic, constantly mutating, artifice of urban spaces lay a nineteenth century lowland countryside that, for all the marks left on it by intruders, resembled the imagined traditional landscape, that generations of artists and writers had firmly planted in the national psyche.

That was so, not simply because farmers and involved landlords carried in their imaginations an ideal landscape where utility and beauty were so often seen to abide together. Hard-edged considerations about markets and profit margins had much to do with decisions to keep and improve older technologies rather than to reconfigure the land so as to accommodate new ones. But, given the peculiar circumstances Britain found herself in during the age of steam, feelings and calculations could often be reconciled.

The expediency of doing so was widely recognized. In his 1849 edition of *The Farm Engineer,* Robert Richie noted that an impediment to the wider adoption of fixed and portable steam power units on English farms was the unwillingness of so many landlords and tenants to disfigure the countryside with smoking chimneys. Perhaps, he suggested "these fastidious feelings" would dissipate if power installations could be masked with "ornamental architecture."[66] Worthy of note is that even this ardent champion of steam agriculture recognized that, given the cultural context, it would be expedient to harmonize the new technology with the "traditional" countryside, its customs, and its rural scenery.

3
Lowland Fields

To build up and never to pull down is a maxim that ought always to be kept steadily in view.

John Watson, land agent, 1845

At a time when massed bomber formations were shaking apart the cities of continental Europe and when shells and the treads of advancing tanks were ripping up hedges and fields, T. Bedford Franklin, a British agricultural historian, published a little book called *Good Pastures*. It recorded another battle, "noiseless" but "none the less deadly," that had taken place early in the twentieth century on his father's farm at Shutlanger Grove, several miles east of Towcester in Northamptonshire. The permanent pasture Farmer Franklin had labored over the years to create was a peaceful, fruitful, attractive, law-abiding, mutually supportive colony of clovers, cocksfoot, timothy, foxtail, and nutritious meadow grasses. It sustained in good health the sheep and cattle who gently grazed. But as they grazed, they tended to select the tastiest plant varieties, thereby disturbing, little by little, the harmonious environmental relationships. A few signs of declining fertility would begin to appear, intently watched for from the surrounding edges by a ragged army of predators: sorrel, reed, bent grass, bramble, and other weeds—an undisciplined band but fitter than their tame adversaries to survive a Darwinian struggle of attrition. Farmer Franklin's task was to intervene, not in order to make the established pasture system work but to protect it from deterioration and the subsequent invasion.[1]

Franklin described in loving detail the strategies his father developed to rescue from earlier neglect some old pastures that had surrendered to weeds and been colonized by rabbits, the soil of the meadows soured, ditches blocked, hedges fouled. By hand, farmer and laborers cleaned out the hedges and filled the rabbit burrows. Next they unplugged and deepened the foul-smelling ditches, mixing into the resulting dirt heaps any manure-rich ant hills they could find. That done, they applied a dressing of lime to the surface of the ground and waited for the snows and rainstorms of winter to work through and loosen the mats and sweeten the soil.

Farmer Franklin used a sharp-toothed harrow to drag out the mat when the spring thaw arrived. By harrowing up, down, and across the field, he accumulated a large heap of vegetable matter mixed with ditch and anthill dirt. To this heap he added lime and animal manure. While all this was rotting, he gave the field a treatment of acid-neutralizing blast furnace slag, and then he chain harrowed and rolled it in. During the summer he penned sheep where they could feed on what turned up and removed them in the autumn when it was time to spread the ripened compost.

With the next spring came a wonderful transformation. As if by magic, dormant red and white clover, trefoil, and rye grass seeds germinated and found the way cleared to grow freely and robustly. By the third year, the old system was back in working order. Franklin's father called this phenomenon, "lifting the face." His care had begun the process that retrieved the countenance of the land from disfiguring blemishes. Nature had been assisted, not mastered. Skill and respect for the land had done what even the most advanced technology could not do: It had increased the soil's fertility and given the local countryside a smiling face. The moral was clear: "Striving after abundance," wrote Bedford Franklin, "by forcing an unwilling crop to grow in an antagonistic soil or an unsuitable climate is almost certain to be a failure." [2]

In *Good Pastures,* Franklin concentrates on the place of permanent pasture in one farm's operation and says little about the other factors in its economy. Therefore his account, if taken as an example of an older lowland agriculture, may give the reader an exaggerated sense of continuity. One notices the reliance on traditional methods, on the use of human and animal energy, on the readiness to recycle the locally available minerals, fertilizers, and biomass. Even at this late phase of the era of steam technology, it would seem, the tools and skills of earlier generations were still at work in the fields. One might be tempted to conclude that farms like Shutlanger Grove had hardly been touched by change, as though the radical improvements since the 1830s in steam-power delivery, machinery and machine tools, metallurgy, soil science, and communications technology had passed them by.

But a closer look at such farms would suggest otherwise. The lime that helped to neutralize the acid soil could have come from a local pit, but the basic slag that intensified the lime's effect obviously did not. It had been processed and then hauled by rail from distant smelters. We may also confidently assume that the manure from livestock (Bedford Franklin called the bullock a "travelling manure cart") did not consist entirely of reprocessed grasses from the farm pastures: it would have been enriched by imported winter feed supplements. Sailing and steam vessels and railways began to import oil cake made from linseed, cottonseed, sunflower, palm, and rapeseed in increasing quantity from the 1840s until the 1880s.[3] Since grazing animals did not completely restore from the rear what they took in at the front, the use of this artificial feed—rich in phosphates and ammonia—more than made up for this deficit—of course, at the expense of the exporter's soil fertility. In *A History of Agriculture* Bedford Franklin gave this summary of the effects of enhancing farm-grown animal food: "more cattle cakes meant more meat, more manure, more corn and straw, mangolds and swedes, and so again more food for still more cattle."[4]

In turn, more cattle meant bigger barns and covered yards to protect the manure (and especially the urine, which contained most of the potash and much of the nitrogen) from rain and leeching. These buildings as well as the new farm houses had to be located inside the farm enclosure rather than in a village. Thus "high farming," in the sense of high investment in more productive techniques, was not simply a reaction to the challenge of low prices and international competition but a response to opportunities created by an expanding domestic market and the construction, in a remarkably short space of time, of a national railway system, a system linked first by sail and gradually by steam to expanding rail networks around the world. In early Victorian years, commercial suppliers of processed fertilizers began to advertise wares drawn from almost everywhere.

Therefore farms like the one at Shutlanger Grove had long ago ceased to extract locally all or even most of the ingredients that went into their productive activities: building stone and wood, roofing straw or slates, lime, marl, fertilizers, implements, and seed. F. M. L. Thompson contends that the traditional, self-contained, "closed-circuit system" broke down during the middle decades of the nineteenth century. From that point, farming turned into a "manufacturing industry" where "purchased raw materials are processed in order to produce a saleable finished product."[5] But the smaller farms of Northamptonshire and most lowland places would have responded to this fundamental change without surrendering all of the aspects of the old regime. Traditional and new farming tools and practices found ways of co-existing.

Coincident with this structural change came significant advances in soil chemistry, and these advances contributed to the trend toward use of imported artificial products. Farmers could purchase packaged bonemeal, either in natural form or, as tended to happen in the third quarter of the century, turned into a superphosphate by the application of sulfuric acid.[6] Many of these innovations were the product of researches carried out from the 1830s on John Bennet Lawes's Rothamstead estate in Hertfordshire. Progress made there in the understanding of how plants convert minerals and chemicals into forms they can assimilate led directly to the development of artificial fertilizers. Improved understanding of soil chemistry allowed farmers to apply specific nutrients to suit different soil conditions. Those few who were willing and able to profit from the advice of scientists learned that soil was not simply a nutritive medium but a complex of processes where the capacity of lower organisms to react to minerals was affected by the amounts of air, heat, and water. "Fine tuning" meant adjusting those processes rather than merely adding to the soil's inherent resources.[7]

Just before the middle of the century, novel forms of nutrients kept appearing, increasing the effectiveness of this technological breakthrough and augmenting the fertilizer supply available to conventional agriculture. Quantities of sea-bird guano, shipped from Peru, became available as did the even richer coprolite—a mineral phosphate, containing the remains of marine animals, dug from shallow mines in Cambridgeshire, Hertfordshire, and Suffolk.[8] These products were supplemented in the 1860s with Prussian potash and Chilean "cubic nitre," along with all kinds of refuse from cities and factories, once thrown away but now packaged and marketed by rail: wool scrap, leather shreds, steel slag, rags, street refuse, coal gas residue, brewery dregs, sulfate of ammonia, dried blood, horns, hoofs, offal, feathers, ashes, and soot from the cities and factories.[9] Human excrement was also utilized, although rarely. Experiments with spraying town sewage on fields showed that the cost of laying pipes and installing pumps usually exceeded the value of the increase in crop yield.[10] The considerable lime-burning industry declined as lighter (thus cheaper to transport) products came on the market.[11] Although quality could not be relied upon until after midcentury,[12] these additions to the farmyard manure pile and to the locally available supplies of salt, sand, marl, chalk, and lime encouraged improving landlords and tenants to experiment with flexible regimes of rotation and pay attention to reports on innovative programs. The resulting spurt in productivity made it possible for large-scale cereal growers to withstand competition from abroad during early and mid-Victorian times and respond effectively to an constantly rising demand, particularly noticeable from the 1850s, for meat and dairy products.[13]

The economy of the Franklin farm would have been directly linked to world markets for food and fibers, and farmers would have reacted like practitioners of any industry to price changes by looking for ways to cut costs and increase productivity. Mechanization was one possibility. Although an impressive amount of hard physical labor had gone into the maintenance of the farm's meadows, that work had been greatly assisted by horse-drawn harrows. Like the other mechanical implements that would have been used on the farm, harrows became common about the time when processed fertilizers and feed supplements were reaching farmers. From the middle of the nineteenth century, mechanical farm implements, whether purchased or rented, were sufficiently cheap and reliable to be good investments, especially since increasing inputs of capital gave landlords, land agents, and tenants an incentive to innovate and consider ways to make factors of production more efficient.

The contemporary expert Lord Ernle pointed out the connection between the cheapness and portability of artificial fertilizers and the decision to acquire mechanical implements: having paid good money for guano or mineral phosphates, the farmer could see the advantage of buying machines to spread them evenly and to make sure that weeds did not profit from this investment.[14] On the other hand, few farms were ideally suited to use, without expensive preparations, the potentially profitable machine harvesters. Where field enclosures were small, horsemen frequently needed to dismantle parts of their reaping machines in order to move them through narrow, muddy, hedge gates to the next field. Because of the rotation system, often the adjacent field would be planted with a different crop. Where the soil was heavy and wet, surface drainage might have been carried out by means of ditches or deep furrows and high ridges—a considerable obstacle to machines made of wood, leather, and iron and pulled by teams of heavy horses. On undulating ground, workmen did not always lay underdraining pipes at the same depth. Consequently farmers either had to put up with the difficulties of using steam cultivators on uneven surfaces or undertake an expensive overhaul of the drainage system before attempting to level fields. Thus it is correct to say that agriculture entered the machine age at about the same time that the railway builders were establishing a rail system. But a modern expert, Paul David, is also correct in stating that the farming landscape of early and mid-Victorian times "was not congenial to the introduction of agricultural machinery."[15]

It was H. V. Massingham's insight that the beauty of the "traditional" landscape was the unconscious product of skilled craftsmen intent on maximizing utilities.[16] Adult male specialized workers took over such tasks as horse-training, machinery operation and maintenance, hedging, and caring for sheep.[17] With skill of all sorts in abundant supply, it was often a rational decision to choose to employ that skill rather than invest in machinery and methods designed to make it redundant. C. K. Harley has put forward a theory that, given the storehouse of skills at their disposal, Edwardian entrepreneurs could reject the American assembly line and still compete successfully on world markets in a number of industrial sectors.[18] Agriculture may have suffered the economic consequences of having such an embarrassment of human riches even earlier than the manufacturing sector, but the land and the landscape were undoubtedly the gainers.

Therefore the contention that "the real mechanical revolution in British farming came in Victoria's reign" is open to question.[19] It is true that ever more sophisticated horse-drawn machinery became cheaper, lighter, and more durable from the 1850s onward and that machinery was widely employed on farms of over fifty acres. Manufacturers of horse-drawn harvesters, rollers, drills, rakes, and hoes (many of them adopted for relatively small farm operations) multiplied after midcentury and found eager buyers.[20] But for this transition to have been a revolution, hand labor, sufficiently plentiful and mobile for most farm tasks until the 1880s, would need to have been displaced more quickly and completely than it was. E. J. Collins has estimated that the 300-acre farm of 1910 had £140 worth of machinery and the average farm of 100 to 150 acres, only £80. He concludes that, while far more was spent on tools and equipment at the end of Victoria's reign than at the beginning, the proportion of farm capital so invested remained much the same.[21]

It follows that the mingling of old hand skills and new technology we noticed at Shutlanger Grove was the norm elsewhere. A farmer might employ a horse-pulled mechanical reaper to harvest wheat standing on sloping ground but then send men and boys with fagging hooks to take in densely packed grain on bottom land. Or he might send them to finish

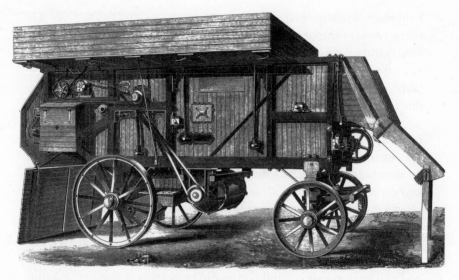

Figure 3.   Combined thresher and finisher (1876). Powered by a separate steam engine, this combine delivered straw in front, discharged chaff behind, and filled sacks with grain. When it appeared, hand cutting and threshing became adjuncts to the machine. (*Engineering* 22, 1876)

off, with scythes and sickles, the "headlands," the corners or edges of fields untouched by the reaper blades. Wind- and rain-flattened grain might need to be hand cut. Heavily ridged and furrowed fields might be machine reaped up and down their lengths and then again cut across by hand mowers. A temperate assessment is that from midcentury to the late 1860s, the machine was an important adjunct to hand cutting; and after that date, to the end of the Victorian era, hand cutting was an important adjunct to the machine.[22] Thus on all but the smallest farms by the end of the century, laborers planted, cultivated, and harvested grain, using horses to convey the crop (in wagons made, as they always had been made, by local craftsmen) to a rented steam thresher. (See Figure 3.)

Few farmers could afford to substitute steam for horsepower even when engineers made steam planting, cultivating, and harvesting cheaper and easier. The agricultural steam engine became more fuel-efficient and portable as time went on, but compared to the petrol-driven tractor of the next century, it remained heavy, clumsy, inflexible, and expensive to operate. If a large farm happened to have flat, rectangular fields about twenty acres in size, if it was situated on heavy soils and grew quantities of wheat, there might be large economies in using steam to get a crop in early and quickly. According to Hugh Prince, steam plowed 200,000 acres of the roughly 50,000,000 acres of arable land in Great Britain and Ireland in the golden days of the late 1860s.[23] Most of that work would have been done by professional contractors who would send engines and tackle, a foreman, two engine drivers, and a plowman. The farmer supplied two carts, one for hauling coal to engine fire-boxes and the other to carry water for the boilers, with two or three men to serve them. Grain prices would need to be steady to afford the advantage such a large expenditure entailed, the reason why so many plowing contractors went out of business when wheat prices collapsed in the 1880s.[24] As Lord Ernle noted, "few farmers can afford to own both horse-power and steam power, and without horses they cannot do."[25]

For these reasons steam farming remained a rarity. By the turn of the century fixed steam engines were the main power source for threshing and barn work (chopping and pulping turnips, crushing cake, grinding corn, lifting hay and straw, pumping and boiling water) on most farms of 100 acres or more—with some exceptions in the west of England, the north of Wales, and the Highlands of Scotland.[26] The experimental "California" engines and chain-driven plow platforms developed by Thomas Gooch at midcentury rapidly improved in efficiency.[27] But steam never threatened to make the horse redundant in rural or urban Britain.[28]

In fact the need for horse-supplied power steadily increased even through the years of agricultural hardship after the mid-1870s. Underdraining made plows easier to pull through wet, heavy clays. Thus one- or two-horse plows were substituted for the large teams formerly needed to lug cumbersome implements through heavy soils. Fewer horses in front of the plow meant fewer trampling hooves to compact the ground.

While the technology of intensive farming saved horsepower, it also created new uses for it. Where, for example, farmers had been reluctant to expend much energy in removing weeds from growing crops only several decades earlier, they now were motivated to keep fields cleaner and tidier than before and to use horse-drawn implements to do the work.[29] Thus between 1811 and 1880 the general horse population doubled. Since railways could seldom deliver goods door-to-door, the number of horse-drawn wagons and carts on the roads kept increasing.[30] Demand exceeded the capacity of domestic horse breeders. By the 1870s, Britain had become a net importer.[31] There were about 800,000 horses at work in agriculture in 1811, 940,000 in 1871, and 1,116,505 in 1901, the peak year.[32]

Had he lived to see this evidence of failure to create a thoroughly

mechanized nineteenth century agro-industry, George Mechi, perhaps
the century's most energetic agricultural modernizer, would have been
deeply depressed, although perhaps not surprised. He was emphatically
not a conservative, nor was he an Arcadian romantic. He believed, and
preached to all who would listen, that paternalism and sentimentality
were outmoded and dangerously irrational mental states, given what he
took to be the commonsense realities of the time. A successful London
businessman (Mechi's Magic Razor Straps, improved gas lamps, high
finance), he purchased a 170-acre farm, Tiptree-Hall, in 1843 on heavy,
wet Essex clays, "in a state between bird lime and putty." He thought it
an ideal place to show what could be done with even the most intractable
environments, given up-to-date methods and close attention to advances
in soil science.[33] Success at Tiptree-Hall would demonstrate, he hoped,
that the "existing *predilection for land as an honorable qualification*"
had become "absurd and inconsistent with our great commercial and
manufacturing dignity."[34]

Determined to act on that conviction, he proceeded to build a "substantial and genteel residence," lay out eighty to ninety miles of drains,
cut every tree, grub out hedges and level boundary banks, line enlarged
fields with roads, and erect cattle sheds with slotted floors so that "every
pint and pound of manure" could drop through and be piped from a collecting tank (as large as a chapel) to be sprayed on the fields. At the center of all these operations he placed a large fixed steam engine, the main
"instrument of progress." He added, "It facilitates intercourse, econo-
mizes time, multiplies labour, and cheapens production." In a characteristic burst of enthusiasm, he declared that "mighty steam," possesses
a "marvellous and almost invisible power which has no opposition,
which never tires. Scouring the plains, piercing the hills, threading the
valleys, and ploughing the wide ocean; mastering with indolent ease time
and space, wind, water, and season."[35] Now that "the feudal, wooden,
and pastoral age" had passed, giving way "to that of coal, iron, steam,
commerce and manufacture," the time had come, he urged any audience
he could persuade to listen, "to rescue land from its feudal swaddling
clothes and give it a modern suit, adopted to modern requirements."[36]

He said this in 1875 after his fortune was lost in the financial crash
of 1866 and his farm was nearing its eventual bankruptcy. In an address
entitled, ironically, *How I Make Farming Pay* he admitted to a gathering of the Midlands Farmers' Club that "there appears to be a total want
of commerciality in the dealing with land" despite the obvious fact that
food-producing had become a highly competitive business, "almost a

manufacture." He pointed out that decades of research and experiment by Liebig, Playfair, Hodge, Johnston, Lawes, and others had turned an empirical art into a "more dependable" craft.[37]

Thirty years earlier, he had discovered that his "desire to apply common sense principles . . . stumbled against the old antiquated castle of prejudice. Instantaneously there descended from its turrets on my poor devoted head such a storm of missiles, indignation, imprecation, ridicule, censure, disbelief, that had I not been clothed with the strong armour of truth, I must have succumbed."[38] But, experience, he conceded, had taught him how obstinately determined were the castle's defenders to fend off even the best-armored of truths. He had not fully appreciated the depth of conservatism in the mentality of his neighbors, not one of whom, he noted ruefully, had "followed my example." Nevertheless he clung to this vision, expressed as follows in the early, more hopeful days of his farming experiment:

> I see, in perspective, a railway activity pervading agriculture. The time is coming when farms will be squared, trees removed, and game moderated—when tramways will intersect estates, and one horse will draw to market the load of four—when the sewage of our towns will ebb back to its original source—when the waters of our rivers and drains will be applied to the irrigation of our fields—when our millers will use caloric engines instead of water—when our farmers and their children will be better educated and rank higher in the social scale—when our labourers will be better housed, taught, and fed.

After those things had come to pass, he continued, "then will antiquated territorial loyalties be superseded by personal responsibility, identity, and possession." He thought it only a matter of time before people would grow used to seeing "mighty engines on railwayed open fields, tearing up furrows a yard deep, making the land look like a sea."[39]

Mechi was able to recognize and perhaps even to feel a twinge of regret that the visual beauty of the landscape would be swept away in this tide, but he asked his readers and audiences to reflect on the Malthusian dilemma. As population increases, Mechi wrote three years after his experiment started, "stern necessity" will compel the farmer "to sweep from the land those pleasing, green fences, trees, and pastures, whose agreeableness blinds us to their cruel unprofitableness. . . . Let us, then, take time by the forelock, and do that willingly and profitably, which otherwise we must submit to grudgingly by stern compulsion."[40]

Probably Mechi was more pleased to sacrifice agreeableness to stern necessity and stern compulsion than he allowed himself to admit. To him, an outsider to landed society, the flowering hedgerow and green, patchwork fields dotted with cattle and sheep signified feudalism. A perceptive Frenchman, Léonce de Lavergne, included a visit to Tiptree-Hall in his 1851 inspection tour of British agriculture. He noted in a subsequent article for *Revue des Deux Mondes* that his host, a bourgeois bent on displacing the aristocratic improver, was "one of those energetic individuals who anticipate the future while seeking by every means to escape from the difficulties of the present." Lavergne recognized that what he had seen on this model farm—the central steam engine, the stall-fed animals, "shut up in melancholy cloisters," and treated as manure machines—was not typical of British farming, being more an exercise in wounded, middle-class pride than in profit-seeking.[41] Equally interesting was Lavergne's observation that the economic realities of the time, forces Mechi so often evoked, were the very factors he tended to ignore in his role as seer. Like so many enthusiasts, Mechi concentrated on increasing productivity rather than adjusting each operation to market forces.

More professional, although not more typical, in his attempt to apply what he considered to be the logic of steam energy and the new soil science technology to food production was John Prout of Blount's Farm in Hertfordshire. Like Mechi, he recognized that the first step required of a progressive farmer was to convert his cold, undrained clay (so stiff and heavy "it would starve a donkey")[42] into productive cornland. Again, like Mechi, his solution was to rely on steam and on the advice of soil scientists, in this case Augustus Voelcker, an expert employed by the Royal Agricultural Society of England, who examined the soil samples and worked out a mix of artificial supplements, designed to allow for continuous corn growing.

Before starting this regime in 1861, Prout invested heavily in drainage for his 450 acres. In this he had an advantage in being able to use a steam mole to lay his pipe drains, having started his experiment twenty years later than Mechi. As at Tiptree-Hall, out went the ancient hedgerows, six and a half miles of them, and down went the trees, 920 falling to the ax. Along the much-enlarged fields Prout stretched ring fences and built roads strong enough to hold portable steam engines. To supply their boilers, he dug reservoirs equipped with pumps, it being his intention to use steam wherever possible. Essential to his strategy was deep plowing to break up the hardpan and make the soil more friable, a task horses would have found impossible. Where he went beyond Mechi was in his decision to eliminate all animals, except for a few horses to sow oats and barley in the wet spring season, and to rely exclusively on imported guano and artificial fertilizers: superphosphates, soot, and nitrate of soda.

Between 1861 and 1880, according to Voelcker, who monitored the effect of this specialization on the soil's fertility, productivity rose by a hundred percent.[43] Were it only possible, Prout wrote in 1881, for tenants to be freed from the drag of indifferent landlords, they might be able to follow his example and thus withstand the barrage of cheap imported grains. As it was, he deplored, as Mechi had done, the fact that so few of his admirers had decided to imitate his methods. Lack of publicity could not be the explanation: thousands of agriculturalists had visited his farm, he said, and chemists had analyzed his soil and published their highly positive findings. In any other business, he mused, successes such as his would have produced a flood of improvers.[44]

Mechi and Prout were among the first to realize and put into action the potentiality of steam agriculture, but their calculations did not take all of the costs into account.[45] Thus they assumed, wrongly, that indolence or stubborn resistance to change caused their neighbors to prefer these compromises: horse-powered machinery, supplemented, mainly at harvest time by steam engines, and continued reliance on a gradually diminishing quantity, but growing quality, of hand labor.[46]

The success of another innovator illustrates the point. Beginning in 1875, when cereal prices began their long fall, George Baylis, son of a Berkshire tenant farmer, built a corn-growing empire. By 1917 he owned or rented 12,140 arable acres. Unlike Mechi and Prout, he looked at new technologies not for how much they would increase production but for how much profit they would bring in. When others were laying aside the plow and turning fields into pastures, Baylis grew rich by turning to wheat monoculture, using ammonia and phosphates from artificial fertilizers almost exclusively to replenish the soil. Where his fields were large, flat, and easily worked, he plowed with steam; on most of his operations, however, he found that, until the 1920s, horse-drawn machinery brought in a higher return, despite rising labor costs. Until tractors and trucks made steam hauling and cultivation technologically obsolete, this consummate rationalizer relied on some 250 workhorses.[47] Only a handful of innovators followed his example and restructured their farm holdings on factory principles. His interest in cost accounting, however, was part of a trend. As he demonstrated during a time when the use of steam energy reached its highest point, reliance on animal power could still be sound business strategy.

Because Victorian and Edwardian landscape was fashioned by horses, pulling machinery designed to make efficient use of animal skill and muscle, field patterns retained, despite all the technical advances of the period, a pleasing variety and a feeling of comfortable intimacy. Field enclosures on the best arable land tended to be larger than they had been in the eighteenth century. In the third quarter of the nineteenth century large farms gained at the expense of small.[48] On the other hand, a constantly accelerating expansion of market gardening along railway links with major urban markets during the latter part of the century led to a division of some properties into small holdings, intensively cultivated by hand. Where machines did the tilling and harvesting, hedges were sometimes grubbed out;[49] but so long as horses were vital and crop routines depended on manure from large stocks of cattle and sheep and so long as estate owners were concerned with providing cover for game, most of those hedges, walls, and ditches survived. They sheltered insects and wildlife while giving definition to the countryside. At the same time, they were essential to the system. Some form of containment was required when sheep were folded on fields during or just before a turnip course and when it was the turn of a field to be put to grasses or clover and grazed by cattle.

Farmer Franklin and his predecessors produced a landscape that reflected their ways of working as well as their attitudes and aspirations. Mixed farming and diverse crop rotations, for example, painted the countryside with a kaleidoscope of colors and patterns: in the spring the rich dark brown of plowed earth, turning smooth and lighter as the sharp teeth of the harrow cut through the clods, the emerald green of young wheat next to the paler green of early grass pasture; in the late summer and autumn, the whitish spread of the barley field, side by side with the blond and copper of ripe grain and the blue-gray leaves of the mature turnips. This harmonious blending of so many patterns, textures, and colors, marked off by lines of darker hedgerow or gray stone, came to be thought of, even at the time, as the "traditional" landscape.

Thus the lowland landscape of mid- and late Victorian times was, in a most literal way, a "synthesis of man and nature."[50] The countryside managed to be both dynamic and stable, partly mechanized yet still organic in so many of its processes, rationalized by earlier standards but still preserving regional variations and traditions, not preindustrial and not fully industrialized. Where high farming was practiced, there was some increase in farm size; elsewhere the scale of farming did not change radically. On most "progressive" estates the work was done by a combination of energies: hand, horse, and steam working together. Because the visible features of much of the land reflected those balances, it could comfort and reassure an age that was well aware of the damage industry and urban growth were inflicting on the environment. This goes far to explain why George Perkins Marsh's warnings tended to be dismissed as exaggerations—when they were received at all. Because the agriculture of high farming returned to the soil what it took out, often improving the soil's texture and fertility in the process, the robbery of the earth's resources by mining, quarrying, tree cutting, polluting, trampling, and house building provoked alarm and indignation but not despair.

It is possible, of course, to overstate this ecological and aesthetic success. The French visitor Lavergne claimed in the early 1850s that "English agriculture, taken as a whole, is at this day the first in the world." [51] This, some thought, was perhaps being excessively enthusiastic. Professor Scott Watson of Edinburgh University was undoubtedly right when he recommended James Caird's 1851 reports on agricultural conditions to the *Times* as a far more balanced appraisal.[52]

The increase in productivity on the high-farming estates in light soil regions of the English Midlands and Southeast and in the Scottish Lowlands was, everyone agreed, one of the wonders of the world. Tenants on high-farming estates managed to survive competition from foreign grain imports between 1846 and the mid-1870s by efficiently responding to the brisk demand for wheat and, increasingly, meat. Their fertilization and rotation regimes built up the soil, and their determination to get as much as possible out of each field fashioned a trim, clean, attractive countryside.

Elsewhere, especially on the heavy clays and areas of marginal fertility, progress was slower and considerably less impressive. By no means did every English estate carry on high farming, and the few Welsh landowners and farmers who did so were concentrated in the Vale of Glamorgan, the southern part of Monmouthshire, and South Gower.[53] At the end of the nineteenth century the agriculture of South Cardiganshire was still a study in "Medieval simplicity." [54] Five- to seven-course rotation systems relying on turnip breaks, heavy dunging, and careful weeding to keep soils clean and fertile were firmly and widely established only in the Scottish Lowlands.[55] In other places the investigator would hardly have noticed that many small-scale farmers were suspicious of new methods and fertilizers and that many land restorers prepared the ground only to exploit it for short-term profit. Nevertheless, the generalization still holds that, until wheat prices collapsed in the last quarter of the century, mixed farming in Britain created an "elegant" balance, although, as it turned out, a precarious one.[56]

Admirers of high-farming methods also need to remember that, with exceptions, the heavy investment never brought a particularly high return and contributed to the sluggishness with which many grain-growing regions responded to the changes in the late Victorian food market.[57] As wheat prices plummeted during the decade after the mid-1870s, "the edifice of high farming," which rested on heavy capital investment in the land's productivity, came tumbling with it.[58] Until 1900 rents and land prices dropped steadily. Owners of large consolidated holdings were not inclined to take advantage of falling prices for chemical fertilizers and oil cake under these circumstances. Spending even more to increase productivity and economize on land use had little appeal. Nor were producers much interested in laying out capital for more machinery to reduce their large and increasing wage bills so long as the heavy and clumsy steam engine was still the main alternative to the motive power of horses and handworkers.[59]

The Great Depression was real for those who, partly for structural reasons, could not or would not convert their operations to produce high-grade beef, or dairy products, or, as on the Cambridgeshire fens, fruit and vegetables for the urban market. Twelve percent of the arable land of Britain in 1872 was in wheat, and in 1913, five percent. The percentage of barley and oats dropped less precipitously from twelve to nine. Estimated farm income fell some forty percent between the mid-1870s and the late 1890s. In the breadbasket of Essex, where heavy clays had always been costly to cultivate, farmers calculated costs of keeping hedges trim and maintaining ditches and drains and decided to retrench. In all parts of eastern and southern England and on sandy soils made productive before by lavish fertilization, fields "tumbled down to grass" or, in particularly depressed areas, to thistles, brambles, and bracken. Water meadows, once maintained by experts, all but disappeared. Between 1871 and 1901 the number of laborers employed on the land shrank by a third; those who remained had to be used by hard-pressed employers in the most immediately productive ways. Man-, woman-, and child-power could not be expended on trimming and tidying up. Therefore in many grain-producing areas the polish did go out of cultivation. Hard times showed in overgrown hedges, dilapidated walls, unweeded crops.

Governments responded to these ominous signs by appointing committees of inquiry. The duke of Richmond's Royal Commission on Agriculture sat from 1879 to 1882 and heard tales of woe from tenant farmers. Lord Ernle summed up the question so many of them, in one way or another, were asking: how could they be expected to "hold their own in a treacherous climate on highly rented land, whose fertility required constant renewal, against produce raised under more genial skies on cheaply rented soils, whose virgin richness needed no fertilisers?"

The subsequent report confirmed that the distress was real, but, believing the trend to be cyclical rather than secular, suggested legislation to lower taxes, adjust rents, and ease burdens. No legislation to expedite transformation to a new economic world was forthcoming. Until 1896, when conditions tended to stabilize, food import figures continued to rise, wheat prices continued to fall, the cost of labor remained high, and rents kept on sliding, although not fast enough to rescue some hard-pressed tenants on grain-producing estates. "Scarcely one bright feature," recalled Lord Ernle, "relieved the gloom of the outlook." [60]

Beginning in the 1960s, economic historians began questioning this melancholy account. One of the first to suggest that "depression" was too sweeping a description was T. W. Fletcher, who noted that bad times for grain farmers in the south and east of England meant that livestock feeders and dairy farmers could fatten animals on cheaper oil cake and coarse grains. He gave, as an example, the cheese, milk, butter, beef, and mutton producers of eastern Lancashire who met the challenges offered by high demand for protein in a highly competitive market by taking advantage of lower feed prices, down by a third during the "depression" years. Dairies, so abundant in the region, had difficulty competing with ever-cheapening foreign cheese and butter. Liquid milk was a more attractive option. Because it was so perishable, it had protection from foreign competition. Demand from city dwellers kept rising. [61] Gradually the Danes and Dutch took over much of the responsibility for providing the English breakfast, but the British hen still provided the egg and the British cow continued to whiten the national cup of tea. [62]

Where crop and farming conditions were roughly similar to eastern Lancashire, farmers developed similar strategies. Central to the Scottish arable system was a regime of rotation based on oats, barley, grass, with a turnip or potato break to recuperate the soil. Meat, not bread, was what delivered the profits. For that reason, the collapse of wheat prices was seldom devastating. Prices for other grains fell as well but less dramatically. Farmers recognized that they could cover some of their losses by increasing their emphasis on animal production, since the market for premium domestic beef stood up reasonably well to foreign competition.[63] In northeastern regions, there were still significant numbers of small farms, worked mainly by family labor. Therefore savings could be made through more intensive exploitation of household members, rigorous belt-tightening, and lower feed bills. There was a tendency to include more grass leas in rotations but not to let the land go to permanent pasture. Few farms remained unoccupied for long. The soil continued to be well dunged and weeded. The number of fat cattle going out from Aberdeen for southern markets rose from 39,000 in the 1870s to 60,000 in 1900.[64] Scottish arable farmers in general struggled and sacrificed to adjust to change and did so with considerable success. There were no complaints in the last quarter of the nineteenth century that these tillers of the soil had ceased to be careful husbandmen.

Lowland Wales, like lowland Scotland, was cushioned against the shock of falling prices by the fact that the climate favored livestock farming and discouraged the growing of wheat. There were some large, high-farming estates in the Vale of Glamorgan, South Pembrokeshire, Denbighshire, and Flintshire, and these suffered from the difficulty of converting away from cereals to other activities; but a large majority of smaller farmers were still semisubsistent producers when the time of troubles began in the later 1870s. The typical small holding would have a few sheep and some store cattle. These they would feed oats and hay from their own hillside fields. A cow or two allowed them to make butter on the farmstead. Thus there would be no need for drastic restructuring. When livestock prices dropped in the mid 1880s, those who produced for distant markets experienced hardship; but it was this class of farmer who benefited most from the improvement in the 1870s of railway communications and the consequent availability of inexpensive imported feedstuffs.

Because Wales as a whole had come slowly, hesitantly, and unevenly into the era of capital-intensive, market-oriented agriculture, its response to the new incentives seemed particularly impressive. Railways, having penetrated so late in the century into formerly isolated regions, brought about striking increases in crop yields. Consequently, growth rates were higher than in England, where the economic benefits of a mature transport system had been felt for decades.[65] Thus observers of the Welsh landscape would have needed to look closely to detect the visual effects of these adjustments to changed agricultural conditions.

By contrast, changes would have been easily noticeable wherever the soil, climate, location, and size of farm units made it practical to grow fruit, flowers, and vegetables. As in the case of milk production, access to rail transport was crucial to success. Orchard acreage nearly doubled in England and Wales in the last quarter of the century. New canning and jam-manufacturing industries created opportunities for Kentish soft fruit growers and market gardeners in the Lea Valley and the Vale of Evesham. Some Norfolk farmers survived by growing mustard for the Coleman's factory. A special train carried produce from glass hothouses in Sussex each morning to Covent Garden, and another brought in celery from the Lincolnshire coast.[66] By the end of the century railways and steamships were filling market stalls with fresh produce from everywhere in Britain and every corner of the world: out-of-season onions from Egypt, apples from New Zealand, potatoes from the Canary Islands. The cultivation of flowers, seeds, and bulbs for suburban homes and gardens added splashes of vivid color to local landscapes in the Fenlands, the Scilly Isles, and almost every place where climate, soil, and, above all, rail transport combined to make specialization profitable.[67] While the gross output of wheat in the United Kingdom, measured by weight in millions of pounds, fell from 27.56 in 1870–76 to 7.72 in 1894–1903, the output of hay, straw, fruit, and vegetables rose over the same period from 19.40 to 21.75.[68]

Mention of exceptions, notice of regional variations, presentation of selected statistics, complicate but do not refute the claim that the long process of taming wildness and reclaiming rough or sodden environments did tend to slow down and, in some places, cease or go into reverse during the last quarter of the nineteenth century and the first third of the twentieth. It is also true that formerly outlawed plant species, birds, small mammals, insects—wildlife in general—benefited wherever brakes were applied, marginal soils abandoned, reclamation projects canceled, coppices and infrastructure neglected, and weeds allowed to invade once well-tended crop and meadowlands. Collins makes the valuable observation that many of the soft, romantic landscape features and ecologically rich environments that preservationists are now especially eager to retain were saved from the plow or allowed to revert to a more natural state when the "biological exploitation of the countryside" lost some of its energy in the 1880s and thereafter. "When agriculturalists despaired, aesthetes rejoiced," is Hugh Prince's version of that idea.[69]

Some late Victorian and Edwardian agriculturalists despaired, a few rejoiced, most struggled and carried on. We should not exaggerate the extent of deceleration and dereliction or fall into the old error of assuming that what happened in places like Essex was symptomatic of all agriculture and all rural landscapes in so richly diverse an environment as the British Isles. During the later years of the steam era, the face of the lowland countryside did change; some luster faded, blotches appeared, but the bone structure remained much the same.

That generalization could not be so confidently made in 1944, when Bedford Franklin wrote about his father's skill as a builder and restorer of permanent pastures. By that time the transformation Mechi had so ardently wished for had become clearly apparent. After 1918, the shift of energy source from coal to liquid carbons accelerated. Between the wars, modern agribusiness, specialization, concentration on reducing labor costs by applying sophisticated machinery, the virtual elimination of animal labor, the massive use of chemical fertilizers, pesticides, and herbicides had advanced far enough to alarm Franklin and make him want to remind his countrymen of what was being lost.

What happened in 1929 in the Cambridgeshire fens to the south and west of the Isle of Ely was an early demonstration of this transformation's ecological consequences. In the late winter of that year, the region experienced the worst dust storm in living memory. As Muriel Arbor noted, local farmers at first blamed a heavy frost for having broken up the fine black peaty soil; but they had to look for other explanations when, in subsequent years, the same thing kept happening during the violent winds of February through May. Swirling dust obscured the sun; seeds and young shoots blew away along with the top layers of soil. Dykes seven feet across could fill in a few hours.[70] Reluctantly, Fenland farmers came to accept that the cause was their decision to convert from mixed farming to the growing of sugar beets, a new crop introduced from Belgium and northern France in 1905.

The difficulty was that this particular agro-industry disturbed a delicate balance that had been constructed and reconstructed. During the first quarter of the nineteenth century, most of the Fenland had been, according to H. C. Darby, "drained in theory but not in fact."[71] By this he meant that existing wind and water mills, dredging equipment, watercourse engineering, and administrative arrangements had made the land dry enough to farm but could not prevent large-scale inundations. New channels and outfalls straightened the sinuous rivers and greatly improved the general drainage system. But it was the steam-driven pump that, above all, gave Fenland farmers reasonable expectations of stability. Experimental steam pumps appeared in 1817 and became well established during the 1830s. By 1852 sixty steam engines had drained 222,000 acres of land in the Bedford Levels and Lincolnshire.[72]

Not unexpectedly, technological solutions to the problem of how to keep reclaimed marshland dry created other problems. One reason windmills were gradually replaced was that they caused subsidence. This meant that pumps would need to raise water from ditches to higher levels in order to discharge it into major channels and rivers. Steam power overcame that difficulty but greatly accelerated the rate of subsidence. When drained and cultivated, the peat contracted as a wet sponge does when gradually squeezed. Darby illustrated this effect with a photograph of an iron column at Holme Fen in Huntingtonshire. In 1851 it had been pounded into solid clay, the top at ground level. In 1860 four feet, nine inches of the column stood above the surface; fifteen years later, the exposed part measured eight feet, two inches. When the picture was taken in 1933, almost twelve feet of post were showing.[73] A recent estimate is that the fens have lost well over half of their volume of peat. Ditches and rivers stand as high as fourteen feet above the fields they pass through.[74] Thus it would be difficult to imagine a physical environment more dependent on human ingenuity for its appearance and its continuance.

To the engineer's ingenuity was added the farmer's. The soil was inherently unstable since its organic particles, when dry, lost much of their capacity to cohere. Therefore, as the peat areas of the Fenlands shrank, they also began to lose some topsoil to wind erosion. There was, however, a compensation: as the clay floor "rose" it became easier to mix marl (lime-rich clay) from that lower layer into the light, organic material on top.[75] J. A. Clarke, writing in 1852, spoke of how, over the past thirty years, the "powdery peat" had been "exchanged for the richly cropped arable of the new corn-bearing mould," giving "solidity and tenacity to the soil." The result, said Clarke, was "the most fertile and productive of soils."[76] In such soil, rotation regimes of roots, grasses, and grains (fertilized by manure from stock) produced, on a sustainable basis, some of the best crops in Europe. Peaty humus absorbed and held moisture and allowed entry for air; the clay supplied potash; animals ingested nitrogen from plants and returned it in the form of dung and urine; the clay, manure, and deep roots of the grain and grasses bound the soil and checked the effect of wind and water erosion. The calcium in the clay reduced or neutralized the acidity of the peat soil, allowing bacteria to convert the nitrogen in the fertilizer into a soluble form, making it available to plants.[77] Victorian farming had disturbed a natural harmony only to create a new one, one that had far more heart than it had possessed in the state of nature.

This flat world, tamed and maintained by human ingenuity, did, over the years, change some of its colors and textures. The fortunes of mixed (a variety of crops and grasses with livestock), high (capital-intensive) farming suffered in Cambridgeshire as it did in most regions during the difficult time of adjustment for agriculture in the last quarter of the century. The more enterprising scaled down their corn growing and converted to intensified production of fruits, vegetables (especially new potatoes), and flowers for the urban market.[78] In the southern peat zone of the Cambridgeshire fens, the growing of sugar beets proved to be, in the long run, one of the keys to survival and prosperity.

For all its merits, the sugar beet, it is generally conceded, is a dull and demanding vegetable. It is a "gross feeder" in that it robs the soil of nutrients and consequently requires heavy doses of fertilizer. Monoculture assured that most of this nourishment would come, not from the stockyard, but in a bag purchased from a retailer. It was much cheaper to use the lighter manufactured lime when it became readily available than to pay expensive labor to dig and spread clay or to bring it in by cart or rail.[79] Powdered lime kept the soil sweet but did not thicken it. Furthermore, before the beet could be planted, the ground had to be plowed deeply. This allowed frost to penetrate to a greater depth than it would have done had the ground been prepared for grain. The effect was to pulverize the soil. The leaves of the growing crop provided less cover than did grain; therefore weeds grew readily and had to be removed, disturbing the surface of the ground. Grain and grass courses of the rotation system had left roots in the ground after mowing; in the case of beets, the root was the product. The old system had acted to fix the surface during part of the windy season; the beet harvest left behind no such protection. Furthermore investment in machinery led in many cases to the grubbing out of hedges and trees.[80] The consequence of this radical change of crops and methods became apparent whenever the cold, dry winds of spring began to blow, seemingly direct from the Steppes, across the level plain.

Franklin had case histories like this one in mind when he predicted that a time would come when farmers and the general public would need to confront the fact that scientifically induced high yields were taking the heart out of the soil. Land was in "good heart," he explained, when it produced abundantly and free of disease the crops and meat suited to its character.[81] An earlier generation of farmers had been obliged by the surrounding culture and the limitations of the available technology to pay close attention to nature's ways and respect her wishes. Should some future generation learn that degree of humility, perhaps then, Franklin hoped, farmers might again see relevance in his father's example of good husbandry: the mixed farming rotations, the utilization of natural fertilizers, the desire to preserve ecological interrelationships, the concern for sustainability, the attention to energy conservation, the loving care of land and landscape.

4
Upland Moors

The chief point is that the incessant selective grazing of sheep
over so long a period must exhaust the soil.
     E. W. Fenton, Scottish Geographical Magazine, *1937*

At its best, Victorian high farming came close to answering Marsh's plea
to "use the world as not abusing it."[1] Although "vanquished by human
art"[2] and made to produce abundantly, nature had been respected and
allowed to retain her healing and harmonizing powers on fertile acres of
lowland farming estates. But on higher ground no such balance between
human ambition and environmental integrity was likely. Many generations of peasant communities, crofters, and other small holders had extracted livings from rough hillside pastures and highland moors by working out methods suited to the character of their land. But the other aspect
of good husbandry, as Franklin had defined it—the capacity to produce
abundantly—had seldom been realized.

New tools, techniques, and incentives for development tempted enterprising people to find ways to squeeze riches out of high, open, wind-
swept environments. This happened with increasing frequency when the
market for fiber and food greatly expanded in the late eighteenth century.
Sometimes improvers and developers met with success, but it was seldom
for long. Within the million or so hectares of heather wastes, stretching
from Land's End to Yorkshire, then north and westward to Cape Wrath,
can be found many testimonials to the moor's vulnerability and to its capacity for inflicting pain on the excessively ambitious. Thus Victorian
agricultural history is, in a variety of ways, highly instructive.

A graphic example of how an upland landscape can teach the observant eye lessons in the wages of greed and hubris appears in the long, straight lines of stone fencing that impose geometry on Somerset's sinuously contoured Mendip Hills. A striking transformation was worked there between 1780 and 1820, during which time land improvers converted some 25,000 acres of rough grazing land into arable fields. They were reacting to high grain prices brought about by the wars with the American colonists and the French. More directly, they were also responding to the enthusiasm of one man, John Billingsley of Ashwick Grove, a landowner from a prominent Presbyterian family, a brewer, a member of a turnpike trust, a canal and colliery promoter, and a passionate advocate of agricultural improvement.[3]

In a report commissioned by the Board of Agriculture called *A General View of the Agriculture of Somerset,* issued in 1797, Billingsley commented favorably on the Mendip venture—not surprising, seeing that he had labored so diligently to persuade Parliament to approve the area's enclosure. The topsoil of the high plateau, he wrote, was, for the most part, deep and loamy, resting on a strong clay base. Although fertile enough, it had never been plowed; instead it was kept as upland common. There an indifferent breed of sheep grazed on coarse grasses and provided an unenterprising community with mean livings. The climate was cold, foggy, and wet; winds, except in the summer months, were so "boisterous" that flocks needed to be wintered over on lower ground. Scarcity of stored fodder imposed limits on how many animals could be kept and sent in the early springtime to high ground. Also, winter feed being scarce, grazers tended not to wait for mid-May when the roots of the new growth would have taken hold.

Overgrazing and soil depletion were the predictable results. Billingsley pointed out these inherent difficulties and argued that a far better use of the land would be to convert the sheep runs into arable fields, grow grain as a cash crop, and put in roots for winter fodder. He recognized that he could not alter the climate and that the farms would need intelligent, prudent, and progressive tenants who understood that this environment would be unforgiving. But he was sure that attention to the new ideas about rotation and fertilizers would produce impressive results—indeed he could report in 1797 that considerable progress had already been made.[4]

Two decades later, peace depressed most agricultural prices. Because landowners and tenants had already poured capital into draining, burning turf, breaking up the clay subsoil by deep plowing, constructing farm buildings and houses, and laying out 1,650 miles of hedges and stone walls, they were strongly tempted to take what quick profits they could regardless of the long-term consequences. They were able to do so because lime was available close to the surface and could be used, at modest expense, to sweeten the soil. With so much of this resource near at hand, farmers could lay on course after course of wheat, oats, barley, and potatoes, without needing, at least for a time, to provide for turnips and other stock fodder. Without a supply of well-fed stock, there would not be an adequate supply of manure. Also, without large flocks of sheep, it would impossible to abide by Billingsley's dictum that folding (penning sheep at night behind movable fences on fields that needed fertilizing) was the "*sine qua non*" of good husbandry.[5] Over the short run, however, it was much cheaper to build a lime kiln than to provide food and shelter for cattle and sheep and then wait for manure to mound up. Billingsley had cautioned that liming would maintain the ground "tolerably well" for the first seven years of successive corn cropping but that retribution was sure to follow in the form of coltsfoot and couch grass, clear signs of a general deterioration.[6]

And so it happened. John Watson, a Westmoreland land agent, could have had the Mendips in mind when he commented in 1845 that for the past eighty or so years many tracts of heath had been reclaimed with "utter disregard to anything beyond an immediate profit."[7] Driven by greed and anxiety about how to pay rents, the Mendip farmers mined the soil's fertility in the 1820s and 1830s and "beggared" the plateau.[8]

By midcentury, large stretches of the Mendips had again become summer grazing ground for sheep and, increasingly, cattle. "Mendip land," noted Thomas Dyke Acland in 1850, "is proverbial for its 'short memory.'" So too were many of the Mendip farmers. According to Acland, some of them decided that the land, in grass for fifteen years, had rested long enough. They proceeded to divide their farms into one-acre plots and, for a pound rent, let them out to impoverished potato growers. The timing could not have been worse: potatoes went into the ground in the later 1840s, just when the ruinous blight visited Ireland and the rest of the kingdom. This circumstance brought the experiment to a swift end.[9]

Later in the century, the quarrying of limestone and lava rock to make railway beds and later, road surfaces, gave the western Mendips a new industry, one that made a major impact on the landscape. It was partly to protect the area from becoming further pockmarked that the government, under a provision of the law that established national parks in 1949, declared the Mendip Hills an Area of Outstanding Beauty. So controlled, the region seems to have become again a "landscape of stone and wind, of space and muted colours."[10] However the gray stone ruins of farmhouses set in the middle of large, oblong fields, marked by straight stone walls, still disclose the many follies acted out in the second half of the eighteenth century and the first quarter of the nineteenth century and testify to the perils of forcing nature to perform unnatural acts.

A far more extensive attempt to exploit meager upland resources took place in the Scottish Highlands during the nineteenth century. Evident in the patterns, colors, and artifacts of the landscape is the impressive extent of this effort. Folk memory, sustained by song, literature, and film, preserves a legend about a unique and culturally rich communal society of small plots and pastures cruelly and deliberately destroyed by alien exploiters bent on establishing a large-scale, sheep-grazing, commercial economy, regardless of human costs. It is a story several generations of geographers and economic historians have tried to demythologize. They show that a money economy based on the breeding and export of cattle to English markets had taken hold in southern Scotland well before the introduction of commercial sheep farming in the 1760s and 1770s and that a class of middlemen had gradually formed to serve the interest of profit-minded large landowners. Thus social and economic forces had long been undermining the clan communality that, according to the legend, the Hanoverians had supposedly set out to destroy after their victory in 1746 over Jacobite forces at Culloden.

Modern specialists on the subject also tend to argue that the nineteenth century Highland Clearances—the displacing of the population from the mountains and upland glens and its resettlement on the coasts and deep valleys or far away in Canada and America—should be regarded as "rational" responses to economic and demographic exigencies, leaving aside the motives or excesses of some individuals. It is customary to end analyses such as these by expressing regret for the suffering that accompanies any displacement.

Again we are reminded that landscape is text as well as color and topography. One can read the landscape of the Scottish Highlands for what it says about historical determinism or, as James Bryce, the Victorian Alpinist and Liberal politician did, as an expression of "joyous freedom."[11] But one can also read it as a record of suffering and injustice.

The argument that this transformation of landscape and way of life was necessary and inevitable would have been stronger had large-scale commercial sheep farming turned out to be a long-term solution to the problem of Highland poverty and had the results benefited the soil and the biosphere. Clearly, no such case can be made. Generalized appraisals have to contend with the diversity of soils, climates, and circumstances; nevertheless, there seems to be a consensus that turning small holdings and common grazing areas into huge sheep runs tended to exhaust the soil, promote erosion, and encourage the spread of bracken, moss, and unpalatable sedges and grasses. There is evidence that grazers continued to take far more from the soil than they were willing to return to it even when the folly of this behavior was obvious and the remedies were reasonably well understood.

Those who go even further and assert that large-scale commercial sheep farming was an "economic catastrophe" are inclined to argue that the old ways were better for the soil and the landscape. Roy Millward and Adrian Robinson, for example, tend to admire aspects of the systems of land use found in many parts of upland Britain during the Middle Ages and surviving in parts of Scotland until the late eighteenth century—even later in the northwest Highlands.[12] The model they and others use to describe this system (called *run-rig*) posits a settlement (called a *ferm toun* in the Scottish Lowlands or *clachan* in the Highlands) with clusters of buildings for six to twelve households, usually placed near the most sunny and fertile tract, or *infield*. In Scotland this was sometimes called the *mukked land* because it received most of the available livestock manure and was used to grow two successive crops of oats and then one of barley. A larger arable circle, the *outfield*, worked in patches or strips, would be sown with oats for five years or until the soil was worked out, left in grass to recover for the same length of time, and then folded just before the next round of oats.[13] Beyond this outer circle would lie the rough, common pastures—usually moorland in the Highlands.

It was on this expanse of high ground that the settlement would establish clusters of turf or stone dwellings and work buildings—the summer *sheiling* in Scotland or *hafodtai* in Wales. Women and children and some of the men of the settlement would migrate to the *sheiling* with their horses, cattle, goats, sheep, and chickens in the late spring and remain until the crops of the inner and outer fields were safely taken in, at which time the poultry and larger livestock would be herded back to the settlement and turned loose on the stubble left over from the harvest. Tenants would be allotted *soums* (areas of summer pasture) proportional to their arable holdings. This practice of shifting the livestock to different pastures depending on the season—called *transhumance*—ensured that the plowed fields would not be trampled while under crops, that fallow outfield patches would be conserved during the summer and autumn, and that heather and grasses on the surrounding slopes would have a chance to grow undisturbed until late April or early May.[14]

So long as population grew slowly, custom and circumstance worked out a balance between subsistence and resources. The relative scarcity of winter fodder acted to control overgrazing. As in the case of the pre-enclosure Mendip plateau, shortage of arable land ensured that the number of animals sent to the hill pastures would be limited. Folk experience established systems for making sure that gazing land was used appropriately: on the summer pastures the animals were separated according to species and age groupings. Newborn lambs, calves, and goats would be weaned early so that their mothers' milk could go into cheese making. The newborn animals would be kept in good health on the best grazing places.[15]

A by-product of this way of living and working was landscape beauty: since the strips or patches would be going through different cycles of vegetation, there would be a pleasing variety of texture and color. The open hills and mountainsides were not barren stretches: there were settlements on inland straths and *sheiling* huts out on the wastes. Around these huts would be small bands of green, marking where cattle had been tethered and small crops of oats taken. Thus the system, with its multiple activities, allocated resources equitably and humanized the landscape.

In the Scottish Highland version of this model of traditional upland life, cattle would have outnumbered sheep four or five to one. This ratio worked in favor of slope stability in the steep uplands since cattle, as a general rule, cannot be wintered over on high ground. Also grazing cattle do not discriminate, to the extent that sheep do, between dead matter and live and therefore are less apt to select out the most nutritious plants and diminish their proportion of the plant cover. Put another way, a rapid increase in sheep population can have a destructive effect on the ecology of moorland because sheep are inclined to avoid the nutritionally valueless mat grass and only feed on purple moor grass when deprived of alternatives.[16]

A kind of Gresham's law can then apply. If the peat face were trimmed back severely, as tended to happen on high, steep, heavily stocked sheep runs, the lower layers would be exposed to the drying effect of sun and wind. Frost would penetrate deeper than before, and vegetation would gradually lose its capacity to protect the soil underneath from wind and water erosion. In such conditions, a spell of dry weather accompanied by high winds could skim off the soil and leave scree behind. If conditions were unusually wet, the reduced ground cover would lose some of its capacity to retain water. Subsurface runoff would increase, washing sediment down into the streams. Although moor and peat bog erosion may be caused by the morphology of the heather plant itself as well as by climatic changes, biotic factors usually begin this degenerative process where slopes are heavily grazed by sheep.[17] Thus another positive feature of the older system was its reliance on cattle rather than on sheep.

But a case can also be made for the fragility of the system, especially when tested by population growth. There is some evidence that, from the mid–eighteenth century, communities tried to feed an expanding but largely immobile population by intensive cropping and subdivision of the more fertile infields. Lower yields per acre were the inevitable result. Another response was to extend outfields and bring more marginal land into cultivation. To prepare this rough pasture for oats, barley, or potatoes, animals would be folded at night during the summer grazing season. To supplement the scarce nutrients and give depth to thin soil, turf would often be "skinned" from rough pasture and mounded up into ridges of soil called "lazy beds." When these "artificial corrugations" came to be used for growing potatoes both in Scotland and Ireland, the effect was to add yet another burden on the soil, since harvesting that crop left nothing for animals and thus reduced the production of manure.[18] Robert Dodgshon, who has given the old Highland farming processes careful study, concludes that such laborious husbanding of arable land meant that hill pastures tended to be "carelessly exploited."[19] Able though the peasantry proved to be at adapting to changing circumstances, their traditional technology could not sustain indefinitely a relentlessly expanding population. In the Parish of Glenelg in the northwest, for example, the increase was fifty percent between 1750 and 1800.[20]

While subsistence agriculture was attempting to cope with population pressures, the capitalist economy was expanding. Cattle raisers and drovers began responding to rising prices in southern markets, and landlords began raising rental incomes (taken increasingly in money payments) by means of enclosures, amalgamations, plantations, rotation systems, and heavy applications of fertilizers. Nevertheless, the decision made by so many to specialize in sheep raising on the uplands was not merely the consequence of a gradual process of applying capitalist values and methods but a radical departure. Large-scale commercial sheep farming was not the only imaginable alternative to famine in the late eighteenth and early nineteenth centuries, but powerful men at the time perceived it to be an appropriate response to an economy in crisis as well as a means to make themselves rich.

Often reluctantly, but sometimes with enthusiasm, Highland landowners accepted that they must choose between ruin or commercial development, even if that meant displacing people for sheep. The heavy-handed methods of eviction associated with the first duke of Sutherland, his duchess, and their agent, Patrick Sellar, were seldom necessary; many landlords preferred to withdraw rights to use the waste for grazing in order to "persuade" crofters to leave, accompanied by such inducements as alternative employment, resettlement projects, or assisted emigration.

Whether the means were gentle or harsh, upland Scotland did become a truly sheep-ridden country in only a few decades.[21] The new landscape that emerged between the beginning and the middle of the nineteenth century was, and to a considerable extent still is, a constant and poignant signifier of a culture torn asunder and a land expropriated. Wrote one indignant Highlander in 1843: "We trace on these islands of sward, the marks of furrows, and mark here and there, through the loneliness, the remains of a group of cottages, well nigh levelled with the soil . . . like those ruins which eastern conquerors leave in their track, still scathed with fire."[22]

For a time, commercial sheep farming on the moorland proved to be lucrative. Lowland farmers were turning away from sheep breeding in favor of using their enclosed and improved lands to fatten animals on grass and turnips. Therefore they needed to import more two-year-old sheep from the open pastures. This shift in the balance favoring upland leanstock encouraged upland farmers to concentrate on breeding and rearing sheep and experimenting with new varieties. The best of the new breeds was the improved Cheviot, a heavier animal than the native Highland sheep and a better producer of meat and wool than the Blackface variety. The Cheviot supplanted its rivals except on the highest and roughest pastures once breeders managed to produce a version capable of withstanding the rigors of winter pasturing on the uplands.[23]

These factors helped commercial grazers to survive the slump that set in at the end of the wars with Napoleon. Better times after 1846 gave them more than two decades of vigorous prosperity, prices reaching their highest point in 1864–65 as a result of the American Civil War and the resulting cotton famine. This prosperity meant that upland pastures had to support heavier feeders and a great many more of them. Five Blackface could live on what would support four Cheviots.[24] Sutherland's sheep population increased by forty percent from 1853 to 1875 and Ross-shire's by fifty percent over that same span of time.[25]

To assist nature in sustaining so many more animals, moorland grazers relied almost exclusively on burning stretches of heather. That way sheep could feed on the more nutritious and palatable new growth that eventually replaced the tough and woody mature plants the fire had destroyed. Modern as well as Victorian experts seem to agree that, managed carefully, this method benefited both the grazing animals and the heather. Since the increasing bulk of the growing plant offsets, for seven years or so, a gradual decline in nutrient, good management strategy aims at a grazing regime that would maintain a balance by removing the older material and by encouraging rejuvenation at a steady level.[26]

But such a "nutrient budget" is not easy to achieve. If the burning is careless, if the timing is off, if a drought happens to follow, or if the fire is allowed to burn too intensely, the stand of heather can be destroyed and the surface left bare and open to soil wastage until the slow-growing plant can regenerate from seed.[27] Even if the burn is successful and new growth responds quickly, there is danger that sheep will concentrate on the site and pull up the tasty shoots by their roots before they have a chance to become established. How to keep hungry sheep and recovering stretches of heather apart on a remote mountain slope tested, and still tests, ingenuity.

On the other hand, if a burning regime does succeed in establishing a heather monoculture, a process of deterioration can also set in. A distinguished botanist, C. H. Gimingham, noted that heather in its growing phase radically reduces the diversity of other flora and the related fauna. Of greater consequence, the litter it produces decomposes slowly; thus it accumulates and produces humic acids that leach out some of the minerals and other nutrient elements, leaving the soil more acid than before. Furthermore the leaching process can result in formation of a hardpan or "moor pan" and thus convert surface humus layers into peat bog.[28]

Land damaged by heather monoculture or left unprotected by careless burning and grazing invites colonizing invaders. What alarmed observers from midcentury on was the steady advance of mat grass and bracken on derelict or damaged slopes.[29] Of the two, mat grass (*Nardus stricta*) is the lesser evil. Sheep will avoid it if possible and eat up competitors, thus encouraging its spread; but the dull yellow tufts of dead stems and coarse grass can be controlled. Cattle can be sent in to help redress the balance; valuable grasses, lying dormant, can be stimulated into growth with treatments of fertilizers like basic slag—provided, of course, such remedies make economic sense. Bracken, however, is a far more implacable foe. It aggressively advances on heather, "attacking along a continuous front," by sending up leaf fronds along lines of sub-surface runners or rhizomes to shade and cripple the smaller heather.[30] Cattle and human beings are bracken's only enemies: cattle because their hoofs tend to break the fronds and stir up the rhizomes, exposing them to killing frost, and people because they harvest bracken to insulate hay stacks and corn ricks or to burn it for potash—that is, they did so be-fore the Leblanc and Solvay processes for making artificial alkali put an end to that rural industry.[31]

Because more and more wool, bone, and meat were being exported from the environment at the same time that the soil of heath and moor-land was losing fertility, it is hardly surprising that observant agricul-turalists should begin to notice, as early as the 1840s, signs of extensive deterioration.[32] In his discussion of past and present moorland condi-tions, Oliver Rackham commented in 1986 that "the profit was short-lived, for the power of sheep to live off blanket-bog had been over-rated."[33] A century earlier, some clear-eyed analysts had noted these signs of exhaustion yet were reluctant to accept the conclusion that an environment such as this imposed strict limits on ingenuity and the ex-isting technology.

Most observers could see by the 1880s that improvements in steam transportation and refrigeration made the future of the domestic wool, lamb, and mutton enterprises precarious, to say the least; nevertheless, they were hopeful that some remedy might be found. Charles Gay Rob-erts was one of these guarded optimists. In 1879, he wrote an article for an English journal about agricultural conditions in the county of Suther-land. His argument assumed that the current troubles of this far north-west corner of the Highlands could be traced to failures of management and character. "The tenants grew rich as the land grew poor," was the thesis.[34]

Commercial grazers had been conditioned, he believed, to reap the benefits of a fertility inherited from the past without expending much of their own effort or capital. Consequently, they had lost, or perhaps never had been able to acquire, a sense of responsibility toward the land. They seemed to lack the maturity to recognize their own long-term interests. He said he could understand why the Sutherland farmer might simply have extracted capital out of the land at a time when access to lime and manures was restricted by an isolation more profound than in many of Britain's colonies. Yet even after the railway had come to Sutherland in the mid-1870s, the same "wasteful and exhaustive system of management" continued. Wool and meat did leave the land by rail, but the goods wagons seldom returned loaded with the lime and phosphates needed to treat the tired, acid soil. Farmers had neglected the arable fields, he added, and had allowed their flocks to destroy the cotton grass as it appeared in the spring pastures; they had permitted the straths and green patches to become "fogged and massed." Consequently the hills were blanketed by inferior herbs and ragged, ill-kept heather.[35]

The following year, 1880, James Macdonald won a prize for another essay on Sutherland agriculture. Like Roberts, he was aware that the arrival in bulk of foreign wool and refrigerated meat made it imperative to revise or replace the existing agricultural system. Like Roberts, he was disinclined to absolve the grazers from blame for their situation. Their single-minded concentration on making profits from sheep had, he thought, blinded them or made them indifferent to clear evidence of deterioration on hill pastures. It was obvious that land formerly under the plow had lost nearly all of its capacity to supply winter feed. As a result, sheep were becoming diseased, and breeders were becoming overly dependent, at increasingly unfavorable terms, on Lowland fatteners. For far too long, he thought, the grazers of Sutherland had chosen to forget that "Nature will have its due."[36]

Explicit in both Macdonald's and Roberts's essays was this message: Hope for the future lay in land renewal and reclamation. The two men believed that the experiment being carried on by the duke of Sutherland was demonstrating that it was possible, even in the most challenging of conditions, to exploit nature successfully while paying her the required dues. What they were referring to was the duke's massive attempt to make arable fields and sown pastures out of 1,175 acres of lonely Sutherland moor and heath six miles from Lairg, an area stretching westward between the banks of Loch Shin and the Tirry River. According to Macdonald, the great landowner's motive was to make his county (he owned ninety percent of it in 1872) self-sufficient in food for the human and animal populations, thus saving the cost of bringing corn, potatoes, and turnips in and sending sheep out for winter feeding.[37]

Another incentive may have been a desire to stimulate business for the railway line to Wick in which the duke had invested heavily. Circumstantial evidence suggests, however, that Sutherland, who greatly enjoyed the technical aspects of estate management, was more attracted by the machinery's productive capacity and the savings it would allow than in calculating whether or not its use would turn out to be profitable. According to Eric Richards, the duke was a "man besotted by steam trains, fire engines and gadgets."[38] This was undoubtedly the case. Therefore the Sutherland reclamations serve to illustrate Charles Kindleberger's dictum: "Irrationality can lead to too much innovation and to concern for physical efficiency rather than economic."[39]

A century and more of trial and error had established a reclamation technology. We can observe it being applied in John Knight's efforts after 1819 to cultivate some 2,500 barren upland acres of bog and purple moor grass in Exmoor Forest on high tableland in West Somerset. The methods Knight used were not much different from the ones employed at Whittlesea Mere in the Fenlands, in the Mendips, or on countless small reclamations carried out on Highland wastes by tenants who had been forced to leave their farms during the clearances. The site had to be ditched and drained; then the turf or top layer of heather had to be pared, piled up, and burned—the nourishing ashes eventually spread on the cleared land. If sand or clay lay within reach below the surface, these materials needed to be mixed with the peat. Next came liming, along with application of manures of various kinds, then plowing and the planting of rape or some other resilient crop before the rotation regimes began— all of this calling for intensive hand, bullock, and horse labor. But when John Knight turned the management over to his son Frederic, the Exmoor reclamation entered the steam era. The inspiration came from Sutherland's project.[40] Sutherland plows were used to break up the hardpan beneath Exmoor until falling prices in the 1880s and 1890s brought further development there to a halt.[41]

In almost every respect the difficulties facing the duke of Sutherland were more challenging. Underneath the surface of his beautiful, desolate Highland basin between the loch and the river were quantities of large rocks and ancient tree roots. To grub these out by hand or use animal power would have been a slow and arduous process, especially since experienced labor in that part of the country was scarce. Here, thought the technology-loving duke, was an opportunity to demonstrate the miraculous strength of steam. Having met John Fowler in Egypt and observed his steam plow at work in the Nile valley, the duke invited one of the Fowler partners, David Greig, to participate in an experiment in cultivating a boulder-strewn area near Dunrobin Castle. Fowler machines performed their task well but at a cost of £50 an acre rather than the estimated £18.10. Undaunted, the duke ordered that the Strath Tirry project proceed.[42] It was this innovation, carried out with imagination under the supervision of the seasoned reclamation expert Kenneth Murray and estate manager John McLennan—shored up by Sutherland's seemingly bottomless purse—that made the Lairg project internationally famous.

Work started in 1871. Murray began by importing workers. They laid a spur line from the Highland Railway terminus at Lairg and dug, with manual labor, a ditch across the basin to the Tirry River. This started the process of drying out the ground, the unearthed stones and boulders being used to build dikes, barns, houses, and roads. Initially two Fowler and Co. steam engines set to work in 1872, pulling, or trying to pull, a set of plowshares by cable, back and forth across the rough ground. But the equipment was designed for flat, well-prepared fields and constantly broke down when plowshare struck boulder. The ingenious solution to this obstacle (Roberts and Macdonald are not clear about who should have the credit but agreed that the duke himself deserved some of it) was to put the carriage for the large plow on broad wooden rollers and to attach steel disks—called coulters—ahead of the front and rear rollers so that they cut the surface a few inches below the plowshares. Thus when the disk hit a large rock it lifted the whole carriage over and left the obstruction behind to be dynamited and carried off on sledges pulled by oxen. It was the duke's idea to improve on this device by attaching a heavy iron hook to the rear—"the Duke's Toothpick." This device stirred up the subsoil and brought some of it, along with smaller rocks, to the surface. After that, special sledges, attached to the cables, would pull the surface debris to the edges where the engines automatically dumped the load. In places, the ground yielded 150 tons of rock to the acre.[43] (See Figure 4.)

Not surprisingly, this remarkable demonstration of how steam could be made to perform tasks thought beyond its capacities caught the attention of other ambitious reclaimers, Frederic Knight being only one of them. The Lairg reclamation became a tourist attraction. The duke, assisted by Robert Fowler, another member of the family plow works, showed a delegation from the Highland and Agricultural Society over the grounds in 1874 and did the same for the Prince of Wales two years later, by which time cottages, a school, workshops, and a church could be included on the tour. Roberts was moved by the transformation, accomplished so quickly and against such odds, to remark on how steam power and the duke's enthusiasm for its use had turned "a lifeless expanse of moorland," into "a scene of fruitfulness and rural activity."[44]

Praise of this kind must have been most welcome, considering that Sutherland began in 1877 an even larger reclamation at Kildonan, a place where the third duke of Sutherland's forbears had gained a noto-

Figure 4.   Steam cultivation in Sutherland (1875). The duke of Sutherland's experiment in using steam to turn rough Highland moors into arable fields and permanent pastures demonstrated that steam could be adapted to almost any task provided one disregarded expense. (*Engineering* 20, 1875)

rious reputation for disregard of life and traditional ways. Nowhere had the excesses of the Clearances been so pronounced or remembered with so much bitterness.[45] Conditions at Kildonan favored steam cultivation almost as much as conditions at Lairg discouraged it. Also, most of the technical difficulties had been overcome on the immensely costly first project (the duke had spent some £110,000 by 1879).[46] But Kildonan eventually took its revenge.

The timing could not have been worse. While Sutherland's toothpick was lifting clay from underneath the one or two feet of surface peat, prices for everything the strath was capable of producing plummeted. For the next half-century, marginal lands in many parts of Britain tended to be neglected. Even if prices had remained stable, it seems highly unlikely that rents could ever have produced a reasonable return on such a princely investment of capital. The new farms could grow oats, barley, turnips, potatoes, and hay, but only if the soil received lavish quantities of fertilizers—most of it brought by rail or boat from a considerable distance. By the end of the 1880s, 7,000 acres of land, reclaimed at a huge expense, had already reverted to rough pasture.[47] Steam technology had been adapted to a new task but in the wrong place, at the wrong time, and at unacceptable costs.

Charles Roberts drew a different conclusion: "the Duke and his predecessors have nobly met the great responsibilities and duties of their position." That noble family had, he wrote, exchanged stone houses and civilized amenities for the turf hovels that once littered the straths. The duke had willingly incurred great losses to demonstrate that the proprietor was the key to the improvement of poor hill and mountain land, without mineral resources or the possibility of industry.[48] Presumably, other landowners should be inspired by this example to use steam technology, agricultural engines, and railways to bring back diversified agriculture. A combination of large and small farms capable of growing food and fodder would return to hills and straths the rural communities of the past, but this time prepared by farsighted paternalism for the modern world.

As it turned out, many landlords found a different, "low-technology," solution to the problem of how to extract income out of great stretches of barren ground. That was to sell or lease (pocketing most of the "unearned increment") all or parts of their estates to rich merchants and bankers who would use the property for deer forests and grouse shootings. Robert Fowler, another of the engine-making family, purchased a hunting reserve from the duke of Sutherland and promptly spent £50,000 to improve it. During the first season, 1866–67, he and his guests shot fifteen stags.[49] In 1920 the Sutherland family was receiving rents from eleven large properties leased out as deer forests by the third duke between 1870 and 1885.[50]

In adopting this expedient, the duke was neither atypical nor first in the field. It is estimated that at the beginning of Queen Victoria's reign there were some thirty-eight deer forests, but rents for them remained low until the development of the high-velocity rifle with a central-fire cartridge in 1861. With deer stalking made so much easier, the sport caught on among wealthy urbanites. From the 1880s until the beginning of the Great War, deer raising replaced sheep raising in many high-country economies. By 1912, the peak year, there were 203 deer forests in Scotland occupying 3,432,385 acres (two-thirds above 1,000 feet) on which, during that year's season (September and the first half of October), 6,900 stags and 5,500 hinds fell to the guns.[51]

Scots who had formerly moved freely across the wastes were convinced that the fingers on the triggers belonged, in large measure, to foreign (including English) urban parvenus. One indignant observer described these usurpers as:

> Plutocrats from America . . . brewers from England . . . successful gamblers from a scoop in the Kaffir market, cotton capitalists, satiated aristocrats; mighty Nimrods from the Piccadilly clubs, nay even the Gaekwar of Baroda hired the Highlands for a solitude, swept away the Shepherd, and at certain stipulated periods of the year came with French cooks and in tartan kilts to slaughter deer and grouse and rabbits.[52]

The slaughter of grouse required almost as much territory as the slaughter of deer, although not all of the land set aside for that sport was in Scotland. Also, sheep and grouse could and did coexist without excessive strain. By the middle years of the century, the opening of the season, August 12, had become a defining ceremony for those with social and political ambitions. To be invited by Edward "the Bear" Ellice, to join a shooting party at his Glenquoich estate signaled or confirmed membership in the inner circles of the mid-Victorian Whig-Liberal Party.[53] The journey north would, of course, be by train. An amateur statistician estimated that around 1890 the elapsed time between departure from Bloomsbury and the moment of killing a brace of Perthshire grouse was sixteen hours, whereas, fifty years earlier, eight days would have been needed. Rents received from sportsmen rose accordingly.[54] The modern technology of the time had made it possible for a primitive pastime to change the economy of many upland regions and to play once again its role in fashioning a new elite.

Those blessed with the detachment time or distance allows seem prone to forgive landlords for having ousted sheep farmers in order to give a small band of privileged sportsmen exclusive use of vast tracks of mountain wastes. They point out that laws designed to protect the tenant decreed that the landlord must take over the flocks of departing tenants, often at above market prices, unless a replacement tenant could be found—an increasingly unlikely possibility in late Victorian and Edwardian times. Alternatives were scarce. Only in exceptional cases was tree farming at high elevations on acid moorland a reasonable investment, especially considering the long wait for a return on capital. Therefore, when faced with the choice of accepting ruin or exploiting rich people's hunger for status, even the most principled of landlords tended to capitulate.[55]

As in the case of the earlier transformation from a crofting to a sheep-grazing economy, the shift from grazing to deer forest put landowners at odds with traditional rights. Areas once cleared for sheep runs were now closed to walkers. The sixth duke of Atholl, owner of 200,000 acres of Perthshire, half of which was in deer forest, waged war, with fanatical ardor, on Professor Balfour and his botanical students when they attempted to assert their rights to follow an old drover's trail at Glen Tilt. Deer forest leaseholders, especially the notorious American millionaire William Winans (whose Braemar enclave stretched over forty miles from sea to sea) rushed to prosecution when bothered by those he considered trespassers. Conflict was also inevitable between hunters and growing numbers of outdoor recreationists. Many owners and lessees closed inns situated inside their jurisdictions and dealt harshly with villagers who opened their houses to visiting ramblers.[56] Trollope's obsessed hunter, Reginald Dobbes, a man "supposed to be capable of outwitting a deer by venatical wiles," believed the only thing standing between the deer forest of Crummie-Toddie ("but twelve miles from Killancodlem") and Paradise on earth was the unwillingness of the law to give him "the right to have all intruders thrashed by the gillies within an inch of their lives." As it was, the forest "had been managed so well that the tourist nuisance had been considerably abated. There was hardly a potato patch left in the district, nor a head of cattle to be seen. There were no inhabitants remaining, or so few that they could be absorbed in game-preserving or cognate duties."[57]

Legislation rather than satire was the tactic favored by the Liberal politician and mountaineer James Bryce. He and his supporters tried, from 1884 onward, to persuade Parliament to grant the public a statutory right of access to undeveloped land for recreational, artistic, or scientific purposes. He complained in 1892 about the scenery having been "filched away from us just when we have begun to prize it more than ever before." Urban growth had, he thought, created a desire among masses of people to escape "the dull monotony of everyday life." At the same time the advance of education was stimulating in them "the taste for poetry and beauty," a sensibility, he told the House, that was now no longer exclusive to "people like ourselves." He and his allies pointed to the ease with which everyone could wander over the Alps and suggested that tourism might bring to Scotland the economic benefits it had brought to Switzerland.[58]

Yes, answered Lord Elcho (one of the staunchest defenders of the rights of sportsmen to privacy), and what had tourists done to that small country? They had turned it into "a sort of glorified tea-garden." He granted that the Swiss had grown "fat on the tourists" and that those tourists could walk freely over the mountain scenery, freely, that is, until they paused to see a famous grotto or waterfall, at which time a concessionaire would suddenly pop out and ask for payment. But at least travelers to the Alps left money behind. Scotland, Elcho warned, could not even count on that: the only contribution likely to be left behind by railway excursionists to the Highland moors was "the family paper and broken beer bottles." [59] Enlightened by this and similar arguments, the landlord and hunting interests in both houses combined for the next fifty-five years to defeat bill after bill.[60]

Naturally, crofters, nature lovers, and most fair-minded people found such sentiments and behavior distasteful, to say the least. Nevertheless, if the focus shifts to the welfare of the land, some support can be found for exclusivity. An argument can be made, for example, that the second Highland transformation of the nineteenth century—described on one occasion as the substitution of gillies and stalkers for shepherds and crofters[61]—did give the upland heaths and moors a chance to recover from the degenerative effects of commercial sheep farming. The French traveler Léonce de Lavergne observed in 1855 that in clearing both people and sheep from the Highlands, the deer forests (those "last vestiges of feudalism,") helped to preserve "the last remains of savage nature in Great Britain"—remains that lent "poetry to country life." [62]

The aims of ecological diversity and poetry could be seen to coincide. Because deer needed winter shelter and protected places to breed, deer forest managers in some case planted groups and bands of trees—even though deer, if given a chance, reduce ecological diversity by destroying green bark and young shoots.[63] Occupiers of some one million acres of upland grouse moors had every incentive to prevent overgrazing. Self-interest led them to insist on careful burning regimes, to restore neglected copses, and to do everything in their power to protect heather from bracken, gorse, fir and pine trees, tourists, and developers.[64] Marion Shoard remarked that the pheasant "has done more to safeguard what remains of the traditional British landscape than all of the voluntary conservation groups put together." [65] Surely the grouse deserves to share that honor.

Most students of the late nineteenth century transformation are inclined to give these claims their due but remind us that assigning deer and grouse priority over all other creatures had a negative side. There was ecological damage as well as gain. Gamekeepers on grouse preserves declared war on rooks, hooded crows, gulls, hawks, eagles, buzzards, kestrels, owls, magpies, ravens, ospreys, foxes, badgers, weasels, martins, house cats, and other "vermin" until restrained, to some extent, by the Wild Birds' Protection Act of 1880. There were also economic and social costs: hunting and hunters did assist landowners in paying rates and provided some income to service industries but had "little local multiplier effect."[66] Furthermore, the saving device of the grouse moor or the deer forest tended to discourage or postpone the search for new land uses and, to the dismay of late Victorian crofter organizations, perpetuated the landlord system.[67]

It is tempting to speculate about what might have been gained had landlordism not been reprieved. Would, for example, the breakup of the great estates into smaller units have induced the government to help sustain subsistence agriculture and small-scale grazing by encouraging or managing tree planting and providing inducements to use silviculture technology? That was the solution proposed by Sir John Stirling-Maxwell in an article that appeared shortly before the outbreak of war in 1914. Conveniently ignoring the usually striking differences between upland and lowland conditions, he recommended Belgium as a model. There government agencies provided the funds and promoted the latest technology, with such success that the state realized a return of between 4.9 and 5.5 percent on its investment. Maxwell thought the lesson was clear: where efficient silviculture became the backbone of a rural economy, the indirect benefits would prove to be as important as the direct ones. Belgian smallholders had gained alternative (and healthy) sources of income; the soil of wastelands had been renewed; and the climate had been improved. He believed that a century of experience demonstrated that small farms provided the best fit between population and the limited capacities of the land, but that experience had also shown that small farms could never survive unassisted.

Maxwell went on to point out that concentration on commercial grazing in Scotland had defeated itself by depleting the already-limited resources of the soil. Market forces had led reluctant paternalists into producing only venison for rich men's tables and stag heads for their smoking rooms. It followed then that some form of state forestry, systematically planned and executed, was needed to restore diversity in land use, the factor upon which a healthy upland economy depended and the means by which a national treasure, the landscape of grandeur and freedom, might be preserved.[68]

In recommending an active role for government, Maxwell anticipated, to some extent, what was to come—gradually after 1921, when his advice helped guide the formation of the Forestry Commission, and then rapidly after the Second World War. But it is difficult to imagine, in the decades before 1914, circumstances so dire as to force even these mild forms of intervention on Conservative or Liberal governments. As later discussion will suggest, free trade combined with an increasingly coordinated international steamship and railway system ensured a cheap and abundant supply of imported softwoods. Before wartime timber shortages alerted people to the peril of depending almost completely on outside supplies, no leading politician would have suggested abandoning an essentially laissez-faire policy or going beyond the occasional experiment in using state-run forests to relieve rural unemployment in sensitive areas. With wood prices steadily falling in the late nineteenth century, further action was hardly to be expected. Ideology aside, a state-directed program for planting coniferous forests on acid moorland at middle to high altitudes would have appeared, at that or any time, a risky economic venture.[69]

Smallholders did occasionally club together in an attempt to overcome the high production costs of small-scale commercial grazing and farming. Willie Orr, who wrote a monograph on deer farms, found evidence that, especially when encouraged by rent reductions and generous terms for borrowing, such experiments in cooperation could succeed. On the other hand, when market conditions discouraged generosity, these experiments usually failed. He concluded that caution on the part of government about returning the deer forests to the crofters "may not have been a reflection of landlord power," but may instead "have stemmed from a genuine concern for the fragile economic structures in the Highlands and a recognition of the adverse effects of depriving local communities of [deer] forest rents."[70]

It is true that some landlords demonstrated how the existing estate system might have adapted itself to small- and middle-sized farming and showed by example that tree planting as well as deer forests could be profitably integrated into such a system. Several studies have selected as a shining exemplar the reorganization program carried out after 1827 by the eighteenth earl of Lovat. David Turnock examined Lovat's North Morar estate in the West Highlands and described how this landlord replaced the traditional run-rig system and the *sheilings* with small grazing and arable holdings and did so without resorting to clearances or exclusive reliance on sheep farming. When the late Victorian economy put pressure on tenants and undermined their ability to pay rents, Lovat came to their aid. He tried to reconcile many of the seemingly inherent contradictions by balancing croft farming, tree growing, and deer stalking. This attempt succeeded, but only for a while. Moreover, the conditions that allowed such flexibility at North Morar were, to some extent, exceptional, as were, perhaps, the earl's virtues. Turnock concedes that, given the economic developments of the twentieth century, even this impressive application of capital, technology, intelligence, and humanity to Highland land reform was not enough in the long run to make up for the inherent poverty of material resources—the underlying problem of the Scottish Highlands and, indeed, of so much of the British uplands in general.[71]

Steam technology stirred hope among enthusiasts in the 1870s and 1880s that a "basically hostile environment"[72] might be adapted to suit human ambitions, but events proved otherwise. Even when ingenious ways were found to make steam cultivation more flexible, the costs proved prohibitive. To trundle his nineteen-ton engines around the fields, the duke of Sutherland built paved roads and invented a self-stabilizing cart to supply boilers with water. Nevertheless, his tenants had to keep horses and oxen to work the land when the fields were soggy. Few reclaimers were equipped with Sutherland's vast wealth and enthusiasm or with Knight's remarkable persistence. At the same time that twenty-nine engines were puffing away at Kildonan and at another of the duke's projects on the Kyle of Tongue, Michael Henry was reclaiming a Galway bog in the Pass of Kylmore using horses and oxen fitted with wooden pattens. The duke of Sutherland's cost was over £30 an acre; Henry's was £12.[73]

Although there were numerous hard-won victories, Oliver Rackham is right when he says that, in the nineteenth and early twentieth centuries, "blanket peat usually defeated agricultural technology."[74] By the second half of the twentieth century, however, machines had become much more mobile and versatile and chemical fertilizers more sophisticated, so much so that even blanket peat could not be counted on to weary and then to repel invaders. Motor coaches and private automobiles enabled tourists to penetrate into places virtually closed to them in Victorian times and to do so in huge numbers. The 555 square miles of the Peak District National Park, for example, received twenty-two million visits by motorists in 1994 in all weather, including those on trail bikes and in four-wheel-drive recreational vehicles. The park's chairman was moved to speak about gridlocked villages, severely eroded footpaths, and air pollution worse than in central London.[75] Whether or not blanket peat can, in the long run, prevail over mass tourism, a mighty abuser, is still an open question.

5

Woods and Trees

In England . . . arboriculture, the planting and nursing of
trees, has, until recently, been better understood than
silviculture, the sowing and training of the forest.
George Perkins Marsh, Man and Nature, *1864*

Extranatural power, iron machinery, artifice, railway speed, innovation,
precision, synchronization, professionalism, rationalization, calculation,
utility, abstractness, efficiency—these phenomena, values, and processes
were what Victorians had in mind when they described their age, as they
frequently did, as the age of steam. That humans could, at last, free themselves from the confines of nature—refashion environments, control climates, redirect rivers, calm torrents, adjust soil chemistry, make deserts
flower, grow food out of season—prospects such as these could be ex-
hilarating, as they obviously were to the duke of Sutherland when he
sent his steam plows to transform the stony wastes of Lairg. But nature
proved to be resilient there and on most high-country places. On fertile
plow lands, nature submitted, agreed to form a bond with humankind,
but only on the condition that her ways of life should be respected.

As for Britain's woods and copses, forests, and hedgerow trees—these
felt the effect of the huge increase in demand for wood products, powerfully stimulated by iron and steam technologies. Professionals called for
steam-era methods and attitudes. But no forest industry developed. Amateurism was tested but prevailed. The landscapes of open heather hillsides and patchwork fields, softened with borders of scattered hardwood
trees and rounded off with hilltop copses, survived largely intact during

the time when steam power became the great moving force in manufacturing and transport.

Why that should have been so is partly revealed in the history of Savernake Forest. Leased since 1938 to the Forestry Commission, this splendid preserve, which lies between the Wiltshire towns of Marlborough
and Hungerford, has been the property of one family—whether named
Esturmy, Brudenell, or Bruce—since the latter part of the eleventh century. Perhaps the happiest period in this long family wardenship was between 1748 and 1814 when Lord Bruce, Thomas Bruce Brudenell, set
out purposefully to shape the forest so that "utility and beauty should
be harmoniously wedded." [1] He planted a grand avenue of trees leading
to his mansion, Tottenham Park, designed by Lord Burlington, and he
created a deer park where these animals—so destructive to young shoots
and forest management—could be concentrated.

In this shaping and planting he had the assistance of Lancelot "Capability" Brown who suggested that the same aesthetic principles that governed the laying out of park and garden be applied to the estate as a
whole. He worked out a strategy for linking coppices with oak plantings,
lining forest trails with beech trees, and providing vistas with "proper
objects" on which the eye might rest. The forest would be made part of
the parkland. The scattered coppices, meadows, scrub, and heath that
Brudenell inherited should be united, Brown advised, into *one great
whole.* [2]

Attracted though he was by this vision of unity, Brudenell was not
comfortable with the idea that the landowner and his seat should be fo-
cal points around which avenues and vistas were made to radiate. That
would call attention to the landowner's capacity to command the estate
and all its surrounds rather than to express his function as steward and
conservator. Brudenell preferred the less assertive statement. He was determined to set his generation an example of the "improving landlord,"
one intent on demonstrating that responsible landlordship served the interests of a wider community. Consequently, he wished his extensive plantations to blur rather than accentuate the boundaries between "working" parts of the estate and parts set aside for enjoyment and display.
Neither beauty nor utility should dictate which trees to plant or how to
group, arrange, and manage them: the aim instead should be to paint
a picture of gentle concord between the two principles. Paradoxically,
notes Stephen Daniels, this determination, shared by many aristocrats of
the period, to be discreet in the use of political iconography, "both soft-

ened the impression of property and, by composing the countryside as a whole as a picture, strengthened it."[3]

When Thomas Bruce Brudenell died, wrote his descendant, the sixth marquess of Ailesbury, "the great planting impulse of the eighteenth century" perished with him.[4] But that is to suggest a linear development, when, in fact, tastes, iconography, as well as the planting urge fluctuated throughout the Victorian years and after. For example, uninhibited Brownian display of pomp and power had something of a resurgence when the second marquess, George Frederick Brudenell-Bruce, took over the wardenship of Savernake in 1856. This ambitious, vainglorious aristocrat had little interest in forest management. He was indifferent to the fact that no new planting of any consequence had taken place since 1814. What he did care about was prestige through conspicuous consumption. There was much rearranging of copses and vistas and setting aside of grass rides so that visitors could see the woods as a whole and be impressed. In carrying this out, George Frederick finally managed completely to do away with the distinction between park and forest. He ordered that the entire estate be fenced and palings be placed around individual trees. That way, the deer might roam freely with a minimum of damage.[5] Visitors were attracted by the reputation of the forest as a sylvan paradise and to the prospect of being, like the deer, free to walk for miles under great trees and along arboreal colonnades.[6] On display was the owner's pride and his ambitions to advance in the hierarchy of nobility.

Then in 1886 the second marquess's grandson inherited. Fate decided that he should demonstrate that the hereditary principle, which in theory and sometimes in practice builds links of responsibility between generations and also makes certain that those links are sometimes severed. To pay his gambling debts, the twenty-three-year-old Willie, openly acknowledged by the family to be "a notorious ne'er-do-well,"[7] tried to break the entail and sell the great trees. "I'll make those damned squirrels jump further!" was his only memorable remark.

But, as it turned out, the squirrels were left in peace. An uncle managed to discourage a prospective buyer, Lord Iveagh, the brewer of Guinness, by entangling the sale in legal challenges. Shortly thereafter, the feckless Willie retired from the wardenship by drinking himself to death. It had been a near thing. By the time he expired in 1894, the family exchequer was much depleted and the forest along with it.[8]

Good fortune then intervened and gave the estate two enthusiastic planters, determined, like the earlier Thomas Brudenell, to marry beauty to utility. The fifth marquess recognized that the woodlands needed to be made commercially viable. Included among the 778,000 trees he planted were a high proportion of softwoods, placed outside the forest's core. Too deeply imbued with tradition to contemplate industrialized forestry, he was, nevertheless, the first of his family to introduce a measure of systematic management. He planted quick-growing larch and spruce. On the other hand, he also let loose in the forest a herd of Highland cattle, thinking that these beasts would add a picturesque touch.[9]

His successor in 1911, Chandos Bruce, the sixth marquess, did everything possible to carry on with this combination of systematic management and concern for amenity and symbolic representation. Eventually, however, he found the burden too heavy, what with increasing costs, Lloyd George's taxes on inherited wealth, and the impossibility of hiring enough labor during and after the First World War. In 1930 he approached the government Forestry Commission but drew back when he recognized that surrendering control would probably bring on an invasion by ranks of straight-backed conifers. Eight years later the commission became more open to the suggestion that recreational uses might be as legitimate as commercial ones and agreed to the special conditions the sixth marquess had stubbornly laid down.[10] As a result, after 800 years of wardenship, the family surrendered control and the public, because of Lord Ailesbury's dedication, gained a handsome amenity.

Immediately apparent in this account of Savernake's changing fortunes is the spirit of amateurism. That spirit had fashioned and preserved many ornaments like Savernake and had a part to play in forming a beautiful landscape, one where hilltop copses and lines of wooded hedgerows supplied contrast and definition. Throughout the century, however, a steady flow of criticism came from those who believed that the country had been forced to pay heavily for such embellishments. Forestry reformers believed that romanticism, sentimental attachment to trees as individuals, excessive concern for aesthetics, and a wasteful obsession with hunting had prevented the development of a national forest policy and had made Britain dangerously dependent on foreign suppliers. Worst of all, such irrationalities had given the world yet another lesson in how much more efficient Germans were at promoting new technologies.

Some of these critics were willing to concede that the energetic but haphazard practices of the estate planters might once have served the needs of the immediate countryside well or well enough. Thin planting encouraged the growth of side branches: these could be used for charcoal, domestic fuel, and manufactured implements. The right to graze cattle, pigs, and sheep on the forest floor made efficient forest management impossible, but it did provide commoners with a margin for survival. In addition, the coppice-with-standards system,[11] as well as the practice of mixing species, produced materials suited to local needs. Standardization was not essential to craft work and early mechanical industry, especially since shipbuilders, wagon makers, and furniture craftsmen required "bends" and "knees," as well as other eccentrically shaped pieces. Local needs of this kind provided the only markets many forest owners could profitably fill. Where heavy logs could be transported at reasonable costs to river, canal, or seaport, it did make economic sense to maximize timber production for sale in distant markets—but nowhere else.

Nevertheless, as the forestry experts from the later nineteenth century insisted, times had changed. They agreed that forestry practices had made some adjustments to new technologies, especially in Scotland, where there was still enough wasteland and rough grazing land to allow landlords to try out new methods and experiment with new species. Still, even there, uncoordinated free enterprise (not to speak of aristocratic insouciance) had failed to create anything resembling a large-scale forest industry equipped with the latest tools and methods. Expanding national and international markets for wood products, improvements made in rail and steamship transport, a growing demand for cheap construction materials created by urban expansion, and continued population growth—these developments had, some claimed, turned sentiment and amateurism into national liabilities.

Hearts of oak were no longer required for the defense of home and empire; the duel in 1861 between the Confederate ironclad, *Merrimac,* and the Union iron gunship, *Monitor,* meant that oaks planted during the early years of the century in the Crown Forests, as well as on private estates, would no longer be required in large quantities by naval shipyards.[12]

On top of that, the steady substitution of coal and coke for charcoal in almost every industry and the importation of cheap bark and artificial tanning materials had undermined many of the traditional markets for hardwoods. A chorus of voices declared that the age of amateurism and arboriculture (the care and feeding of trees so as to bring them efficiently to maturity) had ended and that the time had come to replace it with the age of professionalism and silviculture (the "scientific" management of the plantation unit so as to extract the maximum utility from it as a whole).[13]

Accompanying all these calls for "national efficiency" to meet growing international competition was the complaint that British estate owners and politicians had slumbered while their German, French, Belgian, and Austro-Hungarian counterparts, upon identifying these trends early in the century, had acted promptly and appropriately. Specialists, trained in forestry schools and forestry departments of Continental universities and in the Indian and other colonial forest services, had by midcentury helped to establish a new "science" based on the principle of sustained yield. At home, by contrast, the response had been "sluggish" to the point of "near stagnation." [14] On the occasion of the Report of a Royal Commission on the State of British Forestry, issued in 1909, the *Times* commented that it would have been nearly impossible at the end of the previous century to find a woodland, other than a coppice, managed in regular rotation and according to a fixed working plan.[15]

A few years earlier, a professional forester, Arthur Forbes, had delivered the same message. He equated amateurism with mindlessness: "The general idea which permeates planting operations is that of covering the ground with trees which will ultimately develop into a wood." He thought that negligence of this kind had dotted the landscape with a stunted, distorted, unhealthy, unprofitable commodity.[16] Other experts developed this theme. John Croumbie Brown, who had made a reputation as a conservationist in South Africa, commented that in Britain game was the object of preservation, arboriculture the method, the tree the unit, and amenity the priority; whereas, across the Channel, the woods were the object of preservation, silviculture the means, the forest collective the unit, and the national economic good the priority. It was time, Brown wrote in the 1880s, to abandon tradition and do as others do.[17]

Usually observations of this kind tended to come from experienced foresters, most of them Scots or German-trained academics and administrators like William Schlich. It was only rational, they argued, that foresters learn to use tables for calculating yields, to adjust species to soil and topography, and to manage plantings of uniform species, selected according to soil capabilities and laid out in staggered units, so as to balance planting with harvesting. Some of these experts—especially those who depended on great landlords for their livelihood—hoped that it might be possible to reconcile this rationality with the existing estate system.

One of these was James Brown, head forester at an experimental forest at Arniston, the Midlothian seat of Robert Dundas, a Scottish grandee.

Brown's book *The Forester*, first published in 1847, became the manual consulted by almost every progressive British planter for the next three decades or more.[18] Its purpose was to persuade landlords that trees, managed according to the principles of silviculture technology, could be made into a profitable crop. Brown claimed that in sixty years, a rationally designed plantation should give proprietors an income three times greater than any alternative land use, even on barren hills in the Scottish Highlands.[19] He believed landlords had become skeptical about investing in tree farming because they had, in the past, planted indiscriminately without bothering to study the characteristic growing properties, soil requirements, and life cycles of each species; without consulting mathematical guidelines about spacing, thinning, and draining; without making sure what mixtures of species complemented one another; and without first assessing the conditions of the market and the cost of transporting logs of various dimensions. Agriculture and horticulture had long been the subjects of scientific investigation and had responded to such systematic methods—and with revolutionary effect. Now, he thought, it was silviculture's turn.[20]

The difficulty with this kind of reasoning was that rich landowners, no matter how open to suggestions about ways to increase estate profits, were disinclined to treat their trees simply as commodities. They wanted their woodlands to fulfill a variety of functions, providing opportunities for blood sports being prominent among them. But hunting and silviculture had proved all but incompatible. As the Savernake experience demonstrated, "vert and venison" were uncomfortable partners. Far more compatible was the relationship between greenery and pheasants. These creatures did not destroy new growth; but they did require undergrowth, suitable nesting places, and the right kinds of seeds and berries. The ideal was a mixture of oak, beech, chestnut, with a few conifers for roosting. This was a planting regime certain to conflict with commercial woodland uses.[21]

Interest in bird shooting kept growing while confidence in forest investments continued to decline. Improvements made in shotgun efficiency between the 1850s and 1870s opened the sport to those without abundant leisure to refine their hunting skills. Therefore the recreational value of an estate forest kept rising. Estate owners already had a reputation for sacrificing the health of trees to ensure the health of game—or so foresters commonly complained.[22] The relative status of the gamekeeper now rose even higher. Arthur Forbes spoke for most professionals when he said, "The highest ambition of the modern planter seems to be the conversion of bare ground into something tall enough for pheasants to roost in, and that accomplished, he feels satisfied with his work."[23]

The fondness these sporting gentlemen showed for "overripe" hardwood trees also distressed critics of amateurism. What, they asked, could be more symptomatic of Britain's flagging energies than the attachment felt by the landowning class, not just for game coverts, but for preserving this or that ancient tree, often known by an individual name and associated with some (usually bogus) historical event? Germans, wrote John Simpson in 1909, were not burdened by such "false sentiments and false aesthetics." The "half-military organization of the German forest system," he added, "helps considerably to promote economy and to avoid waste."[24]

Campaigners for silviculture were mindful of statistics showing that the proportion of softwood being used had been rising steadily from the latter part of the eighteenth century and had reached, by the early years of the twentieth century, between eighty and ninety percent of wood products sold. Therefore they deplored this continuing prejudice in favor of hardwoods, this personal attachment to ancient symbols, this antipathy toward anything uniform, this unwillingness to regard trees as "so many cubic feet of timber." They cautioned that irrationalities like these were turning Britain into a museum.[25] What was needed was a dose of hardheaded practicality. If utility indicated that a stand of trees should be cut when it reached optimum size for the commodity market, then down should go the stand of trees, regardless of their degree of maturity. If builders, mine owners, or railway suppliers required cheap, fast-growing Scotch pine, and a particular hillside provided the right soil and drainage, then in should go the Scotch pine. A plantation should, the experts insisted, be allowed to develop only up to the point where interest on the capital that appreciated from tree growth remained marginally greater than the interest that could be realized on proceeds from the product's sale.[26] At the point where growth rates slackened, cutting should take place. Allowing trees the chance to go through a complete life cycle, had, the new foresters insisted, no utility.

Even the most progressive of the Scottish tree planters were unwilling to rationalize to this extent—or so the "modernizers" charged. In their enthusiasm for covering barren land with conifers, these great lords had neglected many of the rules of silviculture. They planted pine and spruce the same way that they planted oak and ash: far enough apart to allow each one to grow to full maturity as individuals. In doing so they ignored the different growth characteristics of various species as well as the mathematical rules of commercial management. Overlooking, for example, the fact that both Scotch pine and larch preferred dry conditions and poor soil, they planted indiscriminately and usually neglected to drain level environments. Among the consequences were devastating outbreaks of heart rot. Amateurism, it would seem, could be a barrier to fundamental change even among those landowners most open to the spirit of enterprise. And, despite the late Victorian concern about national efficiency, few seemed to share the sense of urgency felt by the small body of professional forest technicians.

These experts expressed their frustration, but few of them looked to the fact of empire for an explanation. James Brown was an exception only in that he tried to convince his readers that expanding home markets for wood products would eventually exhaust the reserves of foreign suppliers. He reasoned that these suppliers were bound to respond to the inevitable increase in prices by proceeding to exploit their forests even more brutally. They would be powerfully assisted in doing so by improvements in steam transport and forest machinery. (See Figure 5.) He thought he detected, already in the 1840s, signs that the seemingly inexhaustible North American reserves would soon be depleted.[27] But his timing was not as astute as his analysis: so long as logs, lumber, and potash from Scandinavia, the Baltic, Poland, Russia, India, Burma, and North America kept arriving at prices only a few domestic producers could meet, there was little likelihood his message would receive a serious hearing.

And those products did keep flowing in. Two specialists on the environmental effects of colonialism, Madhav Gadgil and Ramachandra Guha, award Britain the distinction of having become by 1860 "the world leader in deforestation," since by that date her entrepreneurs had managed to exploit ruthlessly the resources of Ireland, South Africa, and the United States.[28] Curiously, these two geographers neglect to list eastern Canada among the places where the connection between empire and land degradation was particularly conspicuous, despite the fact that vast areas of New Brunswick, Ontario, and Quebec had been cut to serve the London market.

In 1884, R. W. Phipps, a forestry clerk for the Ontario Department of Agriculture, reported that piles of chips, tree tops, log butts, and discarded short ends left behind by gangs who logged the watershed of the Ottawa River frequently exploded into flame when they dried out. This forest litter generated heat sufficiently intense to burn the thin layer of humus from the forest floor and to lay bare the rocky undersurface. Pad-

Figure 5. Tree felling by machinery (1878). Gladstone, center, marveled that this saw, attached by a flexible tube to a boiler, cut in one minute what took a hand laborer an hour. That four attendants were needed to use the tool helps explain why forests continued to be logged mostly by muscle power. (*The Graphic* 17, 1878)

dling his bark canoe along the shores of Lake Nosbonsing, Phipps observed such a *brûlé*—"an endless array of ghostly trunks," reaching to the distant horizon. Iron and copper pyrites, mixed with silt, had eroded from this burned country into the lake and turned it brown. "No clear inland water this," he wrote, "our wake is a muddy foam."[29] Similar accounts of land degradation can be found in descriptions of logging operations along New Brunswick's Miramichi River, where the demand from Britain had first used up that area's white and red pine and then, after 1850, its white and red spruce.[30]

As James Brown had foreseen in the early days of the railway, the application of steam to machinery and transport and the resulting concentration of industry in urban centers were certain to create a huge market for softwoods: to build houses, make paper, shore up pit walls in coal mines, and secure tracks for railways. The policy of free trade decided where those softwoods would come from. Home planting and cropping of conifers might make economic sense so long as Scotch pines and larches could reach domestic markets at a price competitive with shipments from New Brunswick, Scandinavia, Russia, and the Baltic. But when steamships were able to reduce long-distance transport costs significantly and when steam machinery and logging railways made it possible and economical to cut and haul trees growing at a distance from North American rivers and lakes, the decision to invest in a commodity that might take half a lifetime or more to harvest became more problematic.

Brown was also right in predicting that a combination of increased demand and new technologies would greatly accelerate the rate of forest depletion abroad. Although steam sawing began early in the century (there were sixty-eight steam mills in Britain by 1850),[31] it was not until the 1880s that North American logging companies began to use steam locomotives and other steam-powered hauling machinery. By 1887 there were 422 logging railroads in the United States. In 1881 John Dolbeer, a redwood lumberman from Eureka, California, invented the first practical steam donkey to yard the great trees of the Pacific coast from where they were felled to collecting places. In the 1890s, those hauling and lifting operations were greatly assisted by the development of steel cable. So equipped, Canadian and American loggers could devour forest resources more voraciously than ever before.[32] At the same time, the roads and pathways they built to bring in the heavy equipment and skid the logs greatly advanced the rate of soil erosion.

World prices fell steadily. By 1914, ninety-three percent of wood products on the domestic market were imported.[33] About thirteen percent of

British tonnage space was being devoted to importing timber, about equal to the space occupied by grains and larger than the space devoted to all other food imports and all imported cotton and wool combined.[34] Faced with this kind of competition, it would have required massive intervention by the central government to convert British forestry into a modern industry and, in the process, to have altered the character of upland landscapes. Protectionist policies would have placed a tax on paper, houses, railways, and coal. In the nineteenth and early years of the twentieth century, neither the government nor the economy were ready for so radical a step.

But, as the story of Savernake Forest suggests, explanations of why something did not take place—always a delicate historical enterprise— must include a consideration of sentiments as well as reasons. The sixth marquess of Ailesbury's reluctance to hand over management to the Forest Commission was based on his fear that his magnificent forest might become an industry for producing softwoods. But his resistance seems not to have been based on hostility to conifers in general. Family tradition, at least the positive side of it, had been built around the idea of "improvement," a movement identified perhaps too narrowly with Georgian England. Thomas Brudenell's use of the concept of harmonious marriage come directly out of that improvement concept: the bride, Beauty, should find in the groom, Utility, a sensitive and respectful partner—the venerable oak, the "joyful elm," the sheltering beech harmoniously wedded to the homely but hard-working and productive fir, pine, or larch.

This was an image landscape painters and garden designers of the period set out to capture. They associated the beautiful in landscape with softer contours, horizontal lines, and seasonal color modulations of the broad-leafed trees. Conifers supplied contrast. Capability Brown used pines extensively in his landscape compositions to provide variety—the cheerful yellow-green of the beech against "the gloomy pine," the "blackening pines."[35] Ruskin pointed to another kind of contrast: the pine's capacity for stoical endurance in the face of the elements, "trained to need nothing, and endure everything," compared to the "timid lowland trees," that "tremble with all their leaves" when visited by any adversity.[36] The *Times,* in a leading article on the subject of coniferization, spoke of "these graceful denizens of barren, sandy soil and infertile granite slopes."[37]

Conifers belonged on the great estates and were admired by generations of aristocrats throughout the eighteenth and nineteenth centuries.

Thomas Coke's vigorous planting regimes at his Holkham estate earned him the title, "King Pine." [38] From the mid–eighteenth century the planting of larches on Scottish moors and denuded hillsides became synonymous with three generations of dukes of Atholl. This planting regime started in 1737, when James, the second duke, made the first experimental plantations near his Highland estate at Blair and Dunkeld. By 1770 the third duke had increased the count to a half million. The pace quickened when, in 1774, John, the fourth or "Planting Duke," succeeded. Before he died in 1830 (wood for his coffin was taken from a specimen 106 feet tall), he had covered some 10,000 acres of Perthshire with over 14,000,000 larches, and his nurseries were supplying seed and seedlings to other Scottish enthusiasts. What had been intended as an ornament became an important feature of Scottish estate management. The suitability of larchwood for railway sleepers and pit props for mines encouraged its plantation, until, later in the century, susceptibility to disease caused a shift toward pine, spruce, and fir.[39]

Reaction against such plantations, and estate "improvement" in general, became fully articulate with the parliamentary enclosures of the eighteenth century—a reaction to be sustained by the romantic poets and conservatives of the left and right who were appalled by the spread of "machinery" and the sacrifice to "progress" of traditional ties and ways. The fast-growing, adaptable, money-making conifers became, in the language of that conservative reaction, the perfect symbol of everything parvenu, precocious, intrusive, pushing, divisive, antisocial, anti-communal, shallowly rooted, American.

"Coniferous rash," was their term for the steady spread of larch and Scotch pine. Antagonism deepened when, at midcentury, the Douglas fir, Sitka spruce, western red cedar, and other conifers arrived in large numbers from British Columbia and the northwest coast of the United States.[40] Generations of commoners who lived in or on the fringes of Royal Forests shared the resentment at the arrival of these relative newcomers. They recognized that plantations of conifers on Crown or common land would put an end to pollarding and forest grazing.

Nostalgia for an imagined *gemeinschaft* of communal institutions, affective ties, and local loyalties attached itself, easily and by a kind of symbolic logic, to oak, beech, elm, and chestnut woods in particular and old mature forests in general. According to Simon Schama, it is the poet who makes landscapes into carriers of memory—"things that are buried but will not stay interred"—and it is the treed parts of those landscapes that are "the truly heroic historians of the drama." [41]

It could be added that this cultural phenomenon, the association of trees with man's primeval ancestry, has its own history as well. Robert Harrison has shown how the forests, especially from the sixteenth century onward, changed in metaphor from places of sinister menace to "sites of lyric nostalgia." [42] That nostalgia reached its height in the nineteenth century. Generations of Victorians had traveled in spirit with Wordsworth to the sylvan Wye and had, like the poet, felt the touch of those gentle powers of tranquil restoration. They responded ardently when Ruskin advised them to seek beauty of form in leaf and branch. Among the educated, articulate classes nostalgia for forest blended together with a rich variety of other emotions: romanticism, patriotism, preservationism, political and social conservatism, varieties of radicalism, concern about losing one's sense of place, a generalized unease about a world that seemed to be moving too fast. Self-proclaimed preservationists were not the only ones to feel these longings. One detects reservations about industrial forestry, particularly its effects on the landscape, even in the writings of many ardent crusaders for the new forestry.

A group of Canadian geographers demonstrated how the transmigration from hostility to nostalgia, effected over centuries in Britain, could be put on fast forward in colonial settings. They examined the behavior of early Victorian settlers on encountering the wilderness in a southern Ontario township.[43] Most of the immigrants were from Ireland, Lowland Scotland, and the English Midlands. They had no experience in dealing with the kind of wilderness they found in their new home—a place where "thick tangles of cedar and tamarack" grew out of the swampy ground and hemlocks and pines stood thickly on the rough sands and gravels of the higher elevations.

The investigators noted that class resentment was part of the baggage settlers brought with them to forested Mono Township. Although trees bore memory for many of these newcomers, it was memory not of "sportive wood run wild" and other "sensations sweet" but of insult and oppression. In the homelands from which they had been displaced, these former laborers, peasants, and cottagers were unlikely to have felt any sentimental attachment to the landlord's woods. Custom had given some of them rights to gather furze or branches or graze livestock on acorns and young shoots, but these rights were often denied by a privileged class determined to assert claims to exclusive use and enjoyment. From the early eighteenth century, increasingly savage punishments awaited the poacher of the landlord's trees and branches. For the rural poor, especially those who had been compelled to leave their homes and find livings across the seas, forests represented injustice, disinheritance. As for the better-off tenant farmers, many of them had resented the hedgerow trees that sheltered pests, shaded crops, and drew nourishment from field edges. Freedom in the Ontario wilds to cut as many trees as he liked could seem to the immigrant an act of justice and revenge.

In their eagerness to tame this savage place, to turn it into familiar fields and pastures, and to overcome the loneliness of their isolated homesteads, immigrants set to work tearing up their fragile environment. They exterminated the bears and wolves, polluted the salmon streams, and, by indiscriminate cutting and burning, exposed hillsides and caused severe erosion. But, ironically, the further their slashing and burning progressed, the less "unfamiliar, implacable, and terrifying" did the retreating forest become, until settlers came to think of the shrinking woodland as a refuge, a place to hunt and explore, a thing of beauty.

Although by no means common, it is possible to find, in the nineteenth century, expressions of our own modern anxiety about the effects of forest depletion on what we (not they) would call the ecosystem. One occasion was a gathering of geographers in 1879, where Professor George Rolleston of Oxford spoke of his concern that steam technology would rapidly put at risk the earth's remaining forest cover and, in so doing, "very powerfully" modify the whole "botanical world"—with consequences that could not be easily predicted.[44] He warned that the driver of modern civilization with "a steam-engine under his foot is daily weaving" the whole globe "into a more nearly all-encompassing web." At the same time, that engine is leaving behind in the remaining wildernesses a path of destruction. Consequently, immediate steps must be taken to mark out and preserve areas of natural forests before industrial exploitation robbed them of their scientific value. Should members of the audience need convincing on this point, Rolleston said, they might want to read George Perkins Marsh's *Man and Nature,* a work he had found to be "highly interesting."[45]

To some extent, the political and economic circumstances at the turn of the century acted to moderate the force of these cultural and scientific reservations. They also encouraged some to advocate direct state intervention to conserve resources and create a modern forest industry. One notices in almost every aspect of British life an atmosphere of introspection as well as worry about eroding power and loss of technological leadership.

Professional foresters found that the way to dramatize what they had to say was to contrast their own government's indifference with the active role adopted by foreign governments toward forestry planning and research. These specialists called attention to the fact that the Danish State Forestry Department had purchased and profitably planted large tracts of the Jutland Moors and that the French government was managing half a million acres in the Alps, Pyrenees, and Central Plateau. They pointed out that the Prussian state had, for many years, not only owned and managed extensive forest lands but had encouraged private landowners to use the latest technology for planting and managing their estates.[46] Reports of this kind deplored the indifference of British politicians. But such documents usually concluded by expressing confidence that an awakening of public interest in the subject would eventually activate central and municipal governments.

Here and there a few pieces of evidence could be found to support that hope. The Royal Arboricultural Society used effective lobbying to persuade the government in 1885 to set up a select committee to report on the advisability of establishing a national forestry policy. Although the committeemen decided that it was indeed advisable, the response was feeble and long delayed. In 1899, after much hesitation, the Office of Woods, Forests, and Land Revenues purchased and planted an estate in Merioneth and subsequently acquired other tracts in Gloucester, in Tintern in the Wye valley, and in Argyll.

A somewhat more daring experiment in state forestry occurred in Ireland, at a wind-lashed place named Knockboys, on the Connemara coast near Carna. Unfortunately, it turned out to be a prime illustration of official ignorance and confusion of aim. In 1890, Father Flannery, the local parish priest, encouraged a public-spirited local landowner to donate 490 acres of boggy hillside, fully exposed to ocean gales. Commissioners at the Irish Land Office spent £2000 in 1893 and 1894 attempting to get the peat cover and the nearly sterile subsurface prepared and planted with two and a half million trees. They and the newly formed Congested Districts Board spent some £10,000 before finally abandoning the experiment in 1900, even though disaster was obvious almost from the start. One critic of the project stated in 1903 that "a rockier or more wind-swept spot than Knockboys may not be found in all Ireland."[47]

Experts who had been consulted beforehand warned that the odds against success were particularly great at Knockboys; but politicians, especially the chief secretary for Ireland, Arthur James Balfour, were disinclined to listen, committed as they were to finding alternatives for marginal agriculture in areas of high unemployment. So eager was Balfour that the project go ahead that he ordered a start without bothering to wait for a survey. Having no idea what might or might not grow, the commissioners put in thirty to forty species, hoping to have success with some. Since the young seedlings had no shelter, they simply blew away.[48] Cattle were subsequently kept off the hill for fear they would fall into the deep drainage ditches left behind after the experiment failed.[49]

Some of the caution shown by the British government before the outbreak of war can be traced to failures of this kind.[50] Responsible officials recognized that a cadre of trained foresters and specialists needed first to be established. A faction inside the late Victorian and Edwardian Liberal Party was in favor of encouraging agricultural small holdings and would only support government afforestation to the extent that it might provide small holders with supplementary income. Socialists of various kinds, although friendly to the concept of government ownership and management of forest lands, tended to prefer that the administrative agents be municipal authorities. An Independent Labour Party publication in 1908 noted approvingly that Liverpool had acquired 22,000 acres in its Montgomeryshire water catchment and was beginning to plant trees there, as were Leeds and Manchester on their extensive holdings.[51] At a conference on afforestation in 1907, John Burns, recently recruited to the Liberal cabinet from the socialist left, pledged support from his local government board to assist municipalities in planting on wastes unfit for grazing or plowing, not a formula proponents of a profitable state forestry industry would be likely to support. He was skeptical of claims that afforestation would be a remedy for rural unemployment but did have hopes that such activities might encourage local handicrafts and industries.[52] Apparently, no constituency existed for government forestry on anything like a Continental scale.

Publicity about the deterioration of forests and the crumbling of coastlines aroused Campbell-Bannerman's Liberal ministry to appoint a Royal Commission on Afforestation and Coast Erosion. An installment of its voluminous report on forests appeared in 1909. Commissioners offered two options: that the government either acquire and plant mostly softwoods on 150,000 acres each year for the next sixty years or purchase 75,000 acres a year for the next eighty years. Unwilling to move so quickly, the government responded by setting up a development commission to overhaul the administration of Crown Forests, to encourage forestry training, and to carry on more experiments with state-managed plantations.[53]

The experience of the First World War changed that mood and weaken preservationist defenses. It drove home the point "progressives" had been making for half a century: that forests were essential to national security in an increasingly bellicose world. By 1915 government planners became aware that a dangerously large proportion of available shipping was devoted to carrying heavy timbers, construction materials, and mine props. Large-scale felling of British forests was the response. Between 1915 and 1918, members of the civilian forestry corps, including 2,000 women and a contingent of imported Canadian lumberjacks, cut some half million acres. Even so, about one ton of cargo in every seven that made it through the submarine blockade consisted of pit props and other wood products essential to the war effort. By contrast, the enemy nations could rely on their domestic supply.[54]

In 1917 a subcommittee of the Ministry of Reconstruction, chaired by Sir Francis Acland, proposed that the state, cooperating with the private sector, plant softwood trees over an eighty-year period, on two million acres of rough grazing land. It recommended that a central authority supervise the task. The idea was to build up a strategic reserve. In 1919 the government responded by establishing the Forestry Commission. That agency was given the authority to begin acquiring properties and supporting forestry training.

Hesitantly at first, then at an accelerating pace, the commission began to plant on ancient woodlands and coppices and especially on moor and heath. Because softwood had been the crucial item during the war and because the future seemed at the time to belong to fir and pine, its agents concentrated on planting conifers, including a great deal of the uninspiring Sitka spruce. These and other hardy softwood trees were about all that could be expected to grow on the thin-soil uplands, the only kind of terrain the commission, short on funds, could afford to buy. A modern landscape historian, Roger Miles, comments on the technical errors made in the early years of the commission's work and adds: "that aesthetic mistakes might also happen was not considered at the time, and there was nothing whatever in the Forestry Commission's brief about amenity."[55]

Therefore Lord Ailesbury had good reason to refuse the commission's initial offer to take over the cost of managing the Savernake Forest. But by 1938, when the commission agreed to preserve the essential character of the estate, its single-minded zeal to cover as much land as possible with quick-growing timber had obviously moderated. From the start that zeal had collided with the cultural image of the landscape inherited from the previous two centuries. Essential to that image was a balance between open space and woodland, intimacy and fastness, order and spontaneity, straight-edged fields and rounded hilltop copses—landscape features that seem to meet some deep-felt need. Resistance could be expected whenever individuals or agencies proved to be conspicuously insensitive to that concept of balance.

One of the first concessions Parliament made to aroused public opinion occurred in the 1870s over the issue of "deforesting" Crown Forests. Proposals to withdraw sections of the New Forest from the jurisdiction of forest law met with angry resistance. This body of law protected to some extent commoners' rights of use, rights that were incompatible with fencing off sections and planting tree shoots. The New Forest Act of 1877 did grant permission to deforest but included a provision requiring that enclosure be carried out with "regard to the ornamental as well as the profitable use of the ground." Another clause stipulated that areas containing ancient and particularly beautiful trees be preserved and kept open to the public.[56]

At the same time, preservationism was becoming organized and efficient in gaining concessions from courts and legislators. New recruits came in the early decades of the twentieth century from countryside rambling and cycling organization. Therefore concessions made by the Forestry Commission to Lord Ailesbury were concessions, not only to a generalized nostalgia for what Savernake represented, but to an increasingly powerful set of interest groups.

Then came the Second World War. In the year it ended, the philosopher C. E. M. Joad published a lament for the passing of this countryside. Fashioned in the eighteenth century and come to maturity at the end of the Victorian era:

> It was, I suppose, some fifty years ago that the fruits of this loving labour of the eighteenth century reached maturity. The trees had grown to their full stature; the grass floors of the avenues were soft and velvety; the houses richly mellow. The motor was as yet unknown, and the depredations of the builder were confined to the towns. Our grandfathers knew England at its best. One could find it in one's heart to blame them for neglect, in that they did nothing to perpetuate or protect the beauty they so much admired. One could, that is to say, if it were not for one's consciousness of one's own guilt; for while the eighteenth century beautified the countryside and the nineteenth century neglected it, it has been left to the twentieth century to ruin it."[57]

Had Joad been granted the opportunity to make another fifty-year retrospective, his tone would probably would have been even more bitter. Nan Fairbrother, who is impatient with this kind of blinkered nostalgia, is willing to grant that the modern amalgamated countryside lacks

the sensitive balance found in the old one.[58] It is generally agreed that
coniferization of upland open spaces, the bulldozing of hedgerows, the
poisoning and ring barking of old forest sites, the practice of intensive,
high-energy-consuming, chemical-dependent agriculture and forestry,
the surrender of governments to the "logic" of cost-benefit analysis, activities so admired by many Victorian forestry reformers, has done far
more during the three decades after the war to change the visual aspect
of the rural landscape, especially the open upland spaces, than anything
the agriculturalists, planters, industrial polluters, and urban developers
managed to do during the time when Queen Victoria and Edward VII
were on the throne.[59]

But at our own turn of the century there are at least some signs that
governments at various levels, the scholarly community, the media, and
the public have become aware of the necessity, not of restoring "the world
we have lost," but of finding a new balance. The 1970s saw a striking
rise in the share of family income spent on transportation, especially
cars, and an equally dramatic rise in the numbers of workers entitled to
four weeks of paid vacation.[60] In 1957 some 50,000 people camped
overnight in the New Forest and the forest parks; thirteen years later,
over a million did so.[61] The connection between these increases is obvious. Recreational use of British forests, once mainly reserved for the few,
had now opened to the many. Legislation aimed at facilitating public access followed this gradual, then rapidly accelerating, trend toward wider
public participation. The result has been that privately and publicly
owned woodlands must now search for ways of resolving tensions between a new set of factors: efficient timber production; demands that
plantations respect the scale, contour, and other visual values of the site;
concerns about environmental impact; problems of vehicle access; and
different, often conflicting, recreational tastes and needs.

In searching for compromises, responsible planners, forestry scientists, landscape architects, owners, managers, and officials have in the
rapidly advancing field of ecology a conceptual tool rarely available before. The older conservationists tended to draw almost exclusively on
the language of public health, amenity, and beauty. Modern environmentalist can add to the repertoire words like *diversity, complexity, sustainability,* and *interaction.*

For example, ecological research has given another dimension to the
long debate about the utility of the conifer and the beauty of the deciduous. Ecologists try to avoid emotive language as they set about chart-
ing the different chemical reaction of varieties of spruce, pine, or larch

with the soil particular to one ecosystem. They measure the effect of these interactions on soil temperature, moisture, and rate of erosion and follow all of these effects and interactions into the drainage system and into the bogs, streams, and rivers. Then they attempt to understand the impact of these factors on local organisms and discover what alterations are taking place in their system of mutual dependencies.[62]

An advantage of this approach is that, when nature lovers, hikers, poets, environmentalists, or economic interests contend about the advantages or disadvantages of planting a particular upland moor or grassland, their discussion can rest on some reasonably firm ground. That a stand of oaks can be shown to support a much greater variety of bird, insect, mammal, and plant life than any of its softwood rivals is now considered relevant information not just to naturalists but to forestry policy makers, planners, and managers. Today promoters of major projects aimed at controlling or harnessing natural processes know that they will be expected to answer in detail questions about long-term environmental impact. To this limited extent at least, George Perkins Marsh's expectation that people would eventually be persuaded to look at the face of the land in a new way—microscopically, subcutaneously, interactively—seems finally to have been at least partly realized.

Historians of the land and the forests have also gained an additional perspective. The late Victorian advocates of the new forestry looked back over their century and saw either stagnation or steady decline. We are inclined to go a bit further and ask about the effects of that history on the physical environment. When the old, largely preindustrial, forestry ceased to be vital to the nation's economic and military interests, neglect, indifference, sentiment, paternalism, concern for sport, amenity, and conspicuous consumption, as well as the possibility of exploiting advantageously other people's forest reserves, combined to preserve much of the "traditional" landscape's harmony—the unity of woods, fields, pastures, ponds, and buildings, arranged so as to respect natural land forms.

But an unwillingness to apply intensive production methods can have other uses as well. We are aware now that rot, senility, and decay bring richness, complexity, and diversity to a forest ecosystem. Knowing that can, and increasingly does, influence decisions about forest uses. Even with the best of will, we may find it impossible to follow Aldo Leopold's advice in *A Sand County Almanac* to "think like a mountain." But we are, perhaps, more open than before to his suggestion that "the role of *Homo sapiens*" change "from conqueror of the land-community to plain citizen and member of it."[63]

6
Cutting New Channels

We flash across the level.
We thunder thro' the bridges.
We bicker down the cuttings.
We sway along the ridges.

A rush of streaming hedges,
Of jostling lights and shadows,
Of hurtling, hurrying stations,
Of racing woods and meadows.

From W. E. Henley,
"Journey By Train," 1876

The passage of time allows us to appreciate how relatively benign were the environmental effects on the homeland of the Victorian transport revolution. We have noted the conservative effect of this technological achievement on forest policy. More direct and significant was the effect of steam locomotion on channels of movement. By diverting long-range travel away from roads onto tracks and from private vehicles onto public transport, railways both facilitated travel and made sure it was confined to narrow corridors, thus tending to preserve the land and landscape.

But few early Victorians could have regarded the railway builders as preservationists. The prospect that railway engineers might soon be able to rearrange the topography of Britain and cut great channels through it inclined people to believe that a major reconstruction of the physical and visual environment was at hand. One reaction was pride in the growing power to manipulate nature and to assist it in realizing its own perfection. In 1837, the year before Robert Stephenson completed his line from

London to Birmingham, Cuthbert Johnson, a Grey's Inn barrister and prolific essayist on matters agricultural, enthused about the possibility of using this newest application of steam technology to redistribute in a massive way the nation's surface crust and, by so doing, eliminate infertility. It might now be possible to correct each local chemical imbalance by borrowing what was missing from somewhere else. He pointed out that the London and Birmingham Railway crossed the gravelly soil of Middlesex to reach, near Watford, the Hertfordshire chalk formation. It then passed over the gravelly chalk of Buckinghamshire to the stiff clays of Northhamptonshire and Warwickshire. Since chalk is an admirable fertilizer for thin soil and the oxide of aluminum in the clay works wonders when mixed with chalk and lime, there was every possibility that, given the versatility and huge carrying capacity of railways, all deviations from the norm might be done away with and the nation's soil be made uniformly productive.[1]

Railway promoters and agriculturalists exhausted all the copies of the first edition of Johnson's pamphlet in the first ten days. One wonders, however, in what mood landowners and their tenants received its message. Even if used for less ambitious purposes, the railway seemed bound to disrupt the fabric of life as well as of the land. It must have been a daunting prospect for most rural residents to hear that engineers and gangs of navvies were soon to arrive in the neighborhood and slice huge gashes (some fifteen acres were required to make a mile of railway) through their ordered countryside. To create these new corridors, engineers would also need to slice straight through land contours.

This was certainly the case with the building of the London and Birmingham Railway. A special feature of that project was that it cut across the grain. Its designer, the young Robert Stephenson, listened to the advice of George Stephenson, his famous engineer father, and kept the grade at an average steepness of no more than 1 in 330. That meant his contractors had to force their way for more than a hundred miles across valleys and through hills that lay, transversely, in their path. They cut deep slashes and filled whole valleys so that locomotives could speed along at a nearly constant level.[2] As one contemporary remarked, the result was that the whole line would need to be either a cutting or an embankment.[3]

Such a drastic act of defiance toward the lay of the land greatly troubled conservative-minded people. According to Sir Francis Bond Head, when Stephenson and his associate, George Parker Builder ("The Calculating Boy"), made a series of surveying walks along the proposed route, they were looked upon by the people they encountered as "magicians, evil genii, or unclean spirits, whose unearthly object it was to fright the land from its property."[4]

In 1851, thirteen years after the line was completed, John Francis remembered that "blinded by ignorance and obstinacy" opponents in and outside of Parliament had made predictions about how fields and valleys would be violated, springs be dried up, soil be eroded, and meadows be made sterile: "Like an earthquake [the railway] would create chasms, it would upheave mountains; and it was pathetically added, the railway promoter was like an evil providence, unrighteously attempting that which nature was too kind to effect."[5]

Francis found this attitude pitiful or narrowly self-serving. He was an ardent booster of steam technology. Nevertheless, he did feel a need to acknowledge that some objections may have been sincere. "There are fancy spots in this our beautiful England which it would pain the most indifferent to destroy; what then must be the feelings of those who have lived and only wish to die there . . . ? If the nobleman disliked the destruction of his fine old English park, the yeoman deplored the desecration of his homestead. The one bore its splendid remembrances, the other its splendid recollections."[6]

From our perspective, what is interesting in this vigorous debate before and after the cutting and embanking began was the form in which the case for and against the new transport technology was made: the concepts and language available to both sides in the early days of the railway era. Already, as Francis's parenthetical aside reminds us, conservative sentiments would be expressed in aesthetic and social terms. We hear that there is a special beauty in the countryside of "this our England"; the landscape through which the rails slice discloses a harmony between nature and the cultivator, the product of intimacy bestowed only by long proprietorship. We note that Francis speaks of the nobleman and the yeoman but not of the tenant farmer, his employees, or any other inhabitants of the country whose connection with the soil, the hedges, the meadows, and the trees is, at least formally, indirect or transitory. Thus it is a continuity of "splendid remembrances" and "affectionate recollections" that makes "fancy spots" (places that are imaginatively evocative for those who know them well) worthy of conservation, or at least makes their destruction a matter of genuine regret.

Francis scoffed when people expressed anxiety that large-scale intrusions into the realm of nature invited retaliation. He dismissed such fears as scare tactics. Nevertheless, there can be little doubt about the genuineness of some of the apprehension. Again and again in the Parliamentary debates and the local protest meetings of 1832 and 1833, warnings about the consequences of arrogance came from disinterested people.[7] The unprecedented scale of the railway works was worrying. Canal builders had also filled in valleys and pierced through inclines but had done so on a far more modest scale. Series of locks provided some compromise between technology and the contours of the land. Railway builders, on the other hand, promised to punish the land unmercifully. The result, it was feared, would be erosion, washouts, soil sterility, and the drying up of springs. The loosened and troubled earth would give way; tunnels, banks, and arches would be certain to collapse.

R. Cort, son of Henry Cort, developer of the combined puddling-and-rolling process in iron making, was sure that excavations would destroy the natural "veins of water" and thus render sterile the pastures and sloping fields along the line. No amount of compensation could possibly make up for the defacing of fields and parks or the destruction of "the haunts of our forefathers": "Woe be to the land, whenever the love of their own green fields, their avenues, their trees, their cottages, becomes cold in the breast of our nobles and our chiefs." Surely the future, the younger Cort wrote, lies not with rails that tear asunder fields and parks, leaving "immense gashes and mounds" behind but with steam boats and steam carriages, moving along improved canals and roads.[8]

Worth noting is how Cort's case for retaining and remodeling the existing road and canal networks rested finally on aesthetic values. After much detailed analysis of the material damage railway builders would inflict, he ended by evoking the love of the settled, unbroken country, the land of our forefathers, noble avenues, green fields. He and other enemies of the railway must have recognized that engineers would eventually work out solutions to the formidable excavation problems facing them. By the late 1830s trust in engineering ingenuity was building, especially after George Stephenson managed to carry his Liverpool and Manchester Railway across two seemingly bottomless quagmires.

Therefore it was good strategy not to rest the case against the railway on technical difficulties but to direct attention to the railway builders' unreflective assumption that what could be done should be done. Influential voices joined in this kind of protest. "Utilitarianism"—wrote Wordsworth in his fiery protest to the *Morning Post* against the intended Kendal and Windermere Railway—while "serving as a mask for cupidity," is an "evil" that now makes railways and their reckless actions "its favourite instrument." The utilitarian mentality behind the railway is,

he warned, heedless of the sacred relics left us by our ancestors; it is incapable of comprehending that there might be "temples of Nature, temples
built by the Almighty, which have a still higher claim to be left unvio-
lated." Wordsworth was certain that if the poet Thomas Gray "were
now living, how would he have lamented the probable intrusion of a
railway with its scarifications, its intersections, its noisy machinery, its
smoke, and swarms of pleasure-hunters, most of them thinking that they
do not fly fast enough through the country which they have come to see." [9]

John Ruskin sounded the same notes thirty-two years later. Upon
hearing that yet another railway was being proposed for the Lake District, he took up his pen against "the frenzy of avarice," that was "daily
drowning our sailors, suffocating our miners, poisoning our children,
and blasting the cultivable surface of England into a treeless waste of
ashes." Since only vice can grow on waste, there must be, he warned, a
"deterioration of moral character in the inhabitants of every district penetrated by a railway." [10]

The distinction between the "utilitarian" outlook and the "aesthetic/
moral" (often referred to in nuanced tones as the "sentimental") outlook
was used to categorize railway advocates and railway resisters. As we have
noticed, sentimentalists did not always express themselves with Ruskin-
ian vehemence and only a few opposed the entire enterprise; likewise
utilitarian engineers and promoters occasionally experienced flickers of
conscience when their navvies and gunpowder obliterated famous beauty
spots or remnants of past civilizations. Nevertheless, in the dialogue between the two sides one detects the same intemperance we have come to
expect in present clashes between developers and their opponents.

Thus framers of the 1832 version of the bill to permit the construction
of the London and Birmingham Railway tended to dismiss expressions of
anxiety as hypocrisy or obscurantism, while, at the same time, making
concessions to individual landowners whose estates lay along the right
of way. They tried to reassure canal companies who feared that their water supplies would be jeopardized. Special provisions forbade contractors
to build deviations that might disturb the surroundings and residence of
Thomas Reeve Thornton at Berkhamstead. No spoil was to be deposited on any part of Chilcot's estate. River water was not to be diverted
through lands belonging to the marquis of Hastings. Trustees of the
Radcliffe estate at Woolverton were to be supplied with culverts to prevent flooding. The quiet and beauty of parks belonging to Lady Bridge-
water, Lord Clarendon, and the earl of Essex, were to be respected.[11]

Missing in the bill, although not in some of the complaints about it, is a recognition that making a cutting or an embankment must disturb, perhaps irreparably, the delicate pattern of relationships between the plant, animal, and mineral components of any site. Instead we find meticulous attention paid to problems of drainage in cuttings and erosion on embankment walls, not because the railway promoters were greatly concerned about the local human, animal, bird, insect, or vegetable populations (except for private game preserves), but because they worried about the effect of earth slippage, subsidence, flooding, and erosion on the excavation site. Committeemen subjected railway surveyors to the most careful questioning about the results of test borings along the prospective line and asked them to predict how various kinds of substrata would react if exposed to air and frost. In reply, Stephenson and his assistants displayed their command of details about the proportion of horizontal slope to vertical rise required for various clays, chalks, and marls.[12] They sounded more confident than they were: a century of canal building had built up no large store of data about such matters, the scale of these excavations having been smaller and the engineering difficulties less daunting.

Also impressive in the testimony was the attention Stephenson and his staff paid to the need to control or prevent earth slippage. When the construction of drainage systems, cesspools, and encasing walls began, no expense seemed to have been spared to get them right. Railway promoters could point to these costs as proof of their claim to be allies rather than foes of the arable farmer. Bristol and London Railway directors later used this evidence to reassure agriculturalists whose farms they intended to cross. If their plans were accepted, they said, it was "not too much to suppose, that many lands will be thereby greatly improved, which indeed has been found to be the case on other Railways." [13]

Other than their sheer extent, this concern about draining and preserving the stability of the cuttings is the most interesting environmental feature at Tring and at Blisworth, where London and Birmingham engineers carried out two of their largest excavations. Brick side drains at Tring ran the whole two-and-a-half-mile length. They were thirty-three inches deep and had capacious storage pools or "eyes." At ten-yard intervals, tiled underground culverts, placed well below the ballast that held the tracks, diverted subsurface water to the sides. Outside the cutting, crest ditches at elevated places drained away water that might otherwise have weakened the banks. Stephenson's dictum was: "Wherever water is known, or suspected to exist, its immediate source should be traced, and every possible means adopted for diverting it from the slopes and adjacent surfaces."[14] In other words, the drainage of the chalk ridge of Ivinghoe was refashioned to serve the interest of the line of communication cutting through it.

The same can be said of the embankment built out of the Tring cutting. Every surveyor of a route had to concern himself with trying to balance, in the most convenient and economical way, what was dug out with what was to be piled up and in what order. This was a particularly difficult strategic exercise for a railway that had almost no level surfaces to build on. Asked what he would do if materials from cuttings were not sufficient to make embankments, Stephenson answered, "The line must be altered."[15] At Tring the exchange was about even. A million and a half cubic yards of chalk were moved to dig the two-and-a-half-mile cutting forty feet deep and another million when a second track was added.[16] Tracked wagons then hauled this material away and deposited it in the next Chiltern valley to make an embankment six miles long and thirty feet high.

The cutting at Blisworth, five miles from Northampton, was a mile shorter than at Tring, but it was deeper (in places, the rails were sixty feet below the surface) and caused the contractor so much misery that Stephenson had to take over supervision directly. Beneath the surface was a layer of sandy clay with loose stones and then a layer of flint-hard limestone that had to be quarried and blasted with 3,000 barrels of gunpowder to reach the thick bed of clay underneath. That bed rested on loose blue shale through which water ran copiously. With so treacherous a foundation, the cutting walls constantly slid or bulged. At great expense, a steam engine began pumping night and day, and 800 men and boys were set to work blasting, shoveling, and lifting a million cubic yards of muck and debris for locomotives at either end to haul away. Thick stone retaining walls buttressed by inverted arches held the clay bank in, and an elaborate system of drains and culverts did eventually prevent deterioration.[17]

The problem of keeping the embankment stable through the two adjacent valleys proved to be nearly as difficult, since the soft valley floors kept swallowing up the debris dumped onto them. Wrote Thomas Roscoe, one of the engineers on the line, "an engineer could wish no worse fortune than to be required to construct culverts upon a soft foundation under a deep embankment."[18] Eventually, however, the task was completed, and the trains got through to Rugby. When they arrived, Thomas Arnold, at one with Wordsworth and Ruskin in his reverence for the holy solitude of the lakes, nevertheless rejoiced that railways would be "destroying feudality for ever"—a reminder of how ambivalent reactions could be to all of this digging down and piling up.

Embankments made far more obvious visual impressions on surroundings than did cuttings; and, because embankments were made of imported material and exposed steep banks to rain and sunlight, they developed special environments of their own. To prevent earth slippage and erosion, railway companies and sometimes private individuals conducted experiments to see what would grow in these miniature environments.[19] A Congregational minister with a passion for railways, Frederick Smeeton Williams, noted that it was common practice in Scotland to cover "travelled" earth on railway banks with the kind of trees that "permeate and interlace" rather than sending their tap roots straight down. He quoted this excerpt from a letter to the *Gardener's Magazine:*

> I had the pleasure of seeing perhaps half an acre of strawberries the other day on a railway embankment. They were planted thickly and broadcast, the whole ground being covered with them, and they were loaded with bloom. Perhaps this is the best way of growing strawberries on railway embankments, as the whole ground is thus covered with them; and the fierce sunshine, though intensified by the slope of the ground, cannot burn the roots.[20]

Authors of early railway travel commented on how quickly the scars had healed, so quickly that travelers might easily forget the heroic labors needed to construct the smooth rights-of-way. Edward Osborne's *London and Birmingham Railway Guide* (1840) informed readers that a once raw cutting just beyond Pinner had already become a "series of beautiful gardens of wild flowers . . . the clusters of violets, the harebell, the forget-me-not, and the germander speedwell." He expressed hope that directors would plant trees and shrubbery all along the line, thus assisting nature in reconciling the railway with the landscape.[21]

Like most of the other guide writers of the time, Osborne was not content simply to reassure the apprehensive that railways had not, in fact, permanently torn the countryside apart; he and the others went on to suggest that railway travel was opening up to the wider community a new way of experiencing and appreciating natural beauty. People, he noted, can now journey for thousands of miles "with greater personal ease than they formerly could over fifty." He was sure that in the process they would shed prejudice, superstition, and all the other evils of parochialism. Visually, too, they would be uplifted by being exposed to the extended rather than the immediate point of view. Looked at closely, Blisworth cutting would disclose fascinating fossils, too small to see from the window as the train sped through the gap. Reward would come, however, the moment the train rushed onto the embankment: "[On] leaving the cutting, a noble scene presents itself; the view to the north is bounded by the distant hills, and the intermediate valley gently undulated and filled with pastures and cornfields."[22]

In *The Railway Journey,* Wolfgang Schivelbusch cites passages from guidebooks to show how the "mechanization of motive power" brought about a perceptual transformation and, in doing so, created a new landscape in which "mechanical regularity triumphs over natural irregularity."[23] Foregrounds flash by. Trees along the way, once experienced on foot or from a coach as discrete entities, become "racing woods and meadows" for railway travelers, The eye of the fast-moving observer reaches out beyond the "rush of streaming hedges" to the "gently undulated" valleys, which seem to be in motion, rising and falling as the train flashes through on its smooth and level course. The "noble scene" on the outside of the window does seem to *present itself* to the seated passenger. The train's velocity reveals the orderly whole even as it blurs the irregularly close and particular.[24]

Most guidebooks of the early railway era express this idea. They assume that the way one experiences landscape depends on one's vantage point but also on the speed of the conveyance and the degree of closeness it allows between the passenger and the natural world outside. Arthur Freeling's *The Railway Companion, From London to Birmingham, Liverpool, and Manchester* (1837), James Scott Walker's *An Accurate Description of the Liverpool and Manchester Railway* (1832), and James Drake's *Road Book* (1839), promised patrons of their respective lines that they would experience something unique in history. On the London and Birmingham they would rush through a constantly changing panorama while comfortably seated in a sealed compartment: now charging along a high embankment with the topography spread out before them, now plunging into a dark tunnel or a cutting, suddenly to emerge again into an entirely different prospect. On the more level terrain of the Liverpool and Manchester, there would be few dramatic plunges and rises but, instead, the "steady succession of scenery," the springy sensation when riding across Chat or Parr Moss—like "skimming over a sea of oil." For the price of a ticket, ordinary people, once restricted by cost and stunted imaginations, could now be moved by impressions "at once pleasing and sublime" and at the same time be protected from the rigors and terrors once endured by seekers after sublimity.[25]

One of the most insightful commentators on the connections between speed, conveyance, and landscape was Francis Roubiliac Conder, the apprentice engineer on the London and Birmingham, whose enthusiasms about steam agriculture have already been noted. Like others in his profession, he could be lyrical about the transforming power of steam energy; what was unusual about him was his capacity to see that some of the exhilaration would go out of travel once people were able to dash through the countryside in hermetically sealed containers. His duties for Stephenson required that he move quickly from place to place along the line of construction, using a four-in-hand coach. When the weather and road conditions were just right, he recalled, such vehicles were capable of moving along as fast as sixteen miles per hour. On such occasions, the experience of speed from the top of a coach was thrilling because directly received by all the senses—"so much more enjoyable," he recalled in 1868, "than that to which our iron roads have accustomed us." Given "four well-conditioned horses" and a "crack whip," he testified, nothing "has yet been discovered to equal the physical enjoyment" of rushing down country roads on an old first-class coach at sunrise. One of his favorite stretches was between Cheltenham and Tewkesbury. Along that road, he said, the rider is in nature:

> The fresh morning air, the fragrance of the wide hedgeless bean-fields, the distant ragged outline of the great Malvern range, clear in the early morn before you; the purple glory of the sunshine bursting over the Cotswolds behind; the steady, unswerving, rapid motion, combined to give a sense of exhilarating power for which the greater speed of the dusty, noisy, uninteresting train can afford no substitute.[26]

Conder thought railway travel was boring. Not only are the senses of the seated travelers dulled but so is their understanding of the landscape, since they are only able to see the passing scene in glimpses and have no way of anticipating what lies ahead. In the old days, he recalled, it was possible to prepare the eye and the mind. He offered as an example the approach to the Black Country as it used to be made by road travel. Then transitions were gradual. Long before entering that intensely industrial landscape, distant smoke and flame would have warned observers that they were about to pass through the gates of Lucifer's palace. But now, he wrote, the passenger looks up from his page to behold a suddenly "carbonised landscape" with "a pair of lofty cupolas vomiting flame. All around, the earth is black; the hideous, unarchitectural buildings are black; the half-stripped men, toiling to fill the ever-devouring furnaces, are black; the sky is a dense canopy of smoke, glowing and angry with the reflected light of the undying furnaces." Having been suddenly offered this scene out of *Paradise Lost*, the rider then has it snatched away and turns back to book or newspaper, not having smelled, heard, or felt the reality of the scene. Thus the modern traveler, Conder concluded, must, unfortunately, be reconciled with the "natural abhorrence of the steam-engine for the picturesque." [27]

In 1857, a decade before Conder's reflections appeared, Thomas Hughes had made a leading theme in his *Tom Brown's School Days* the need to adjust institutions and perceptions to the steam era. As the narrative proper begins, Tom is leaving home by stagecoach to start his life at Rugby School; at the end Tom and his fellow graduates are breaking off their cricket match unfinished so that the visiting team can catch its train to London. But before beginning to trace Tom's spiritual and physical growth under "The Doctor," Hughes leads his schoolboy readers on an excursion, by means of the Great Western Railway, to the White Horse Hill just beyond Swindon. He asks them, "if they have a few hours to spare," to disembark at the Shrivenham station and walk with him to the highest point. He promises to show them the glorious view and then some of "the relics of bygone times," relics that only practiced eyes can see. In the voice of an old man, carried away by nostalgia, he exclaims: "O young England! Young England!—you who are born into these racing railroad times, when there's a Great Exhibition, or some monster sight, every year, and you can get over a couple of thousand miles of ground for three pound ten, in a five week's holiday, why don't you know more of your own birthplaces?"

In his day, continues the narrator, when the old coach disembarked schoolboy passengers at the crossroads on the first day of holidays, no modern entertainments awaited when they reached their homes. There would be little to do but walk or ride on country lanes, listen to country stories and ways, and make friends of "the fields and woods and hills. . . . We were Berkshire or Gloucestershire or Yorkshire boys," he says, "and you're young cosmopolites, belonging to all counties and countries. No doubt that's all right,—I dare say it is. This is the day of large views and glorious humanity, and all that; but I wish back-sword play hadn't gone out of the Vale of the White Horse, and that confounded Great Western hadn't carried away Alfred's Hill to make an embankment." [28] Of course Alfred's Hill was only carried away figuratively by the Great Western's speeding locomotives. Brunel and his contractors would have used human and animal muscle to level the hill and fill the next valley. "Racing railroad times" did not set the pace of construction and steam technology did not, except on rare occasions, greatly lighten the task.

In *The Railway Navvies,* Terry Coleman describes how one navvy was expected to fill fourteen sets, a set being a string of wagons brought in on rails to the cutting or along an embankment. This meant lifting twenty tons of earth a day. If the excavated earth was not intended for the construction of an embankment but needed to be deposited at the sides of the cutting, a workman would guide a barrow, pulled by a horse-powered windlass up a steep plank run.[29] An engineer named James Day wrote a book about excavation and embankment techniques and included a drawing of an ingenious device by means of which a horse could, alone, pull a barrow to the top, dump its contents, and lower it empty. Although the inventor won a gold prize from the Society of Arts, his invention apparently did not find favor with contractors. The sight of men rapidly and skillfully guiding barrows up and down slopes continued to be a sight-seeing attraction at excavation sites all through the century.[30]

These links with older technology and with older ways of perceiving remained (since trains were, except in London, mainly for distance travel) well after steam excavation had come of age. That age began in Britain with the construction in 1887 of a canal to bring oceangoing ships thirty-five miles inland and turn Manchester into a major ocean port. There were precedents for using machines. According to an article in the *Builder* for 1846, an "American Devil," a sixteen-horsepower "steam navvy", was brought from the United States to construct the Victoria Dock at Hull. It had a crew of five and could do the work of thirty men.[31] Only a few years before, William Smith Otis had developed the prototype of this machine to help build a railway line from Springfield to Worcester in his native Massachusetts.[32] But such early innovations were exceptional. Steam excavators were a rarity on construction or excavation sites until 1876, when the Lincoln firm of Rushton and Proctor introduced its efficient steam shovel. Several of these excavators were used to make cuttings during the construction of the West Lancashire Railway, where stiff brown clay made hand digging difficult and where the absence of boulders made conditions ideal for the rail-mounted machines.[33] (See Figure 6.)

The first real test in Britain for steam excavating came a decade later with the digging of the Manchester Ship Canal; indeed, this huge project would not have been undertaken had steam shovels and dredges not already demonstrated their capacities. Sixty Rushton and Proctor excavators, supplemented by seven larger French and German machines, were trundled along tracks to the site. Working with them were 194 steam cranes, 2 floating steam dredges, and 173 locomotives. Two hundred and

Figure 6.   Excavating scoop (1878). Heavy excavators, moving on rails, could only be used economically on major projects like the Manchester Ship Canal. This scoop, pulled back and forth by two steam engines, aimed at the earth-moving flexibility eventually achieved by the bulldozer. (*Engineering* 25, 1878)

twelve steam pumps assisted in the process of digging 53,500,000 cubic yards of earth, transporting 460,000 bricks, and pouring 1,250,000 cubic yards of concrete. Three hundred and twenty Wells's portable oil lights of 2,000 candlepower and three electric light installations allowed some of this work to go on at night.

Steam machinery finally had an opportunity to demonstrate its ability to cut deep grooves through the surface of the earth, yet it would not be strictly true to say that steam built the Manchester Ship Canal. One hundred and twenty thousand men, most of them using shovels, barrows, and other hand tools, also took part in the digging, building, and hauling, as well as 2,000 horses and 6,300 sturdy wagons.[34] All through the nineteenth century, machines acted as extensions of, and supplements to, muscle power. In turn, the operation of machines depended upon a large reserve of manual labor. Every steam excavator required a crew to shift the tracks it moved upon and to dispose of the material it scooped up. A steam land dredger, developed by Messrs. J. Boulet and Co. of Paris for use on the Suez Canal, was put to work on the Manchester Canal project. Known as "the Frenchy," it needed from twenty-eight to forty-three attendants and a locomotive to pull it.[35]

Machines like these displaced hand labor and created additional uses for it. In earth moving as in agriculture, mining, quarrying, and transport, steam gradually took over certain functions and skills but did so without displacing or even threatening to displace almost the whole range of traditional implements and handcrafts. Most workmen who built the London and Birmingham Railway in the 1830s or the Great Western shortly afterward could have set to work on the Manchester Ship Canal and found accustomed tasks awaiting them. Only a few would have needed retraining.

There were other continuities. As in the case of the London and Birmingham Railway, the proposal to build the canal stirred furious debate between vested interests. Liverpool shipping firms were understandably apprehensive about the emergence of so close a rival, as were railway owners and existing canal and river navigation companies. Manchester businessmen, politicians, and the less timorous among their bankers and stock promoters were excited by the prospect of an economic revival in their city. Each of these interests brought forward its own specialists to show why and how the project would be the making or breaking of the region's economy, even the nation's.[36] Talk about self-interest was restricted to the board rooms. Both sides were far more conscious than early Victorians seemed to have been of the need to appear public-spirited rather than narrowly self-interested. Consequently, they rested a fair proportion of their arguments on estimates of how little or how much the canal would affect the physical environment. For this reason the discussion can give us some notion of the range and scope of late Victorian environmental consciousness and competence.

Spokesmen on either side had little to say about the ethics of interfering with natural processes or about the aesthetic effects of creating new channels for the Mersey River and its tributary or for the river Irwell, which flows (if that is the word) through Manchester and Salford. They were aware that natural process, in the sense of a river being allowed to take its course without human intervention, had ceased long ago. On the scale of artificiality, the Mersey and the Irwell would have found places at the top. From the eighteenth century, dredging and other means of channelization had made this river system navigable for barges and small cargo ships; but after the railway went through in 1829, navigation ceased to be as profitable as before and the disposal of industrial and urban waste gradually became its most important function. The textile mills of densely industrialized south Lancashire dumped dyes and other chemicals, Manchester discharged untreated sewage, and Salford deposited partly treated sewage. This sludge collected on the river bottoms, raising them, in places, four to nine feet.[37] As one might expect, the Irwell, which drained this urban area, was the more polluted of the two. A report in 1860 estimated that filth was accumulating on its floor at a rate of two or three inches every year.[38] When riverside mills were forbidden to dump their refuse directly into the river, they simply placed it on the banks and waited for flood waters. One way or another, 33,000 tons of cinders found their way into the river yearly.[39] One sanitary expert claimed in 1907 that it was "the hardest worked and foulest stream in the world."[40]

In his *Endangered Lives,* Anthony Wohl used the subject of river pollution to support his generalization that "the Victorians were probably far more successful at improving their urban, than protecting their natural environment."[41] He pointed out that rivers were turned into sewers because reformers, alarmed at death rates in cities, placed urban sanitation higher on their priority list. They could rationalize this decision to remove human and animal wastes from city streets and drains and dumping it, untreated or only partially treated, into water courses by pointing out (as some still do)[42] that rivers contain natural self-cleansing processes. Since, to quote Lord Salisbury, "drainage must be put somewhere,"[43] it seemed to follow that fouling notorious rivers like the Irwell was a legitimate exchange for allowing the residents of Salford and Manchester to live longer.

During the debate over the canal, such reasoning as this was more subtextual than explicit. Occasionally critics of the proposal, particularly landowners whose estates fronted on the Irwell or the Mersey, spoke of the terrible stench and predicted that the canal would concentrate the effluvia and, being an artificial watercourse, would have negligible purifying capacities.[44] The 1870 Report of the Rivers Pollution Commission contains the facsimile of a letter written using fluid from the Irwell instead of ink.[45] Sir Edward Leader Williams, the engineer-designer of the project, tried to reassure a House of Commons committee by stating that much of the dark color came from dye works and that the probable effect of this additive was to deodorize and to act as an antiseptic, or, as he put it when questioned at another hearing, a "mordant." Canal supporters produced a chemist to support this contention that the stench given off by industrial wastes actually promoted good health. He added that his own garden ended at the edge of the Irwell, so he would be certain to know if noxious vapors had any ill effects.[46]

Salford spokesmen used the occasion to criticize Manchester for making no serious attempt to treat sewage, and Manchester spokesmen promised that sewage works would soon be on their way. An act of 1892 followed up on that promise, but, as in the case of clean air legislation, the effect of improving standards and vigorously enforcing them was more than canceled out by large increases in the volume of pollutants produced and discharged. The canal took over the evil reputation of the rivers it absorbed. A fairly recent contributor to the "Notes and Queries" section of the *Manchester Guardian Weekly* remembered seeing, when a boy in the North Riding of Yorkshire, a sign in a local bus that directed, "Do not spit in the bus. Use the Manchester Ship Canal."[47]

The deadly equation continues to apply in the present: increasingly higher volumes of increasingly less contaminated emissions damage the environment more than the less restricted but smaller volumes of liquid, solid, and gaseous emissions. Where we appear to have an advantage is that the concept of an ecosystem is now more familiar to conservationists and the public. That means it can be used as a conceptual framework for understanding the consequences of pollution and for suggesting control guidelines. George Perkins Marsh had, of course, already demonstrated how an environment might be perceived as a unit in which organisms interact and exchange material with the physical surroundings. But the engineering profession in the half century between the building of the London and Birmingham Railway and the Manchester Ship Canal had tended steadily toward specialization, not integration.

Two of the leading experts on hydraulic engineering in the 1880s and 1890s, Leveson Francis Vernon-Harcourt and W. H. Wheeler, wrote detailed texts on the motion of water in rivers; the action of tides and currents; the effects of dredging; the mechanics that govern the buildup and shifting of bars in tidal rivers and estuaries; the effects of embankments and "training" walls on sedimentation, channel depth, and rate of flow.[48] For both of these authorities, rivers and their basins, sources, and mouths formed discrete systems, each with complex mechanisms. They cautioned about the difficulties of predicting the effect of management and control in a complex system where one intervention was bound to have such a variety of consequences. Vernon-Harcourt, like Marsh, spoke about the effect of deforestation on the rate of evaporation and water runoff and its consequence for river velocity and about the connections between the permeability of the underlying strata of the drainage basin and the characteristics of denudation and sedimentation.[49] He said nothing, however, about the place of other living things in these systems. Both Wheeler and Vernon-Harcourt believed (again like Marsh) that a "good" or "natural" river was one where all or most parts were in a dynamic but stable balance and that a well-managed river was one where the engineering works opened a channel for navigation and at the same time maintained or promoted that balance. Thus the approach of the two engineers was systematic. But their system was not an ecosystem.

Engineers who took such a prominent part in the discussion about the merits and defects of the various Manchester Ship Canal proposals confined their testimony to estimates about the effects of this or that feature on the Mersey estuary and the capacity of that volatile estuary to carry ship traffic. They also gave their judgment upon what effects the canal might have on the propensity of the Mersey basin to flood seasonally.[50] Scarce indeed, however, is any mention of possible consequences for fish, bird, insect, animal, or vegetable life, even though it was known at the time that estuaries and marshes are usually rich in nutrients and support a diversity of species. Overshadowing every other concern was Liverpool's fear about an exodus of commerce and Manchester's hopes for a revival of her export industry. In the controversy, economics was the senior partner, and the environment appeared in a supportive role.

That role, however, was far closer to center stage than it had been in the equally spirited struggle over the building of the London and Birmingham Railway. Fifty years later, all sides in the argument had available well-articulated rules about the behavior of rivers and estuaries and an abundant supply of engineering expertise. All sides recognized the need to invoke the authority of science and technology to legitimate their appeals.

Since much of the public discussion took place in committees of Parliament among many who had no direct stake in the economic welfare of Merseyside, it does seem curious that so few conservation-minded politicians or groups raised the issue of the possible aesthetic consequences. Apart from a few landowners who objected to damage to amenities on their estates, one of the few occasions where anyone expressed regret about the destruction of some beauty spot is a brief observation in Sir Bosdin Leech's history of the canal. This vigorous champion of the project did at one point regret the necessity of spoiling the landscape around Eastham. "It almost seemed a desecration," Leech wrote, "to invade such a pretty rural spot with its beautiful woods and foliage stretching down to the estuary." He noted that Liverpool ramblers and picnickers called the spot "The Richmond of the Mersey." [51] But he hastened to remind his readers that great engineering works have an aesthetic quality of their own. He recalled being stirred, while on a night visit to the construction site for the canal entry at Eastham in 1888, by the sight of the Rushton and Proctor steam navvies digging into the landscape under the brilliant illumination provided by Wells's oil lights.[52]

Presumably Liverpool residents who used the fields and lanes of Eastham for weekend excursions also regretted the loss of this stretch of greenery. There is no evidence, however, that they articulated their feelings in any organized way or that spokesmen with access to print took up the cause. There is abundant evidence, on the other hand, that the public was attracted in the same way Leech was to the spectacle of the surface being violated by huge and powerful machines. If there was organized tree hugging around Eastham or any other place, it went unreported. Trees had, after all, a long history of suffering in that part of Lancashire and Cheshire. Widnes, Runicorn, Ince, and other notorious examples of industrial dereliction along the Mersey had for years been written off as possible beauty spots. The damage done to nature there had been so thorough and prolonged that nostalgia must have seemed, even to those temperamentally inclined toward it, decidedly misplaced: indeed, watching great ships move in a straight line far inland through so thoroughly industrial a landscape must have had considerable appeal.

Therefore it proved to be effective strategy on the part of the canal's critics to concentrate on the possible danger to the special environment of the Mersey estuary. Through the narrow mouth, flanked by the Liverpool and Birkenhead docks, heavy tides flowed into the bottle-shaped basin and, by tidal scour, kept the sandbar at the entrance open to ocean ships. From the mid-1820s, engineers had debated how the channel into the Mersey River might best be improved without disrupting this vital current. One engineering expert, John Frederic La Trobe Bateman, who will appear later in his role as master reservoir builder, noted that most of the scouring took place when the ebbing tide left the sandbanks and concentrated its flow in the channels. In 1840 he proposed that a barrier be placed across the river entrance at Runicorn, creating a navigable lake stretching as far as Warrington. When the ebb was midway, the barrier could then be opened, briefly, several times a week, to flush accumulated sediment out into the ocean. This and other schemes were considered by the Mersey and Irwell Navigation Company and then shelved.[53]

When the Ship Canal Bill was being prepared forty years later, its drafters faced up once again to the now much-discussed problem of how to manage tidal flow in the Mersey basin. One of the company's engineers, Hamilton Fulton, suggested that a deep, straight, tidal canal be dredged all the way to Manchester so that scour would keep both canal and estuary open. The difficulty was that such a cut (Manchester was

sixty feet above sea level) would place docks and quays far below the surrounding surface. Therefore the planners gave approval to another plan,
developed by Leader Williams, who proposed to bring a set of retaining
walls, with a dredged channel in between, from the Mersey at Runicorn
to the middle of the estuary and by means of a series of locks and sluices
to raise and control the canal waters leading to the docks at Manchester.
This decision to prefer an engineered rather than a somewhat more natural form of estuarine and channel management became the sticking
point between the two sides when the bill was ready in 1882.

Early the next year, committees of the Houses of Commons and Lords
listened to testimony from a parade of witnesses, including most of the
leading British hydraulic engineers of the time and Captain James Buchanan Eades, the extraordinarily versatile American engineer who had
succeeded in keeping the mouth of the Mississippi clear for navigation.
Although Eades was forced to admit that the tides affecting the Mississippi delta were comparatively weak and other experts had to concede
that well-understood hydraulic principles had to be applied to entirely
different sets of circumstances in each case, the weight of the argument
went against the promoters. Witnesses reminded questioners that the
harbor at Chester silted up because an eighteenth century navigation
company had ignored the natural channel and made a "trained cut"
through the Dee estuary.[54] So, on the reasoning that inactivity was the
best policy when the risk of calamity was great and when the testimony
of experts conflicted, Parliament refused to pass the first Ship Canal Bill.

The leader of Liverpool's resistance was Sir William Forwood, a
wealthy merchant. He recalled later that he knew his cause was lost when
an engineer for the Mersey Docks and Harbour Board was asked what
he would do to protect the bar at the entry to the estuary from silting
up. In what Forwood thought an excess of professional zeal, this supposed Liverpool ally answered: "I should enter at Eastham and carry the
canal along the shore until I reached Runicorn, and then I would strike
inland."[55] The point having been conceded that a safe solution was possible, Williams revised his plan accordingly, thus preserving, or so he argued, existing tidal conditions.[56] Despite this concession, the battle between the experts or, more accurately, between the interest groups and
their experts, continued; and it took two more bills, the expenditure of
even vaster sums, and another year before Parliament gave, in 1885, its
authorization to Williams's revised plan.

In a way this was a considerable success for Victorian environmental
reform. Neither Parliament nor the national press was swayed by the ar-

gument that since all progress involves risk, the benefit of doubt should go to the promoter. A majority rejected the contention that a cautious response would be like saying, as one witness before a committee put it, "good-bye once and for all to the material progress of Great Britain."[57] Politicians retained a healthy skepticism about engineering expertise and evocations of professional authority. Lords and Commoners seemed to have had no inhibitions about confidently offering personal experience as evidence. Lewis MacIver, M.P., felt perfectly free to instruct the House of Commons on the strength of long experience as a participant in sailing regattas about the condition of the harbor bar and the contortions of the estuary. Since his constituency included a section of the Port of Liverpool, he could hardly have been regarded as unbiased; yet many of his colleagues must have agreed with his warning about a bill that would allow contractors to dump several million tons of stone into the Mersey when "no person in the world, whether he be an engineer or anybody else, knows what the effect would be."[58] In a special edition at the time of the canal's opening in 1894, one of the leading professional journals, *Engineering*, admitted that the judgment of the politicians had been the correct one and that the threat to the estuary had been real.[59]

In view of the fact that the construction of the canal depended on the participation of steam technology for its successful completion (even a steam cement mixer was experimented with)[60] and that this technology was in the process of extending in a radical way the capacity to change the character of river channels and estuaries, the often-lamented late Victorian and Edwardian wariness about engineering innovations had something to be said for it. A century after the Manchester Ship Canal project got underway, a Dutch expert on estuaries cautioned about the potential harm in constantly tampering with environments where the "see-saw" effect of experiments and the disrupting power of our modern earthmoving machines—so much more agile, mobile, and versatile than their counterparts in the steam era—are apt to upset delicate balances and do so in unpredictable ways.[61] Our present awareness of ecological complexities gives that warning additional force. Argument and pressure have caused companies and agencies to concede that care of the environment is a legitimate obligation. Yet the carrying out of great excavations remains far too serious a matter to be left to the excavators.

7

Holes

[B]y draining the useless inlets of the Cumberland, Welsh, and Scotch lakes, and turning them, with their rivers, into navigable reservoirs and canals, there would be no difficulty in working the whole of our mountain districts as a gigantic quarry of slate and granite, from which all the rest of the world might be supplied with roofing and building stone.

John Ruskin, "The Two Paths," 1859

No account of the completion of a major Victorian engineering project—a great canal dug, a railway trunk line opened—was complete without long statistical accounts of the quantities of muck lifted, rock blasted, and bricks imported. Comparisons with the great accomplishments of ancient Romans or, more often, ancient Egyptians, almost invariably followed. Those who read these celebratory descriptions or listened to triumphant opening-day speeches could expect to be congratulated on living at a time when new skills and machines had opened the possibility of rearranging the surface of the earth to make the way smooth for the wheels of progress. On these occasions, much would be said and written about the huge holes dug. The huge heaps left behind were seldom mentioned.

The contrast between the forces of human beings and the forces of nature is the central theme of a work we have already noticed, Robert Sherlock's *Man as a Geological Agent,* published in 1922. Its author agreed with Hutten and Lyell that nature's efforts might be described as uniformitarian and deliberate. Human endeavor, Sherlock pointed out, worked in exactly the opposite way, being intermittent, erratic, constantly changing in direction. While the action of wave, wind, rain, and frost wears away at the soft parts of the land, Sherlock wrote, miners and quarry-men attack the "bony framework" instead. "Where Nature would leave a hill or hard rock, there Man leaves a hole." [1]

As this distinguished geographer was intent on demonstrating in detail, few places on earth had, over the centuries, been more hacked away at and burrowed into than the British Isles, that small but resource-rich part of the global anatomy. Especially in Cornwall, the pockmarks left by Phoenician tin exploiters and Roman lead and iron miners could still be detected. Fresher were the remains of hillocks that had been turned over for their minerals in the eighteenth century. According to Sherlock's calculations, over the course of that century, some 1,700,500 tons of copper ore had been raised from underneath Cornwall and neighboring Devonshire.[2] And near St. Austell, the deep craters left by the still-flourishing china clay industry were ever deepening and production ever expanding. But concentrated though this disemboweling might be in Cornwall and Devon, as well as in Anglesey and Glamorgan, in Lancashire, Durham, Staffordshire, the West Riding, and Northumbria, scars could be found everywhere: little of the epidermis on the national body had been left entirely smooth and unblemished.[3]

Transport being expensive, builders, processors, and farmers looked to their immediate neighborhoods for supply. Almost every city building site had its own clay, stone, or limestone quarry. Tillers of acid soils, needing marl for fertilizer, or masons, needing limestone to make mortar, dug as close as possible to work sites. Road builders and menders pitted the land alongside with sand and gravel holes. Peat diggings, large and small, dotted many landscapes. Saucer-shaped depressions marked the sites of former bell chambers, small mines that were narrow at the top, wide at the bottom, and up to fifty feet deep. Farm laborers who usually worked these deposits might or might not trouble to fill up the holes with rubbish.

These often-unstable cavities occasionally swallowed sheep and cattle, particularly in the clay areas of Hertfordshire and Buckinghamshire.[4] Walkers in Cornwall needed to watch their step. According to a 1858 edition of *The West Britain* newspaper, a "whirlwind" from a bell pit got beneath the crinoline of a young lady, lifted her over its mouth, and dropped her nine fathoms to the bottom, not seriously injured but "much affrighted"[5]—a particularly jolting reminder that the land surface of Britain had, over the centuries, not only been thoroughly denuded, converted from one purpose to another, plowed, grazed upon, cut over, and replanted but also thoroughly drilled, gutted, and hollowed out.

Time set to work softening the blight remaining after these older excavations, carried out by hand labor, ceased. Surface wounds tend to heal
quickly in Britain's moist climate. Even where the scars still show, it is
seldom unambiguously clear where the hand of the digger left off and
where the powers of nature took over. This is particularly the case in areas of the Norfolk Broads, where the work commenced by medieval peat
cutters was then refashioned by the sea. When does the artificial become
the natural or the natural the artificial in such an environment?

Some eighteenth and nineteenth century holes, on the other hand,
remain conspicuous features of local regions and do disclose an unmis-
takable human paternity. One thinks, for example, of lunar landscapes
made by the St. Austell china clay diggings, the old slate workings in
Wales's Snowdonia, or the brick fields of Flintshire. These were places
so dramatically plundered that they became, and some remain, tourist
destinations. Centuries of quarrying in Cornwall, it has been claimed,
actually "enhanced" its landscape.[6] There, as in ravaged areas of North
Wales, visitors were attracted by the "sublime" effects created by some
Victorian quarrying operation, particularly where (as was often the case)
deep, terraced pits of exposed stone were surrounded by wooded hillsides, smiling fields, and lush pastures.

The sensuous curves of so much of the British topography evoke
metaphors having to do with the female form. Sudden and forceful intrusions into valleys, folds, and mounds become, by metaphorical logic,
acts of rape. Thus hole diggers "ravish," "defile," and "violate"; yet the
long-term effect of these acts of violence, carried out before the age of
the bulldozer, have proved to be, if not benign, at least not permanently
devastating. Although heaps are the consequence of holes, nineteenth
century diggers seem to have fared better in public esteem, over time,
than dumpers. Visitors can still admire the great chasms fashioned by
Welsh and Cornish slate workers, but even the most enthusiastic among
the industrial archaeologists tend to deplore the dead, rubbish-strewn
scree around the rims.

This is not to suggest that the Victorians themselves were untroubled
when they encountered the raw gashes around the edges of their cities
or the cratered surface of the Black Country or the scrofulous stretch of
brickfields west of London, extending from Southall to Slough, or the
gutted terrain of the lower Medway Valley.[7] Little that could be called
sublime, heroic, even tragic, was to be discovered in those dreary wastelands. The *Penny Magazine,* dedicated as it was to enlisting its working-
class readers in the cause of progress and civilization through industrial

"improvement," nevertheless reprinted in 1835 an extract from an article that first appeared in *Knight's Quarterly Magazine*. The author spoke of the "miserable tract of country commencing a few miles beyond Birmingham and continuing to Wolverhampton. . . . It was," he wrote, a "dismal situation waste and wild." He remembered that he and his party shuddered to "observe the surface of the desert around them scarred and broken, as if it had just reposed from the heavings of an earthquake." Particularly grim was Bilston, a town that sat on top of coal mines and was steadily subsiding. Foundations of houses and shops, wrote the correspondent, were shrinking, "leaving them in . . . a state of obliquity with the horizon." Another traveler to Bilston a decade or so later reported that subsidence had recently caused an inn near the town's center to fall in. He stated that "many houses in the place may still be seen nodding to each other, fearfully out of the perpendicular." In the surrounding area, in places where the earth had sunk enough to destroy the natural drainage, pools of stagnant, festering water, called *swags*, shaped what another contemporary described as "a vast rabbit warren." [8]

Undeniably repugnant though such reminders of human destructiveness could be, there was always the comforting thought that without a certain amount of dereliction there could be no civilization. Furthermore there was always the rationalization that, in places like Bilston, the inhabitants seemed willing to sacrifice amenity and even the security of their house foundations for the promise of employment. It could also be argued that many mining families managed to hold on to their small holdings and surrounding gardens and to reclaim patches of broken land for cultivating gooseberries and currants because they had alternative sources of income in the nearby mines and quarries.

In the valley of the river Weaver in north central Cheshire such exercises in positive thinking underwent a particularly severe trial. On one memorable day, 6 December 1880, in an outlying district near the town of Northwich at the Ashton and Sons Salt Works, a ninety-foot chimney, observed for several years to be gradually leaning, collapsed with a roar. Following that dramatic episode, two streams, Wadebrook and Wincham Brook, the latter twenty feet wide, were seen to plunge straight down into a crack that had opened in the earth. Soon after, the Weaver broke through its banks and began filling the emptying stream beds. Between 2:00 and 4:00 in the afternoon watchers were treated to the "grand sight" of water and mud rushing into holes in the ground at an accelerating pace and filling the hollowed-out salt mines. Then, as in Shakespearean tragedy, a deep rumbling groan issued from the depths fol-

Figure 7. The Great Subsidence (1880). Panels from the *Illustrated London News* show the spectacular results of pumping brine for the alkali industry from flooded salt mines underneath the Cheshire town of Northwich. (*Illustrated London News* 78, 1881)

lowed by a violent bubbling in the many small lakes and pools nearby. Some minutes later twenty- to thirty-foot high geysers of mud and gas, accompanied by the smell of rotten eggs, began to burst through fissures in the earth. A large lake, known locally as a "flash," quickly formed as the surface sank. At the same time the levels of the Weaver and of another already-existing flash dropped when their waters poured into the hollowed-out chambers below. The sinking continued for more than a month, although on a diminished scale. Of the many subsidences that had occurred in a 200-square-mile area around Northwich for centuries, this was the Great one.[9] (See Figure 7.)

A local newspaper noted that a Northwich evangelist standing at the verge of the "yawning chasm . . . improved the occasion" by giving an impromptu sermon. "Now, my friends," he intoned, "the ground you are standing on is the rottenest in the world and it may all go down with you in a moment while you stand listening to me." In that event, he warned, a fair proportion of his listeners would follow the path of Lucifer and keep falling until they reached Hell's floor. He invited them to reflect on the certainty that "when the end of the world does come, it will come as suddenly as this terrible accident, but instead of the water there will be fire."[10]

Physically, but probably not morally, this part of Cheshire had indeed become one of the rottenest regions in the kingdom. Mining the vast salt field underneath Northwich and neighboring Middlewich, Winsford, and Holford got under way twelve years after explorations for coal in 1670 disclosed a bed of rock salt some 200 feet from the surface. Manufacturing salt by boiling water taken from natural brine streams had been an important part of the local economy, probably from pre-Roman times. By the early eighteenth century, entrepreneurs had made the region into the nation's leading supplier. For the rest of the century small mining enterprises hollowed out underground caverns, held up by pillars of salt. Careless, "hit-and-run" mining methods as well as leakage from the surface and from underground streams gradually wore away or dissolved these supports, causing mine roofs to fall in. One collapse led to others because miners seldom bothered to seal off an exhausted shaft from those adjacent. As these cave-ins were happening, prospectors discovered a second bed 120 feet lower, and from the 1780s most of the rock salt extracted came from the lower level. Inevitably, however, the disintegration and flooding of the chambers above began to break down the cavern roofs of the Bottom Bed, and by the mid-nineteenth century all but a handful of rock salt mining operations had ceased.

But that did not put an end to the industry. Late in the eighteenth century, salt manufacturers had began to pump the brine from a natural underground reservoir above the Upper Bed. In time this method became standard practice. But reserves of natural brine being limited, salt manufacturers experimented with ways of tapping the layers of rock salt. By the 1850s they were using increasingly powerful steam pumps to reach into the flooded mine chambers to bring up what was called "bastard brine," produced in some cases by inducing freshwater and waiting for it to turn into brine.[11] As the volume being pumped increased and as the wells sunk deeper and deeper below the water table and below the floor of the river Weaver, increasing volumes of unsaturated water began seeping in and turning into solution with the rock salt, thus commencing a period of spectacular subsidences that continued for about eighty years.[12]

Affected most violently by the influx of freshwater were the salt deposits nearest, not the wells, but the places of entry, so that cave-ins often occurred at considerable distances from the pumps. Some local inhabitants assumed that what they were experiencing was the working of nature, a misapprehension the manufacturers were at no great pains to correct.[13] Nevertheless, disquiet had been growing for over a decade as landowners watched their fields sink and fill with water. Farmer Clough, for example, had decided in 1853 to fill in a large hole on his leasehold. Four years later the hole was deeper and bigger. He repeated the process with the same result. In 1867 he dumped in 200 cartloads of clay and some rubbish left over from highway repair work. By the early 1870s the crater in his field was four feet deep and seventeen feet wide. Rents dropped as such pits, often surrounded by widening fissures, became increasingly common features of the countryside.[14]

Residents of Northwich had even more cause to complain. Their buildings, like those in Bilston, began to bow deeply to one another.[15] One public house, the Wheat Sheaf, lasted only fifteen years before disappearing from sight. A company of volunteers came within a minute or two of disappearing with it when a large cavity opened up just after they left their drilling ground in the pub yard.[16] Whole streets of workers' cottages and a great many small shops were lost in the third quarter of the century, although, surprisingly, no lives. In spite of these warnings, town dwellers failed to protest, at least in an organized way. The explanation is obvious: what was causing properties to crack and collapse was what kept the town and increasing numbers of workers alive. Stopping the damage meant stopping the pumps.

Property owners and railway and canal interests did ask for compensation but, in any individual case, had great difficulty discovering the culprit. Many independent saltworks were pumping from the same brine reservoir, and the resulting subsidences appeared as far as five miles from any wellhead. Simply connecting cause and effect did not, therefore, fix responsibility in such a way that courts could easily provide relief. As a result, most townspeople of Northwich and surrounding communities had learned to accept the fact that infirm foundations were simply realities of life in that part of Cheshire and that anyone who knowingly chose such a place to reside should learn how to adapt. Inspector Dickson reported in 1873 that the new Northwich town hall was being constructed on a strong wooden frame so that when it began to lean, it could be brought back to plumb.[17] Given such a cast of mind, one could no more expect the people of Northwich to be champions of environmental protection than one could expect loggers in a Canadian milltown to be militant protesters against clear-cut forestry.

In looking for a way to make those who profited from brine pumping compensate those who suffered from its effects, Dickson came to the conclusion that blame could only be assigned collectively. A toll on pumped brine should be paid by the salt manufacturers to offset the damage they could not help but inflict. But Dickson also used this occasion to make the point that it was time the whole nation became engaged in an effort to husband mineral resources. He wanted the state to establish some kind of policy to cover all cases where the extraction of minerals from the earth must inevitably cause major damage. It was not good enough, he maintained, for the government merely to place limits on how much might be extracted in any given period: slowing the rate of damage did not affect the long-term results. Such a policy might only delay catastrophe. In the Cheshire salt fields, where steam pumps were extracting much of the brine from below sea level, there was a possibility that brine leakage and subsidence might eventually submerge "very large areas of the salt districts." It was time, Dickson thought, for the state not only to take some responsibility for environmental damage but also to respond to a growing apprehension that coal and other vital resources were not inexhaustible and that mineral shortages might reach crisis proportions in the foreseeable future. Central authorities, he declared, should alert the public and assume control over "the national waste of minerals in general."[18]

The Home Office was not inclined to heed Dickson's call for a national policy on management of mineral resources. Nevertheless, officialdom in general did come gradually to accept that subsidence in the Cheshire salt fields was more than a local matter, that vital economic interests were involved. Alkali manufacture, the backbone of the British chemical industry, depended on a secure and reasonably priced salt supply and the makers of textiles, glass, soap, and paper depended, in turn, on access to the products of the alkali makers. In 1874 John Brunner and Ludwig Mond set up a new plant to produce soda ash by the Solvay process and chose for their site an estate called Winnington, near North-

wich—prudently just outside the subsidence area.[19] The Winnington
works, which became part of I.C.I. in 1926, employed 2,000 workers at
the time of the Great Subsidence and doubled that number by the outbreak of the First World War.[20] Needless to say, members of Parliament
had no intention of placing heavy restraints on the irresponsible "bastard brine" pumpers simply in the interest of preserving the beauty and
stability of the Cheshire landscape. A bill to compensate property owners, introduced while new flashes were forming after the 1880 disaster,
was stalled by the appointment of a select committee and eventually
failed when the industry warned that cessation of pumping would simply allow brine to run into the sea.[21]

A surge in salt production in 1890–91 brought in its train another
wave of subsidences. In 1891 Parliament set up a compensation board
and empowered it to levy a rate of three pence on every 1,000 gallons of
brine pumped. However, framers of the bill made sure that the act only
applied to a small area around Northwich. The act also authorized the
board that administered this levy to monitor operations and recommend
precautions. But the pumping of brine from collapsed mines continued
and so did the subsidences.[22] What did eventually control the situation
was not government intervention, although that possibility may have
been among the incentives, but a new technique for brine pumping first
introduced by Brunner-Mond in the 1920s. Known as "controlled pumping," this method sent water at high pressure down boreholes into the
rock salt, which, as the freshwater went into solution, fashioned self-
contained chambers. Subsidences gradually decreased as more brine
pumpers came to adopt this technique.[23]

Significant here is the fact that initiative to control environmental degradation came from a large, highly capitalized company with a long-
term stake in the region and a technical staff that functioned as a regular component of the general production process. These advantages were
not shared by the partially integrated Salt Union, a loose amalgamation
formed in 1888, of many small companies. However, Brunner-Mond's
initiative could not be called environmentally sensitive, at least by the
present usages of that term. An attraction of the Winnington site was
that flashes and sunken fields seemed to be ideal dumping grounds for
industrial wastes. Although the Solvay process used far less coal than the
older Leblanc method, quantities of ashes and cinders still had to be disposed of. For years this refuse as well as waste products of salt boiling
had gone underground.

But much more troublesome was calcium carbonate, a useless by-product of alkali and soda manufacture—three quarters of a cubic yard of this effluent for every ton of salable product. This lime waste material is deliquescent, meaning that it becomes liquid upon absorbing moisture from the air. It is gray, slimy, and semiplastic. If it is spread out on the earth, it must be covered with several feet of earth; otherwise a deathlike pallor will settle over the landscape. And this was the product that filled sunken fields, sometimes diked to extend their capacities, along the river Weaver. The company sealed off several flashes and dumped chemical wastes into them. The effect, when touches of rubble from decayed saltworks were added, has been described as the very "picture of desolation," and a "nightmare landscape of devastation."[24] A decision, adopted in the 1950s, to pump this glutinous mess into the bore holes created by the controlled pumping method was a "solution" of sorts, but not one likely to reassure the ecologically minded.[25]

Sherlock used this relationship between man-made holes and subsidences and man-made waste disposal to demonstrate the "apparently erratic manner in which Man interferes with nature." He also wanted to emphasize that this kind of behavior made it "particularly difficult to estimate the net result of his activities."[26] He took as his prime example Ashton's Flash near Northwich, a product of the Great Subsidence. In 1896 soundings taken in a straight line showed the flash to have depths ranging from 80 to 110 feet; in 1906 the deepest measurement was 50 feet. In the intervening years, quantities of sandstone scraps left over from excavations to make docks at Liverpool and leavings from the construction of the Manchester Ship Canal had been transported up the Weaver in an attempt to give the constantly subsiding flash bottom firm underpinnings. On top of that went about one and a quarter million tons of waste, mainly dredgings from the river, along with ashes and clinkers from coal used in salt and alkali manufacture; but, as in the case of Farmer Clough's hole, so much weight caused more subsidence and, by 1906, maximum depth had fallen to 110 feet. In the meantime, considerable subsidence had occurred in those Lancaster coal fields that had supplied energy to Northwich industry. Sherlock's conclusion was: "Man's great engineering feats are so widespread that it would be a Herculean task to sum up their total effect on Nature."[27] And, as he admitted, when some Herculean geographer had completed that task, it would then be time for the biologist to begin.

Such a consciousness of the intricacy of the relationship between geological and biological processes and the fragility of what we now call the ecosystem might be thought of as typical of the twentieth century

approach to geomorphology and the place of humans in it until one re-
members that Sherlock's inspiration had come from Marsh's writings in
the 1860s. What then do we find in the story of nineteenth century subsidences that seems peculiar to the time? One obvious answer is that governments, at all levels, took a far less active part in regulating and were
not pushed to adopt a more active policy by highly organized pressure
groups and well-informed public opinion. It was not until the Control
of Pollution Act of 1947 that the law required waste disposal sites to be
licensed and not until the Deposit of Poisonous Wastes Act of 1972 that
the precautions resource extractors would need to take before being licensed were made specific.

Regulations governing underground and strip mining and quarrying procedures appear to contrast sharply with the Victorian policy of
laissez-faire. Modern governments, in principle at least, accept some responsibility for protecting the environment; nineteenth century governments only acted to control polluters or defacers in exceptional cases.
But the contrast is perhaps not really so sharp as that. The older hands-
off policy encouraged powerful interests to develop in ways that had
profoundly disturbing effects on the landscape; late twentieth century
ministries and bureaucracies do the same, only more directly and actively, subsidy to agricultural "improvements" being the most prominent
example.

A clearer contrast between then and now is that subsidence, a major
environmental issue in the nineteenth century, has now all but ceased to
be so.[28] The explanation is obvious: subsurface mining has lost its emi-
nence as a British enterprise. John Barr's passionate indictment of modern despoilers in his *Derelict Britain* (1969) does not even mention subsidence in his catalogue of horrors. Today, exploiters of mineral resources
tend not to hollow out or pump out the material beneath the earth's surface but are inclined instead to use powerful machines to dig into and
expose the coal or other mineral deposits. Thus it is the new technology
of resource exploitation that marks our time off most conspicuously from
the past.

Only indirectly was steam technology a crucial factor in the huge
nineteenth century expansion of the mining and quarrying industries. It
is true that the application of steam energy to industry and transportation caused an enormous outpouring of coal, iron ore, copper, stone,
clay, tin, lead, zinc, salt, sand, and slate. Rapid improvement in pumping and hauling technology, especially in the early part of the century, allowed mines and quarries to reach deep below the water tables, but by

no means all of these pumps and hoists were steam driven. Waterpower had a longer life than most people, until fairly recently, have been aware.[29] In general the effect of this deepening and enlarging process was to allow more and more workers to reach the face or wall and saw, hack, drill, and chisel—using traditional tools, skills, and muscle power. One innovation, Nobel's dynamite, began to be used in blasting from the 1870s onward; but techniques for digging, cutting, and lifting, although assisted occasionally by steam power, hardly improved until late in the century. As we have already noted, steam-powered earthmoving machinery was invented surprisingly early, but it was not a significant factor in either quarrying or strip mining until the early decades of the twentieth century.[30] We hear of accidents being caused by hand-operated, brakeless cranes in slate mines and quarries as late as 1895.[31]

Given enough time, of course, the constantly increasing application of animal and human labor could produce some prodigious dents in the land surface. Two quarry industries in particular, granite and slate, created some spectacular holes and in a variety of ways left conspicuous imprints not only on the countryside but both directly and indirectly on almost every cityscape as well.

A combination of a fictional and geographic Sherlock would be required to follow all of the essential clues leading to the great expansion of the first of these, the granite industry, from the late eighteenth century to the late nineteenth. A good place to start would be London and its remarkable nineteenth century physical expansion. Even before a dozen railway stations ringed the central area in the 1830s, 1840s, and 1850s, horse-drawn vehicles had been crowding the streets at an alarming rate: cabs, omnibuses, delivery carts, heavy freight wagons. Horsepower brought supplies to factories and food to wholesale markets, did most of the transshipping and, until electrified trams entered the streets late in the century, moved a large proportion of the nonpedestrian commuter population from suburbs to underground stations or to workplaces. The resulting traffic crisis, coinciding with the first in a series of cholera epidemics in the 1830s, alerted the influential part of the public to the urgent need for public health reform and street improvements, among them efficient street-cleaning techniques.

The need to ease the way for ironclad wheels and hoofs and to provide hard surfaces for scavengers led various parishes within the city to begin paving the most heavily used passageways with granite setts from the 1760s on. On secondary streets they laid down macadam surfaces. These were composed of broken granite pieces, rammed until their rough edges crumbled to form a more or less impermeable, but far from permanent, carriageway. As these passageways filled with traffic, there was a tendency to differentiate the parts of streets required for human and for animal feet and this created a demand for stones and paving materials suitable for curbs and footpaths.[32] By 1911, Aberdeenshire quarries were sending 30,000 tons of granite setts to London annually.[33]

Less utilitarian considerations also created new markets for granite. Churchyard burial inside the major urban areas ceased at midcentury and the era of the great Victorian cemeteries commenced. The desire of middle-class people to leave behind a permanent record of their existence made them or their families willing to pay for elaborate memorial tombstones and monuments. Granite's durability made it the stone of choice. At the same time, the urban rich sought to express their sense of civic pride in the great municipal halls and other public buildings that still give distinction to the old centers of provincial cities. City fathers also sought durability. Thus a longing for material reminders of both public and individual immortality as well as the wish to keep urban streets and groundwater supplies clean put skilled craftsmen to work blasting, chiseling, grinding, and polishing in Cornwall and Devon quarries and mills and especially in the great granite deposits on both sides of the river Dee in Scotland's Aberdeenshire.

Now, well inside the modern urban sprawl of Aberdeen lie the remains of the most famous of these, the Rubislaw Quarries. From above, the huge cavity looks like the crater left by a meteor strike. Standing on the edge of the sheer drop of this "muckle hole," one looks directly down at a pool of dark water that hides the old quarry bottom, 180 feet below.[34] Perhaps no other city has so conspicuous an exhibit of its origins—the "Granite City" constructed out of itself. According to a former stonemason, William Diack, quarrymen used to claim that "the half of Aberdeen has come oot o' that hole." Diack thought that far too modest an estimate.[35]

From the eighteenth century well into the nineteenth, some six million tons of granite had been lifted to the surface, much of it carried on two-man litters. As the pit deepened, hand cranes and then, in the 1850s, steam cranes replaced some of the muscle power; although Diack, who worked at the quarry in the 1920s and 1930s, remembered watching teams of horses carting "junks," "half ware," and "litters" up the old winding roadway.[36] Long before, muscle power had been assisted by an invention made in 1872 by John Fife, the owner of nearby Kemnay Quarry. This was a device called a "blondin," after a French tightrope walker who had crossed Niagara Falls on stilts.[37] It consisted of two wire ropes, the lower one having a skip attached that could be lowered to the quarry floor, loaded with stone, and raised by machinery to the surface.[38]

Quarry companies sent finer stone from the lower levels almost everywhere. Fashioned into blocks, this material faced buildings and built bridges, docks, and lighthouses. Charles Rennie and Thomas Telford used Rubislaw granite and the silver gray stone of Kemnay for their Thames bridges. Some of the world's finest stone craftsmanship can be seen in the beautifully fitted blocks of the Thames Embankment, also quarried at Kemnay. It is Aberdeenshire craftsmanship that finds an enduring memorial at London's Kensal Green and Highgate Cemeteries.

Although it got its start much earlier, in so many ways, the Aberdeen granite industry was a Victorian industry. Rubislaw, for example, prospered by the conversion of city centers from residential areas into offices, shops, theaters, monuments, and other civic amenities. Construction of massive viaducts, embankments, and tunnels to serve the new railway system also made heavy demands on suppliers. The quarry, like other extractive operations, depended on skilled craftsmen and on subcontracting rather than on standardization, piecework, and centralized management.

"With the Victorians, and how appropriately," wrote Jacquetta Hawkes, "granite came into its own." This rock, "the pillar of Victorianism"[39] had its heyday in the 1890s and then declined in popularity when asphalt surfacing became more common and when artificial building materials and the use of thin veneers lightened the fabric of steel and reinforced concrete structures. As the substantial old bourgeois class declined in influence, the taste for solid granite monuments and buildings declined as well.

Also like most heavy Victorian industries, granite quarrying was noisy, dirty, messy, and unsightly. Lying above the Rubislaw granite deposits were some thirty feet of "tirr," or hard boulder clay. This needed to be brought to the surface. Coal miners could often deposit waste materials in worked-out chambers, but granite workers needed to keep the way clear to the quarry floor where the best quality of stone was to be found. Quarry companies were then under no legal obligations to restore the landscape to something resembling its earlier state. So the great hole deepened and expanded until Rubislaw's final demise during the Great Depression. When the pumping stopped, the quarry filled halfway up with water. While still functioning, Rubislaw was one of Aberdeen's main tourist attractions; once the quarry ceased to be active, the city, perhaps embarrassed at having in its midst so conspicuous a reminder of declining enterprise, ringed it with a thick border of trees and later a high wire fence, effectively sealing it off from the surrounding houses, commercial enterprises, visitors, and passing traffic.

That the gaping cavity left behind by the quarrymen of Rubislaw could be so easily isolated from its modern environment by some relatively simple screening points to one feature of granite quarrying that makes it different from Victorian coal, slate, mineral ore, and clay extraction industries. It tended not to ravage an entire area or to poison the environment so severely that the technology then available was unable to hide the dereliction, prepare the site for some new use, or find ways to market the rubble left behind. Granite scraps could be ground in mills at the quarry lip and used to make mortar and road beds and surfaces.[40] In the late Victorian period, managers responded to the demand for suburban gravel walks and garden paths by installing special grinding machinery. They also turned waste into profit when they discovered that fine granite powder could be mixed with cement and formed under great pressure into those hard, dull gray blocks still used extensively on city pavements. Dust from this grinding and pulverizing was a menace to the health of the humans who did the work, but it tended not to contaminate the soil. On the contrary, feldspar and mica, two of the components of granite, break down into carbonates, which are plant nutrients.

Waste taken from quarries and mines could seldom be profitably disposed of, but the holes left by abandoned workings proved highly useful. Detritus from cities could be dumped there. Ashes and cinders made up more than eighty percent of household refuse at the end of the Victorian period. Some of this material found its way into plaster and bricks, but most of it went into landfill or disappeared down a convenient hole. Although the quantity of rubbish per person much increased in the later twentieth century and contained far more durable and toxic material, the possibility of disposing of it underground, often in abandoned Victorian excavations, meant that Britons, who discarded 3.2 pound of solid waste per person every day in 1988—nearly the same quantity as the world's leaders, the Americans—spent less to dispose of it than any other Europeans.[41]

Holes left unfilled could often be used to provide recreational facilities, increasingly in demand from the middle of the nineteenth century, when more time could be spared for leisure pursuits and when civic reformers became interested in supplying the urban working class with facilities for "rational recreation." A favorite of do-gooders was swimming. Old quarry holes were ideal for this purpose, particularly ones much more modest in size and depth than Rubislaw—as the great majority of stone quarries were. Copper, lead, iron, and zinc digs often exposed minerals that reacted with air and water and released toxic chemicals, making them unsuitable for reservoirs or swimming holes. Coal and clay tips usually contained at least some iron pyrite. This oxidizes into sulfuric acid. Stone wastes, on the other hand, were relatively nontoxic; thus water accumulating in abandoned quarries was usually safe and clear.[42] Cavities left by quarrying this material could also be safely fashioned into small urban parks or playing fields. Sometimes they were converted into cemeteries. A particularly impressive one is St. James's churchyard, built between 1825 and 1829, next to Liverpool's Anglican cathedral.

Thus in leaving behind a permanent legacy of dereliction, Rubislaw tended to be an exception. Many rock, sand, and gravel holes, especially if they were close to urban areas and not too densely concentrated in one region, eventually added variety and amenity to the landscape.[43] The Victorians carried out no conversions on the scale of, for example, Thorpe Waterpark, just outside London, where a large area that had been pockmarked with gravel pits was turned into a large lake surrounded by 200 hectares of sporting grounds after the Second World War.[44] Nevertheless Victorians began the process of reclamation and did so on a scale that merits recognition.

No such credit can be given the Victorian exploiters of slate deposits located in some of the loveliest parts of North Wales. Several of the quarries there were so massive that they turned men and machinery into tiny dots. Viewers registered shock and gave signs of having experienced intimations of mortality. Poets of the sublime were moved to speak of "the gulf profound" and painters and engravers were moved (one thinks especially of John Martin) to convey on paper or canvas the human capacity to create Pandemonium here on earth. From the late eighteenth century on, no tour of the mountainous ranges of Caernarvon or Marioneth was complete without a visit to these vast, artificial cavities. Visitors were, as often as not, struck by the disconcerting contrast between the beauty of the countryside and the man-made scars it bore. At the same time, they were impressed by this evidence of human capacity to form caves almost as mammoth as those fashioned by nature. A German tourist in the 1840s remarked that the slopes of North Wales looked like they had "been bitten into."[45] A contributor to *Macmillan's Magazine* in 1864 spoke of how "no mountainside is so inaccessible that the slate prospector has not reached it." The "thunder of the quarrier's blast," he continued, echoes through "the most secluded glens and passes."[46] Visitors were awed by the sculptural effects slate workers had created and often dismayed by the litter they left behind.

The reason why the shattered detritus around slate quarries accumulated is that only five to ten percent of the material that was chiseled, blasted, chopped, and raised had any use.[47] The brittle rock breaks down slowly and, unlike granite, provides little nutrient for plants.[48] Waste could not be disposed of in the deepening holes so long as work was going on. Also, the waste dumps for most Welsh quarries were located in remote places, usually on steep inclines, that could not be conveniently or economically used for landfill. Here and there, as at Blaenau Ffestiniog, the slate was mined. But according to Sherlock, of the nearly 17 million tons of usable slate taken from the ground between 1874 and 1913, two-thirds came from open pits from which overburden had to be removed before any valuable rock could be taken out.[49]

In the most efficient quarries, quarrymen needed to excavate something like a hundred tons of useless rock for every three and a half tons of marketable product. To make sure a deposit was worth exploiting, prospectors first stripped away and dumped this rubble and decomposed slate. This made prospecting a risky venture and caused hillsides to be disfigured even when no fireplaces, roofing materials, or school blackboards and writing slates ever came out of them.[50] Before Richard Pennant could begin quarrying on a massive scale at Penrhyn or Thomas Assheton-Smith could do the same at nearby Dinorwic, workmen had first to cut out and haul away an "inchoate mass of rubbish, heaps, and holes" left behind by generations of "old people" who dug into hillsides and pried out what lay conveniently to hand.[51]

As in the granite industry, most prospectors and developers were small operators who leased or rented the mineral rights and contracted out the actual work, sometimes vein by vein or gallery by gallery. That meant that work might start and stop and proprietorship might change hands many times, depending on shifts in the market. Under those circumstances, it would be the rare entrepreneur who would even think to repair damage that so many different agents had inflicted. The government did take a belated interest in the welfare of quarrymen. In 1879 mining inspectors laid down a set of safety rules, and Parliament passed an act in 1894 establishing special quarry inspectors. Nevertheless, it will come as no surprise to learn that, during the discussion preceding this legislation, no one even suggested that the health and safety, as well as the beauty, of the countryside should also be a concern. It was only following the Second World War that strip mining and quarry ventures were required by law to carry out any form of reclamation after operations ceased.[52]

Where slate quarrying was rationalized, the landscape gained some spectacular chasms. But there was a downside: since even the most highly capitalized operation never discovered a way to convert waste into a useful product, the landscape also gained mountainous piles of gray detritus. On his way to visit the famous Blaenau mine in the 1870s, a tourist approached nearby Ffestiniog village. What first caught his eye were the huge piles of rubble, squatting like dark blots on a remarkably beautiful landscape. The monochromatic effect was, he discovered, sustained inside the town: parapets, curbstones, roofs, chimneys, mantlepieces, kitchen tabletops, the mud in the road—all were slatey blue.[53] By then that color was imposing itself almost everywhere, but it was especially noticeable in the terraced housing of industrial towns and villages. Builders had been roofing with slate for centuries. Canals and coastal carriers had made slate roofing available to the well-off, but it was not until the arrival of railways in North Wales during the third quarter of the century that this uniformity was imposed on so much of the nation.[54]

"The Industrial Revolution may have been founded on textiles and powered by steam," writes Merfyn Jones, but "it was roofed with slates skilfully wrenched from the Welsh Hills."[55] This is true in spirit but not in letter. The factories and mining towns of the industrial Midlands were commonly built of local materials until steam transport in the mid-Victorian period made slate cheap enough to roof mills and worker housing in inland areas. Blue, was the pigment Wales added to the national palette but not until the first industrial revolution had been consolidated.

Steam technology brought cheap slate roofing to the national and international markets but, as in the granite industry, played only a supportive role in bringing the product out of the ground. This was so even at the great mines and quarries of North Wales: Penrhyn, Ffestiniog, Dinorwic. Steam- and water-powered saws usually worked side by side on the finishing level. An American invention, the steam-driven Burleigh rock drill, was tried out in several Cambrian quarries in the 1870s.[56] Penrhyn acquired its first steam pump in 1807.[57] Occasionally, steam cranes or windlasses did some of the lifting. But experience showed how awkward it was to transmit steam-generated power over distances. When electric motors became available as early as the late 1870s, they were quickly taken up. This happened about the time that slate production, which had reached its peak in 1898, began to experience competition from artificial roofing products and a consequent decline in demand.[58] The great mine at Blaenau Ffestiniog practically skipped over the period of steam technology, advancing almost directly from muscle and water-powered devices to electrical ones shortly before the First World War.[59]

Until then, waterpower remained crucial, especially the water balance. This was an iron tank equipped with wheels, running up and down the quarry side on rails. Filled at the top with water, it descended and pulled slate and rubbish to the top. When it reached the bottom, workmen drained it and sent it back up.[60] This was a slow process and required quarries to construct extensive reservoirs, which meant that drought or frost could put a halt to operations. Even so, steam technology proved insufficiently flexible to allow for a thoroughgoing mechanization of the rock and ore extraction industries. The overwhelming spectacle presented by the great amphitheater at Penrhyn, until the mid–twentieth century the largest excavation in the world, was literally sculpted out of a mountainside by human hands, aided by horses and by machines nearly as old in their workings as civilization itself.

A lithograph of Penrhyn, made by W. Crane in the early 1840s, places the viewer on one of the lower shelves of this amphitheater.[61] In the foreground is a group of visitors, one a woman in shawl and bonnet. On their level, wagons, loaded with slate, are being pulled by a two-horse team down the gallery incline on metal rails.[62] Below and above, other teams are also moving their freight around and around the circling ledges (or benches) before cranes lower it to the quarry floor. Once there, it will be split or sawed into roof slates, gravestones, chimney pieces, tabletops, and counter tops, and sent, usually along horse- or locomotive-drawn tramlines, to railheads and ports. Puffs of smoke on opposite sides of the great semicircle mark the places where blasting powder is loosening slabs of black slate for the skilled rockmen, using hammers and wedges and crowbars, to process into blocks.

The impression Crane gives is of a great, terraced chasm, fashioned by antlike perseverance into a hugely dramatic artifact. This artifact we, like the well-dressed tourists seated before us, are meant to view with awe and, having viewed it, to consider how wondrous are the works of man. Continued reliance on hand and animal labor supplemented with steam pumps and lifting devices meant that great holes like this one could be viewed as dramatic incidents in an otherwise untroubled landscape. Whole regions left flailed and derelict inspired other, less exalted, emotions.

8

Heaps

Industry has ravished it; drunken storm troops have passed
this way; there are signs of atrocities everywhere; the earth
has been left gaping and bleeding; and what were once bright
fields have been rummaged and raped into these dreadful
patches of waste ground.

J. B. Priestley, "The Black Country,"
English Journey, 1934

On a summer tour of England's manufacturing district in 1835, Sir
George Head made his way north from Halifax on the Bradford Road
to Wibsey Low Moor. The moor, he found, had become a cauldron of industry. Arriving there, he said, was like entering a volcano's crater: a broken landscape heaped with cinders and calcined shale from the ironstone
mines. What impressed him was that each one of the "four ancient elements," earth, air, fire, and water, had, in this one locality, been subdued
and made subservient "by human power and intelligence." It was, he
wrote, "a noble sight to stand here and see the devastating elements in
such radiant glory, yet at the same time under perfect subjection." There
was so much energy in the scene, he tells us, so much drama: "Here, the
ore dug from the bowels of the earth; there, the steam-blast rushing
through the furnaces; together with various contrivances for the economy of water, and application of its power to the machinery—all these
sights and sounds are sufficient to raise, even in the apathetic mind, the
sentiment of veneration." [1]

The bowels of the earth laid open for viewers to admire, to be stirred
with feelings of admiration and profound respect? No sense of shock or
outrage? We recollect that his account appeared at a time when a num-

ber of poets, novelists, and social commentators were expressing with
great force the dismay they felt on encountering such images, sounds, and
smells of industrial blight. There is that unforgettable scene in Charles
Dickens's *The Old Curiosity Shop* when Little Nell and her grandfather
walk through a nightmare landscape "where nothing green could live but
on the surface of the stagnant pools, which here and there lay idly swel-
tering by the black roadside."[2]

One possibility is that Head was simply a champion of free enterprise
in its most unrestrained, early Victorian manifestation. He almost certainly subscribed to the rationalizations commonly offered by defenders
of mining and heavy industry and their methods: that the iron and coal
lying under the surface only became valuable when extracted from the
ground; that employment of the workers who did the extracting and
smelting depended on an economy that was growing as a result of their
labors; that an expanding population needed to consume more energy
and iron or risk decline; that it was responsible behavior, inside a free
market economy, to pursue self-interest and maximize profits; that market mechanisms, when allowed to run freely, not only encouraged innovation but also eventually rewarded the thrifty and punished the wasteful. Moreover, the rate of technological progress was bound to keep
accelerating. Consequently, human ingenuity could be counted on to find
new ways to reprocess waste and rehabilitate the land. What appeared
at the moment to be ugly, noxious heaps could, in time, turn out to be
valuable after all.

He might also have made the case that such views were widely shared
by the communities most directly exposed to those heaps. Given the gift
of a bit of hindsight, he could have offered supporting evidence. Victorian
entrepreneurs were seldom subjected to pressure from public opinion
unless, like the early alkali manufacturers, their pollution constituted a
hazard to the health of a region or unless their effluents threatened salmon fishing and other privileged pastimes.[3] Individuals did occasionally
come under organized attack. There was fierce resistance in the 1860s
and after when manor lords claimed the right to dig gravel or clay from
a common. But one must search hard to find instances where such pressure was applied against those who dumped mine, quarry, and furnace
waste in or near mining and manufacturing towns.

Were Head in need of further rationalizations, he might also have
pointed out that efforts to interfere with the right to litter received little
overt support from those who chose or were forced to live with blight.
So long as carts were tipping their loads, mining and quarrying families

could be assured that they were reprieved from the doom that inevitably awaited their communities. Many who grew up in mining and smelting towns no doubt associated the heaps and tips that surrounded them with home and its comforts. It was possible to regard tailing mounds as interesting and familiar features of the local landscape. If spontaneous combustion set the shale on fire at night, the effect could be dramatic, even beautiful.

One can imagine John Thornton, Elizabeth Gaskell's principled, intelligent, hard-headed Manchester mill owner making these points and Head nodding in agreement.[4] But then we come to another passage in the description of Wibsey Low Moor that suggests there might be something more to be discovered about Sir George's understanding of nature and his way of relating to it. After his panegyric about man's conquest of the elements, he added that it was "awful to reflect, that science will never, probably, wholly avert those catastrophes which, either by combustion or explosion, in the melancholy reverse of fortune, serve to remind man of his finitude of his wisdom, and occasionally obtrude the fortunes of the victim on the victor."

Sir George was an experienced soldier and world traveler. So was his younger brother, Sir Francis Bond ("Galloping") Head, at one time a mining engineer in South America and in 1835 Lieutenant Governor of Upper Canada. Both brothers gained reputations for their abilities to describe working environments at home and abroad in graphic detail. They were enthusiastically optimistic about the direction the march of progress was leading. Yet when George Head saw what had happened to that Lancashire moor, he was fascinated but also aware that nature had been victimized and that the result was catastrophic.

Head recognized that his generation was saddling posterity with frightful environmental problems. Apologist though he was, he felt the need to remind readers that one day, in this place, Prometheus would be compelled to return the fire he stole from the gods and leave behind a once-pastoral scene now transformed into a rubbish heap of calcined shale, a reminder that man had once governed the elements there but did so no longer. Before that happened, nature, the victim, would from time to time recover her strength sufficiently to strike back and teach her masters lessons in humility. What Head invites us to venerate is not just human ability to control the elements but also nature's patient endurance, her tenacity, her capacity for revenge, her final victory. In his eyes tortured nature was as much a sacred text as was nature in full health and vigor.

A more secular age finds this juncture of optimism and fatalism, this

way of understanding, difficult to grasp. We know that feelings and attitudes cannot be left out of the attempt to explain why toxic heaps were
allowed to accumulate and why so little was done to put these ugly and
dangerous leavings to some use. But we usually find it difficult to con-
nect these emotions and rationalizations directly to behavior. Therefore
we search for structural explanations to help guide and buttress our inquiry—in this case, into the reasons why a moralistic age failed to control its litterers and clean up the messes it left behind.

A look, for example, at the scale and organization of mining enterprises provides some valuable clues. We see how precariously most entrepreneurs carried on their businesses. Especially where the seams of ore,
limestone, or coal were close to the surface, any risk taker able to save or
borrow several thousand pounds, possibly much less, could lease or buy
the mineral rights of a property and then contract out the task of exposing the seam and setting miners to work. The contractor, or "butty,"
might supply some of the capital: tools, blasting powder, horses, and
wagons. He would hire and pay laborers (often at his own pub) and send
an overseer (called a "doggie") to supervise their work. His object was
to keep the cost of production below the agreed-upon price. Since there
could be no margin for miscalculation or adverse market fluctuation, the
butty might frequently find himself delivering coal, stone, or iron ore to
someone other than the original lessee, or the butty who made the contract might not be the butty making the delivery.[5] Under these circumstances, it would have been, if judged by conventional wisdom, unrea-
sonable to expect leaseholder or butty to be concerned about the looks of
the environment or interested in spending money experimenting with recycling waste, waste that some other entrepreneur might have left behind.

Although fly-by-night operations were common throughout the century in the extractive industries, as the century progressed they tended
to be overlaid with somewhat larger and more heavily capitalized enterprises. Presumably, these enterprises could afford to think ahead and
spend money on waste management and reclamation. Occasionally this
did happen. The most obvious example is the use found for basic slag,
the product of blast furnaces. Sometime in the 1880s, soil chemists discovered that this material contained ammonia and phosphorus and recognized that if ground up, it would make an excellent fertilizer, more effective than lime in sweetening the acid soils of rain-soaked Britain. As
we have noticed earlier, farmers discovered that treatment with slag encouraged dormant "leguminous herbage" to sprout and eventually to
choke out weeds, especially on pastures where stiff clays became water-

logged in winter and parched in summer. Industries appeared to supply a growing demand. In the 1890s several factories that ground slag and sold it to fertilizer retailers and glass and cement manufacturers opened in Middlesborough and Wednesbury.[6] The hill farms of Wales still depend on slag for fertilizing permanent pastures.[7]

Science and industry came together in this case. But it was an exception. Compared to much of the Continent, bridges between industry and scientific laboratories were few in number and poorly signposted. Unless stimulated by protest or threat of regulating legislation, businessmen's interest in recycling waste lagged behind developments in the relevant science and technology. It should also be kept in mind that few mid-Victorian firms had accounting systems sophisticated enough to alert managers to the total costs of waste.

Cost of transport was, on the other hand, well known. As ways were discovered in the latter part of the Victorian era to use mine and furnace wastes, proximity to water or rail transport became crucial. These factors determined whether utilization would pay. Since cinders and furnace slag were heavy and had low unit values, they could only be profitably shipped to places conveniently served by water or easily reached by railways. The same could be said for coal spoil heaps. As in the case of the Cheshire flashes, waste left over from coal mining, although likely to be highly acidic, could be used for relatively safe fill. It could also make firm railway beds. But demand for this material was much smaller than was demand for blast furnace slag. Location was the determinant. Particularly in the Welsh valleys, where mine shafts were dug into hillsides, tips would be grouped nearby. That meant rubble would often be piled up on remote and dangerously unstable sites and allowed to remain there after the mine closed.[8]

Where the lifeblood of communities was supplied by collieries, smelters, and stone, clay, and slate quarries, residents would be slow to complain. If reclamation projects were begun, they were usually undertaken by individual landlords and their agents or the occasional mine or quarry owner. Where outside pressure was a factor in these experiments; it would most likely have come from a sector or sectors of the community and not from the whole. That meant that reclamation usually had to wait until the mines, quarries, and blast furnaces shut down and ceased to add fresh waste to the heaps. Only when these mounds had became relatively stable could they be cleared away or planted.

Until the middle years of the twentieth century, no laws required that reclamation be carried out; contractual agreements to do so were usually settled with cash payments. Thus it is not difficult to understand why mining and quarrying companies did so poor a job of cleaning up after themselves. There was usually little or no material reward for being environmentally responsible, and there were few deterrents to irresponsibility. So most large and small extractive and metal refining industries simply piled tips higher or shot slag into ravines or the sea. Peter Simmonds, editor of *The Journal of Applied Science,* estimated that in 1876 it cost about a half million pounds a year to dispose of six million tons of the "metallic encumbrances of the smelting works." [9]

It follows that the circumstances of the mining and metal smelting and processing industries are as crucial to understanding the history of reclamation and pollution control as are the development of agencies for promoting these causes. During the final quarter of the nineteenth century, concern about the effect of these industries on the environment coincided with concern about their long-term future. Testimony before investigatory committees suggests that few employers acted on the premise that cleaner and safer surroundings would increase the productivity of labor and make their industries more competitive. Structural factors stood in the way of such reasoning. As we have seen, the subcontracting system removed many owners from management. A resident of South Staffordshire remarked in 1843 that more work could be extracted from the men by butties than the owners "would like to extract themselves." [10]

Up to this point, we have focused the discussion mainly on people to whom the land was leased, those who dug mines and built smelters, or on workers and middlemen who did the digging, shoveling, and hauling. Those who owned the land leased it to mining companies, advanced capital for mining enterprises, and occasionally took over some of the active direction of operations also shared in the responsibility for turning the fields, pastures, and wooded areas of the South Staffordshire, Glamorgan, County Durham, Lancashire, Nottinghamshire, and Northumbrian countryside into industrial dust heaps. For the most part, landlords as a class were despoilers, not reclaimers. If there were valuable deposits of sand, stone, gravel, slate, salt, or ore underneath their properties or if enclosure settlements had given them some pretext for claiming control of mineral rights over former wastelands and commons, men of property were usually more than ready to convert parts of the landscape they owned into money. No doubt, many of them took pride in the mounds, cavities, and chimneys that pocked or littered portions of their estates. They might look on these indications of industry as visual testimony to the progressive, improving spirit of their class.

It may seem inconsistent that a great landlord should wish an estate to express his or her good taste, importance, wealth, and paternalistic concern for local values and at the same time wish to associate that estate with the spirit of industrial development. Such an apparent confusion of symbolic landscape meanings did often trouble Victorian squires and aristocrats but seldom to the extent that they refused to grant lucrative leases to resource exploiters.

It did not escape the notice of contemporaries that professed paternalists so often showed a crass disregard for the traditional values of rural society. Reflection on Adam Smith's dictum, "Wherever there is great property, there is great inequality," could dampen appreciation of the refined proportions and textures of an elegantly contrived vista. Not long ago a contributor to a gathering of scholars spoke of the "evil selfishness of generations of landowning gentry . . . those who ruined Nottinghamshire and County Durham (not to mention enslaving their inhabitants)." [11] It is well to bear this judgment in mind when admiring the view from the porch of a great country house as it sweeps from the shrubbery to the park to the farmers' fields and the village, half hidden, by bosky groves. The view back from the cottage doorstep to the forbidden park and plantation may not always have conveyed the same gentle message.

But it can be productive to think about these matters in less categorical terms. Individual landlords could be at the same time ruthless exploiters and imaginative reclaimers of the lands they controlled. Until the beginning of the twentieth century, it was almost invariably a landowner who began a reclamation project. The earl of Dudley, for example, was the most vigorous and by far the largest resource exploiter in South Staffordshire. His entrepreneurship did much to produce one of the century's worst areas of dereliction.[12] Yet it was that same earl of Dudley who, about the time of Waterloo, carried out experiments on the site of one of his limestone quarries to find out which grasses and trees might best heal surface wounds.[13] Shortly before 1914 a visitor remarked that Dudley's plantation, then a century old, could be mistaken for a "virgin" forest. Apparently the visitor did find incongruous in so peaceful a setting the "crash of hammers and shriek of railway whistles." [14]

A more systematic experiment with techniques for returning despoiled land to productive use occurred on the duke of Buccleuch's Boughton estate in Northamptonshire in the early years of this century. In much of the East Midlands and especially in the area around Kettering, ironstone lay only a few feet below the surface. By the 1850s contractors were strip-mining large patches along the route of the London and North West Railway. For the most part, workmen used picks, hammers, shovels, and wide-tined forks; but by the end of the century the steam-powered "face shovel" was removing the overburden. This machine traveled along the working face and dumped the spoil in parallel ridges, leaving behind it debris mounds, resembling giant washboards. At Boughton, however, the ore was so close to the surface that most of the excavating could be done by hand and horse labor and the waste shoveled into carts and dumped. This meant that the ridges in this "hill-and-dale" configuration would contain a mixture of top soil, heavy clay from farther down, and rubble from the lower ironstone seam.[15] Thus when the lease was up and the duke again took possession in 1909, the land offered considerably better opportunities for reclamation than would have been the case had machines done most of the stripping.

Other landowners of the region had attempted to plant trees on similar sites, with mixed success. What was unusual about the duke's project was his determination to make the Boughton plantation into a laboratory where experts could experiment with suiting tree species to the different chemical properties of the rubble mixtures and with finding the most efficient and cost-effective fertilizers. After lowering some of the hills and partially filling some of the dales, workmen fenced the site to keep out rabbits. After that they put in the shoots, having made sure that plenty of soil from the bedding flats remained on the roots. Results exceeded expectations. Alder did well on heavy boulder clay; sycamore, ash, beech, and European larch flourished on the limestone and ironstone rubble.[16]

As the years went by, those involved in the project were gratified to note that most tree varieties grew better on this reclaimed land than they had done in the period before the site was disturbed. Hand strip-mining had left enough nutrient in the soil for the shoots to take hold and had broken up the layer of clay that had formerly caused mature trees to be shallow-rooted. Thus at Boughton exploiters had thoroughly ravaged an ecosystem, and a landowner had created a new one of considerable beauty and integrity. René Dubos once pointed out that disturbed biotic communities sometimes "undergo adaptive changes of a creative nature that transcend the mere correction of the damage"[17]: the Boughton ironstone fields, it would seem, were cases in point.

Both the duke of Buccleuch and Lord Dudley were model restorers, but few great landlords followed their lead. Most nineteenth century reclamations were undertaken by individual landlords whose object was beautification rather than utility and carried out in a hit-or-miss fashion and with little attention to cost. A General Carolyn, for example, was determined to build an estate on what had been the site of Crinnis copper mine at Tregrehan, near St. Austell Bay, on the south coast of Cornwall. Fumes and leaching from piles of copper ore waste had created a barren surface. Next to the old shafts were the ruins of smelter buildings and chimneys. Since copper slag is, along with zinc, especially toxic to vegetation, there seemed to be no point in treating it with fertilizer. So Carolyn leveled the ground, had the slag carted away, and then imported uncontaminated soil. Only then could he plant trees and establish a garden, one of particular beauty and eventually a showplace of the region.[18] Owners of derelict sites who needed to keep careful watch on profit-and-loss columns might admire such efforts, but they would hardly be inclined to emulate them.

A similar desire to cover up unsightly heaps caused Lady Frances Osborne to plant on colliery slag near her Northumberland home. In 1887 at a nearby mine, the agent for the owner, the Greenwich Hospital in Chelsea, turned a particularly dismal mound into a tree-clad hill. About the same time, another local experimenter managed to get Scotch pine established on shingly refuse. In Cumberland, experimenters working on the leavings of a colliery abandoned in 1897 were initially discouraged by the high proportion of toxic pyrite in the caked surface but discovered that if they started the process of disintegration with rape and grass and then planted larch, Scotch pine, and birch in holes filled with fertile soil, they could overcome even this inhospitable environment.[19]

But these labors seem to have been carried on in a near vacuum. Isolated reclamation projects failed to generate institutions capable of sustaining this kind of research and publicizing the results. Therefore there was no repository of information readily available to landowners, smelting companies, municipal authorities, or mine and quarry developers.

However, by the 1890s there were signs, that some collieries and corporate landholders were becoming interested in finding ways to make reclamation pay. A few of them turned for advice to those professional foresters and soil scientists who had begun to gain footholds at several universities in the 1880s. William Schlich and William Rogers Fisher of the Forestry School at Oxford were closely involved as consultants in the Boughton experiments and received regular reports from the estate agent on how the seedlings were faring.[20] Several books and a few articles also described experiments and made specific recommendations.[21] Their authors assured prospective reclaimers that they could be confident of success when planting on coal wastes, especially if some of the sulfur had first been burned out, providing they finely tuned the needs of each plant variety to the properties of the site.

According to these specialists, experimenters must proceed empirically when looking for the best fit between host material and plant species, since every tip would have a slightly different chemistry, depending on age, the composition of the material, and the degree of compactness. Where a coal shale heap had a high content of pyrites and was loosely packed and receptive to water infiltration, harmful acidic residues could be expected. Disturbing that tip might speed up oxidation. Those about to begin a reclamation project were advised to neutralize this acidic condition with applications of lime and the planting of black and white alder. Experts pointed out that these remarkably undemanding trees gradually built up a layer of humus and thus prepared the ground for other, less hardy, species. In addition, their matted root formation was effective in keeping the subsurface moist.[22] If a tip had a relatively low degree of acidity, particularly on heaps that had been burned, reasonably good results could be expected from Scotch pine, birch, willow, and poplar. Such guidelines as these were doubtless useful to those already determined to experiment. What was lacking, however, were organizations formed to bring the message of reclamation to the unconverted.

Except for the Lower Swansea Valley in South Wales, nowhere was dereliction more concentrated than in the Black Country of South Staffordshire and North Worcester. Inside this fifty-three-square-mile region were more than 30,000 acres of pit banks—slag, shale, and coal waste— resting, for the most part, on heavy boulder clay.[23] Travelers through the Black Country were invariably inspired to vivid rhetoric by the sight of smoldering slag heaps. There, industry had created not just an "artificially made desert,"[24] but a wasteland "where everything is black with the blackness of coal dust," and "where birds, sun, and civilisation are alike absent, and where barbarism unmitigated maintains its improvident pomp."[25]

Quarrying and subsidence had spotted the surface with thousands of slimy green "swags"—sunken pools. To James Nasmyth, the early Victorian machine tool maker, the whole area looked as if it had "been turned inside out, its entrails strewn about, nearly its entire surface covered with cinder heaps and mounds."[26] According to a Birmingham newspaper, a tallow chandler named Thomas Holland suddenly disappeared early one morning in December 1903, while walking down St. John Street in Northwood. He had been swallowed up by an old pit bank beneath the pavement.[27] This accident was unusual only in that it resulted in loss of life. According to Thomas Tancred, who prepared a detailed report on mining conditions in South Staffordshire in 1842, it was "a matter of everyday occurrence for houses to fall down" as the ground sunk beneath them. He cited the testimony of a lay rector in Wednesbury that "twenty or thirty houses in the centre of town were thrown down by the mining the other day."

The whole country, wrote Tancred, "might be compared to a vast rabbit warren." Mixed in indiscriminately with workers' cottages were blazing furnaces, fumes from coking mounds, and calcinating ironstone, forges, pit banks, engine chimneys and, in odd corners, patches of corn and grass, all "intermingled with heaps of the refuse of mines and slag from the blast furnaces." [28] By the time wrought iron manufacturing had reached its peak (about 1870), smoke from some 2,000 puddling furnaces had erased even these last traces of an agrarian past.

Elihu Burritt, a New Englander, spent several years in mid-Victorian Birmingham, acting as his country's consul. In 1868 he published his impressions of several tours through the region. The title of his book, *Walks in the Black Country and Its Green Borderland,* indicates the theme: the stimulating contrast between what Burritt considered to be the most charming and the most shocking features of the English landscape. At the center of the composition appeared "a section of Titanic industry, kept in murky perspiration." It was "black by day and red by night," a "*sierra negra,*" yet the whole burning panorama was "beautifully framed by a Green Borderland." [29] (See Figure 8.) He invited his readers to board a train with him and experience the sudden transition from nature "scourged with cat-o'-nine-tails of red-hot wire, and marred and scarred and fretted, and smoked to death" to nature "in the various dresses she has worn from her birth":

> ... in an English Autumn you have all the colours on an equal footing, and no one has an absorbing place or power in the landscape. .... You see a green in the middle of November which the grass or grain fields never show in spring. For nothing in May or June can equal the green of a field of Swede turnips, or the vivid hue of mangel-wurzel . . . when alternated with the bright stubble of recently harvested wheat and barley-fields, and fields of lake-coloured soil harrowed and smoothed to a garden's surface for the harvest of another year. ....

In America, noted Burritt, one did not encounter such sudden contrasts between kinds of landscape and between the costumes nature wore at each of her seasons. Root crops were not a feature of the American autumn countryside. The rural spaces of his homeland were seldom sharply

Figure 8.   Manchester from Kersall Moor (1857). This study in contrasts suggests two things: that most areas of pollution and industrial detritus were concentrated and closely ringed with greenery and that city dwellers were within
walking distance of the countryside. (*Illustrated London News* 31, 1857)

defined; whereas in England, he noted, hedges, "like gilded frames, enclose these various fields" to "give to the whole vista an aspect which no
other season or country can equal." [30] Burritt's perception that contrast
and variety gave the Midland countryside its particular character and
interest did not lead him to call for the preservation of those "ranges of
blue-black hills, looking like huge barrows, which have been windlassed
up from unknown depths." [31] He looked forward confidently, he said, to
the day when this ugly waste would find an agricultural use. But the idea
that so black a country might itself be made green again apparently
never crossed his mind.

That suggestion first appeared in the *Birmingham Daily Mail* during
the summer of 1884, in a leading article entitled "Beautifying the Black
Country." It began by admitting that "the idea of conferring beauty of
any kind on such a hopeless agglomeration of the unbeautiful will doubtless seem not a little laughable." But the writer thought that the time had
come to consider the possibility seriously: in recent years many mines
had ceased to pile up sterile ash mounds, and many foundry chimneys

had ceased to cloak the blue sky with a "reeking canopy of black and grey smoke." Readers were asked to consider that wherever individuals and groups had tried to plant shrubs and flowers on burned over heaps, they had discovered how ready nature was to "repay any care bestowed upon her." Let the skeptics take heart from those hopeful signs, the article concluded, and let the region's leaders rise to the challenge of restoring "one of the Malebolgic districts of the Inferno" to the delightful Eden it once had been.[32]

One reader, Frederick Hackwood, responded enthusiastically to this exhortation. He appealed to the local government of his hometown, Wednesbury, for help in converting twenty-two acres of ugly pit mound into "a smiling pleasure ground for the people."[33] A crowded public meeting at the town hall gave its endorsement in 1884, and Brunswick Park was the result.[34] It proved so popular that the district council of nearby Tipton decided to follow suit and other Black Country towns began to experiment with planting trees along streets.[35]

Encouraged by this response, Hackwood then tried to generate local support for legislation aimed at encouraging colliery owners and municipalities to cultivate wastelands in mining districts. In an article written in 1886 for the *Midland Advertiser*, he attacked the "gross carelessness of colliery managers and the callous indifference of coal-owners." The manager, he wrote, is bent on "ripping open the bowels of the earth in the readiest and cheapest manner possible." The owner is content to pocket whatever compensation he might receive for permitting exploiters to ravage the surface of his mining properties, only to spend it where "his fastidious taste had led him to take up his residence—in most instances in some paradise of a park, or amidst the luxuriance of nature's verdant beauties."[36]

Philip Stanhope, Liberal M.P. for Wednesbury, brought Hackwood's views to the attention of Charles Bradlaugh, best remembered for his successful struggle to sit in Parliament as a professed atheist and for his collaboration with Annie Besant in disseminating information about family planning. In 1886, soon after winning the battle to take his seat as member for Northampton, Bradlaugh brought in a private member's bill to make failure to cultivate usable land a misdemeanor, a move that succeeded in embarrassing and infuriating the landed classes. This was, of course, his main purpose, although he must have been aware that a group of Liberal land reformers, including Scottish M.P.s from places where anti–deer park sentiments were running high, could be counted on for support.

Having caused a satisfactory stir, Bradlaugh withdrew his bill. But the following year he tried again. The second proposal was to empower local councils to condemn cultivable wastelands and divide them into allotments for distribution to small farmers. On this occasion, Hackwood and Stanhope persuaded Bradlaugh to accept an amendment giving local authorities the right to condemn and acquire thousands of derelict acres in South Staffordshire and to permit authorities to raise rates and use that revenue to assist small landholders in leveling heaps, filling holes, and restoring the soil. The hope was that councillors would be attracted by an opportunity to use town sewage in so positive a way. Bradlaugh's argument was that property values would rise as soil fertility increased, and consequently, costs would eventually be offset by increased income from rates. He made the point that at modest or no expense and with far-ranging benefits, waste itself could be the means for reclaiming wastelands.[37]

Few were persuaded: Men of property were not attracted by talk about extending powers to condemn land, even sterile, derelict land. So this second try also failed, although ninety-seven members actually voted for it. Criticisms in the House and outside tended to concentrate on the absurdity of suggesting that ratepayers be asked, especially given the depressed condition of agriculture, to subsidize crackpot schemes for making profitless land marginally productive.[38] Nevertheless, these two bids for attention were symptoms of a perceptible quickening of interest in the possibility of restoring derelict areas.

This development had much to do with growing concern about the depletion of resources, especially in areas like the Black Country where foundries were beginning to import coal, ironstone, and limestone as early as the 1860s.[39] Also in the background was a sense of anxiety about the nation's economic future and a corresponding interest in improving efficiency and eliminating all kinds of unnecessary waste. The later 1880s was also the time when influential people in government, in universities, and, to a limited extent, in industry and agriculture became aware of the progress being made on the Continent with techniques for enlisting the aid of governments and the public in restoration projects.

The Danish *Heleselskab*, or Heath Society, provided a particularly interesting model. Founded in 1866, this organization came about through the efforts of an army engineer named Enrico Dalgas who had helped to prepare a fortified line across Schleswig shortly before the Prussian army swept through it in 1863. Dalgas came to the conclusion that what his nation required to compensate for its humiliation in war was a cause around which all factions could rally: a state-sponsored project to make Jutland's heath productive by cultivating it and planting it with trees. When the government failed to respond, he joined with a lawyer and amateur natural scientist, Georg Morville, and a wealthy landowner, Ferdinand Mourier-Petersen, to rally support and put pressure on officialdom.[40] The society recognized from the start that success depended on demonstrating that the Jutland plain was not hopelessly infertile. Members enlisted in its cause some of the leading figures in the earth sciences, literature, the fine arts, and the fields of educational and religious reform. So aided, the Heath Society and its cause of reclamation became a major focus of patriotic feeling and prospered to the extent that it could undertake a series of drainage, irrigation, and afforestation projects and encourage other local groups to do likewise.[41]

The success of the Heath Society came to the attention of a Tory M.P. for Birmingham, Herbert Stone, who had been trained in forestry and had become interested in experiments in growing pit props on coal spoil mounds carried on in the Forest of Dean and abroad. He discussed with geographers and scientists at the University of Birmingham the possibility of using similar methods to reclaim the most derelict parts of the Black Country. The most prominent of these experts was Sir Oliver Lodge, a physicist of international reputation. As a result, an organization called the Midland Reafforesting Association came into being in 1903.[42]

This group of some ninety academics and concerned citizens recognized that the first hurdle to be overcome was the widespread skepticism about the possibility of renewing so ravaged a landscape. Unlike the Danish movement, the English association had no soaring ambitions, no expectations for a nationwide reclamation of derelict land. What attracted them about the Heath Society was its method: its emphasis on education aimed at convincing people that reclamation was an act of patriotism, of social responsibility. They also approved of the Heath Society's decision to manage restoration projects directly as well as its decision to combine on each of these projects woodland, arable land, and pasture. They determined to adopt its tactics for avoiding excessive red tape, its strategy of incremental rather than large-scale planning, and its emphasis on community involvement.[43] But unlike the Heath Society, the Midland Association would start small. Rather than announce that they intended to make the industrial desert bloom, association members bought four and a half acres of spill banks at Travellers' Rest Mound in the heart of the Black Country and set to work, determined that the name should once again fit the place. If reclamation could succeed in so blasted and dehumanized a scene as this, presumably it could succeed anywhere.

Since the primary aim was to overcome the legend that nothing would ever grow again in the Black County, the society bought or supervised on contract the planting of small tracts of land that were covered with coal-measure shale rather than with potentially toxic heavy metal tailings. On shale some degree of success could virtually be assured. The trees grew reasonably well, and a few donations allowed for some modest expansion. By the outbreak of the First World War, the association owned or managed sixteen plots, sixty-three acres in total.

There seems to have been little attempt to conduct scientific experiments in soil science and botany. Using the familiar trial-and-error procedure, association agents discovered anew which species of grass or tree did best on the various kinds of wastes, depending on elevation and mound configuration. They carried out tests to see how acid the material was, how much potash and phosphorous should be added and in what form, which plants best withstood a smoky atmosphere, and which were the most effective at building up nitrogen and covering the ground with humus. They confirmed what others had noted about the virtues of black alder, poplar, willow, wych-elm, birch, ash, and sycamore and tried out ways of keeping rabbits and human trespassers away from the young trees and grasses by fencing and planting thorn-bearing bushes along borders.[44] In 1914 the association won a medal at an agricultural show for an exhibit of articles made from their pit bank plantations: handles for small tools, electric switches, and kitchen utensils.[45]

Considering that the first priority was to overcome pessimism and apathy, the association was probably right to be content with such small successes and to begin by planting on furnace slag and burned-out coal waste where they knew trees would grow. A greater challenge was finding ways to reclaim ground contaminated by waste materials from copper, lead, and zinc mines, materials that were far more toxic to vegetation than coal waste. Trees would survive on highly toxic ground only if quantities of fertilizer were added. Since it was unlikely that the sale of such things as tool handles would repay the cost of growing willow or alder on these sites, association members hoped that municipal authorities would recognize that improving the appearance of their towns would be sufficient recompense. If they felt themselves to be too poor to afford expenditure on beauty, they could, at least, contribute reconstituted town sewage.

Like many other reform-minded citizens, association members assumed that local governments would respond if shown that reclamation had direct local benefits. From the 1880s cities had been increasingly active in acquiring and managing gas and water supplies, urban transportation facilities, parks, and sporting grounds. Decades earlier, the larger cities had begun to develop water catchment areas to meet rapidly expanding needs. One of the points the association had been trying to make was that reforestation of derelict areas would greatly improve the capacity of watershed areas to absorb and retain water. The difficulty was that local authorities in the area were too hard-pressed to take interest in making investments in such long-term benefits. Except for a few words of encouragement and several joint projects in tree planting along city streets, they failed to get behind the idea of Black Country reclamation. Even those branches of local government with the most to gain, the municipal water authorities, proved to be indifferent.[46]

More encouraging was the response from some of the Black Country school boards. When a new school opened in 1909 on Doulton Road in Rowley Regis, a few miles from Dudley, the educational committee of the district council approved a suggestion made by the Midland Association that students be encouraged to plant whatever space was not needed for playing grounds. Mr. Teague, the headmaster, with the blessings of the association, decided to make the occasion of the planting part of an Arbor Day festival.

This idea of devoting a day to the celebration of the tree had originated with Julius Sterling Morton, head of the Board of Agriculture of Nebraska. Energetically promoted by Morton, the Nebraska legislature made the event an official holiday in 1885, and other American states soon followed. The idea also caught on in Sweden, in France, where children planted two million trees in 1910, and here and there in England.[47] As its contribution to the 1897 Diamond Jubilee celebrations, the village of Eynsford in Kent decided to have children plant a school ground hillside with an arrangement of maple, yew, sycamore, oak, negundo, birch, elm, weigela, ivy, sumac, and elder to make an acrostic for the text from *Proverbs,* "My son, be wise." This deeply Victorian rite attracted considerable attention, and Arbor Day became an Eynsford event, villagers digging holes, gaily dressed children planting the seedlings, the village band playing.[48]

At Rowley's Arbor Day, teachers, students, and members of the council planted 500 trees in the school's barren surroundings on mounds of fired shale mixed with slack. Attached to each seedling was a label with its planter's name. A "progressive" educator, Teague incorporated into

his curriculum what students observed in this and a nearby small plantation. Children were shown why it was best to grow alder on gray shale,
birch on the burned-out shale, and black Italian poplar on the lower
slopes of the mounds. As the young grove developed, it became the
school's laboratory for geology, botany, and chemistry lessons. Boys and
girls learned how to measure rainfall, wind direction and force, and
degrees of frost. In what seems like a modern ecology assignment, they
were taught how to observe changes in the environment and how these
changes affected the relationships between fungi, insect, bird, and small
animal populations. Somehow Teague even managed to work in hygiene
lessons. As a result of this experience, he proudly reported, there had been
a noticeable improvement in the manners of the children. They seem, he
said, in better health and less drawn to town amusements like the cine-
matograph. Furthermore, they had developed a civic sense through par-
ticipating actively in their own reclamation project.[49] Although he does
not say so directly, Teague's object was clearly to teach children who had
grown up in a blighted environment respect for nature and nature's healing powers.

At least one other teacher in the Black Country responded to the association's encouragement and initiated a similar program. Mr. Evans of
Wright's Lane Council School in the Staffordshire town of Old Hill had
his pupils plant and study a grove of 100 trees on the edges of the play-
ground. He, too, reported improvement, both physical and moral. He
found it impressive that there had been no act of vandalism even though
most of the children came from families of a "rough class." Drawing from
these examples of the association's successes, Augustine Henry, a professor of forestry at the Royal College of Science at Dublin, came to this
ambitious conclusion: "To get the scholars and the teachers into the open
air, and in touch with farming, gardening, and forestry, will be the great
step towards the hygiene of the Social Organism." [50] He did not go on
to speak about how such lessons might also improve the hygiene of the
earth itself. For him, good stewardship was valuable because it made
practitioners into good people and good citizens.

Measured by its effect on the Black Country landscape, however, the
association was a failure. Whatever impetus there was just before the
First World War dwindled in the aftermath and the economic troubles
that followed. Because of this discontinuity, many of the lessons learned
during the experiments of the earlier period had to be repeated—from
experimenting with varieties of grasses and their capacity to withstand
toxic materials to involving schoolchildren in planting mounds and hill-

sides. The economic troubles of the 1920s, the depression of the 1930s, another war, concentrated attention on attempts to increase employment by fashioning metal instead of making it. Black Country smelter workers became skilled at "bashing" metal. Since the end of the 1970s that new kind of industry, too, has declined, and another phase of dereliction has set in. This time, however, it is generally recognized that reclamation must be large-scale and government-supported and not carried on bit by bit by voluntary organizations more or less in isolation.[51]

An era of reclamation can be said to have begun when central and local governments begin cooperating with university-organized planners, engineers, and scientist in restoring and rehabilitating blighted regions and when scholarly journals, technical publications, books aimed at the general public, and the documentary media begin to pay attention. That happened in Britain two decades after the end of the Second World War. The tragedy of Aberfan in October 1965, so movingly reported by the television camera, touched and shocked the nation as few disasters have done before or since. Occurring at a time when fears about the possibility of nuclear catastrophe and the effects of air and chemical pollution were creating a culture of protest, this event acted as a catalyst. Specialized treatises on techniques for reclaiming spoiled or seriously disturbed land began to appear. An aroused public demanded regulatory legislation, and Parliament responded by requiring mining and quarrying companies to submit comprehensive reclamation plans when applying for permission to begin digging and blasting.

It was in this climate, so different from what the Midland Reafforesting Association had to work within, that the first of the large-scale renewal programs, the Lower Swansea Valley Project, began to submit its reports.[52] Eight hundred of the valley's 1,175 acres were completely derelict, half of this area covered ten to ninety feet deep by coal shale, furnace ash, and the mixed leavings from extracting copper, arsenic, zinc, silver, lead, cobalt, and iron.[53] Those who issued progress reports described in detail the initial sense of hopelessness that suffused the valley. Wreckage was everywhere: ruined works, vegetation "blasted" away, rills and deep gullies scooped out by erosion, acid soils, bare slag heaps, coal tips, rubbish dumps, seven thousand tons of clay and furnace waste, toxic seepage, atmospheric pollution. The place was an industrial Gehenna: "the most extensive contiguous area of industrial dereliction found anywhere in the United Kingdom."[54] It is doubtful that even those able to appreciate the "lunar beauty of industrial dereliction" could have responded positively to this cluttered wasteland.[55] As John Barr wrote in 1969, "nowhere in Derelict Britain is there a more dismaying example of man creating wealth while impoverishing his environment."[56]

One explanation is that wealth was created in the Lower Swansea Valley by smelting copper—an activity that left highly toxic residues on the surface of the land. When John Vivian arrived in 1810 to build the first of the large-scale copper smelting works at Hafod in the valley, nine smaller smelters already lined the river Twae. Other large companies followed. By the peak years in the late 1860s and early 1870s, over half of all copper ores imported into the United Kingdom and an even higher proportion of partly refined imported copper was coming into this small triangle of land.[57] Two hundred furnaces on some 1,200 acres of former floodplain filled the valley night and day with acid smoke. Charles Frederick Cliffe, who visited Swansea in 1846, said that what appeared to be "a dense thunder cloud" was visible "at a distance of 40 to 50 miles."[58] The sight and the smell, he wrote, formed "no bad representation of the infernal regions":

> Large groups of odd chimneys and rickety flues emit sulphureous arsenic smoke, or pure flame; a dense canopy overhangs the scene for several miles, rendered more horrible by a peculiar lurid glare. The day-light effect is not much more cheering. All vegetation is blasted in the valley and adjoining hills, and immense swellings in the joints of horses and cattle occasionally attest to the pernicious nature of the vapour.[59]

What seemed like hell to owners of those horses and cattle represented prosperity or at least jobs to residents of Swansea and the valley. Supposedly, the whole community rejoiced when the courts rejected an action brought against Vivian in 1833 by a group of farmers whose fields had become desert. According to a highly biased press report, the news of the court's decision "diffused the greatest joy throughout this town and neighbourhood, which has been manifested by the ringing of bells and firing of cannon throughout the day."[60]

Nevertheless, objection to toxic smoke continued. Increased use of copper ore containing concentrations of arsenic pyrites sent white clouds of stinging oxide over the valley. Complaints were sent to the Noxious Vapours Commission, then hearing testimony about pollution created by the alkali industry. Commissioners sympathized but, noting that no technology existed for neutralizing sulfurous fumes and arsenic gases, recommended that copper smelting be exempted from legal penalties.

Landlords, who had been suing and petitioning for thirty years, were less passive. They organized themselves and continued to agitate. Henry

Hussey Vivian, heir to the family business, tried to respond by raising the height of his chimneys, but only succeeded in poisoning a wider area.[61] At the suggestion of Sir Humphry Davy and Michael Faraday, he tried, unsuccessfully, to recover some of the valuable sulfur by passing smoke through a water filter. Eventually, Vivian did find a way to control the amount of air needed to bring about combustion in the copper and zinc ores and to make sulfuric acid out of some of the effluent, but this improvement had no significant effect on the quality of the atmosphere.[62] As for the natural habitat, the damage had already been done. All vegetation had long since disappeared, even the weeds from the churchyards. In the wet climate of the valley, sheet and gully erosion had left behind a surface of hard, sterile boulder clay.[63]

On this desolate scene, changes in the color of waste heaps recorded changes in the history of metal refining. Copper waste produced tips that were at first orange-colored and later, black. Superimposed on these heaps were layers of gray. Shades modulated as the smelting industry gradually shifted from copper processing to zinc refining and then to lead, arsenic, tin-plate, and steel manufacturing. A poisonous environment became more so. Relief came only in the aftermath of the First World War, when all but a few of these industries closed down. The air improved, but the Victorian and Edwardian legacy of barrenness and grime remained behind, seven to ten million tons of it. Dereliction in the Glamorgan Valley, because of the higher toxicity of its residues, seemed more durable than elsewhere, even in the Black Country.[64] Therefore pessimism about the chances of bringing this place back to some kind of life seemed well-founded. Robin Huws Jones, the inspiration behind the Lower Swansea Valley Project of the 1960s, knew that overcoming this sense of hopelessness should be his first priority.[65]

Thus it is surprising to find that as early as 1912 the Swansea City Council received a proposal for reclaiming the banks of the Twae. The originator was the borough surveyor, George Bell. His plan, bearing the sumptuous title *Floreat Swansea*, proposed to clear one part of the valley for an industrial park, expecting that secondary industry would then be encouraged to replace the nearly extinct nineteenth century dinosaurs.[66] Recognizing that prospective developers could not be attracted to such a forbidding site, Bell proposed that the borough undertake to fill the holes and cart away the heaps. He envisioned a "garden suburb" for the eastern side of the valley that would be integrated into metropolitan Swansea by means of new roads and a tramline. He proposed a comprehensive remaking of the whole region. In its statement of objectives, its analysis of the obstacles to be overcome, and its recommendations, this plan was nearly as imaginative as the one finally implemented in the 1960s and 1970s. But Bell's rationale was strictly utilitarian. In his view the purpose of reclamation should be new development in the form of housing, high-technology industry, and recreational facilities. He recognized that land so completely despoiled could never be returned to its preindustrial condition.[67]

Bell's plan was shelved; Robin Huws Jones's plan, similar in conception, succeeded. Two world wars were fought during the half-century interval and helped to bring about important changes in how governments understood their responsibilities toward society, the economy, and the natural environment. After 1945, technological advances led to public anxiety about the planet's future health. Prosperity stimulated interest in recreational resources. The science of ecology became more sophisticated. University specialists gained experience in conducting group research. As a result, the Lower Swansea Valley Project of the 1960s had available to it a new configuration of forces willing to promote large-scale reclamation and to support it once under way.

The local authorities who received Bell's plan in 1912 could not have relied on meticulous research information from an interdisciplinary team of university botanists, biologists, geologists, soil scientists, ecologists, and social scientists. They could not have anticipated timely donations from private foundations interested in promoting environmental causes. They could not have been confident of assistance in the form of money or advice from central government agencies or of support from local industries and businesses. They could not have expected to receive publicity from scientific and technical journals specifically devoted to the subject of reclamation or from national media that recognized that news about the state of the environment attracted viewers and readers. Therefore those who write about the history of reclamation are right to concentrate most of their attention on the 1960s and afterward—so long as they recognize that the subject has a longer history than many suppose.

It is tempting to read in that history confirmation of Sir George Head's optimism about the widening out of knowledge and the eventual redeployment of new technology to clear away the noxious heaps an older technology helped to produce. But prudence cautions against so Whiggish a view. As we have seen, discoveries made were interrupted by wars and had to be rediscovered. Public support at all levels, acknowledged to be crucial to success in the Lower Swansea Valley and elsewhere,[68] still ebbs and flows with the shifting tide of events, the economy, and the political climate. Then there is the condition of the land. Modern research shows that damage caused by toxic seepage from heavy metal tips, although not theoretically irreversible, is far greater and more long-lasting than Edwardian reclaimers seemed to have been aware.[69] Meanwhile, drums full of nuclear waste steadily accumulate.

That some Victorians and more Edwardians looked for ways to clear away their detritus does not mean that they had found a way of reconciling the development of heavy industry and the inevitable pollution it entails with the basic need for a livable environment. They were not even well started on that path. In that area they had created no balances, no harmonies. Largely isolated and small-scale reclamation efforts did little to balance the effects of dereliction. But at least these efforts demonstrate that by no means all Victorians or Edwardians were indifferent to the wounds they inflicted on the surface of their land, not all shared Head's reasonably good conscience about leaving so many of those wounds unhealed. Many people of the time saw what was before their eyes and described what they saw with passionate indignation and in vivid detail: the ugliness, clutter, banality, and dereliction that were left in the wake when, what Marsh termed "the motive power of elastic vapours" was firmly connected to the gears of change.

9

The City in the Country

By this raising, the lake [Thirlmere] will be greatly extended,
and will be more in harmony with the surrounding scenery
than the narrow riverlike mere which now exists.

John Frederic La Trobe Bateman, 1868

Indignation about the ravaging effects of smelters and chemical manu-
factures—the holes and heaps of St. Helens or the Black Country or the
Lower Swansea Valley—did not supply the impetus for an organized
preservationist movement. The moving force was the perception that the
city was intruding everywhere, sending out its tentacles to grasp even the
most precious of the remaining natural sanctuaries. This apprehension
stirred resistance and supplied it with an agenda. As a result, organized
preservationism became, from the decade of the 1860s onward, a political force promoters of development and their allies needed to reckon with.

Paradoxically, this sense that the countryside was in danger grew during the extended period when activities connected with growing cereals
and raising birds and livestock became increasingly the source of livelihood for rural people. F. M. L. Thompson has reminded us that industry,
including cottage industry, gradually departed from the country when
steam energy came to be applied to machinery, thus leaving the countryside more agrarian than it had been before or ever would be again.[1]

Throughout the nineteenth century, city and country managed to keep
their distance and distinctness. Thompson estimates (or conjectures) that
Victorians added about 300,000 acres to the 100,000 acres of urban
streets, housing, and other buildings existing in England and Wales at
the beginning of the reign.[2] Those who experienced that unprecedented

spread of city into country space were understandably concerned about the blurring of margins. George Cruikshank expressed that anxiety in a famous cartoon, drawn in 1829, called "London Going Out of Town." It depicts an army of chimney pots marching on defenseless hayricks, cows, sheep, and fields while the city, behind a screen of poison gas laid down by tall smokestacks, fires off salvos of bricks. However, as the country retreated before this onslaught, Thompson again reminds us, it gathered its forces and placated the advancing enemy by cultivating more intensively and extensively and shifting some of its production to animal husbandry, vegetable and fruit growing, and milk, cheese, and butter processing.

In addition, the power of this attack was not overwhelming. There is general agreement that the great urban invasion took place, not in the nineteenth century, when towns were comparatively tightly packed, but after 1918. Urban land space in Wales and England increased by nearly a million acres during the first half of the twentieth century, the rate of conversion from agricultural and wasteland to urban uses reaching a peak in the 1930s.[3] Fringe areas, not suburb, not country, but scabrous mixtures of gravel pits, vacant or "dead" land, noxious industries, and small dairies, poultry cooperatives, pig farms, and highway-oriented businesses did not surround cities to anything like the same depth they do today in Britain and, to a greater extent, in North America.[4] By contrast, Victorian cities and the rural countryside managed to abide together as separate entities even while the population was increasing fourfold and becoming overwhelmingly urban between 1800 and 1900. Into the early twentieth century, a clearly discernible line divided the built-up area of Manchester, the symbol of urban industrialism, from surrounding farmland.[5]

While the country was becoming more countrified, it was responding in every part to the city's gravitational pull. Railways made it profitable to enlarge slate quarries in North Wales and to roof the new suburbs. As cities grew larger and richer, Aberdeenshire stoneworkers cut more blocks and slabs to build city halls and bridges, pave city streets, and commemorate the dead in city cemeteries. Because urban building contractors required softwoods for new housing tracts, some landowners experimented with planting pines and firs on their estates.

In turn, demand from city meat markets preserved grazing lands in remote and peaceful landscapes. By the 1880s large companies were supplying dairy farmers within range of railway depots with strainers and cans, collecting and cooling the milk, and distributing it to distant urban markets and to cheese, butter, and biscuit establishments. Other farmers, strategically placed to send small fruit to city jam factories, began, as early as the 1850s in Cambridgeshire, to specialize in strawberries, raspberries, plums, and pears. The coming of the Great Northern Railway to Bedfordshire at midcentury caused landowners along the line to divide farms into small holdings for intensive growing of onions, new potatoes, and sprouts. To nourish these vegetables, the railway wagons that carried the produce to Covent Garden returned with horse manure from London's streets. A Captain Peel even built a branch line to make sure his tenants had a supply. Thus from the beginning of the railway era, the food chain between country and city grew ever longer.[6] Having greatly furthered specialization in the nation, urban markets, served by steam railways and then by steamships and refrigeration technology, eventually extended that process worldwide.[7] Indeed, it is difficult to imagine any aspect of the countryside that remained entirely impervious, isolated from, and unresponsive to, the city's attraction.

While cities were drawing material in, they were also reaching out, far into the countryside, to dump sewage and refuse and to tap resources. Of these resources, water was the most sought after. Surface and underground supplies were exploited from areas near the major cities. When London, for example, had polluted the Thames and the Lea, it began tapping the underground sources of those rivers in Hertfordshire, to the dismay of that county's town corporations and agriculturalists.[8] But it was the building of reservoirs or the conversion of lakes into reservoirs that demonstrated most conspicuously the effect of city growth on the surface of the countryside. A growing number of these reservoirs added to or detracted from, depending on one's point of view, the landscape features of some of the most "naturally" beautiful parts of Scotland, North and South Wales, Dartmoor, the Lake District, and the Pennines.

Beginning in the 1830s, cholera and typhoid outbreaks and confusion about the source and means of contamination caused city dwellers to grow anxious about the purity of local water supplies, and these anxieties were graphically confirmed by the reports in 1844–45 of the Royal Commission on the State of Large Towns and Populous Districts. Since existing techniques for water purification were not sufficiently far advanced, reformers felt they needed to look ever further afield. Furthermore, the thirst for water was increasing with population growth and a rising rate of domestic and industrial consumption—and doing so at the same time that pollution of subsurface reserves and the depletion of water levels by pumping were diminishing usable supplies. These factors came together to create a major, if not the major, challenge for urban re-

formers.[9] It was "now well understood," an engineer told the directors
of the New Glasgow Water Company in 1837, that "no community can
have a reliable water supply when it comes directly from a stream or
river."[10] Observed another midcentury engineer: "The same causes that
have rendered a larger supply necessary, have tended to render the water
thus obtained, unfit either for domestic use, or for many manufacturing
purposes."[11] If rivers and streams flowing through or near cities were
the natural avenues for disposal of sewage and industrial chemicals, then
how could these watercourses also be the sources of water supply?

In London the search for a way around this dilemma began in the
Middle Ages. Early engineers looked away from the Thames to streams
and springs in the surrounding countryside. The most impressive of these
engineering works was carried out by Sir Hugh Myddleton who built a
system of pipes and aqueducts to bring pure water from Hertfordshire
to Islington in 1613. Later in the same century residents of Manchester
queued in the Old Market for already inadequate supplies. In the 1670s
a local doctor commented on the poor quality of water trickling from
the conduit and warned that it was the cause of "glandular obstructions
and scrofulous swellings."[12] A response came from Sir Oswald Mosley,
whose estate lay on the river Medlock. He connected the river with the
town and distributed its water through pipes, a project carried out both
as a civic service and as a source of income.

In 1809, when Manchester's population was about 100,000, a private company took over this system and supplemented it, in 1825–26,
by building a reservoir at Gorton, four miles from what was then the
town's edge.[13] Nevertheless, demand during the next few decades kept
well ahead of efforts to increase supply. As more homes connected water closets to sewer pipes, more water was required to move the waste
along. Textile manufacturers became aware that acute shortages of clean
water imposed limits on industrial expansion, limits that private enterprise had shown itself incapable of overcoming.[14]

Remarkably early, in 1808, a public gathering passed a resolution
claiming that private water companies could not be expected to serve the
public interest and calling for public water management; but Parliament,
intent on privatization, refused to listen.[15] Then in 1847, nine years after the city's incorporation, the Manchester Corporation did get permission. It set about purchasing the water company and began acquiring most of the 10,000-acre Longdendale Valley drainage area (usually
called, at the time, a "gathering ground") on a stretch of the Etherow
River, from ten to twenty miles northeast of the Gorton Reservoir. The

site had much to recommend it: a fairly high annual rainfall, few plowed
fields to send topsoil mixed with manure into the river and its tribu-
taries, and, best of all, no mills and therefore no "greedy mill-owners." [16]
The duke of Norfolk, who owned the land on one side of the Etherow,
and Mr. Tollemarche, who owned the land on the other, were easily persuaded to cooperate.[17] In 1847 Parliament gave permission to borrow
money and assess rates, and the city corporation's engineer, John Frederic
La Trobe Bateman, began work soon after. By 1851 water from most of
the seven other impounding reservoirs along the Etherow began flowing
into Manchester, eventually doubling the city's supply.

Bateman, still a young man, was one of the most experienced international reservoir builders of his day. He was an important early figure
in the slow process by which hydraulic engineering changed from what
he called the "guess or 'rule of thumb'" period of the canal builders to
the somewhat more systematic, statistically based, approach of midcentury.[18] He commenced his researches into the feasibility of converting
the Longdendale Valley into a reservoir for Manchester by measuring
rainfall rates in the gathering ground, calculating how the feeder streams
could be directed and coordinated, and studying the absorbing qualities
of the vegetation and the soils. There is no indication that he cared about
the basin's environment for its own sake; his object was to manage the
supplies of the watershed so as to obtain the maximum possible quantity of water of the softest and purest quality and to send it by the force
of gravity to the homes and industries of Manchester.[19]

What did concern him was the possibility that his high reservoir dams
might not be able to stand up to nature at its most extreme, although in
his public statements he tried to be reassuring. He recognized that flash
flooding was a real danger. The gathering ground of the Longdendale
Valley rises from 500 to 1,900 feet and receives drainage from the west-
erly slopes at the southern end of the Pennines, so flooding was a common occurrence. To meet that danger, Bateman constructed ten holding
reservoirs and fitted the impounding reservoirs with outflow pipes. The
dams, however, were embankments made of earth and rubble and faced
with puddle—dampened clay, sand, and gravel trodden into a semi-
impermeable mixture by laborers wearing special boots. This technology was centuries old and was used to build the many low reservoir dams
(rarely more than five feet high) needed to keep the canals of the eighteenth and early nineteenth centuries filled during dry seasons. What was
special about these Victorian dams was their greater size and the stress
caused by the weight of the core, or puddle wall, at the center, extend-

ing well below the stream or river bottom into a stone-lined trench. Problems sometimes occurred when water seeped into the cracks between the trench lining and eroded the clay at the point of contact with the puddle wall. The much higher dams needed for the Longdendale project greatly increased the danger that the heavier core would settle unevenly, crack along the deep cutoff trench, and weaken the dam's underpinnings. Furthermore, gathered behind these strong yet potentially capricious barriers at Longdendale was "the largest aggregate capacity of any artificial sheets of water in the world," according to the *Manchester Guardian*.[20]

Only good luck prevented a disaster when these dams were first put to a test. In 1849 a flood washed away one embankment, and the stored-up water destroyed a downriver school, wrecked several bridges, and covered a number of fields, but, the timing being fortunate, drowned no one. Bateman repaired the damage and this time embedded discharge pipes in masses of concrete. Nevertheless, when unusually heavy rains fell steadily for six days on already saturated ground in early February 1852, there was a chance that the whole system might be destroyed. According to reports, crowds gathered all night in the rain to watch the effect of rapidly rising water on the reservoirs. Cottagers began removing their furniture. Just when Bateman became most apprehensive, the heavy rain eased, and, except for small landslides, the reservoirs remained intact.[21]

Much of the anxiety that night was the result of a catastrophe that had occurred four days earlier when the sixty-seven-foot-high earthwork dam of the Bilbury Reservoir gave way above the manufacturing village of Holmfirth in the West Riding of Yorkshire. In retrospect, disaster seemed inevitable. Starting in 1838, a consortium of mill owners built a series of reservoirs along two small rivers. The contractors they hired threw earth and rubble barriers across the top of a deep gorge through which water had formerly rushed in torrents down to Huddersfield. The dam at Bilbury Reservoir was the largest of these. Its construction was carried out as cheaply as possible. Builders poured loose rubble into the earthen embankment and mixed small stones into the puddle facing. A coroner's jury subsequently found that the project's backers had spent only half of what it would have cost to do the job properly and then had refused to carry out any repairs, arguing that money spent on maintenance could only come out of wages. Presumably, this threat succeeded, even though it was obvious that cracks were forming and the discharge pipes had silted up. Everyone predicted that "something would happen."

At 12:30 A.M. on February 5, the expected took place. The unusually heavy rains had filled the reservoir to the top for the first time and spill-over water had seeped into the cracks in the puddle wall and through the rubble interior.[22] Nevertheless, the valley people retired to bed, ignoring "with supine indifference," one report commented, the obvious signs that waters were rising rapidly and that the valves were choked. Most villag-ers had already fallen asleep when a wall of water hit Holmfirth, sweep-ing away whole streets of cottages and then carrying on for a further five miles until the valley broadened out and weakened its force. Approxi-mately 100 people drowned. Whole families died in their beds; boilers of steam engines were stranded in gardens; skulls and bones from grave-yards were strewn about.

It was a national event. Subscriptions from the major cities raised £60,000 to help the survivors, a testament to the rarity of natural disas-ters in mid-Victorian Britain. The jurymen who heard evidence of what had caused this one expressed regret that the directors of the commis-sion responsible for this criminal neglect could not, under the law, be found guilty of manslaughter.[23]

In spite of this evidence in the 1850s that high dams made of clay, earth, and gravel were, in areas where rainfall was heavy, apt to disinte-grate unless painstakingly built up and constantly maintained, they con-tinued to be so constructed in Britain long after the use of masonry and concrete had become common elsewhere.[24] Thomas Hawksley, one of the most prolific of the dam builders, consistently refused to use con-crete even for the cutoff trenches or for grouting in the stone footings, although Bateman began to apply portland cement occasionally after the 1870s to places that needed to be especially watertight.[25] In France engineers did not use earthwork dams if the height was more than forty feet.[26] Earthen reservoir dams in Victorian Britain frequently were more than double that height. Conservatism about adopting new materials and methods in a country that had so long an experience in construct-ing canal and water mill reservoirs may have been a factor, but it seems much more likely that tight budgets forced engineers to follow custom-ary procedures. Ratepayers in localities might be persuaded to support long-term investment in new water supplies, but there were limits to that revenue source, and, except for private enterprise, there were no other sources.

Municipalities, on the other hand, could make such investments at fa-vorable rates by offering local taxes as collateral. The more enlightened among the municipal governments were willing to realize profits, not from the utility itself, but from its indirect benefits to the economy and society as a whole. From the midcentury on, other cities followed Manchester's lead and took control over their water supplies, so that by the end of the century about eighty percent of the water companies were owned by the cities they supplied. This represented a major investment of public funds. However, there were constraints imposed by the necessity to raise large sums locally so that engineers like Bateman were restricted in their use of new construction technology.

Bateman's Longdendale project was fairly sophisticated, measured by the standards of the time; even so, Robert Rawlinson, distinguished geologist and expert on river pollution, criticized Bateman for having cut costs on some of his many other municipal supply systems to a dangerous extent.[27] Rawlinson did not, however, put all the blame on Bateman. Municipal authorities simply could not be persuaded, he said, to spend more on reservoir dams than contractors customarily spent on railway embankments, even though it was understood that the action of reservoir water on clay or mortar created far more complicated engineering problems.[28] Some cities, particularly those with comparatively small industrial units or where water supply was not as crucial as in textile towns, were reluctant to make such a heavy commitment. They usually compromised by giving support and services to private monopolies.

Sheffield was a case in point. Its city council waited until 1888 to purchase the Sheffield Water Company, even though the bursting of one of that company's reservoirs in 1864 caused the greatest single "natural" catastrophe of the century. The circumstances were not unlike those at Holmfirth. In 1853 Parliament gave permission for the Sheffield company to build a series of reservoirs along the steep hills and gorges of the Loxley Valley. One of them, the Bradfield Reservoir, contained by the Dale Dyke Dam, held more than 700,000,000 gallons. The dam was located 450 feet above Sheffield and at a distance of six and a half miles from the city's outer edge.[29] Considerably higher than the ill-fated Bilbury Dam, the embankment at Dale Dyke was also built of earth, rubble, and puddle. Unfortunately, at Dale Dyke, this material was simply dumped from carts onto the site.[30] "It is not a reservoir embankment," a Scottish engineer was later to remark, "it is a quarry tip."[31] One result of such carelessness was that the foundation settled, possibly causing the brittle cast-iron outlet pipes inside the embankment to fracture.[32] Villagers of Bradfield, downstream from the dam, spoke among themselves about how carelessly the work was being carried out, and the resident engineer named Gunson seems to have been aware of the risk but to have decided that the cost of strengthening would be prohibitively high.[33]

Thus when flood waters, accompanied by gale winds, filled the reservoir to the brim on the evening of March 11, workmen opened the pipes. They became alarmed when the buildup continued, especially when one worker discovered a fifty-foot crack in the dam wall. A messenger rode to Sheffield to summon the chief engineer. On hurrying to the dam, he noticed that the villagers of Damflask, the nearest community below the reservoir, were moving their cattle to higher ground. It was good that they did so, because shortly after the engineer reached the dam, it collapsed with a terrible roar, and the trapped water of the Loxley River charged toward the sleeping citizens of Sheffield, brushing away trees, villages, bridges, and factories in its path. The first victim was a newly born child, pulled from its mother's arms when the flood hit Lower Bradfield. By the time the torrent, on its rush through Sheffield, had spent itself, 270 people had perished. One body was carried to Doncaster, fifteen miles away.[34] The company admitted to having been negligent and raised city water rates twenty-five percent to pay the £373,000 compensation bill. Only after years of debate and delay did the city council decide to ask Parliament for permission to buy the company out, permission that was granted nearly twenty-four years after the disaster.[35]

This episode was the century's most dramatic demonstration of nature's supposed retaliatory powers. Editorialized the *Builder,* "It is particularly interesting to observe how nature punishes the *moral errors* on the part of great societies." [36] It was also a demonstration of the consequences of purse tightening by city officials, many of whom were holders of water company stock. But evidence of this kind did not slow the process of municipal reservoir construction or persuade many aldermen to experiment with safer construction technology. Cities continued to extend their reach farther and farther out in order to divert water from countryside to city and frequently from one watershed to another. Where rivers and streams were converted into lakes, this intervention could be regarded as an enhancement of the beauty and amenity of rural areas, but where the resource being tapped was an already existing lake and beauty spot, the reaction could be angry and vociferous. This the Manchester City Council discovered when it decided to listen to Bateman's advice and extend the city's water system ninety-six miles out to Lake Thirlmere in the heart of the Lake District.

Bateman's recommendations were contained in a report to Manchester authorities in 1868 in which he detailed increases in water consumption since 1855 and listed the advantages to be gained by adding Thirlmere to the existing system. He spoke of the extremely heavy rainfall in the area and showed how the level of the lake could be raised forty-five feet without damaging adjoining property, this part of the Lake District being sparsely inhabited and seldom visited by tourists. He added that in its natural state Thirlmere was of little use even to sightseers, but as a reservoir it would be accessible. An encircling carriage road would provide one of the loveliest drives imaginable.[37]

Most of the city councillors were convinced. After trying, and failing, to persuade Liverpool to go along with a scheme for jointly developing both Thirlmere and Haweswater, Manchester decided in 1876 to ask permission to go ahead with the acquisition of Thirlmere alone[38]—only to meet with strident opposition inside and outside Parliament. This opposition Bateman characterized as either self-interested or inspired by "the sentimental idea that it was sacrilege to invade the precincts of the lakes for any such utilitarian purpose as giving a supply of fresh water to famishing thousands of the manufacturing districts."[39] Seldom had the issue of values been more concisely stated. What has been called "the greatest battle of the picturesque front"[40] during the second half of the nineteenth century was between developers on the one hand and preservationists on the other. In a particularly graphic way, it pitted the need of urban industrialism for additional natural resources against the need of nature lovers to retain unspoiled the rare beauty of the lakes, the most poetic of landscapes, a symbol of the possibility that human beings and nature could abide together in productive harmony.

Speaking on behalf of the Manchester City Council in 1925, Michael Anderson recalled the public rejoicing in Albert Square when Thirlmere water first reached the city in 1895. However, he admitted that the public reaction to the project had not always been so enthusiastic. Despite the fact that time and use accustomed the public to the thought that it was proper for engineers to set about "improving on the work of the hills,"

> but when to that is added a proposal to drown a beautiful valley, putting a small hamlet, the Dun Bull Inn, and a church beneath the flood at the behest of the thirsty industries and scullery taps down on the distant plain, the sentiment that townspeople feel for the country-side is thoroughly awakened. Many of the people who can escape with their wounded nerves from the world of Watt and Arkwright look upon the lake district as a sort of half-way house to heaven, and they were naturally concerned as to the effect the scheme would have on the landscape.[41]

Anderson was, perhaps, being gently ironic when he mentioned the attraction of the lakes for wounded sensibilities, nevertheless his remark is a reminder of how important this particular Arcadia was in the history of Victorian preservationism. Since the eighteenth century, travelers, most of them from the higher reaches of society, had sought out the lakes in their search for the sublime. In the next century, middle class travelers, influenced by Wordsworth, Coleridge, and Ruskin, had tended to look, not so much for the vast, the intense, the terrifying, as for the beautiful, the picturesque, the harmonious. No place in England seemed closer to embodying all the values attributed by the imagination of the time to a landscape ideal—a landscape that seemed to many a "halfway house to heaven." Because the romantic poets had made the lakes sacred, proposals to exploit the aesthetic or physical resources of the region were, by definition, acts of sacrilege. Passionate and articulate reaction could be expected.

Wordsworth set the pattern of resistance when he spoke out early in the nineteenth century against vulgar villa builders and later against the railway promoters. He fired off two eloquent letters to the *Morning Post* in 1844 on hearing that a spur line might link Kendal with Lake Windermere and spoil forever the solitude of a wilderness "rich with liberty." It was on that occasion that he asked, in an accompanying sonnet, whether any treasured place was safe "from rash assault?" [42]

That question arose again forcefully when a royal commission made inquiries into proposals for transporting "surplus" water from the north to London as a substitute for using the polluted Thames. Although Bateman's proposal to build a series of reservoirs in a catchment area near Snowdon in North Wales received the commission's blessing in 1869 (but not, as it turned out, Parliament's), commissioners gave serious attention to its closest rival, a plan prepared by George Hemans and Richard Hassard to make a reservoir for the Manchester Water Commission out of Ullswater, one of the ornaments of the Lake District. Recognizing that so famous a beauty spot had to be treated with some respect, these two engineers suggested piping in water from Thirlmere and Haweswater, thus keeping Ullswater at a reasonably steady level. Supporters of this alternative pointed out the disadvantages of building reservoirs where tilled fields, pastures, villages, churches, and graveyards would need to be flooded. Far better, they argued, to enlarge and control natural lakes, especially since the strategy in this case would be to convert the other two lakes into balancing and distributing reservoirs. That way, they claimed, little that was romantic need be lost, since Haweswater and Thirlmere were seldom frequented and had no "particular beauty about them." [43]

Because Parliament decided not to act on the commission's recommendations, there was no need for highly organized protest; nevertheless, lovers of the Lake District had received warning that solitude would need vigilant protection. Thus when Bateman's plan to turn Thirlmere into another reservoir for Manchester became public in 1876, those with long memories knew what to expect and quickly organized themselves. Wordsworth had earlier asked the winds and torrents to protest against "a false utilitarian lure,"[44] and many of his admirers were prepared to join in.

The campaign to save Thirlmere was organized by Robert Somervell, whose family owned a shoe business in Kendal. Before leaving his Lakeland home to become a Cambridge undergraduate, he had been converted to Ruskinianism by reading *The Political Economy of Art*; so after taking his degree and becoming a schoolmaster at Harrow (where he taught English composition to Winston Churchill and instructed three Trevelyans), he became one of the original Companions of Ruskin's Guild of St. George.[45] Because Somervell's pamphlet *Water for Manchester from Thirlmere* contained an endorsement by Ruskin, the press assumed that it spoke the Master's voice and paid attention.[46] The result was that one of the first organized attempts to preserve natural beauty for its own sake became associated with Ruskin, who was at the time suffering from stress brought on by Whistler's action for libel. That and an attack of mental illness prevented him from taking a leading part. The youthful Somervell, who had taken the initiative and had worked out most of the tactics, got far less credit than he deserved.

His struggle to save Thirlmere grew out of an earlier struggle to protect it from mining interests. On hearing in 1875 that railway developers planned a line to exploit an iron ore deposit on the side of Helvellyn, Somervell said "[I] felt, like Elihu in the book of Job, that I must speak out or burst." He drew up a protest, appended a petition to Parliament, and circulated hotels and lodging houses in Windermere, Ambleside, and Grasmere. A copy reached Brantwood on Coniston Lake, where Ruskin had recently taken up residence. "Fancy our joy and pride," Somervell recalled, when the great man asked if he could append a supporting circular. As it turned out, the petition, signed by three to four thousand, including Carlyle and other literary notables, never reached Westminster, the railway proposal having been dropped; but the names and machinery were in place when the Manchester Corporation disclosed its latest designs on Thirlmere two years later.[47]

At a meeting in a Grasmere hotel, Somervell and a number of businessmen who catered to the tourist trade formed the Thirlmere Defence

Society and raised £1,000 on the spot. Somervell drew up another petition and sent it to those who had signed the previous one; more money
soon came pouring in. Octavia and Miranda Hill invited him to strategy
meetings at their house in London, where discussions took place about
what line to take before a select committee set up to hear testimony and
make recommendations. Somervell's petition had concentrated on the
"aesthetic and general public argument." Robert Hunter, who had conducted so many successful campaigns for the Commons Preservation
Society, thought this approach to the committee would be the most productive in the long as well as the short run. But he was overruled by businessmen pragmatists who supplied most of the finances.[48]

In the meantime, the debate between the developers and preservationists grew more and more passionate. Dr. James Fraser, Bishop of Manchester, became a target for preservationist ire when he told an audience
in 1877 that two million urbanites had a right to draw water, a prime
necessity for life, from any place where they could get lawful access. He
then went on to endorse claims made by Bateman and other promoters
that the exercise of this right need not impoverish the exploited area.
Man, acting as God's steward, could, he thought, improve on wild nature and in so doing expose an ever-widening segment of the population
to the loveliness of lake and mountain.[49]

The *Spectator* responded to this claim that natural scenery existed to
enhance the well-being of the city dweller by printing a caustic article
called "Manchester and the Meres." What does it matter, its author
asked, that doubling the size of Thirlmere will submerge the little church
of Wythburn, since the engineers promise to build a prettier one higher
up and carry the surrounding gravestones to a "fresher bit of ground"?
Must, then, the old winding road go? Never mind; the problem hardly
exists: a straight new carriage drive can be cut level around Helvellyn.
What about the enlargement of the lake? Clearly a positive step, considering that nature has erred in placing so disproportionately small a
body of water in such magnificent surroundings. Here was an aesthetic
infelicity human ingenuity could correct. True, the need for a strong and
high embankment might be an intrusive element in the charming scene,
but, "by scattering a few large boulders over its front, and planting a few
trees in the midst of them," the dam can be made to fit into its setting,
"if indeed it does not approach in grandeur to its proud neighbour the
Raven Crag."[50]

In letters to the press and repeatedly in *Fors Clavigera*, Ruskin was
equally sarcastic and far more blunt. The appropriate sentence to be

passed on that city of Balaam ("cowardly in war, predatory in peace") for its criminal act of invasion, he wrote, should not decree that the "Lake of Thirlmere be brought to the top of the town of Manchester, but that the town of Manchester, or at least the Corporation thereof, should be put at the bottom of the Lake of Thirlmere." Earlier, on hearing about Bateman's plan, he wrote: "But landscape, and living creature, and the soul of man,—you are like to lose them all, soon. I had many things to say to you in this *Fors*—of the little lake of Thirlmere, and stream of St John's vale, which Manchester, in its zeal for art, is about to drain from their mountain-fields into its water-closets."[51] He was no Roman Catholic, Ruskin wrote in *Fors Clavigera*, "Yet I would not willingly steal holy water out of a font, to sell;—and being no Roman Catholic, I hold the hills and vales of my native land to be true temples of God, and their waves and clouds holier than the dew of the baptistery, and the incense of the altar."[52]

Deep in the culture of the time was this belief that nature's sacred places must be preserved from desecration. Even Mr. Punch could be serious through his comic mask on such a subject. Thus this last stanza of a verse, written and illustrated by Linley Sanbourne on the occasion of Somervell's pamphlet about Thirlmere:

Though Commerce claim free course,
    and subtle Greed,
In mask of Progress, her convenience plead,
Should Wisdom not be chary
In casting Nature's dearest dowers away?
Leave Lakeland still to elf, and fawn, and fay,
For Art, Thought and Toil self's place of play,
And Sanctuary.[53]

Implicit here is the Wordsworthian view that nature needed no improvement and that arguments from utility rested on an arrogant assertion that the progress of civilization justified any abuse of nature. Against this assertion, the Ruskinians maintained nature's intrinsic value. Prominent among this group were Octavia Hill, Hardwick Rownsley, and Robert Hunter—the triumvirate who were to form the National Trust in 1895 and who, along with people like George John Shaw-Lefevre, James Bryce, and William Morris, were at the heart of Victorian and Edwardian preservationism and conservationism.

Less vituperative and adamant than Ruskin but hardly more conciliatory was the Bishop of Carlisle. In a much-discussed letter to the *Times* in October 1877, he asked if Manchester really believed that God had

created the site and elevation of Thirlmere as "a providential arrangement for the satisfaction of the wants" of one grimy city. In fact, he continued, the special virtue of the lake was that it had, over the years, so
little to do with humans. Somehow it had managed to keep itself free
"from villas and all that is villainous." Invoking the "shades of Wordsworth," the bishop stated that "the substitution of engineering contrivance and utilitarianism for Nature in her most primitive and untouched
beauty" was to be countenanced only under "some great pressure of necessity," a concession his critics were glad to exploit.[54]

On the leader page, the *Times* gave the Bishop of Carlisle's position
its endorsement, but, adopting its best magisterial tone, went on to regret that a major contest between Beauty and Utility seemed to be shaping up. "All beauty," pronounced the editorial writer, "is essentially incapable of demonstration."[55] As for the argument from utility, according
to the *Times,* that went against Manchester: when submitted to the fe-
licific calculus, the harm done to a national recreation ground and thus
to the profits of a growing recreation industry must weigh more heavily
than the pain imposed by compelling the Manchester City Corporation
to pay for more expensive water. Water supplies were, the *Times* conceded, growing scarcer and thus more valuable. But rarer still in an increasingly artificial world, its editorial writer observed, was "recreation
that is really refreshing." Therefore, applying the doctrine of "utility
rightly understood," it must follow that the water commission ought to
look elsewhere for a place to build its "tank."[56]

This and similar notices in the press, the bishop's letter, Ruskin's de-
nunciations, an article in the *Spectator* and another in the *Saturday Review,* the public questioning of the capacity of self-interested municipal
corporations to manage the nation's water supply, had their intended effect. They provoked John Graves, Chairman of the Waterworks Commission of Manchester, to send back a spirited counterbarrage. Who gave, he
asked, these priests, romantics, intellectuals, art critics, poets, and agita-
tors the right to sneer at villadom? (He admitted to being a villa owner.)
By what right do these "sentimentalists" disparage the claims of trade
on water resources: where but in industrial expansion will a growing
population find employment? It was Ruskin, he was sure, who was behind much of this ill-informed emotionalism; Ruskin was the man "who
delights in charging the windmills of political economy and common
sense" and longs to submerge Manchester at the bottom of Thirlmere.
As for the Bishop of Carlisle, "The Bishop of the Lakes," he invokes the
spirit of Wordsworth to impress Parliament with "ignorant clamour."

But do these dilettantes "know what they mean by ridiculing the wants of trade?" [57]

Sentimentalists, he continued, have a distorted view of nature, supposing, as they do, that its forces always are enlisted on the side of beauty. Ignorant of geology, they are blissfully unaware that heavy rainfall has, over centuries, eroded the banks of Thirlmere and piled up sediment on the swampy end of the lake. Nature creates beauty but also destroys it. Nature can be improved. The proposed dam can be made irregular and picturesque; by deepening the lake, engineering can restore it to the full health it enjoyed in its prime. Now only the single proprietor is allowed to take his boat out on the lake; the proposed new road will allow thousands to enjoy what privilege now denies. Furthermore, the reservoir will act as the best of all preservationists: no lead mine developers will ever be allowed to pile up tailings and thus send toxic fluids to seep into the source of Manchester's water supply. [58]

As might be expected, the Thirlmere defenders treated with more disdain than it merited Graves's assertion that nature destroys what she builds. By far the most interesting of these responses came from one of the century's finest practitioners of the art of writing letters to the editor, Octavia Hill. She had established her reputation as a reformer by purchasing (with Ruskin's money) slum property in the Marylebone district of London and, instead of razing the old buildings and starting over, rejuvenating them, thus preserving some neighborhood continuity. Consistent with this respect for artifacts that contain within them evidence of their own past was her comment that the slow process of sedimentation that had narrowed Thirlmere and built up the swampy area meant that nature's lake "contains its own history." The process of change in nature has its own aesthetic, she insisted, although not one that admirers of things new are apt to detect. To discerning eyes, things of value can arise out of natural decomposition:

> Again, some of us liked the sedgy margins of our lakes, where great reeds and rushes grew, and had been rather glad to remember there were still left in England some few swamps where grass of Parnassus and bog-bean and bog-myrtle could be found. Here too, it seems, we were wrong, and Manchester will help us by draining or flooding over our lake shore, and giving us instead a bare bank of mud or of shingle. [59]

Those Manchester men, she concluded, who instruct us in the nature of beauty, who think a dam strewn with a few boulders can rival Raven Crag, who believe more is necessarily better, who prefer straight roads to winding, little-frequented bridle paths, who have no concern about wild swamp flowers, and who boast that they will improve our old lake by making it new: "are these the men to whom we are going to commit one of the loveliest lakes and valleys our England owns?" [60]

Hill was aware that such appeals would have a greater effect on readers of the *Times* than on those members of Parliament who represented urban constituencies. Politicians capable of appreciating swamp flora would think twice before expressing this interest in a public forum. Therefore she tended to side with the pragmatists rather than with Hunter and Somervell. Aesthetic arguments, she believed, would have no effect on politicians unless it could be shown that the health and future prosperity of Manchester did not depend on the destruction of wild beauty. Thirlmere defenders would present expert witnesses who could show that wells sunk in the new red sandstone area of Lancashire would be an adequate, although somewhat more expensive, alternative. What the effects of abstracting water would be on that less celebrated landscape seems not to have concerned them.

For these tactical reasons, opposition witnesses tried to indicate where alternative supplies might be found when a Commons select committee, chaired by the noted scientist and promoter of technical education Lyon Playfair, began its hearings. Others who appeared suggested that Manchester was more interested in making profits from selling water to purchasers along the line of supply than in assuring economic growth and improving the sanitation of her citizens. In reply, supporters of the bill cited demographic statistics and compared costs. The committee found for the bill promoters and dismissed the notion that heavily polluted South Lancashire and industrial regions north of Manchester might be viable alternative sources of water in the future. It stated that "any of the Westmoreland and Cumberland Lakes" were legitimate areas of water exploitation.

However they did concede to the protesters that the region was "a valued possession of the whole nation," that proposals to intervene in such sites must demonstrate that no injury will be done to natural beauty, and that the facility should act to preserve such beauty for future generations. Commissioners were satisfied, the report continued, that the Thirlmere project answered these conditions: it would bury one island but create two new ones; the fluctuation of water levels would expose no unsightly mud banks since the lake edges were shingle; doubling the size of the lake would create—and here commissioners cited the authority of a landscape gardener named W. Broderick Thomas—a better proportion between water and land masses and restore the lake "to its ancient condition." [61]

This language about the value to the nation of aesthetic resources was new to official publications. It represented a victory of sorts for the growing influence of the kind of environmental argument used so effectively by the Commons Preservation Society in its battles against enclosing landlords during the 1870s. When speaking about "preservation of the scenery," the Liberal politician W. E. Forster felt the need to add, "to use a phrase now current." [62] This concession to aesthetics served the preservationist/conservationist causes but brought little comfort to residents of other beauty spots threatened by urban-industrial growth, especially since the report and subsequent legislation invited further exploitation of the lakes. Friends of the Lakes realized correctly, as subsequent events proved, that Haweswater, Ullswater, and Windermere would be next.

Although the preservationists lost the battle for Thirlmere, they did win another skirmish. Reacting to pressure, Parliament inserted into the 1879 Manchester Water Act the commission's "environment clause" stipulating that "all reasonable regard" be shown for preserving the scenic beauty of the place and another clause protecting existing rights of access. [63] Preservationists also emerged from the struggle experienced in organization and tactics and equipped with a ready supply of rhetoric.

Whenever threatened with some new threat of invasion during the 1880s, the Friends of the Lakes chose confrontation. Canon Hardwick Rownsley came forward as their spokesman and rallying point as Ruskin, suffering from depression and bouts of mental disorder, tended to withdraw. But the "Seer of Brantwood" could occasionally be roused. In a letter dated April 7, 1884, to *The Manchester City News,* Ruskin imagined a future "Lift," which would carry enthusiastic travelers to a "Refreshment Room on the summit" of Helvellyn before it made a "'drop' to Ullswater; while beyond the rectilinear shores of Thirlmere reservoir, the Vale of St John will be laid out in a succession of tennis grounds, and the billiard rooms of the Bridal of Triermain Casino be decorated in the ultimate exquisiteness of Parisian taste." [64]

A later chapter will address the object of this heavy sarcasm: the popular recreation industry and its effect on the environment. Worthy of note here is the failure, on the part of Ruskin and the many others who adopted his tone, to leave much room for compromise. The preservationists showed nothing but contempt for Manchester philistinism in particular and proletarian tastes and urban values in general. Nature must be protected from the moral as well as the physical poison spreading out from cities in ever-increasing volume. Developers, "not content with vomiting pestilence,"[65] are intent on destroying the purity and simple faith that had imprinted itself on the landscape of remote places. Urban predators will, Ruskin warned, "deface your ancient hills with the guilt of mercenary desolation," determined as they are on driving an "ancient shepherd life into exile, and diverting the waves of . . . streamlets into the cities which are the very centres of pollution, of avarice, and impiety . . . [and] blasting the cultivable surface of England into a treeless waste of ashes."[66] These were strong words. In his angry wish to show contempt, he denied the possibility of working out some pragmatic way to reconcile a set of legitimate but conflicting demands: of an increasingly urbanized population for pure water and access to places of natural beauty, of rural people for some security in their way of life, of cultivated people for peace and quiet, and of naturalists and historically minded people for continuity and variety in species and places.

Ruskin's uncompromising position was consistent with his general attitude toward capitalist exploitation. Just before the Thirlmere threat, he had been carrying on a protracted feud with the Bishop of Manchester over the subject of Christianity and usury.[67] However, there was some justification in the allegation that his attitude to reservoirs was of the "not-in-my own-backyard" variety. Had he not once enthusiastically promoted a scheme for damming an Alpine valley of the Rhone and turning it into "one Paradise of safe plenty"?[68] Some critics have suggested that his anger, and perhaps Carlyle's, was less purely environmentalist than it was anti-Manchester and what that city represented to so many professional middle-class intellectuals.[69] Motive aside, the fact that such an array of eminent Victorians took part in the campaign meant that the national newspapers would carry the discussion to a wide audience throughout the 1880s.

The Battle of Thirlmere between Beauty and Utility was never resolved on the theoretical front. If, however, we consider behavior, a somewhat more optimistic reading of the event is possible. It is obvious that the reservoir promoters did not anticipate the strength of feeling their bid to appropriate a renowned beauty spot would stir up. They still seemed clumsy and inept at public relations when the time came, just after the First World War, to make the next move, this time on Haweswater. On the other hand, it was obvious, even in the Thirlmere construction plans, that Manchester wanted to be a good steward (or thought it prudent to appear like one), as its water commission understood that concept. It

Figure 9.   Lake Thirlmere becoming a reservoir (1891). We look south from
the lake's outlet to the site of the Manchester Corporation's new dam—a project for raising the water level fifty-one feet and transforming Lakeland poetry
into urban resource. (*Engineering* 52, 1891)

made minor and spasmodic attempts to heal or disguise the scars made
by dam building and the construction of tunnels to take the water on
its three-day journey to its destination. The project supervisor, George
Henry Hill, stipulated that local rock be mixed into the concrete used to
construct aqueducts so that they might harmonize with their surroundings.[70] (See Figure 9.)

In 1908, advised by Professor Fisher, one of the leading forestry experts of the day, the commission set out on a ten-year plan to plant trees
on the steep slopes of the catchment area. The object was to stabilize the
soil, improve its capacity to hold moisture, turn a profit, if possible, and
keep sheep from polluting the water. A six-acre nursery supplied most
of the saplings, shrubs, and grasses for the planting operation and also
served as a botanical laboratory. Although the outbreak of war in 1914

put a temporary end to Fisher's plan, some 2,000 acres of the 12,000 owned by the city were successfully reforested by the mid-1890s.[71] This allowed commissioners to claim high ground as preservationists: had their decision to convert grazing land back to forest not acted to purify the region? Had they not rationalized the region's water system by "altering nature's plan" and "diverting helter skelter streams into more profitable courses"? Their practical, not sentimental, conservationism had, they pointed out, managed to control rapid runoff and its erosive effects while at the same time, through planting and restricting public access, succeeded in leaving the site more "wild" than it had been for many centuries.[72]

Thirlmere's defenders did not applaud the commission's accomplishment in reforesting the slopes. They held up this aspect of water commission policy as a prime example of how even well-intentioned governmental (in this case, municipal) intervention was almost certain to be physically and aesthetically destructive. Virtually all of the trees planted under Fisher's direction were alien importations: firs and spruces from Alaska and the American and Canadian Pacific coast, Scotch pines, and European and Japanese larches. In 1906 a visitation of saw flies (*Nematus erichsoni*) defoliated most of the larches and spun cocoons in the litter and moss of the plantation floor. Specialists from Manchester University recommended spraying with arsenate of copper, but the knapsack sprayers used could not reach the tree tops, so "insectivorous" birds were introduced and housed in 400 nesting boxes to keep them from migrating. The city council was pleased to report that by 1912 the saw fly epidemic seemed to have passed and the forest had gained new species of bird life.[73]

What lessons the "nativists" among the late Victorian and Edwardian Friends of the Lakes, and they were the majority, drew from this "success story" were decidedly less positive. Discouraged with planting larches, the water commission concentrated on Sitka spruce, perhaps the most unpopular of all conifers with visitors because of the brooding quality of its dark foliage. Some came eventually to regret the demotion of the more cheerful larches.[74] Even the care the Manchester landlord took in keeping the area neat and tidy had its detractors. So "prim" and "paper-planned" is the place, noted Norman Nicholson in 1963, "that you expect to find a public convenience behind every tree."[75] W. G. Collingwood had written several decades earlier: "The old charm of its shores has quite vanished, and the sites of its legends are hopelessly altered, so that the walk along either side is a mere sorrow to any one who cared for it before." [76] Asked B. L. Thompson in 1946, do we really want another Black Forest? [77] Canon Rownsley would have not hesitated to give his answer. After surveying the region once the scars had a chance to heal, he concluded that "henceforth neither painter nor poet will come for rest and song, where the pack-horse bells at far intervals were once 'The only sound that dared intrude / Upon the Sylvan solitude.'" [78]

That so exuberant an enthusiast as Rownsley could emphasize the value of peace and quiet has caused some who have written about the Lake District to reflect on how strongly the Wordsworthian tradition influenced the late Victorian and Edwardian preservationist movement. [79] Few Wordsworthians would have been open to the suggestion that the lakes should be allowed to evolve to suit democratic tastes. It has been pointed out that the Thirlmere defenders felt a tension between their contempt for proletarian manners and their insistence that the Lake District was a national treasure for all to enjoy. They saw the contradiction but could find no way to resolve it. [80] Nevertheless, critics and defenders of the Thirlmere project seem to be in general agreement that Manchester's first intervention in the Lake District had been less than a success from almost any but an engineer's or a forest manager's point of view; as an exercise in public relations it had been, by general agreement, a "debacle." [81]

A century later, this Victorian and Edwardian contest between Beauty and Utility continues but the contestants and the issues are no longer quite the same. Concern about the appropriation of famous beauty spots by city developers has lessened now that the National Trust, the Council for the Preservation of Rural England, and other countryside protection groups provide leadership and direction to preservationists. Also, a great increase of interest in hiking, bicycling, climbing, and camping, clearly discernible from the 1880s on, gave the cause (once largely the preserve of the middle-aged and the professional middle class) youthful energy and change of focus. Then the advent of popular environmentalism in the 1960s again enlarged the recruiting grounds.

Thus a proposal the Manchester Corporation made in 1961 to tap Ullswater provoked a well-orchestrated outcry and was defeated in the House of Commons. Blocked for the first time, corporation engineers and public relations experts came up with an expensive new plan to send water from Windermere and Ullswater by way of Haweswater to a treatment works at Watchgate before sending it, along with the water from Thirlmere, on to Manchester. Chemical treatment would make it possible to permit public access to the three new additions to the system, the alternative of fencing these tourist sites being impractical anyway. Elaborate devices for hiding away pumping stations and masking the sound of their machinery won over enough support finally to carry the measure through Parliament.[82]

Therefore the struggles on the picturesque front had not been entirely in vain. Consciousnesses were undoubtedly raised. On the other hand, the battle to preserve Thirlmere and the skirmishing that followed demonstrated to all combatants, preservationists included, the conceptual limitations of romantic conservationism.[83] The appeal to beauty could not hold fast, in the forum of contending interests, against the argument from necessity. Neither could it hold its own against the resource conservationists—those who championed the cause of sustainable development and advocated wise, rather than reckless, exploitation.

In claiming respect for the Thirlmere, which time and natural erosion had fashioned, on the grounds that it was an entity with its own history, its own ends, its own system of self-regulation, Octavia Hill seemed to have approached what we now think of as an ecological perception, a sensibility that conceives of natural environments as biotic communities characterized by diversity, complexity, and symbiosis. Had she gone on to regret the passing of the bog myrtle and the bog bean, not simply as valued individuals, but as indicators of the existence of a unique, self-regulating community, and then warned the Manchester Corporation that indifference to such communities can have dire and unpredictable results for human beings, she might have shown the country how to construct firmer strategic defenses against the city. In this sense, at least, the environmental forces are now in a somewhat stronger theoretical position than they were in the past.

10
Greening the City

We are forced, for the sake of accumulating our power and
knowledge, to live in cities: but such advantage as we have in
association with each other is in great part counter-balanced
by our loss of fellowship with Nature.

John Ruskin, Stones of Venice, *1853*

As the countryside became more "countrified," the cities became more
densely citified. Here and there a village green or a country path managed
to survive when cities spread out and swallowed communities on their
edges, but these relics from the past were always in danger of being "assaulted" by brick walls and paving stones. Eventually Victorian cities responded to the retreat of natural sights and sounds by constructing green
places and incorporating them into the urban fabric. One kind of artifice—parks, street plantings, ornamental flower beds, mown lawns, window boxes—was introduced to balance the advance of another kind of
artifice—"chartered streets," densely packed housing developments, enclosed shops, markets, and recreational facilities. The commons around
the edges were preserved but gradually made tidy, more parklike. To
claim that the greening of cities compensated for increasing density and
pollution would be going too far. Yet what the Victorians did to provide
some sort of equilibrium altered and humanized the urban landscape in
important ways.

Steam power was one of the prime movers in making cities thoroughly
urban. It brought foundries and mills from the sides of rural streams and
rivers into city centers, adding to the other factors that were causing cities to expand and change shape—prominent among them the quicken-

ing of domestic and international trade, the concentration of industry, huge increases in land values, and unprecedented population growth. Banks, offices, exchanges, and warehouses squeezed out residential populations in the central areas; dockers, warehousemen, street and fixed-market sellers, and others who needed to live near their places of work packed into congested inner rings around and just outside. The well-off moved farther out onto higher, brighter building sites upwind. Developers paved and built on what open spaces remained inside.

The introduction of railways carried on this process. Rarely did their intrusion into the peripheries and then closer to the center do more than accelerate these trends. But if railways were not determinants, they did affect traffic volumes and patterns, land uses, and residential densities. On entering, they slashed and arched their way through commons and market gardening areas where property values were low. A longtime resident of London's Blackheath recalled in 1865 having watched as railways "entirely altered the suburban open spaces" and "the whole *entourage* of London." [1]

Closer to the center, railway engineers deliberately cut rights-of-way through congested working-class housing areas. Since slum properties were owned by a few great landlords, negotiations for purchase were relatively uncomplicated. Unfortunately, this crude instrument of slum clearance only produced greater overcrowding since the people it displaced (probably around 120,000 in central London over the second half of the nineteenth century) were forced to huddle together more closely next to the railway cuts. There were hopes that cheap fares might relieve the problem by allowing the working poor to move farther out where rents were lower; but it was not until after the turn of the century that these expectations were, to any significant extent, realized. Thus the centrifugal push of suburban rail service failed to compensate for its centripetal pull. In the city center and the inner districts around it, railway building added greatly to the snarl of people and vehicles by appropriating space for termini, viaducts, rail linkages, and shunting yards and by attracting to these facilities storage buildings, cab stands, omnibus stables, and loading areas for carts and wagons. [2]

As the city was covering over the remaining patches of nature and setting goods and people into motion along the ever more congested streets, it seemed in the eyes of many to have become a great pump that, in the morning, drew in people, goods, nutrients, and, in the evening and after dark, expelled wastes of every kind. Engineers from the beginning of the Victorian period became fascinated with the mechanism of this complex artifact, especially its circulatory patterns and its hydrological systems. Contributors to journals like the *Engineer,* the *Proceedings of the Institution of Civil Engineers,* or *Engineering* carried on debates about how to deal with the increased runoff from roofed and paved surfaces; and, as time went on, they accumulated data about the effects of this runoff on downriver sedimentation and flooding and about the effects of water imports on water distribution. Engineers became aware that extensive pumping as well as decreased infiltration of rain, dew, and snow acted to lower local water tables. From early in the century, measurements of temperature, humidity, and wind velocity had indicated that cities generated large amounts of artificial heat, that they tended to reduce wind speeds and acted to increase precipitation. Specialists experimented with the best and most economical ways of filling in marshes, embanking or completely enclosing rivers and streams, flattening relief features, building up depressions, and disposing of the vast amounts of dust, ground-up stone, organic refuse, and muck that were, as their experience as well as their senses indicated, accumulating at alarming rates.

Being optimists by profession, civil engineers took pride in their contribution to this transformation. The resulting environmental problems they regarded as challenges to be met with further technical ingenuity. In their nonprofessional lives, engineers might share with other urban dwellers anxieties about the social or psychological effects of the artificial mechanism they were trying to understand and redesign, but in their roles as builders and fixers they were impressed by and proud of technology's ability to command nature.

Occupied as most engineers, urban investigators, and reformers were with practical matters like drainage, water supply, sanitation, street traffic, and slum clearance, they seemed to lack sufficient perspective to write about urban geomorphology—one branch of what Lewis Mumford called "the natural history of urbanization." [3]

In the 1920s Robert Sherlock did, at least, make a start. He showed how London constructed the ground it stood on out of its own debris and subsoil as well as out of the rock and baked clay it imported. He noted how the metropolis redirected the water flowing through or under it, how it radically augmented the natural denudation of its site, how it deposited its wastes in every bit of low ground it could find, and how it then piled on top of this reconstructed surface millions upon millions of bricks. [4]

Sherlock's *Man as a Geological Agent* had mainly to do with nonorganic matter—its displacement and piling up—and not with ecological processes. However, his research broke new ground, even though it did not produce an immediate crop of follow-up investigations. In the 1950s, thirty years after Sherlock had led the way, Mumford could still comment that only the preliminary work on the subject had been done.[5]

Although short on relevant statistics, Victorians were aware of the capacity of cities to level, fill, drain, erode, heap up, and set in motion. Some of them were deeply troubled by accumulating evidence that masons, bricklayers, and railway contractors were choking out all things natural. Writing in 1875, the journalist W. J. Loftie thought he knew what had become of the fen in Finsbury, the conduit in Conduit Street, or the mount on Mount Street: they had been swallowed by an artificial monster: "It spreads north and south, east and west, creeping onward like the tide of the sea, slowly but surely, year by year, and obliterating as it goes, all the original features of the country."[6]

Artists, poets, essayists, and novelists drew public attention to this phenomenon; dozens of parliamentary and private investigations made recommendations about how to cope with the consequences. Carlyle, Ruskin, Edward Carpenter, and their many followers called for a return to life's simplicities, away from the smoke and anonymity of the city. H. G. Wells foresaw the whole of lowland Britain transformed into one leafy garden suburb. William Morris imagined a deurbanized London, "small, and white, and clean." Paternalistic employers like Titus Salt, W. H. Lever, and George Cadbury sought to recapture for their workers the community and natural amenities of village life by building Saltaire, Port Sunlight, and Bournville. In the early years of the twentieth century, the Barnetts, Raymond Unwin, Barry Parker, and Edwin Lutyens realized their dreams of integrating town and "country" at Hampstead Garden Suburb, and Ebenezer Howard saw his image of a garden city come to life at Letchworth in Hertfordshire. The idea was to improve the city by importing what Michael Hough has called the "pedigree" landscape, not the vernacular or working countryside, but the planned spaces of gardening design convention.[7] These green communities would be places of escape from an otherwise synthetic environment.

This negative view of the city, especially the metropolis, became more pronounced as the population lost its ties with the country and with country ways.[8] It was usually in the interest of reformers, even those who had an appreciation of urban values, to emphasize what was destructive and dangerous about allowing cities to grow at such an alarming rate. They spoke of the cluttered streets and lives; the fetid turnings and foul air; the tense, noisy atmosphere; the "sick hurry"; the "divided aims." A familiar refrain runs through all forms of criticism and re-portage: the city exacts for the freedom and creativity it enjoys the pen-alty of physical and spiritual debility. "We find," wrote Ruskin in 1853, "all men of true feeling delighting to escape out of modern cities into natural scenery."[9] Health as well as feelings, it was generally agreed, deteriorated when deprived of greenery and freshness. The compiler of the Metropolitan Public Garden Association's report for 1887 spoke of the dangers of remaining constantly inside a place devoid of anything natural:

> The ever-widening girdle of bricks and mortar—the ever-increasing height of dwellings and warehouses—the tendency . . . for the current of human life from all directions to flow towards the metropolis as a centre [will] render London less and less the place where bodily functions can have full and nat-ural play, where bone and muscle may be developed, and where constitutions are able to ward off disease and decay.[10]

Sentiments and pronouncements of this kind being so abundant, it is easy to understand why Victorian environmental reform should be de-scribed as essentially antiurban.

Not surprisingly, architects who specialized in large-scale urban proj-ects or engineers hired by municipalities to plan and supervise sanitation improvements and carry out public works rejected this way of thinking. They were drawn to the notion of the city as an organism that operates according to intelligible systems. They were confident that such symp-toms as lethargy or antisocial behavior could be diagnosed and treated. That involved identifying the problem, locating the inflammation or malfunction, and then radically curtailing the range of factors operating on the particular organ, artery, or gland in question. The object was to select from the many factors acting on the affected part the ones that were capable of being remedied or surgically corrected and then con-centrating attention on this small set of variables. If, for example, this process identified the withdrawal of nature from the daily experience of slum dwellers as the treatable factor among the various causes of some particular symptom of ill health, then the specialist on civic spaces and structures would set about devising remedies, prominent among them strategies for bringing "the country" back into the city. The availability of a practical remedy set the reform agenda.

Victoria Park, London's first "people's park," materialized in 1846 as a consequence of this problem-solving method. Sir John Pennethorne, the park's designer, was architect to the chief commissioner of woods and forests. He was convinced that he could rejuvenate the overbuilt, unsanitary, generally run-down areas of Hackney, Bethnal Green, Stepney, and Bow. He would do so by giving its people an East End equivalent of the West End's Hyde Park and by connecting it to the Thames by means of a splendid, tree-lined, landscaped boulevard. Believing that much of the area's blight and unrest resulted from its abandonment by wealthy respectables who had moved westward to more salubrious districts, he proposed to line both park and boulevard with fashionable homes. He thought that by giving surroundings the same picturesque treatment his mentor, John Nash, had used in designing Regent's Park, he could entice upper-middle-class families back, closer to the center. Land values would rise and with them rates. Increased revenues could then be used for improvements of every kind.

Pennethorne assumed that, once set in motion, this engine of renewal would become self-perpetuating. In addition, slum dwellers who formerly had no choice but to use the streets or the public houses for leisure activities would have a fine park with rolling lawns and shaded copses where they could walk in family groups and fill their lungs with nature's sweet breath—and closer at hand, a leafy promenade, a corridor of freshness and brightness.[11]

When confronted with human complexity and unpredictable circumstances, technological planning frequently produces some unexpected results—a truism that city planners and engineers, in particular, continually rediscover. Pennethorne's experience was no exception. In only one important respect did he create what he intended: a replication of the landscape values of Regent's Park. On a large tract of market gardens punctuated with houses and outbuildings, he was able to superimpose the picturesque features associated with, not the fields and pastures of the country, but the country estate and the landowning aristocracy: meandering lanes, artificial hills, carefully positioned clumps of trees, expanses of mown lawn sloping down to ornamental lakes. The effect was pleasing and much admired. Yet the rich were not seduced into forsaking Kensington or Bayswater. As for his ambition to transform the whole area, that foundered from the start. Cutting a broad swath through the East End was beyond the means and imagination of local authorities. No leafy boulevard ever brought greenery close to the doorsteps of Bethnal Green and Stepney.

Pennethorne did succeed in constructing, within the walls of his "people's park," an environment that East Enders found attractive. Victoria Park was hugely popular from the start. But users proved unwilling to receive passively what had been bestowed. They enjoyed strolling and admiring lawn and foliage but wanted, in addition, opportunities for more active leisure pursuits. Groups petitioned for sporting fields, gymnasia, docks for boats, swimming areas, centers for the study of natural history, places for public celebration and debate. Park authorities, having lost some of their apprehensions about the possibility of social disorder, responded positively. As concern about riot and revolution receded, interest in "improving" the tastes and habits of the poor advanced. The "gardenesque" style—herbaceous borders, elaborate and vividly colored bedding arrangements, specimen trees and shrubs—seemed to express this moral purpose. Besides, the many amateur horticulturalists among the park users seemed eager for such displays. Therefore the ornamental had to be fitted into Pennethorne's naturalistic setting.

What happened to Pennethorne's vision tended to be repeated whenever architects and engineers attempted to treat urban ills by providing "lungs" and green oases. Designers would begin with a coherent, rationally conceived answer to a clearly defined problem, only to see their designs evolve through practice into parks that expressed eclecticism and confusion of purpose in their structures and ornaments.

Intended to be refuges from artifice, parks were in themselves highly artificial and increasingly ornamental. Moreover they quickly adapted themselves to the urban fabric. Lawns, carefully placed trees and shrubs, mounds, curving drives and walks had to be modified to accommodate more and more artifacts: fenced tennis courts and fields for games, gymnasia, bathing facilities, swings, sandboxes, refreshment stands, statues, clocks, box-edged beds, galvanized-wire floral vases, Moorish-Gothic drinking fountains. Commenting on this process by which "fragile enclaves of countryside" grew more crowded, manicured, segmented, and architectural, David Nicholson-Lord writes: "Parks thus became entertainment, placing the municipal marigolds firmly in an urbanized tradition stretching back to the *panem et circenses* of imperial Rome." [12]

Green oases gradually assumed more and more the features of the built environment, but at the same time they turned away from the cityscape and erected barriers against the surrounding streets. Designed by architects to give city dwellers relief from urban constraints, spaces turned into highly structured, biologically and botanically simplified areas of greenery, requiring sophisticated technology, heavy expenditures of energy, maintenance, and strict surveillance.

Some Victorians noticed these contradictions—although mainly the aesthetic and social ones—and searched for more effective antidotes to congestion and the loss of fellowship with nature. They all agreed that nature was a balm to urban sores but had reservations about the ways the remedy was being applied. They were also troubled by the thought that in concentrating on building parks and sporting grounds, opening private squares to public use, converting disused graveyards into gardens, and putting effort into saving commons and footpaths, reformers were treating symptoms rather than confronting real issues: poverty, cruel exploitation of labor, and miserable housing.

One of the most systematic of these critics was George Godwin, a longtime resident of central London, architect, expert on the properties of concrete, champion, in the 1830s, of railway building, social investigator, lobbyist for sanitary improvements, art and architectural theorist and patron, playwright, designer of model agricultural buildings, and editor, from 1844 to 1883, of a highly influential journal, the *Builder*.[13] Indeed, it would be hard to imagine a figure out of the nineteenth century better equipped by temperament and experience to act as a commentator on urban questions and values. Although acutely sensitive to aesthetic issues and intensely engaged with social ones, he was at heart an engineer and master builder, not a romantic naturalist. He loved urban spaces, particularly London's. Nevertheless, he conceived of the city as a problem for which architectural arrangements were the solution. In his vision, the gardener was there to assist the architect in making the city not only more livable but more urbane.

A central theme informs the *Builder's* editorial line and all of Godwin's writings. "It cannot be too often repeated," he wrote in 1854, "that the health and morals of the people are regulated by their dwellings."[14] At a time when that cause-and-effect relationship was often understood differently, this proposition seemed more challenging than it does to us. Crime, epidemics, shortened life, drunkenness, child neglect, indifference to religion, sexual exploitation, low self-esteem, slovenly habits, lack of self-discipline, negligent citizenship, and all the other evils so commonly believed to be especially urban were not, in Godwin's view, the results of increasing segregation of classes inside cities, or the influx of Irish immigration, or sin, whether original or learned, or absence of nature's remedies. Neither did those evils arise out of bad drains, polluted water, inadequate provision for education, capitalist exploitation, exposure to excessive stimulus, or fragmentation of traditional cultural and communal ties. Antecedent to all these symptoms of ill health was overcrowding.

He believed the afflictions commonly associated with city living were directly attributable in the first instance to the fact that poverty-stricken people were crowded in upon each other "like pilchards in a box." Children creep out of "close courts and alleys" to escape into "confined streets," passing from one kind of contamination to another. Given any chance at reaching fresh air and sunshine, they respond readily, with "the instincts of nature." [15] Children do not need to be taught to prefer light to "shadowy corners" any more than poor people in general need to be taught to dislike dirt and disorder. On the contrary: "Dirty, dilapidated, and unwholesome dwellings destroy orderly and decent habits, degrade the character, and conduce to immorality. Bad air produces feelings of exhaustion and lowness of spirits, and these tempt to the use of stimulants—the fruitful parents of all crime." [16]

It followed that the provision of decent housing should, ideally, precede or at least coincide with other reform agendas: temperance drives, provision of ragged schools for street children, supply of parks, commons, and playgrounds, as well as attempts at moral elevation. If these worthy causes were to have any lasting impact, architects must first design housing, and politicians must make it possible for the poorest classes to live at affordable rents in what they constructed. "When the house ceases to be a sty, and possesses the conditions which render it capable of being made into a home, then, but not till then, may it receive, with some hope of benefit, the schoolmaster and the minister of religion." [17]

This ordering of priorities did not prevent Godwin or the *Builder* from giving fervent support to other environmental causes; what it did do was to supply the journal and its editor with a critical edge. Every campaign to save, convert, open, or construct green spaces could count on encouragement from that quarter. Godwin even indulged himself with the occasional panegyric about "the cradle of nature" and the "mysterious bond between man and animals." [18] But always there was this reservation: exhortation, example, influence—even the influence of nature—will prove "useless against a damp, dilapidated, ill-drained, miserable dwelling, where decency is not possible, and immorality inevitable." [19] Success for the gardener, in other words, depended upon the close cooperation of the architect: the park could never, itself, be an effective antidote to the slum. If, on the other hand, poor slum dwellers could be decently housed, then manifold were the possibilities for enriching the urban experience. It followed that since they were occasional spaces and incapable of being incorporated into the design of domestic living space, large parks or commons were not of first importance as instruments for urban renewal.

This interest in suiting recreational spaces to housing and neighborhood conditions made the *Builder* a strong and early champion of the small local park. Anything that extended domestic living spaces should have highest priority. Attempts to bring trees and flowers to the people least able or least motivated to seek them out were sure to be fully reported and commented on. Several leading articles Godwin wrote in the 1870s began with praise for the success of the London civic park builders and commons preservers but then went on to show how their efforts had contributed little to the lives of the poor majority. One editorial noted that a "grand chain of parks" now reaches from Regent's Park in the north to Kensington Gardens, Hyde Park, Green Park, and St. James's Park in the west to Battersea and Southwark Parks in the south, to Victoria Park in the east, some 2,000 acres in all. Yet parents from green-sounding places like Hatton Garden, Hughes's Fields, or Whetstone Park lack the time or energy to take their young children to true greenery.

Godwin agreed that users were doubtless improved by reading Latin tags on trees and shrubs. But what, he asked, does all this contrivance mean to the neglected child who has never seen a lawn; whose world is ruled into squalid streets, alleys, courts, and rows; and whose sky is "a few square yards of smoky canopy"? You can see, the editorial continued, these slum children peering through the fences of Lincoln's-Inn-Fields or Russell, Bedford, Bloomsbury, Euston, Soho, Red-Lion, and Golden Squares, where from one day to another, the only sound to be heard is made by a gardener's foot. Between the links in that great chain from Regent's Park to Victoria Park there is no natural thing, only a "wilderness of bricks." The same can be said, an editorialist noted on another occasion, about the stretch from Battersea to the open market gardens at Peckham or the eight miles from Clapham Common to Finsbury Park. What a boon it would be to those who need the influence of nature most if broad, tree-lined highways connected those points and brought green things close to the doorsteps of the poor.[20]

Whether or not reform-minded readers of the *Builder* agreed with its editor's emphasis on congested housing as the root cause of urban ills, most agreed that greenery should be introduced directly into the homes and neighborhoods of poor people. Visitors returning from the 1867 International Exhibition in Paris spoke enthusiastically about how the trees on Baron Haussmann's new boulevards were already attracting promenaders. One of these commentators, William Robinson, curator of Kew Gardens, reported that as soon as a new avenue is laid out in the French capital, "in go the trees," lovingly protected with cast-iron gratings.[21]

Suggestions that London do likewise received only a lukewarm response from the Metropolitan Board of Works. It authorized a double line of plane trees for the Thames Embankment, opened to the public on both banks by 1872. A correspondent to the *Builder* noted in 1862 that stretches of trees on Piccadilly, Cheyne Walk in Chelsea, Brompton Road (where Godwin lived for many years), parts of Highgate, Hampstead, and Hackney had been spared "the ignorant vandalism of modern builders" and had grown to form "pleasant oases in a wilderness of slovenly abominations in brick and cement." [22] Why the city seemed so unwilling to spend money on trees puzzled the writer, especially since concern about damp had diminished once people came to recognize that trees absorb moisture as well as give it off and that deciduous varieties shade only in the seasons when shade is appreciated. Also he believed there had been a general rejection of "sterile Georgian" taste, everywhere, that is, except in the minds of parish officials. Therefore prejudice against trees was not "deep-rooted" but merely a "vestry tradition," one that "took its rise in the modern English dark age of the last great war." The article ended by asking that the "tedious highways" of the central city be transformed into "gay and pleasant *boulevards*." [23]

Voluntary organizations appeared from the 1870s to achieve similar purposes. Societies formed to bring flowers to workhouses, hospitals, and slum dwellings and to organize rural outings. Convinced, like Godwin, that little permanent good could be expected from "monotonous lives punctuated with sprees," Octavia Hill campaigned vigorously for including small gardens and playgrounds in slum renewal projects and raised money to save plots of open land near slum areas. [24] She was assisted in these efforts by similarly motivated individuals: Robert Hunter, George John Shaw-Lefevre, Lord Robert Grosvenor, Samuel and Henrietta Barnett, Hardwick Rownsley, Lord and Lady Brabazon, Henry Fawcett, various members of the Buxton family, Lord Mount-Temple, and James Bryce. This circle appeared on committees together and worked cooperatively to get legislation passed facilitating the conveyance of neglected squares and graveyards into the hands of public bodies, saving this or that field or common from the developer, sponsoring programs for teaching gardening principles, taking slum children on weekend picnics in parks or commons, and requiring builders to make provisions for gardens and small parks in their housing developments.

One specific recommendation was that estate planners be required to make their window ledges wide enough to hold window boxes. This advice appeared frequently in the *Builder*. "Window Horticulture" was a greening program Godwin's journal took credit for initiating. [25] An article in 1849 described how Belgian ladies used double-glazed windows to grow flowers all year round on their balconies.[26] But it was in 1857 that the journal set out in earnest to interest Londoners of all social classes in bringing nature really close to home. Before then, as a leading article explained, the "infernal fogs" of the capital and provincial cities had discouraged central city gardening. Only when Parliament passed a measure in 1853 to reduce smoke in London had it become possible again, the writer thought, to grow roses and other delicate plants. In the last year or so, the article continued,

> We see in very many mean streets and lanes, narrow window openings adorned in the prettiest manner with such floral vegetation as the scant means of the industrial tenant can supply: a ledge board extends across; it is fenced with ivy palisades, repeated to every window, with miniature five-bar gates to complete the hanging garden—all that can be realized of examples seen at the Crystal Palace, or in the floral balconies of other roomkeepers, an interest in those germs of nature which have arisen from their own care and attention.[27]

Several years later, the *Builder* sent an artist to a spot near Cripplegate Church to sketch "A Poor Woman's Garden in the City." The accompanying article reminded readers that Milton had once lived in this now "dark and smoky region" when it was full of pleasant homes and gardens. Since then, drabness had descended. But standing out as one bright spot was the roof of a small washhouse, covered with jars, boxes, butter tubs, and cracked tea pots filled with mignonette, wallflowers, hollyhocks, and stocks. Ivy climbed the abutting wall and a cage for a blackbird hung in the midst of the flowers. The contrast appealed to the staff artist. While he was sketching, said the writer, a little boy pointed at the bird and said that it sang so well in the mornings that "it was almost as good as being in Highgate Woods."[28] (See Figure 10.)

The tone here was not patronizing. The *Builder* was not above moralizing about the "humanizing effect" of home gardening but seems to have assumed that, given a little space and a supply of cheap seeds and bedding plants (nurseries like Anderson's, Bull's, or Whimsett's sold a one-shilling packet of variegated seeds, enough for eight window boxes),[29] poor Londoners would respond with enthusiasm. Over the years, the journal printed letters and excerpts from speeches that adopted the language of what used to be called "social control" before the term went out of favor. The architect Sydney Smirke was of the opinion that working-class horticulturalists stayed out of pubs and were never lazy. He cited the testimony of Samuel Broome, gardener at the Inner Temple and the leading enthusiast for chrysanthemums—"essentially a working man's plant," and "ideally suited to London's climate."[30] One of the first

Figure 10.   Poor woman's roof garden (1862). To promote flower growing
in slums, the *Builder* sent an artist to show what one woman had managed
to create with a few plants and a collection of old pots. (*Builder* 20, 1862.
Reproduced by permission of the Guildhall Library, Corporation of London)

to organize flower-growing contests for slum children, Broome testified in the *Builder's* pages that on occasions when he had been invited by eager Cockneys to show them how to grow plants on backyard "dust-holes," talk of strikes was never to be heard.[31] In a similar vein, a speaker at a meeting of the British Association said "it was a well-established fact that whenever a pink, or a carnation, or a rose was seen outside a cottage, there was a potato or a cabbage for the pot within." He also favored his audience with these lines:

Yes, in a poor man's garden grow,
    Far more than herbs or flowers,
Kind thought, contentment, peace of mind,
      And joy for weary hours.[32]

No doubt Godwin did share the assumption that the personal contentment gardening bestowed had a calming effect on society; at least he never bothered to question on his editorial page that commonsense but untested proposition. However, his real interest was in the capacity of home gardening to make high density into a positive feature of city life. He recognized that bare façades and turnings seem to constrict spaces; patches of bright color, on the other hand, seem to have the opposite effect. In this respect, if in no other, he believed living conditions to have improved in his lifetime. Ten years ago, he noted in 1866, one rarely came across houses, even in the West End, embellished with window boxes, balcony gardens, or ivy-covered walls. By contrast, he said, the pedestrian could now pass by splendid displays of flower baskets on balconies, tendrils of Virginia creeper on trellises and railings, and, on the window ledges of Piccadilly and Cavendish Square, glass herbaria, warmed by boilers. Godwin was also glad to report that in far less fashionable areas—Aldersgate, Bermondsey, Hackney, and Islington—there was hardly a street without flowers.[33] He believed that this love of flowers was building bridges across the class divides.

Godwin returned often to the theme that London and the other major British cities were importing green nature at an ever-increasing rate over the course of the nineteenth century but that speculative builders with their doctrine of "bald utility" were, at the same time and also at an increasing rate, pinching it out.[34] Depending on perspective, either side could be said to be gaining.

Anyone capable of looking down on London, Manchester, Liverpool, Birmingham, or Nottingham (with its 10,000 allotment gardens)[35] at the end of Queen Victoria's reign would probably have been struck by the amount of greenery there was below, not just in the suburbs but also in the central parts of the cities, especially if a particular balloonist had made the same assent nearer the beginning of the long reign. At the end of the nineteenth century, some Londoners were claiming that in no other city, not even in Paris, was flower cultivation, "in every available nook, and in the windows, alike of rich and poor, carried so far." [36] In the central part of London there were 2,000 or so acres of large public parks. Of these, Victoria Park, Battersea Park, and Primrose Hill had been constructed in mid-Victorian times, and the older Kensington Gardens and Hyde, Green, St. James's, and Regent's parks had been extensively replanted in the 1850s and 1860s. To the already-existing private squares had been added a variety of green "open spaces" maintained by the Metropolitan Board of Works and then by the London County Council.[37]

Added together, the various smaller recreation grounds—converted graveyards, public squares, playgrounds, shrubberies, road triangles, and enclosures—made up about 350 acres before the outbreak of the First World War.[38] Outside that central area, campaigns by horticulturalists and advocates of "rational recreation" for the multitude had made impressive contributions: publicly owned and administered commons like Wimbledon or Hampstead Heath, Epping Forest, Kew Gardens, Blackheath, and Bushey and Greenwich parks, to name only some of those larger open spaces that had been preserved or embellished. Although not visible from the air, there would have been patches of color in the lines and bends of terraced houses put up by speculative builders, little roof, window, balcony, and backyard gardens that would not have been there before midcentury. Greenery had returned to the heart of the Victorian city in profusion, gathered from the most remote corners of the world. As Godwin had hoped, these importations had been adopted and refashioned to form part of the urban fabric.

At the same time Godwin shared with the more romantically inclined the belief that uncultivated landscapes had a particular therapeutic value for a closely contained populace. He was inclined to agree that planned and contrived green spaces could not provide strong contrasts to the surrounding streets, brick walls, back alleys, and factories. In 1847 the *Builder* gave space to a letter expressing regrets about the imminent development of Copenhagen Fields. The correspondent noted that to lose this bit of wasteland would be to destroy a "play-ground of the northern part of the metropolis," where residents of Holloway and Camden Town come to pick daisies, buttercups, and wild hyacinths—in a setting more beautiful than any park. That same year, a letter from "A Faithful

Observer" described a visit to the site being prepared for Victoria Park and complained that "none of the advantages of the locality have been understood or turned in to account." The area being smoothed and reconfigured had been, the observer noted, "a favorite, a beautiful spot, rather wild, varied, and luxuriant: it is now comparatively dreary, tame, and of course insipid." [39]

Other journals sounded this same note. Parks, commented the *Lancet,* a leading medical journal, were "cages of a larger kind." [40] Might it not be a good idea, asked the *Morning Advertiser* in 1874, to fence off at least one park and leave it more or less to nature's devices? "There is absolutely no poetry," the article continued, "in the modern garden, which at best but apes a Kaleidoscopic combination, and appeals to our most prosaic attributes." Thus a healthy dose of neglect might allow our "good old fashioned" flora to return. [41]

The founders of the Commons Preservation Society made a similar claim about the value of luxuriant wildness in their campaigns, begun in 1865, to save the commons on London's periphery from manor lords who wanted to enclose them or dig down in them for sand and gravel, from railway builders looking for inexpensive rights-of-way, and from speculative builders eager to lay out housing tracts. One society member observed that railways had annihilated space only to cramp the space available to the poor. That being so, he thought it would be unjust for the rich landowners who profited from suburban sprawl to deny others "the privilege of roaming far and wide, without hindrance or interruption." [42] The "smoke dried citizen," wrote the society's attorney Robert Hunter, wants "to rest himself," not in some place of "artificial beauty," but "on the green sward of untutored nature." "Free and well-regulated usage" of some "rural haunt" must be, he thought, a far better restorative than a sedate walk along graveled lanes, past neatly planted groves and flower beddings. [43] Presumably Hunter noticed no contradiction between free usage and well-regulated usage or between the related idea of preserving commons exclusively for recreation and presumed longing of pent-up city dwellers for things bucolic.

This ambivalence about what constituted the best restorative for urban workers and dwellers could be noticed in the landscape of suburban development. Especially after the 1870s, builders and designers of suburban enclaves for the numerous new recruits to the middle class incorporated landscape design aimed at suggesting rural values of community and organic growth: curving, tree-lined streets and carpets of lawn— features intended to provide transition between the public street and the private realm, to knit suburban developments together, and to shield them from the harsher realities outside.

Technology had something to do with this trend. Until the last quarter of the century lawns had been maintained by gardeners using scythes and brooms, an expense only the rich could afford. The introduction of cheap, efficient lawn mowers bridged that suburban social division. As early as 1830 a textile engineer named Edwin Budding had adapted a machine for shearing nap from cloth and rugs to the task of mowing grass, but it was not until the lighter and much cheaper Follows and Bates lawn mower appeared in 1869 that the average homeowner could afford to display what came to be the symbol of suburbia—"a kind of verdant moat," an orderly green barrier against the central city's hard-edged jumble.[44]

Expanses of manicured turf were meant to suggest those country estate parks where lawn, clumps of trees, and shrubbery extend themselves without obvious transition into copses and meadows grazed by livestock. The well-manicured green carpet conveyed a different message. When the estate park was miniaturized into a suburban lawn, a playing field, or a golf course green, these immaculate stretches or patches of green tended to symbolize detachment from the immediate environment, not continuity with it. Grazing animals were not present to suggest harmony between two different but related meanings of "cultivation." By contrast, the suburban lawn suggested discontinuity with its surroundings.

Especially with the advent of the lawn mower, expanses of grass became simple, high-maintenance monocultures, environments that actively discouraged variety. "As a high-cost, high-energy floor covering," writes Michael Hough, the lawn "produces the least diversity for the most effort."[45] It follows that the cult of the manicured lawn, a Victorian legacy, acts as a formidable barrier to habitat complexity and less energy intensive forms of horticulture.

In the urban environment, the rural meadow, like the estate park, underwent a transformation. By midcentury, city dwellers began to notice other signs that the country was retreating from the city. This perception forms a major theme in Henry Mayhew's four-volume *London Labour and the London Poor*, published in 1861 and 1862. A section devoted to "Street Sellers of Green Stuff" contains transcripts of interviews with people who made their livings gathering turfs and plants from commons, the few remaining wastelands, and "eligible sites for villas"—areas cleared by developers but allowed to run wild until building commenced. Mayhew interviewed a partly paralyzed former brace maker who had been reduced to selling chickweed and grunsell as feed for larks. He also had a sideline in turfs to line cage bottoms. Each morning at seven he took his stick and limped to Chalk Farm, where there was an abundance of chickweed. That done, he made his way to a private garden near Hollo-way, where he was allowed to gather grunsell. He bought the turfs from a boy who dug them at Kilburn Wells and Notting Hill. If there were a special order, he would add nettles to his basket so that lady custom-ers could make a blood-purifying tea.[46] Here was an example of old-fashioned rural pursuits being carried on in the city, although they were hardly the kind Hunter probably had in mind.

Testimony given by another turf gatherer shows both that the city en-vironment was still being "farmed" and that this kind of activity was steadily diminishing. He said that the small rings of sod he peddled had to contain shamrocks, or "small Dutch clover," otherwise keepers of sky-larks, who used the turfs to line the cages, would refuse to buy. The best "harvest field" for specialty turfs used to be Chalk Farm, but it was now "fairly flayed." Parts of Camden Town, once prime sources, had been built over. As for Hampstead Heath, a place where shamrocks flourished, turf purveyors were now prevented from "so much as sticking a knife." [47]

Ironically, the manor lord who probably did the forbidding, Sir Thom-as Maryon Wilson, was engaged at the time in a fierce and protracted struggle with irate commoners and concerned citizens over his right to dig gravel from the heath to sell to developers of a railway line and over his announced intention to appropriate parts of the common for specu-lative housing. Sir Thomas's death in 1868 opened the way for negotia-tions between his heir and the City of London, which ended in the heath's being set aside as a public recreation area. From then on "untutored" nature was there to be enjoyed but not to be gleaned or dug into. The heath remained a common, but its functions narrowed. Refashioned with Corot and Constable in mind, it became almost parklike.[48]

Mayhew does not comment directly on the disappearance of country ways from the experience of urbanites, but his fascination with "sur-vivals" shows how aware he was that an era had past. We find, for ex-ample, an analysis of why there had been a steady decline in the street sale of live poultry. Geese, he writes, used to be brought to London's Leaden-hall Market where they would be purchased by vendors and driven through the streets, often in flocks as large as five hundred, to the sub-urbs where purchasers kept them until it was time to wring their necks or chop off their heads and prepare their corpses for the dinner table. In the same way, live ducks and chickens would also be transported from

Surrey, Sussex, or as far away as Ireland into the city center and then driven or carried out again through the public throughways to suburban backyards. Mayhew interviewed a middle-aged man, engaged in this trade since childhood, who reminisced about serving one young bride who ordered six couples, three hens and three cocks, in order to procure a supply of fresh eggs. When he explained that a ratio of one to five would be more productive and far more peaceful, she appeared less than pleased. But of late, he said, suburban wives prefer to buy their eggs so as to keep their gardens "nice"; as a result, orders had fallen off sharply. Obviously, squeamishness and the cult of tidiness and gentility must be included, along with the shrinkage of open spaces, among the explanations for why *rus* and *urbe* lost so many points of contact.

Mayhew noted these developments but looked to the advent of the railways for an explanation. He saw that this new technology tended to centralize both retail and wholesale marketing. "Resource blindness" was one of the results.[49] Increasingly, shoppers bought their ducks, chickens, and rabbits already butchered. Customers for live hedgehogs fell off radically when stores began offering packaged powders to control black beetle infestations.[50] For a similar complex of reasons, street vendors of seeds began to complain that people of all classes seemed to prefer buying flowers in pots.[51]

We have progressed so far along that road that Mayhew's London seems to us, by comparison, redolent with the sights, smells, and sounds of rural life. In 1855 the live meat market moved from Smithfield in the City to the Caledonian Market, reachable by rail lines. However, lack of refrigeration meant that well into the third quarter of the century, during the hot months, cattle and sheep would be driven through street traffic in London and other cities, on their way to inner-city basement slaughter houses. Because milk soured quickly, a few dairies remained near the city center well after the notorious swine herds of the Kensington Potteries had been banished. Until late in the century, cows were kept under license in St. James Park. When taken there as a boy in the 1880s, Thomas Burke recalled always being given a penny glass, "fresh from the cow." At the end of that decade, more than twenty percent of London's milk supply still came from urban cowsheds.[52] It should also be kept in mind that so long as most street traffic moved, literally, by horsepower, all city dwellers shared, to some extent at least, the farmer's intimate relationship with animals.

Yet there could be no question that a separation of realms did take place during the nineteenth century, although a full account of that process would need to begin much earlier. Those born when the century was new recognized as adults how detached their lives had become from country lore and pastimes. It may be that bemoaning the loss of contact with elemental things is a perennial sign of advancing years, but this kind of lament seems to have had a special poignancy in the 1860s and 1870s. In 1871, a middle-aged resident of North London sent the *Builder* a letter recalling the pleasure of swimming as a boy in spring-fed ponds on summer mornings at Hornsey-Wood House. Since then, he noted ruefully, the forces of "improvement" had intervened. Wishing to provide and at the same time control recreation, the Metropolitan Board of Works had absorbed the house property and spring system into its new Finsbury Park. So he knew what had happened to the original fen in Finsbury: it had either become part of London's reservoir system or had been fashioned first into a bucolic tea house retreat and then into a park with an "ornamental water." "No Swimming" signs were soon posted.[53]

There was a sad irony in all this, the correspondent thought. Having displaced people to build the park, thereby increasing congestion in the surroundings, officialdom had proceeded to cut off access to fields and bathing places, and doing so after having increased by their actions the desire and need for informal recreation. He recognized that, in this case, it had been park planners and municipal engineers, not housing speculators, railway builders, or industrialists, who had been the agency by which a semirural environment came to be blotted out and refashioned into a carefully designed artifact. He would probably not have been cheered had he known that the informal playground of his youth would eventually be turned into, among other things, a concentration of sporting facilities. He thought that parks and playgrounds were certain to be "less enjoyable than the old fields."

We are now more conscious than was this Victorian Londoner of the subjective nature of enjoyment: choice between active and passive recreation seems to most of us a matter of age and lifestyle. Still alive but much weaker is the feeling that the city represents corruption and the country, virtue. And even the most nostalgic recognize that North London suburbs and their equivalents elsewhere are unlikely ever to be linked to the countryside by a vernacular landscape of fields, ponds, and hedges. Yet the ecologically minded do feel a bond with those in the past who saw value in what has been called the "unofficial countryside"—the marshes and fens, the unmown and untrimmed verges and edges of the urban environment where nonhuman life often flourishes.[54]

11
The Environment of Leisure

These be thy wonders, O Steam! And so let the shades of
Fuller, and Watt, and the genius of Stephenson and his competitors, be properly revered and appreciated, for thus, as
'twere, so far annihilating time and space, and promoting
social intercourse, civilization, and a speedy retreat from the
plodding cares and cankering toils of commerce, trade, and
labour!

J. S., A Guide to Southport, 1849

Genuinely rural places all but disappeared from most Victorian cities;
Yet they remained close at hand and available to visitors from the cities
they surrounded. Elizabeth Gaskell begins *Mary Barton*—her close observation of Manchester working-class life in the early 1840s—by taking us outside the city along a public footpath to Green Heys Fields, an
easy half-hour walk. We are joined by a group of "merry and sometimes
loud-talking" factory girls and "numbers of boys, or rather young men,"
out for a ramble and ready to treat the girls to their "noisy wit or ob-
streperous compliments." It is toward evening in early May. Perhaps the
masters have granted a half-holiday, or perhaps these young people have
seized a holiday "in right of nature," the day being so mild and the "young
green leaves" fluttering into life. It is too early in the year and late in the
day for "the country business of hay-making, ploughing," but towns-
men know that at other times they will be able to stand and watch "such
pleasant mysteries."[1] (See Figure 8.)

Gaskell does not tell us how the villagers received these visitors from
an alien world or how they felt when boisterous shouts shattered "the
delicious sounds of rural life." No doubt the tensions were considerably

greater outside the realm of fiction, even before the advent of day trippers and excursion trains. When that time did arrive, the demands of leisure began to make a larger claim on the countryside. Therefore it is remarkable that from the beginning to the end of the Victorian and Edwardian eras, a constantly readjusting compromise could be maintained between the demands of sustenance, amenity, and recreation.

Steam boats and trains made formerly remote beaches, heaths, moorlands, mountainsides, and valleys easily available to urban populations. Believing recreation in natural surroundings to be the best antidote to city-induced moral and physical malaise, reformers organized themselves to bring urban workers and their families into contact with bracing salt air, green nature, and rural tranquillity. Rising real incomes and a modest relaxation of work discipline permitted a popular tourist industry to develop. Tourism taught a widening circle of people to appreciate the beauties of the countryside for its own sake.

While popular tourism was developing, so too was apprehension about its effect on the rural environment. The urban multitudes might need nature's sweet lore, but what would become of fresh valleys and mountain solitudes if tourists in great numbers were given easy access to them?

Doubts about finding a solution to that dilemma surfaced even before factories and societies began organizing steamboat and railway excursions. In the 1830s Dr. Kay-Shuttleworth testified that "the whole population of Manchester is without any season of recreation and is ignorant of all amusements, excepting that small portion which frequents the theatre." [2] This was an exaggeration. Decades before railways reached the coastline in the 1840s, textile workers from Lancashire towns walked or came by the cartload to Blackpool, Lytham, and Southport on warm Sundays and "darkened" the beaches. [3] As early as the 1820s, weekend excursionists were leaving London by sailing vessel and paddle steamer for Margate, the Thanet resorts, Gravesend, and Richmond. Steam packets brought 650,000 clerks and artisan families to Gravesend in 1835. [4] Four years before the railway reached Brighton, Thomas Creevey was complaining that "the crowd of unknown human beings" pouring down from London by coach was becoming unendurable. [5] But if the era of popular excursions began in the 1820s, it is certainly true that the railway system, developed in spurts of energy during the early Victorian years, made the family, works, church, chapel, or club excursion part of urban working-class and lower-middle-class cultures.

Nevertheless, until the last quarter of the century, it was the patron-

age of middle- and upper-class vacationers that had the main transforming effect on the leisure environment.[6] Rapid though the change was from
elite travel to popular tourism, it was not until the interwar years of the
twentieth century that mass recreation and the modern leisure industry
fully developed. Long working hours, low wages, the slowness of the paid
holiday to become common practice, still tied a great many Victorians
and Edwardians to home, workplace, and neighborhood streets.[7]

There were, however, enough city dwellers with leisure time and the
means to enjoy it by the 1860s to distress nature lovers and cause them
to issue warnings about the threat popular tourism posed for the land
and landscape. By then middle- and upper-class anxiety about a possible
Chartist revolution had died away. The sigh of relief from London's
West End had been almost palpable when workingmen and their families, arriving by the trainload in London to visit the Crystal Palace Exhibition of 1851, had proved to be good-humored and orderly. But evidence
that a mobile populace was unlikely to promote riot and revolution
failed to reassure those who feared for their tranquil refuges. In the Lake
District, one Ambleside resident remarked: "[A] great steam monster
ploughs up our lake and disgorges multitudes upon the pier. . . . our hills
are darkened by swarms of tourists; our lawns are picnicked upon twenty
at a time, and our trees branded with initial letters."[8] Excursion trains,
recalled an upper-class woman about her once-serene Derbyshire valley,

> used to vomit forth at Easter and in Whitsun week, throngs of mill hands of
> the period, cads and their flames, tawdry, blowsy, noisy, drunken . . . tearing
> through the fields like swarms of devastating locusts, and dragging the fern
> and hawthorn boughs they had torn down in the dust, ending the lovely spring
> day in pot houses, drinking gin and bitters, or heavy ales by the quart, and
> tumbling pell-mell into the night train, roaring music hall choruses; sodden,
> tipsy, yelling, loathsome creatures, such as make the monkey look a king, and
> the newt seem an angel beside humanity—exact semblance and emblem of
> the vulgarity of the age.[9]

So dim a view was not, of course, shared by all. Hugh Shimmin, a mid-
Victorian journalist who wrote a number of books about Liverpool life,
made a distinction between the *Lumpen* element of "Cottonopolis" with
its preference for the Saturday night spree down at the local pub and the
"Sunday guzzle," and the respectables, those "swarthy and hard-handed
labourers, decently clad, with their wives, children, or sweethearts," who
were gradually expanding their recreational orbits with trips to places
like the Isle of Man, intent on enjoying its creeks and romantic glens. He
expressed regret that "our rulers" seemed content to abuse the "drinker"

and ignore the "thinker" when they should be searching for ways to promote a taste for "enjoyment without vice" among the new consumers of
recreational facilities.[10]

But what might be the erosive effects of feet, hoofs, or wheels on moorland vegetation, rural footpaths, coastal dunes, forest tracks, or mountain trails if the urban populace did develop that taste? Since every user
left a trace, the wearing effect of large numbers on the most attractive or
archaeologically or historically interesting sites threatened eventually to
degrade such places, thus lessening their appeal and weakening some of
the incentives to maintain or protect, especially in a climate friendly to
private enterprise.[11] Here was a dilemma that no amount of education
in how to enjoy nature was likely to solve.

That large numbers of tourists could be major morphological agents
would have been obvious to anyone who troubled to look. A particularly conspicuous example of their capacity to alter details of local landscapes would have been apparent, for example, on Snowdon, Britain's
highest mountain, once called Eryi because of its eagles' nests. Snowdonia, the region around this glacier-sculpted peak in Caernarvonshire,
North Wales, is a rugged expanse of rough grasslands, kept free of underbrush by grazing cattle and sheep and crossed by stone walls, sharp-
edged ridges, and steep-sided valleys. Travelers have been drawn to the
beauty of this place since at least the time of John Leland's journeys in the
1530s.[12] Most who came, especially in the late eighteenth and nineteenth
centuries, felt obliged to climb to the mountain's 3,560 foot main summit or be hauled up by ponies. When Dr. Johnson passed through in
1774, he recognized no such duty. "Above is inaccessible altitude, below
is horrible profundity," he observed.[13] "Fag End of Creation; the very rubbish of Noah's Flood!" snorted an equally unimpressed contemporary.[14]

However, by 1831, a year after a steam packet service brought tourists within close range, the top of Snowdon had become almost too accessible, especially for those who had come with hopes of experiencing
the sublime. The Rev. John Parker noted in that year, "there is no place
more public than the higher ground of Eryi during the summer." When
George Barrow paid a visit a decade after railway connections were established in the 1850s, he remarked that, as far as his eyes could see,
other walkers, in groups or individually, were passing up and down the
paths in steady streams. At mountain top, a small walled area called
Wyddja, he recited a poem in Welsh and was rewarded with a glass by
the keeper of a crude refreshment building. It should also be noted that
while descending, his young female companion so admired what turned

out to be a rare species of plant that the young guide who had accompanied them from Llanberis clambered over a crag to pick it for her.[15]

A special attraction for hikers and rock climbers, then and now, is the ease of access provided by generations of slate quarry workers and copper ore miners who made stone surfaces for paths over which they wheeled and carried their heavy burdens or led their pack animals.[16] Commented J. G. Kohl, a German tourist, after a visit in the early 1840s: "In all direction, in this part of the country, the mountains may be seen to have been bitten into by the slate quarries." He also noted that the ponds near several copper mines next to his path of ascent "had been dyed green by the metal." An army engineer who was in charge of a survey team at the top told him that the last of the eagles who had nested on the mountain had recently been wiped out. Gone, too, were the vestiges of woods that once covered the steep slopes. Herds of goats had in the distant past carried out deforestation with great efficiency. That animal, Kohl wrote, had proved to be "not only a bad gardener, but also a bad farmer." Therefore he thought it fortunate that the less destructive sheep had taken over.[17]

But such an interest in the effects of direct and indirect human intervention was rare. It is doubtful that many, drawn to a place where, as Barrow remarked, "nature shows herself in her most grand and beautiful form," [18] paused, as Kohl did, to reflect that the surface texture of the landscape they were moving through owed perhaps almost as much to artifice as to the hand of nature.

Railway connections brought in tourists of a less hardy and adventurous sort than steamboats had done. Seeing an opportunity, the owner of the Llanberis slate industry built a rack-and-pinion railway in 1896, reaching from the valley floor to the summit, a distance of just under five miles. Canon Rownsley roused the forces of resistance. Why must "one of the chief glories of our country," he asked, be degraded to "the level of a tea garden"?[19] But this time the forceful Rownsley did not prevail. Soon a café next to the station at the top ensured that no tourist need endure hardship while enjoying "scenes inexpressibly grand." [20] Over the next century the number of visitors grew steadily. During one year in the early 1980s, 80,000 riders joined with 110,000 walkers, many of whom had queued near the valley parking lots to wait their turn on the trails. A decade later, nearly a half million were making the ascent each year by foot or train. One expert on park management thought the summit was in danger of becoming an "environmental disaster area," while another called it "a mass of unvegetated boulder scree." [21]

Experience had shown Victorians how the compacting effect of tread-
ing feet and the puddling effect of hoofs, especially on wet clay, could
cause steep hillsides to erode along the lines of transverse or steeply as-
cending paths. But it was not until countryside rambling began to be
popular near the turn of the century that the typical nature lover became
anxious about the wear and tear recreational use inflicted on the land.[22]
Before the advent of off-road vehicles of various kinds after the Second
World War, it is more than likely that the outpouring of urban bicyclists
and ramblers onto the hills and dales from the 1880s on did more to
strengthen support for conservation of the countryside than it did to
damage moorland and mountainside. As in the case of Snowdon, it was
the buildings and transportation facilities constructed to serve or exploit
the outdoor movement, rather than hikers and bicyclists themselves,
that had the greatest impact on the visible features of the Victorian and
Edwardian inland landscape.

Fears about the effects of steamboat and railway tourism proved to be
exaggerated; the same might be said about the hopeful expectations.
These were neatly summarized in 1861 by Thomas Cook, the pioneer of
popular tourism. In promotion material for package tours to Scotland,
he noted:

> Railways have not only revolutionised the ordinary modes of travelling, but
> have also affected most powerfully the ideas, habits and pursuits of social life.
> A quarter of a century ago, travelling for health and pleasure was a luxury
> enjoyed by only the wealthy and the privileged class; and places . . . but dis-
> tant a hundred miles or more, were known only in history.[23]

Cook rejoiced at the prospect of this transformation and invested in it.
Nevertheless, if examined soberly from the perspective of an era in which
people use automobiles for local errands, visiting, and sight-seeing, this
assessment seems overblown. Radical variation in pace was a peculiar-
ity of the Victorian and Edwardian journey. Travelers were carried from
home station to a distant destination at railway speed but, on alighting,
walked or drove slowly along streets and country lanes. In the experience of most, the new way of traveling was occasional; the older ways
were everyday. Railway time forced the pace of life, collapsed time and
space, but did so episodically. It is true that travel for health and pleasure expanded and established itself in the culture of almost every social
group and, in doing so, produced significant changes in the landscape.
Nevertheless, so long as steam drove the wheels of long-distance transport, there were limits to the ability of individuals and families to go
wherever they chose and limits to their impact on the countryside.

Qualifications need also to be made about the effect of railway tourism on habits and social attitudes. Obviously, steam technology had profound effects—a widening of horizons being one of them. Local cultures had no choice but to react to the new technology and the influx of strangers it introduced, but these receiving communities usually discovered ways to exercise control over the pace or direction of change. In 1850 Carlyle perceived that "railways have set all of the Towns of Britain a-dancing," but, as Jack Simmons has noted, each town managed to pick its own tune and dance steps.[24] The reciprocal relationship between a local culture's capacity to define itself and the imperatives of technological change are particularly clear in the case of destinations that depended on tourism and the provision of holiday attractions.

The arrival of steam packets and then steam railways caused many older inland spas to languish and coastal or scenic upland communities to flourish. Thanks to cheap fares and steam transport's comfort and speed, urbanites of moderate means began spending days, weekends, or longer holidays on ocean beaches. Those whose means were abundant could expand their leisure repertoire with train trips to some northern grouse moor or inland or coastal golf club. Steam did offer the rich and a growing number of not-so-rich travelers "speedy retreat" from "plodding cares and cankering toils." In that sense improvements in communication did spread the "habit of enjoyment" through the ranks; but, paradoxically, these improvements also furthered the segregation of leisure activities according to social class.

F. M. L. Thompson, whose research has ranged so widely over Britain's rural, suburban, and urban landscape, develops this theme. He points out how misdirected, for the time at least, were Wordsworth's fears about railways turning loose hordes of day trippers upon defenseless "Mountains, and Vales, and Floods." "The millowners of Yorkshire and Lancashire," Thompson writes,

> did indeed launch their masses by the trainload, but the trains headed for Blackpool or Scarborough; by the 1890s Bass, the Burton brewers, were sending twelve special trains, marshalled with military precision, on the annual works' outing, but the destination was Skegness. Railways, in fact, protected the Lakes by funnelling the masses to the seaside, which from his argument about working-class tastes and preferences is what Wordsworth should have expected. He was, perhaps, premature by a century in his forebodings, shooting at a target he could not have foreseen.[25]

The new technology forced diversification and expansion of services on resort communities. It also was a factor in shaping the physical arrangements of resorts. In many cases, steamboats set the pattern several decades before railways arrived. To receive the excursion boats, towns would need to construct a pier; a promenade along the beach would follow and serve as the focus for development. Rail connections expanded this development rather than directed it. Train passengers were likely to disembark from a terminus, positioned at the top of a main shopping street, leading directly to the promenade and pier.[26] Because visitors continued to arrive by sea in considerable numbers all through the century, the pier retained its original function, but added restaurants, kiosks, concert facilities, and other entertainments. It would seem, then, that steam transport tended to conserve what it did not invade. The steamboat picked up passengers at one point and deposited them at another, leaving no permanent trace of its passage. Railways further increased the mobility of holiday travelers but channeled that mobility through narrow corridors.

Seekers of gaiety and respectability alike were restrained in their mobility by the fact that nearly all of them had arrived by some form of steam-driven public transport. Having arrived, they had little choice but to make further explorations on foot. Restless souls might arrange excursions to nearby beaches, piers, promenades, and pavilions, but only rarely would they spill over to places outside the territories prescribed by walkways or special boat, train, or carriage services. For that reason, accommodations and seaside pleasures needed to be concentrated. Closely ranked hotels and boardinghouses, arranged in a thin line along the town beach or cliff, intruded only here and there into the hinterland.[27] Beyond the ends of the promenade, there might be clusters of shacks or cabins, but private "villas" tended to be placed within the resort's orbit, strung out along cliff or beach foreshore. These larger houses would be inhabited, for the most part, by wealthy families, many of whom treated the seaside town more like a long-range exurb than a resort. Since most Victorian income earners worked as close to the end of their lives as possible, it was not until the late 1920s that elderly people in large numbers began building permanent residences along the "natural and secluded buffer" zones between resorts.[28] The advent of the private motorcar, was, of course, another prerequisite, which also explains why caravans and beachside bungalows and chalets did not appear in large numbers until well after the First World War.[29]

The development of Herne Bay on the north coast of Kent shows how steam locomotion could alter an environment, but it also shows how effectively residents could exercise choice in how to respond. One would think Herne Bay's geography might have been its destiny. Within easy reach of London, it had come into being in the 1830s, when Thames steam packets began bringing passengers to that part of the coast. Growth was steady but moderate. By the end of the decade, Herne Bay's facilities included a mile-long parade, an assembly room, a pier, swimming baths, and two libraries, as well as a plentiful assortment of churches and chapels.[30] Two decades later, railways connected London and the north Kentish coast, making day trips feasible. But Herne Bay refused that option. City officials and businessmen, instead of adjusting their facilities to appeal to low-income visitors from the city, successfully fought off proposals to put on cheap excursion trains. Their object was to create a quiet atmosphere calculated to attract young middle-class families. Accordingly, when the number of visitors began to increase, they deliberately fashioned additional buildings and amenities to that end and succeeded to such an extent that the town came to be known as "Baby Bay." [31]

Entertainments on offer remained eminently quiet and respectable. Families making extended visits to this and similar white-collar seaside watering places were encouraged to spend their entire holidays in or around the grand hotels or modest boardinghouses and to use the tepid comforts they offered. A few visitors, having come unprepared for such an atmosphere, complained about the "aggressive piety" that closed down the pier on Sunday. But town spokesmen were unmoved. If tourists want "bands, gaiety, itinerant Christy Minstrelsy, and such like, they must go elsewhere," the *Herne Bay Argus* was still advising the resort's critics in 1880.[32] It was clear that in Herne Bay and most other seaside resorts the amusements on offer would only partly depend on the tastes of the clientele the railway was capable of bringing in. What social tone those in charge of development decided to promote was another, often more important, determinant.

The evolution of Southport illustrates this point particularly well. It was a ready-made destination resort, fashioned out of a vast, flat stretch of sand just south of where the Ribble estuary opens out to the Lancashire coast. Speculating on profits to be made out of the fast-growing popularity of ocean-bathing therapy in the late eighteenth century, an enterprising landlord, William "The Duke" Sutton, built a hotel, nestled among the sand dunes. Residents of Meales (later called Churchtown), a tiny hamlet nearby, referred to the project as "The Duke's Folly," and so it seemed to a number of early visitors. For years, it stood alone near the top of a wide stretch of pure sand, some twenty-three square miles in extent, reaching twenty miles south to the Crosby Channel and the mouth of the Mersey at Liverpool.

In prehistoric times a once-forested inland coastline had given way to deep layers of peat. Strong westerlies had blown sand inland, covering the peat floor. During the seventeenth century, descriptions of the region spoke of a wilderness of shifting sand dunes and undrained "moss." [33] Planting of marram or star grass along with a few pines and willows in the eighteenth and nineteenth centuries did manage to check the sand's invasion, so that the region itself was fairly stable, even though the dune area was, of course, fragile. In front of the town of Southport, which grew up around the hotel, undulating sand banks spread so far out between high- and low-water marks that it was difficult to tell where the land ended and the sea began. Between the shoreline and an older beach farther inland a line of salt marshes made a hollow or valley. At first, Southport grew in conformity to this natural configuration. But not for long.

What Sutton and especially the intertwined Hesketh and Scarisbrick families (the heads of which were the local lords of the manor) sensed was that close proximity to Liverpool and Merseyside made this seeming waste a convenient destination for jaded urbanites in search of the supposed restorative powers of sea bathing, seawater drinking, and sea air breathing. However, the family compact was not particularly keen to cater to the fluctuating holiday trade; its members were far more interested in making profits from leasing land to "cotton princes" in search of exclusive secondary residences. Therefore they laid out their sandy wastes in large plots and attracted prospective tenants by offering generous terms and guarantees that leasehold controls would be strict enough to guarantee future exclusivity. In turn, wealthy speculators, most of them nonconformists concerned with establishing a high moral tone, recognized that money could be made out of developing a holiday trade based on the resort's reputation for respectability and good taste—as people like themselves understood those terms. [34]

This correlation, not of strategies or values but of mutual interest between aristocratic landlords and the middle-class elites, brought about the rapid and purposeful development of a planned gardenlike resort. In 1814 a visitor, Richard Ayton, came across the Royal Inn and its cluster of eccentric "villas" and expressed surprise at seeing "art and taste" in such a "scene of desolation." [35] A few years later a new canal between Wigan and Manchester drew visitors and a few more settlers. Stimulated by a reputation for promiscuous mingling of bathing machines for both sexes, this town—which subsequently worked hard at becoming a "bastion of select respectability"[36]—grew and acquired, in the 1820s, its famous eighty-eight-yard-wide, straight, mile-long, tree-lined Lord Street, placed just behind, and parallel to, the shallow, marshy declivity that marked the line of the old beach. In this hollow between the new street and the new beach, which had formed farther out, builders put up a line of detached houses.

Since the natural process of sand dune formation was still at work, this site turned out to be highly volatile. Sir George Head, who included Southport in the peregrinations he undertook in the 1830s, reported that gale-driven sand was threatening to bury the gardens and lower the floors of some of these structures.[37] The resort's promoters reacted by constructing a protective wall on the strip between the hollow and the offshore dunes and then adding, as an afterthought, a wide promenade on top. Shortly afterward, in 1839, they included, among other improvements to the hollow, the Victoria Baths. Permanent and semipermanent residents along with boardinghouse and hotel proprietors were encouraged by large-scale plotting to build substantial structures over what had been marshland.

An unusual feature of this development, after railway connections with Liverpool and Manchester were made between 1848 and 1855, was the degree of control the property-owning interest managed to exercise. In 1842 Sir Peter Hesketh Fleetwood, having got into financial difficulties as a result of a project to build a new port called Fleetwood on a point of land north of Blackpool, sold his Southport holdings to his brother, the Rev. Charles Hesketh, and to Charles Scarisbrick, a wealthy landowner and entrepreneur who had been involved in an ambitious land-reclamation project at Martin Mere along the banks of the Ribble estuary. They agreed about the direction of future development and in 1846 received Parliament's permission to set up an improvements commission, controlled, of course, by themselves.

These tight reins were loosened gradually after Southport was incorporated in 1866, but, despite intense rivalry between estate trustees and town corporation, a measure of continuity, based on a determination not to become another Blackpool, was maintained. From the middle of the century to its end, a firmly organized group of developers created a garden city: a tree-lined shopping boulevard, two main residential areas plotted for villas, detached houses surrounded by flower beds and trim lawns, and a promenade that sheltered the planted spaces from the blowing sand.[38]

The American writer and diplomat Nathaniel Hawthorne, whose wife had been prescribed a lengthy dose of saltwater bathing and sea air, chose to move, with his family, into a Southport boardinghouse for ten months in 1856–57. On weekdays he commuted to his consular office in Liverpool by train ("through a most uninteresting tract of country"—"a wide monotony of level plain").[39] Southport, he wrote, was "as stupid a place as ever I lived in," adding, "it was a place where everybody seems to be a transitory guest, nobody at home." From his vantage point along the promenade, the shore "stretched out interminably seaward, a wide waste of glistening sands." But he did approve of the neat way the town was laid out and the "well-paved streets, the principal of which are enlivened with bazaars, markets, shops, hotels of various degrees, and a showy vivacity of aspect." "Except where cultivation has done its utmost," he concluded, "there is very little difference between winter and summer . . . there being nothing but a waste of sand, intermixed with plashy pools, to seaward, and a desert of sand-hillocks on the land-side."[40]

Before the Hawthornes arrived and for many decades after they departed, artifice, incrementally but radically, replaced nature. By the 1840s Southport had ceased to be a place where developers accommodated their projects to the existing conditions and topography. Promoters, planners, engineers, gardeners, and architects labored instead to refashion the site so that it would conform to the pattern of resort geography established elsewhere.[41] Shifting sand dunes became lawns and gardens; tropical plants bloomed under glass in wintertime; man-made lakes and heated baths allowed oarsmen, swimmers, and amateur sailors to ignore the weather or the condition of the sea.

The shoreline retained some of its attractions. A photograph taken in the 1930s shows the beach at Ainsdale, just to the south of Birkdale, blackened almost to the sea's edge with lines of motorcars;[42] but, of course, Victorian beaches had only human feet, donkey hoofs, and carriage and bathing-machine wheels to contend with, although in Hawthorne's day a large boat on wheels and equipped with sails, called "The Flying Dutchman," rolled up and down the beach in front of Southport whenever the wind was brisk and thrill seekers had pennies to spend. Heavy use of this kind could flatten the marram grass that fixed the dunes, but erosion did not become a matter of much concern until well into the twentieth century. As for the site of the growing city, the transformation brought about by the promenade barrier, the filling in and planting of the hollow, as well as the laying out of garden city housing developments, failed to provoke reprisals from nature, particularly since the long foreshore broke much of the force of the Irish Sea's relatively gentle waves.

Southport citizens did become concerned about a possible environmental, hence a potential economic, disaster in the 1880s when the Ribble Navigation Bill seemed to threaten the stability of the estuary and, consequently, the security of the resort's waterfront. Tidal waters reached five miles above Preston and brought cargo, off-loaded onto barges, to that cotton mill town. During the second half of the eighteenth century, the south channel through the estuary and into the Ribble shifted closer to the middle of the tidal basin, leaving a blind channel in front of the site on which Southport grew. The resort's pier therefore ended not at the open sea but at the Bog Hole, a long narrow arm in the midst of sand banks that, except at high tide, reached about eight miles across to the north side of the estuary mouth.[43] The Bog Hole was not a conspicuous landscape feature; indeed, depending on tides, Southport had more of a sandscape than a seascape. Paul Theroux, who paid a visit in the early 1980s, thought the beach resembled "a long ludicrous desert," only flatter—a "seaside resort without much sea."[44] Yet Southport really was a port in the Victorian era, and its pier received steam packets from Liverpool well into the twentieth century.

At various times in the first half of the nineteenth century, navigation companies had carried out extensive improvements: dredging, building retaining walls, and reclaiming marshland along the river just below Preston. In 1882 the Preston City Corporation, unimpressed by the results of these attempts to straighten and deepen their town's sea approaches, decided to purchase the Ribble Navigation Company. They obtained permission from Parliament to extend and deepen the channel sufficiently to bring large steamers to the Preston docks at high tide. They were also permitted to stabilize the channel banks by building an additional three and a half miles of retaining walls.

Over the next decade these works were carried out in spite of vigorous hostile lobbying by Southport landowners and developers who feared the possible consequences for the Bog Hole and the resort's sea connection.[45] A three-way tug-of-war followed between the corporation who saw the necessity for refurbishing the town's threatened seaside attractions, the Hesketh/Scarisbrick trustees who claimed ownership of the foreshore, and a group of wealthy opponents of the Ribble Naviga-

tion Bill, who were concerned about the possible effects on their investments that changes in the estuary might bring about. This last group, believing that trustee ownership would strengthen their hand in the political contest with Preston, eventually sided with the landed interest in their
successful effort to buy clear title to the land from the Duchy of Lancaster, a victory that radical land reformers everywhere greeted with angry
protest.[46]

As it turned out, these maneuvers failed to halt the rechanneling project. The consequences were not to be as dire as opponents predicted, although the refashioning of the estuary did cause some narrowing of the
blind channel leading to the pier. Dredging operations at Liverpool had
the same effect. Nevertheless, steamboats found they could still reach
the Bog Hole and unload passengers at the Southport pier.

Continued sea access did not compensate for the fact that the sea was
steadily retreating from what was supposed to be a seaside resort. The
corporation responded energetically to that challenge in 1887 by building the first of two extensive lakes and gardens just to the south of the
pier and on the inland side of the promenade. In the 1890s they added
another lake and garden north of the pier.[47] These were to make sure
that holiday makers would have places to row, sail, and bathe even if the
sea moved beyond convenient reach.

So by the century's end, well-off visitors and residents of this former
sandy waste could spend a brisk afternoon in a winter garden, stroll
through the geometry of the botanic garden or the picturesque rockery
of Paxton-designed Hesketh Park, enjoy the amenities of ornamental inland lakes, plunge into one of the six large, steam-heated seawater pools
at the Victoria Baths, immerse themselves in warm mud and afterward
be hosed down at high pressure, view a collection of ferns in the conser-
vatory of Churchtown Botanical Gardens, attend an annual flower show
almost on a par with Chelsea's, and enjoy all of this improving culture
without needing to go near or even managing to see the ocean.

Most other holiday towns had been able to exploit naturally attractive settings. Not so Southport. As a late nineteenth century guidebook
pointed out, "Nature had done for [rival resorts] what Art has had to
do for Southport."[48] Yet just to the south of this man-made bourgeois
paradise much of the duneland remained during the century in something approaching a natural state almost as far as Seaforth on the outer
edges of Liverpool's turn-of-the-century outreach. Along the whole
stretch of this part of the Lancashire coast, no seawalls or groynes were
needed.[49] Here, at any rate, a reasonably long-lasting truce seemed to

have been worked out between the contending forces of land and sea and a kind of *modus vivendi* established between nature and artifice.

Eventually, a compromise was also worked out between the holiday tastes of the various social orders. Once railways offered excursions, total middle-class exclusivity became impossible to maintain. During one week in 1855, 41,000 day trippers from Liverpool, Manchester, Salford, Preston, Wigan, and other Lancashire manufacturing towns poured into Southport. Until late in the century, planners adopted Herne Bay's tactics and did what they could to discourage this influx. But difficult economic times in the 1880s cut into revenues from the trade in holiday exclusivity and respectability, and city authorities and the interest they represented decided to remove some of the impediments they had placed in the way of the popular recreation industry and concentrate on shielding the long-term vacationers and residents from its effects. On the pier side of the central shopping and hotel district, sandwiched between the two main middle-class residential areas, they constructed a fun fair. In this smallish area could be found the entertainments in which, according to a promotional guide published in 1897, "the not too exacting holiday maker delighteth":[50] merry-go-rounds, swings, a switchback railway, a camera obscura, minstrel shows, photographic studios, donkey rides, a water chute, an aerial ride over a lake (the Maxim Flying Machine), and an Aunt Sally.[51]

On the north and south flank of villadom, city fathers eventually constructed two golf links as *cordons sanitaires* between affluent residents and the noisy day trippers and, as early as the 1890s, the especially noisy automobile racers.[52] The pier, which opened in 1860, acted as a social neutral zone. It was a cast-iron structure 1,460 yards long, the longest in the country until Southend extended its pier later in the century. In 1872 Southport's pier replaced its manually operated railway with a steam cable railway. Its waiting and refreshment rooms were patronized by everyone. Although the class recreational divide was not wide in a geographic sense, it was broad enough to allow for a fair degree of mutual tolerance (rare for seaside resorts).[53]

By the 1890s nearby Blackpool, "a very pandemonium of amusements,"[54] had gone well beyond tolerance to extend an exuberant welcome to Lancashire mill workers and their families, leaving Southport to embellish its reputation as a desirable destination mainly, although not exclusively, for the well off. For residents and visitors who had no great interest in sea bathing, sketching, or poking about in rock pools and who were easily bored by a routine of promenade and band concert, the golf course, the practice green, or perhaps a round of tennis followed by a drink at the golf club among "one's own sort" became all but indispensable.

A rush of interest on the part of the Victorian and Edwardian middle class for competitive games of skill opened up new markets for resort developers. Especially favored were those sports that promised a cluster of advantages: a degree of social exclusiveness, opportunity for social advancement and individual expression, reasonably easy access for amateurs possessing no unusual amount of skill and strength, and the capacity for being rationalized by all but the most puritanical as healthy, fresh air exercise for office-bound people with only a limited amount of "disposable time."[55] Tennis offered these attractions. But golf, as Horatio Hutchinson, an early enthusiast, pointed out, had an additional one: it was a game that an individual could enjoy alone, with only "Colonel Bogey" for an opponent.[56]

Southport was one of the first to react to the golfing boom of the later 1880s and 1890s. Its businessmen recognized that off-season golfing weekends might help the larger hotels to survive the winter doldrums.[57] The resort's first golf club opened in 1885 and another, one of the country's most prestigious, in nearby Birkdale in 1889. Two more links were laid out on land reclaimed from the foreshore of the estuary in the years just preceding the outbreak of war. One of these was owned by the municipality and open to short-term visitors; but, beyond that small concession, the rapid promotion of golf created social and physical barriers in Southport as well as in every other place where private courses and clubs were established.

Before the 1860s golf had been largely confined to "real," not "virtual," places: the river estuaries and sandy foreshores of eastern Lowland Scotland and a few rough commons in England, Ireland, and Wales. A historian of the St. Andrews Golf Club noted that a meeting was called in January 1803 to discuss what to do about a Mr. Dempster who had imported rabbits and was turning the links into a warren.[58] Eventually the players prevailed over the rabbits, but until the mid-Victorian years most golfers maneuvered their feather-stuffed leather balls around dunes, hummocks, patches of bracken or heather, and what other hazards nature happened to have provided.

The introduction of a much cheaper and more durable gutta-percha ball in the late 1840s made the game more attractive to suburbanites with ordinary skills. At the same time, railways began to offer special fares for weekend golfers and carried spectators to professional exhibitions at such famous courses as St. Andrews or Musselburgh. Again, railways acted to widen participation in what Thomas Cook called the pursuits of social life and also reacted to a trend already under way. Clubs slowly began to multiply and to construct new courses on dunes, heaths, farm-land, and woods, placed near rail connections with the major cities, within range of businessmen who were looking for ways to combine "moderate exertion with social exclusiveness." [59]

When growth in the sport's popularity radically accelerated in the 1890s, the construction of new courses increased accordingly. (See Figure 11.) Hutchinson estimated that by 1906 there were some 1,800 golf clubs, using some 1,000 courses. Those with nine holes needed a minimum of thirty to forty acres and eighteen-hole courses needed at least seventy-five. [60] Most were considerably larger. The introduction of the livelier "gutties" called for wider and longer fairways. When the even more spirited Haskell ball, made by winding rubber thread tightly around a rubber core, arrived in Britain from America in 1902, many clubs found it necessary to widen and lengthen once again, so that some courses came to occupy two or three hundred acres. Before 1914, only provisions for game shooting covered more of the recreational land surface in England and Scotland. [61]

Until the early years of the twentieth century, professional golfers or club greens keepers planned most of this construction and extension. Only a few of them did so with aesthetic considerations in mind. Being experts at the game, they tended to position hazards to punish players for making clumsy drives and approaches rather than using them to induce players to plot out a strategy. [62] The result, according to H. S. Colt, who had by the 1920s established himself as the Capability Brown of golf landscaping, was that most Victorian links were rectangular. Sod bunkers all faced the same way and were fronted with traps filled with a "dark, red sticky substance." Greens tended to be flat and squared-off; bunkers were arranged to be approached at right angles. These links, Colt thought, were unimaginative and boring: blots on the landscape, insensitive to their environments and to the social aspirations of the game's new, suburbanite recruits. [63]

Colt and such other professional designers as Willie Park Jr., J. F. Abercromby, and W. H. Fowler set out to correct this. Their dicta were: return to the notion that nature should be the guide; make an effort to disguise artifice; contrast patches of regular, green turf with a background of heather or other rough and darker vegetation and make the edges of sandy areas look as though swept by the wind; reshape harsh natural

Figure 11. Ladies' golf championship at Portrush, Ireland (1895). Enthusiasm for outdoor sport in the 1890s, shared by both sexes, added many golf courses to the landscape. Lady Margaret Scott won this and two other championships in 1895, then chose to retire as the first woman golf champion. (*Illustrated London News* 106, 1895)

features but strive to avoid the "horrible symmetrical"; and try to give the course and the clubhouse the visual values of a traditional landed estate.

When the site chosen happened to be timber, arable, or grazing land or when the desire for expensive exclusiveness clashed with popular recreational uses, protest, even sabotage, could be expected. Once land that had grown crops or supported grazing animals had been reshaped, top soil hauled in, and irrigation and drainage systems installed, its value would have risen far beyond the point where conversion back to food production could ever be feasible. Country people and residents of fishing villages understood this. Many of them were suspicious that a new course and club might be a Trojan horse containing cohorts of housing and resort developers. These premonitions were well-founded. Experience has shown that the loss of agricultural land to golf courses has tended everywhere to be permanent and that the opportunity golf offers city dwellers to enjoy exercise in a controlled, exclusive, idealized countryside must be measured against their contribution to the erosion of agricultural or fishing communities.[64] Hutchinson noted in 1911 that "many a fishing village has risen into a moderate watering-place by virtue of no other attractions than those which are offered by its golf course." [65]

Not everyone could have been expected to share the obvious pleasure he took in making that observation. Colt wrote that the two most formidable obstacles to his course constructions were "the commoners and the commonable beasts." [66] He was referring to villagers who retaliated by turning animals loose on fairways or by digging holes in awkward places. Thus at the end of the nineteenth century, a new enclosure movement again provoked clashes between traditional forms of land management and traditional "rights," only this time the expropriators came from a different social and geographic position. In the earlier period, defenders of the public right to use open spaces had evoked the ideal of consensus achieved through shared participation in outdoor activities and had attacked the landowners who they believed selfishly stood in the way of achieving this renewed sense of commonality. The rhetoric that served the cause of the Commons Preservation Society still applied in the 1890s, except that the parvenu, rather than the established group, had become the enemy.

When omnibuses, trams, suburban railways, and retail traders penetrated exclusive enclaves like Birmingham's Edgbaston and Liverpool's Everton, the local elites resisted, then decamped for greener pastures: "segregation and co-operation were replaced by conflict and departure."[67] As the older group identity conferred by place weakened and as the ranks of the middle class swelled and became more differentiated, sports clubs tended to become important social centers around which suburbanites could organize their social activities, make friends, meet eligible marriage partners, be recognized, and have their status reinforced. Attempts to make golf courses and clubhouses into replicas of country estates were responses to this widening of function. John Lowerson, who has done more than any other to place the history of golf in a social context, thought that the shift in golf course architecture from the utilitarian to the picturesque had as its object the provision of "a pseudo-gentry life-style" for socially mobile urbanites. Businessmen, professionals, their sons, and, with increasing frequency, their wives and daughters, had at their disposal (for a stiff fee) "a country house and park controlled by a committee of pseudo-yeomen who lived in the surroundings but whose use of the land was recreational rather than productive."[68]

Because this particular land use was unproductive and low intensity, golf courses could sometimes act as a refuge for wildlife. The fairways and putting greens would be grass monocultures and, from an ecological point of view, sterile. But the rough and wooded areas included in the newer kind of design protected and encouraged species diversity, especially when a course incorporated some existing countryside features and when greens keepers were not overzealous.[69] Not surprisingly, this kind of pro-exclusivity argument was seldom, perhaps never, made at the time and would not have softened antagonisms had it been.

Resentment against colonization of the countryside by suburbanites was not confined to those who used the land productively or locals who resented having their rights over common lands ignored. Organized cyclists and country ramblers frequently objected to the placement of golf courses in their paths and expressed distaste for this kind of intrusion into marshes, heathlands, and sandy stretches. At the same time that some members of the middle class were discovering the pleasures of golf and lawn tennis at seaside resorts like Southport and going home to form and join clubs, others were becoming members of the Cyclists' Touring Club, setting out for a Sunday tramp, subscribing to the *Rambler,* and taking part in one or another of the Footpath Preservation Society's campaigns to reopen blocked trails.

Late Victorian and Edwardian golfers, cyclists, and ramblers may have been alike in their enthusiasms for exercise in the fresh air of the country, but they differed radically in their conception of what the countryside should represent. According to David Rubinstein, in an article called

"Cycling in the 1890s," it was the opportunity cycle touring offered for personal mobility and freedom from convention that attracted "advanced spirits," male and female, particularly among the "fin de 'cycle'" lower-middle and upper working classes. He includes a passage from H. G. Wells's *The Wheels of Chance* where the young shop assistant hero speaks about the joys of the open road and the forests, "heathery moorland and grassy down, lush meadows," and "shining rivers" he passes through on his way to the sea.[70] Not for him or those like him the contrived landscape of the links or the elaborate rules, dress, and code of etiquette prescribed for the golfer and tennis player. Young men and women who pedaled out together from town were looking for flower-dappled meadows, quiet villages, nature clothed in innocence, release from artifice of every kind.

Even stronger was this "yearning for the rural" among ramblers, the term most often used from the 1880s for those who joined clubs to explore the countryside on foot.[71] Not everyone who joined in this tramping fellowship was moved to do so by ideology—socialist, humanist, or otherwise. Nevertheless, an interest in folk culture and local history, admiration for the arts and crafts of preindustrial times, longing for the pastoral simplicities of village life, desire for contact with natural textures, foods, sounds, and smells were strong elements in this less self-conscious British version of the German *Wandervogel* movement and its preoccupation with comradeship and close contact with folk and fatherland. Thus ramblers could become militant when golf club managers as well as proprietors of deer forests and grouse and pheasant shooting grounds, with their appetites for exclusive space, carved out picturesque settings from rough pastures or restricted access to heaths, mountains, commons, and wastes.

An instance of this tension can be found at Weybridge, in the heart of the Berkshire golf course belt. When a local club placed a chained gate across a public footpath in 1909, a thousand people gathered and forced the gate open.[72] Defenders of the game replied to this kind of protest by claiming to be model countryside conservators. They made, and still make, the point that golf courses served to protect green spaces from developers or mineral exploiters; they also claimed that the game encouraged an appreciation of landscape quality and therefore enlisted its players in the cause of landscape preservation.[73] But few conservation-minded people were convinced. It was the cyclist and the rambler, only some of whom were *Clarion* readers or had heard of *News from Nowhere,* who became the constituency for late Victorian and Edwardian conservation

and preservation causes and not, as a general rule, the weekend or seaside holiday golfer.

Rivalry between different leisure groups for the use of the countryside
became as intense as the rivalry between leisure interests and those of
agriculture, forestry, or urban development. Nevertheless, so long as the
age of steam lasted, there was still room enough for compromise and ac-
commodation. Because the bulk of passenger and freight traffic between
cities and the larger towns moved on rails rather than on paved surfaces,
cyclists had the open road largely to themselves. Walkers, carried to attractive parts of the countryside by rail, could discover the authentic rural scenery they had set out from the city to find.[74] Cheap excursion fares
and, by the 1890s, low-cost hiking and cycling clubs gave both male and
female factory, shop, and office workers access to beaches, mountains,
and heaths and, at the same time, placed some limits on the numbers
who would visit those places and wear them down.

Hardly of the countryside had been developed with recreation in
mind. Contrived show places, "counterfeits of real objects," filled with
"pseudo-events,"[75] were mainly confined to seaside resorts. Having decided on a seaside holiday, the first-class traveler could put himself in the
hands of travel specialists and decamp with his large family and mountain of trunks and cases, confident that all would be taken care of by an
army of porters and by expert staff in hotels that looked and performed,
to use Peter Bailey's term, like "social fortresses."[76] Golfers, who needed
to plan and schedule their leisure as well as their work, could, with the
help of Bradshaws, fit a day of outdoor exercise into their busy weeks. At
their clubs they would be certain to meet people like themselves and be
secure against contact with the less-affluent leisure-consuming populace.

Whatever the defects might have been with respect to social justice
and cultural hegemony, a balance of forces did tend to protect the physical environment. The equilibrium was, however, an unstable one, having been achieved when the age of steam was nearing its end and before
rising real wages, a further expansion of leisure time, the diversification
of leisure services and forms, changes in the social climate, the widening
of democracy, the advent of the motor bus, and, after that, the triumph
of the private automobile—all of these interacting—released the full
force of mass leisure upon the land and the seashore.

12

The Hungry Ocean

When I have seen the hungry ocean gain
Advantage on the kingdom of the shore,
And the firm soil win of the wat'ry main,
Increasing store with loss, and loss with store . . .
Shakespeare, Sonnet 64

Toward the end of the Victorian period, it was becoming apparent to those who cared to notice that the concentration of so much of the new recreation industry at coastal destinations was interfering with the self-correcting capacity of wind and wave. One kind of balance—among the various demands on the agricultural countryside—seemed to have been achieved by placing in jeopardy another balance, one that nature had established on the margins. Meanwhile, advances made in dredging technology and the construction industry were making it increasingly profitable to undermine beach sand and shingle. At a time when Britons were beginning to find their isolation from the rest of Europe less and less "splendid," some geographers and geologists among them were issuing warnings that the defenses around the "kingdom of the shore" were being undermined. Thus, on a number of levels, concern was growing about the integrity of the ramparts guarding the British Isles.

Earlier specialists on shoreline geography had been comforted by the thought that the forces of nature could usually be relied on to rebuild what they tore down. Writing in 1831, the noted geologist Henry De la Beche developed the theme that artificial interventions in the form of built barriers or pumps and dredges were not vital to winning this war of attrition: that there were natural restraints on the ocean's capacity to inflict damage on the solid earth. Where coastlines had ample supplies of sand

and shingle, he noted, the waves breaking on the shore tended to "pile up barriers against themselves." He explained that the crash of shingle-filled waves during a storm causes sand and pebbles to mound up just beyond the break line, creating a barricade against future onslaughts. Storm waves take sand out to sea, then calm waves slowly bring the sand back, thus restoring the normal beach slope and preparing the shore for the next onslaught.

De la Beche offered Chesil Bank on the Dorset coast as a particularly striking illustration of this "strategy" of advance and retreat. There, pounding waves had gradually raised a sixteen-mile-long shingle bank to a height, in places, of fifteen feet. Storm waves, loaded with small quartz pebbles, had also created Slapton Sands by crashing on the beach. This shingle bar, stretching some six miles along the Devon coast from Start Bay, had preserved the mouth of five valleys for centuries. Ferocious winds had broken through the sands in November of 1824 and filled a freshwater lagoon behind with brine. But then, De la Beche noted, the sea had immediately set about the task of repairing the beach, assisted on this occasion by a few bags of pebbles carted in by people who wished to preserve the lake fishery.[1]

Assured by the thought that the ocean itself was the best protection against its own destructive force, writers on agricultural matters directed public attention in the early and mid-Victorian years to projects aimed at reclaiming farmland from the sea. Not surprisingly, enthusiasm for such reclamation diminished when the fortunes of agriculture began to wane in the 1870s. Engineers then tended to concentrate attention on developing technology for safeguarding valuable resort property.

Essential to that task was an understanding of what takes place when an artificial barrier interferes with natural checks on coastal erosion. Knowledge about these matters had been accumulating,[2] although a leading authority on seacoast engineering at the turn of the century, W. H. Wheeler, commented in 1902 that in no branch of his profession "is there so little unanimity of opinion, or in which so much money is from time to time expended on works that are useless."[3] He found it puzzling that a sea-girt kingdom had contributed so little to the science of oceanography or to knowledge about processes of erosion and accretion, Dutch, Danish, German, and French specialists having made most of the advances in theory and practice. Furthermore, what had been learned about the action of wave, tide, and current had not, he believed, been communicated to those public authorities most directly concerned with coastal matters.

Wheeler had in mind the projects undertaken by seaside resorts to shield their frontages. His book *The Sea-Coast* is filled with instances where, in the "fight between the sea and the land," victory had gone, not to the resort promoters, but to the waves. The difficulty was that groynes (barriers reaching from high-tide line down to low waterline), piers, jetties, and walls tended to starve downwind beaches. As one contemporary put it, engineers employed to shore up a stretch of resort beach seemed willing "to rob Peter to pay Paul." Building a pier at Storeham had deprived Hove and Brighton of their shingle supplies, and Dover had suffered when Folkstone, "a principal delinquent," got its pier.[4] Nine feet of shingle had once protected the beach at Hove. Then the town built a seawall, and within a year severe scouring had removed the entire stock. Dredges had to be brought in to replace the supply and prevent the wall from collapsing. Concrete walls at Sandgate, Seaforth, and Poole produced the same effect. Bridlington's sea bulwarks endangered thirty-four miles of the already fragile Holderness coast. Digging and dredging shingle for cement aggravated erosion at Lyme Regis and cost the Essex town of Walton, between 1874 and 1906, fifty-six acres of land.

Evidence of this sort kept accumulating, so that by the turn of the century seaside residents had become aware that they were being asked to make some sacrifices for technological progress.[5] Commented a member of the British Association in 1885, "as respects groynes there is hardly a watering place on our Southern coast where they have not become a burning *rexata quaestio* of the day."[6]

But the most unfortunate results of engineering interventions were to be found, Wheeler thought, at Blackpool. There promoters had experimented with a variety of protective devices. Their first step was to construct a rough stone footing to keep the sea away from the cliffs. This led to a rapid denudation of shingle: when scouring deepened the water in front of the parapet, wave action grew stronger. Engineers responded by taking shingle from the beach to repair the wall and by digging the foundations lower; but they managed, in the process, to remove all material along the frontage down to the clay base. To make matters worse, in the mid-1840s railway builders were busy assisting the force of the waves by carting away loads of beach material to construct a line from Poulton to Blackpool.

The conclusion Wheeler wanted his readers to draw from this debacle was that intervention into the natural processes of denudation and accretion was bound to be risky and should only be undertaken to safeguard crucial natural barriers like Spurn Point at the mouth of the Humber or

to stabilize unprotected beaches in front of the new resorts where wave
action might be ruinous. Always, he advised coastal engineers, be sure to
factor in the inevitable, sometimes remote, environmental consequences.[7]

Wheeler's warnings coincided with a growing sense from the mid-
1880s and through the period of international tension during and after
the Boer War that "strife is always raging" along the edges of "our island home."[8] Journalists, politicians, and engineers expressed fears that
the island itself might be shrinking, both physically and figuratively.
They acknowledged that preventive measures had actually aided the enemy as often as not. It was time, they thought, for island residents to reconsider their situation. In earlier days Britons had been able to think of
their coastline as "the enclosing walls of a garden";[9] perhaps it had become appropriate now to think of the seashore as a bastion under siege.

This apprehension became more widely felt when Germany began to
challenge the Royal Navy's rule over the waves. In 1902 a Canadian-
born journalist named Beckles Willson published a book called *Lost England* in which he warned that "Old Ocean" was advancing against the
land. This advance, he thought, prefigured an erosion in the political and
moral fabric of the nation. It seemed as though Neptune, once Britain's
ally, was no longer willing to play that role, but had determined instead
to sweep away "into the insatiable salt flood," the "green verge of the
realm."[10] Overheated rhetoric of this sort was by no means rare. A sense
of beleaguered isolation and physical vulnerability entered into nearly
every form of discourse. Several years later, a magazine article entitled
"Crumbling of the Coasts—Vanishing England" speculated in verse that
by the time the Germans were ready to invade, they might discover that

> The coast line had vanished, the cliffs with a crash
> Had yielded to billows that bellow and bash;
> And afloat far away where the whales wallow free
> Was the last bit of Britain that fell in the sea.[11]

In 1904 an engineering journal made the point more soberly. It claimed
that "in the perennial struggle between sea and land, the frontiers of England are being continuously pushed back" and called for the kind of
national mobilization already under way in continental Europe.[12] Two
years later, the *Tribune* in London warned that the sea was breaking
down the coastline and "threatening to steal whole villages under the
very eyes of the nation that boasts itself its ruler." The editorial concluded by urging that the national government follow the example of

France, Italy, and Belgium and take responsibility for defending the realm's frontiers.[13]

The government did respond, after a fashion, by setting up a royal commission in 1906 to investigate the rate and consequences of coastal erosion. Commissioners were influenced by talk about the island in danger and presumed at the outset that the war of attrition was being lost. Thus they were surprised and, at first, skeptical when presented with some confusingly compiled statistics suggesting that England and Wales had, between 1880 and 1905, actually experienced a net gain of about 30,000 acres.[14] The commission was not reassured by this information. Members thought that the figures were distorted by the fact that most of this gain was concentrated in the area of the Wash—the large tidal basin between Norfolk and Lincolnshire.

Elsewhere, as many witnesses before the commission testified, exploitation of shoreline resources seemed to be assisting the sea in undermining the shore. To a certain extent, that had always been the case. The farmers of Devon and Cornwall gained, as the result of a license granted in 1261, the right to take sand from beaches so long as they used it to improve tillage.[15] Beaches had long been mined to supply shingle for ship's ballast as well as to provide sand for agricultural purposes: to lighten and fertilize soils and to bed cattle. Demand increased significantly from the 1840s, when railway contractors sought material for track beds. When the rail network was completed, the needs of an expanding concrete industry for sand and gravel more than took up the slack.

Concrete had been available for centuries but was not widely used in Britain. Early in the nineteenth century, several experimenters, including a Leeds bricklayer, Joseph Aspdin, developed portland cement. This invention greatly expanded concrete's versatility. Ancient builders had discovered that cement would set in water if made from carbonated lime containing a high proportion of clay. But the difficulty of obtaining natural material with the right mixture tended to limit the use of concrete in constructing harbors and sea defenses. Portland cement, so named to suggest to builders that it produced concrete the color of portland stone, was a powder matrix made from lime, silica, and aluminum heated at a high temperature. This artificial product was cheaper to make than natural cement and was harder and dried much more quickly. In 1851 I. C. Johnson set up the first mill at Frindsbury to produce an improved version of portland cement made with chalk and Medway mud.[16] Some of his products were on display at the Crystal Palace Exhibition. Within a decade or so, hydraulic concrete, a mixture of cement with sand and small stones or gravel, became an increasingly common substitute for brick and stone, particularly in massive dock works where utility was of greater importance than finish.[17]

Despite these improvements, the use of concrete did not become widespread until the 1860s at the earliest. Difficulty in manufacturing a product of standard quality seems to have been the inhibiting factor. Eventually, methods for testing quality before pouring were worked out but not until several decades after the portland cement industry had been established.[18] In 1881 Dr. Erdmenger, a German expert, contrasted the fast pace of the industry in his country with the slow progress in Britain and attributed the lag to the failure of British industrialists to employ men with scientific training in their cement works. He said that German technicians had worked out the exact chemistry of the ingredients and were thus able to adjust the mix to the requirements of a particular job while British manufacturers simply used their kilns to test quality.[19]

Nevertheless, use in Britain was sufficient by the 1880s to awaken the interest of administrators of Crown properties and those lords of manors who happened to have acquired proprietary rights to foreshores. Considerable profits could be gained from supplying materials to be mixed with hydraulic cement and used to make concrete for harbor jetties, seawalls, dockyard works, and groynes. From the 1860s what had been on many beaches almost for the taking turned into a valuable source of income—a clear illustration of how technological innovation can create property rights over resources once regarded as free or communal.[20]

Building contractors leased the mineral rights and brought in steam dredges. The consequences for the beaches and the shorelines soon became apparent. Experts on shoreline erosion sounded alarms: greed and economic development were threatening to remove the ground on which an island people stood. A spokesman for the British Association in 1885 emphasized that erosive processes had, like everything else, become more artificial than natural and blamed the precarious state of the southeast coast on the creation "of works of defence in a selfish spirit, unaccompanied by concerted action."[21]

The Royal Commission on Coast Erosion issued reports, along with testimony, in 1907, 1909, and 1911. They show how poorly the existing laws and rival agencies defended the shoreline. Asked by a commissioner whether he was aware that the removal of shingle from a beach might have effects higher up the coast or farther down, C. E. Howlett replied,

"No, I am afraid that is rather a new point to us." Howlett was the principal clerk to the Commissioners of Woods and Forests, and the "us" he referred to was his special branch, charged with protecting and exploiting Crown property along the shoreline.[22] His counterpart at the Board of Trade was aware that interference with beach materials or with their pattern of drift might have unexpected consequences but added that this awareness had really only percolated down to his department seven or eight years previously.[23]

On the same occasion, the head of the Survey Committee of the Board of Agriculture and Fisheries had great difficulty in explaining to a group of questioners the difference between a foreshore (the zone between high and low tides) and the beach area above the high-tide line.[24] It should be borne in mind, however, that testimony of this kind may reflect departmental tactics as much as ignorance, since Board of Trade officials had, with unfortunate consequences, granted a number of licenses to allow mining of building materials. Therefore they had reasons for appearing less well informed about coastline erosion than perhaps they actually were.

One instance of this danger particularly interested the commissioners in 1907. They heard a detailed story about how Sir John Jackson, a contractor, had received a license in 1896 from the Board of Trade (a body that advertised itself as the protector of the public interest in coastal matters)[25] to take shingle from a bar known as the Greenstraight in Start Bay, just offshore from the old Devon fishing village of Hallsands. It was a tiny hamlet, little changed over hundreds of years. Walter White described how, on his walk from London to Land's End in 1855, he came, late in the afternoon, to this lonely, wild-looking place where several dozen cottages stretched along recesses in the cliff above a shingle beach. In exchange for accounts of events in the Crimea, the proprietress of Hallsands' tiny London Inn agreed to put four chairs together in the parlor; on that rude bed White had slept soundly, lulled by "the solemn plunge of the surge upon the beach, not forty feet from the window."[26]

It was this shingle, which absorbed the force of the wave and kept the inn safe, that Jackson proposed to mine. His intention was to use the material to make concrete for improvements at the Admiralty's Keyham Dockyards at Devonport on Plymouth Harbour. Having received permission from one arm of government, Jackson then negotiated a contract with the Commissioners of Woods and Forests, whose sole interest seems to have been to ensure that Crown properties brought in the best possible return. Seemingly as an afterthought, commissioners did, however, include a clause requiring Jackson to refrain from doing any injury to the village of Hallsands.[27]

Steam dredging operations began in April 1897. Steam dredgers had been used, here and there, since the early years of the century. As early as 1805 a remarkable American inventor, Oliver Evans, constructed a seventeen-ton steam-propelled dredge called "Orukter Amphibolos," which trundled itself over land to the Schuylkill River in Pennsylvania and then, true to its name, turned into a stern-wheeler and paddled itself to Philadelphia.[28] Several decades later a Boulton and Watt engine attached to a windlass pulled a "spoon-and-bag" dredger along the bottom of the harbor at Sunderland, the first instance of steam-powered dredging in Britain.[29] But it was not until the last quarter of the century that sophisticated chain bucket, grapple, and suction devices capable of clawing, scooping, and sucking up huge quantities of sand, mud, and rock were employed on a large scale. (See Figure 12.)

At Hallsands, Jackson first used a bucket loader, probably of the St. Austell type, to fill barges and then brought in two suction dredges. The buckets on the first machine had more than twice the capacity of most dredges used in the 1870s; they could lift in a day what would previously have taken nearly a week. The suction dredges were even more efficient, being able to fill between them thirty-four barges in ten days. Waiting until high tide, these powerful devices moved in and stripped shingle in front of the Hallsands beach from the top down. By 1901 Jackson's company was barging away 22,000 tons a week.

Over the next four years machines scooped up 650,000 tons of shingle, lowering by fifteen feet in some place the shore in front of the steep cliff with its rock platform and nestling cottages. One hundred and fifty feet of beach above the high-water mark disappeared, carted off to be made into an artificial product and used in a place far from its origin. The rapidity of this process testifies to the devastating effect of advanced steam technology on a coastal landscape. The champions of the land in the contest against the sea had developed a potent new weapon, but, as the Hallsands example demonstrated, one that could turn against the land's defenders. "The beach went to Keyham," wrote Richard Hansford Worth, a Devonshire geologist, "and the houses to the sea."[30]

Within the first two months fishermen discovered that the wide, dry beach where they pulled up their boats was fast disappearing. Their protests brought a visit from a Board of Trade inspector who decided that the alarm was exaggerated and ruled against the fishermen. Over the

Figure 12.   Bucket-and-ladder dredging machine (1867). Constructed to cut a submerged sandbar, this dredge and others like it could also mine beaches— thus weakening natural defenses and assisting the ocean's erosive power. (*Engineering* 4, 1867)

next three years, waves reached and undermined the low seawall protecting the village. Jackson paid some compensation and put in a concrete wall; but, because there was no longer a protective beach, the result was to increase the scouring effect of the waves and to cut the ground and rock out from under the concrete.[31]

A second formal complaint brought a second inspector. At the hearing, Jackson's agent claimed that damage was due solely to natural forces. This caused one of the sufferers to remark that if such were the case, "nature has been extremely well assisted."[32] The Board of Trade this time agreed that the complainants had a case and placed restrictions on the dredging operation. In January 1902 the board decided to cancel the license, although Jackson seems to have assumed that he could still carry away sand and did so for two more years.

The dredging of shingle stopped in 1902, but the damage was already done. Wave energy, which had previously dissipated as it pushed across the gradual slope of the shingle, now struck the rock bench with full force. When there were gales, the buildings received a buffeting as well. In September of 1903 the kitchen, beer cellar, and a bedroom of the London Inn collapsed. Finally in 1917 an easterly gale gave Hallsands its coup de grâce. As two modern historical geographers have commented, its ruins "stand out as a reminder of man's folly in interfering with the natural setting of the coast."[33]

At the time, questions were asked in the press and in Parliament about why this reckless treatment of a sensitive environment had been allowed, especially since tests previously carried out by the Marine Biological Association suggested that the shingle had been deposited in much earlier geological time and was not being renewed—a conclusion Worth confirmed in a series of articles first appearing in 1904.[34] Much was said about the greed of private exploiters and the feebleness and ignorance of all levels of government, but few practical remedies were brought forward.

The North Wales seaside town of Rhyl offered another example of what Worth called "the consequence of theft." John Ellis, of Rhyl's Urban Council, described how a dredging company in the late 1870s leased the gravel deposits at the mouth of the Clwyd River from the owner of its riparian rights and took two million tons of gravel to make concrete for Liverpool's Mersey Docks. The result was that some of the supply was cut off from Rhyl's beaches. This weakened the sand spit that kept high-tide waters from inundating low-lying ground inland—including, eventually, the town's golf links.

To meet this threat to the beaches, the council paid the Commissioners of Woods and Forests, who acted as agents for the Crown—the titular owner of the foreshore, a license fee to construct groynes. These devices acted to retain the sand and shingle in front of the town but did nothing to protect the shore outside town limits. Ellis thought it patently unfair that the action of one arm of the government—the Board of Trade—should force the ratepayers of Rhyl to pay protection money to another arm—Woods and Forests—particularly since those ratepayers, after having submitted to this injustice, still found their collective livelihoods threatened. The golf links were one of the resort's major attractions. Some 25,000 summer visitors arrived annually and needed to be entertained.[35]

This statistic provides a clue to why so many coastal places began investing heavily in sea defenses from the 1870s on. Sand, shingle, and gravel were being mined from beaches to improve harbors and to make walls and groynes, partly because so many towns were responding to an expanding demand for seaside holiday facilities. Investors in those facilities called for safeguards. Paradoxically, the more the protectors removed material to build groynes and seawalls, the more protection the beaches required. As fishing villages and minor ports turned into seaside resorts, they expanded to include vulnerable stretches of shoreline previously allowed to shrink or enlarge as nature dictated. Engineers then were called in to extend the protective system. Doing so often had an adverse effect on neighboring shorelines, so more expensive protective devices were called for.

At Herne Bay, one of the places along England's coastline most affected by erosion, local officials felt themselves trapped in this seemingly endless cycle. So frustrated was Harold Ramsey, a town councillor, that he formed in 1906 the National Sea Defence Association to enlist the aid of other towns in lobbying the central government for financial assistance. Representatives from thirty-five seaside councils met in Westminster to support Ramsey and to give accounts of their efforts to secure their beaches. They complained about the unfairness of placing the burden of securing the nation's shorelines upon local ratepayers and doing so at a time when a shrinking island was supporting more and more people. T. H. Baker from Clacton-on-Sea spoke of the wholesale removal of beach material and estimated that the town, at the end of the day, had paid out £10,000 for every £100 worth of shingle carted away. Martin Cheverton-Brown of the Withernsea Urban Council warned that his town was in imminent danger of being "outflanked" by the sea. He also argued that it was entirely just to require that taxpayers from large cities pay for the protection of the "lung" resorts they repaired to in such large numbers during the holiday season.[36]

As spokesman for the Sea Defence Association, Ramsey was asked to appear before the Royal Commission on Coast Erosion. His testimony gives us a feeling for how spongy the administrative marshlands must have been. Asked about changes over the last fifty or sixty years, he gave a brief account of how a bare stretch of beach had become a seaside resort, catering to a middle-class clientele. In 1907 Herne Bay had a wintertime population of 8,500, but in the warm months the influx caused it to swell to hold 40,000. This pattern of dramatic seasonal ebb and flow had only established itself, Ramsey said, over the last fifteen years or so and had completely changed, in that short time, the town's looks and character. As the town expanded, so did concern about the fragile foreshore.[37]

Erosion had always been heavy along this part of the Kentish coast.

The cliffs were made up of loamy soil on a substrata of London clay. Not only were banks prone to slip toward the sea, but they broke down in wet weather and exposed soft debris to wave action. In 1894 a developer's tract collapsed before he had paid all of his installments. The court decided that he must continue to pay since it had been common knowledge that the cliffs were unstable when he made the purchase.[38] This was a sensible decision. Residents were all aware that their foundations were anything but firm. Records kept at Herne Bay between 1872 and 1896 showed a loss of about a thousand feet of land. North and east winds caused the beaches of the area to "travel." Before development engulfed the older core of the town, the constant coastal downdrift seems to have caused no great concern.

That changed when boarding houses and summer cottages began to appear on exposed places at either end of the beach. Speculators, buyers, everyone interested in promoting resort facilities, urged local authorities to secure these considerable investments. A sympathetic Urban District Council worked out an elaborate and expensive protective system: a series of groynes to intercept longshore drifting and hold beaches fast, a fence made of woven faggots parallel to the shore, a massive concrete breakwater at the western boundary, a strong "breastworks" at the east end, and conversion of an old oyster pier into a groyne to check the movement of the beach. At first, all seemed to go well: these measures worked as they were intended, and the areas under council control remained stable. The difficulty was that sand and shingle soon began piling up on one side of the groyne and the pier, causing severe scouring on the other side and weakening the capacity of these structures to resist battering from severe storms.[39]

But the major threat came from just outside the town's jurisdiction. Rural councils on the flanks saw no reason to ask ratepayers to finance expensive sea defenses that would benefit speculative developers from the town. Speculative developers had no wish to saddle themselves with huge expenditures, preferring instead to pass on to prospective customers the cost of securing building sites. On the western side the situation was, from the town's point of view, much worse than on the east. Interfering with lateral drift in front of the town meant that the soft cliffs would not renew those shingle beaches and sandbars that provided the cliffs with natural protection. To make matters worse, the Commissioners of Woods and Forests and officials at the Board of Trade behaved as they had done at Hallsands and Rhyl and, ignoring protests, permitted concrete manufacturers to remove quantities of sandstone from low-lying stretches of foreshore.

Everyone had someone else to blame for depriving Herne Bay of its original crescent shape, thus creating, over the years, a "misnomer." One member of the Royal Commission, however, went close to the heart of the matter when he asked Joseph Jubb, solicitor to the Herne Bay Council, this leading question: "Then it is your own prosperity that has really aggravated the problem?" Jubb had to admit that by protecting its eastern flank and safeguarding it for development, the town had injured the land farther west.[40] On the other hand, as his colleague, Councillor Ramsey, pointed out, once the process of building sea defenses began on any large stretch of coastline, resorts were obliged to respond or risk economic or even physical oblivion. Towns were only allowed to tax those who owned or leased buildings. Landowners, including those who profited by selling their beach resources, could not be forced or prevailed upon to contribute to the cost of protecting the shoreline. Ramsey reminded the commissioners that the Belgian government had recognized the domino effect of large-scale protective efforts and the responsibility for assisting with costs. He implied that if Belgium's central government was willing to spend a million pounds a year for these purposes, then Whitehall could at least consider granting subsidies to local authorities, guaranteeing loans, and providing experts to make sure that dilemmas like the one his town faced did not keep arising.[41]

In only one instance in the nineteenth century had the government departed from its laissez-faire policy: at Spurn Point on the end of a long, thin sand-and-shingle spit at the northern entrance to the Humber estuary. Being really the coming together of the Trent and the Ouse, two rivers that drain fenlands, the Humber carries a heavier burden of silt than any other river in England. Since Stuart times, land reclaimers had "warped up" the tidal marsh land by digging earthen banks, allowing spring tides to flood in, and then closing sluice gates. When the sediment had a chance to settle, the water was then allowed to escape, leaving behind up to three feet of rich mud. In three years the soil would have dried out sufficiently and lost enough of its salt content to allow for the planting of rape seed, then oats, beans, potatoes, and other root crops. On the northern shore of the estuary, Sunk Island grew in this way from an area of about nine acres to become, by 1911, part of a reclaimed area extending over more than 7,000 acres.[42] For this large expanse of man-made land, Spurn Point and its long beach acted as a "natural" groyne. Ebb tides scoured the navigable channel near the point and flood tides brought in additional shingle and sediment from the erosion of the Holderness coast to the north. The result was a fortunate balance of dynamic elements, to which human artifice contributed.[43]

Thus it was with alarm that the Admiralty learned in 1849 that individuals were removing shingle from the narrow spit at the rate of 60,000 tons annually. That year a storm forced a breach that threatened to undermine the already weakened natural barrier.[44] Arguing that to preserve the Humber as a harbor of refuge was in the national interest, a Captain Vetch laid out a plan for building fifteen groynes, the government to pay one half of the costs and those lords of the manor who would benefit, to pay the other. The Admiralty agreed to put up £10,000, and the work commenced. In 1852 the contractors asked for a further £5,000 to £6,000. The Admiralty Lords agreed, providing that Trinity House, the seaman's guild in charge of lighthouses, supervise construction and maintenance. Eleven years later, all appropriations spent and little accomplished, the government ordered the Board of Trade to take charge. This time the work was carried to a successful conclusion. Even so, an official from the Board of Trade admitted before the Royal Commission in 1907 that this success in preserving Spurn Point and its lighthouse had "starved" the coastline farther north.[45]

The lesson the Board of Trade seems to have drawn from this experience was that powers and jurisdictions were so hopelessly confused that it would be best not to encourage further direct interventions. A solicitor to the board was asked what his department might do if it discovered that a groyne it had licensed interfered with a beach farther down. He replied that, since an individual had the right to protect his property, "the effect further down does not arise"—not, one would have thought, a particularly forceful conception of the board's stated determination to protect the national interest.[46] The fact that no legislation aimed at establishing a national coastline policy appeared until the Town and Country Planning Act of 1947 shows that politicians were in no hurry about urging civil servants to more aggressive efforts.

There was a positive side to this otherwise depressing story of Victorian and Edwardian greed, apathy, myopia, confusion, and bureaucratic bumbledom. Alarm at the possibility that economic development, assisted by rapid advances in technology, might be literally undermining the British Isles at their edges did drive home to many the fact that humans, for a long time critical elements in coastline ecology, had now become the main morphological determinants.[47] Even people who had no

interest or background in geological or geographic issues were coming
to realize that the coastline landscape was, like all other landscapes, ceas-
ing to be in any sense natural. This realization served to alert groups and
individuals to the need for conservation and preservation.[48]

A refrain in the testimony heard by members of the Royal Commission on Coast Erosion was that nature had once worked out its own way
to deal with attacks from the sea but was no longer being allowed to do
so. They heard from experts that, if left alone, erosion prevented erosion
in the sense that the crumbling cliffs fed debris to starving beaches, debris that absorbed some of the sea's power to erode. Thus, as one writer
on coastlines noted, the sea "fortified the land against its own powerful
incursions."[49] Clement Reid advised the British Association that "we
should strike a balance between loss and gain before we attempt to stop
erosion."[50] Accounts from Hallsands, Rhyl, Herne Bay, and many other
places around the edges of England, Wales, Ireland, and, to a lesser extent, Scotland brought home those points in graphic detail.

At the same time, those who paid attention to the Royal Commission
hearings were reminded that the time had long gone when the shore's
protection might be left to natural forces. William Whitaker, a past president of the Geological Society, an expert on coastal geomorphology
who had spent thirty-nine years on the Geological Survey, tried to impress on his hearers that, over the course of the last hundred years, human interventions had converted a natural coastline system into an artificial one. To speak about a natural coastline was like referring to the
natural process of the Thames—forgetting that this water course, like
all the other so-called rivers of the land, had long ago become a canal.
This meant, said Whitaker, that rivers "do not do what nature would let
them; they have to do what we allow them." Similarly, "our coast is
artificially treated to a very large extent."[51] Thus he tried to impress on
his listeners that to talk about "sea erosion" confused the issue, since
much of the erosion was caused not by the sea but by industrial enterprises; by disruptions of natural drainage systems brought on by deforestation, cultivation, ditching, excavating, and paving; and by the action
of farmers in plowing or allowing animals to graze near cliffs. He thought
the great effort at constructing barriers against wave action during the
last century, although uncoordinated and piecemeal, had made the concept of "natural seacoast" a contradiction in terms.

However, Whitaker offered no comfort to those who might conclude
that, having made much of the coast into an artifact, they might as
well go ahead and "put a cast-iron band all way around." To do that,

Whitaker cautioned, would only increase the force of the waves and eventually weaken the fortress walls.[52] His counsel was to abandon the notion of "absolute protection" and to concentrate scientific knowledge and engineering experience on strategic defenses for vital harbors and town frontages, leaving the rest alone. He thought it crucial that farmers be encouraged to leave strips along cliff sides uncultivated in order to preserve the long-established natural herbage. He would prohibit the dumping over cliffs of mining and quarrying debris, rubbish, and industrial wastes and only allow beach materials to be removed where experts had done studies of sediment sources and flow patterns to determine possible consequences. How these worthy guidelines were to be implemented he did not venture to say; but at least he managed, along with others, to articulate the dangers of continued virtually unrestricted development and to suggest a set of remedies that still constitute much of the modern conservation program.

What to do about the damage already inflicted was a question that also concerned individual Victorians and led some of them to experiment with reclamation projects. The person and project most often referred to in 1907 were the earl of Leicester and his experiments on the coastline of Norfolk. Probably it was Sir Henry Rider Haggard who made sure that Lord Leicester's plantation of the Wells sand hills got as much publicity as possible. The author, who gained fame by writing the robust schoolboy classic *King Solomon's Mines*, was chosen to sit on the Royal Commission on Coast Erosion on the strength of his two-volume work about the condition of agriculture. In *Rural England* Haggard had described a visit he made to the earl's Holkham estate, where he inspected progress being made in planting a variety of pines to help fix the shifting dunes of the estate's ocean frontage. He made sure that passages describing his visit were included in the appendix to the commission's report.[53]

Haggard was impressed by the fact that trees, planted in sand and shingle, had provided an environment where lichens, then marram grass and St. John's wort, had been able to establish themselves. These plants had generated sufficient soil to allow the pines to reseed. As a result, the 300 acres of plantation had become self-sustaining. Having held up this experiment as a model, he must have been disconcerted when Lord Leicester's agent, J. M. Wood, testified at the commission hearings that the plantations had little to do with safeguarding the beach; that they inhibited growth of the marram grass that did fix the dunes; that they offered little prospect of becoming commercially viable, and that they had proved to be a costly, although amusing and attractive, hobby.[54]

The earl of Leicester was only one in a long line of aristocratic coastline reclamationists. As in the case of experiments in planting on industrial and mining wasteland, it had been landlords—Lord Palmerston was one of them—who had made the first attempts to win back dunes and marshes from the sea.[55] Some did so as a speculative venture, but usually the motive was to improve the appearance of estates. Others, like the proprietors adjoining the Culbin Sands, struggled to save properties from encroachments.

No region offered a greater challenge to reclaimers than this long expanse of blowing, shifting sand stretching northwest along the south coast of Scotland's Moray Firth from the Highland town of Nairn and Findhorn Bay. According to a seventeenth century map, the village or barony of Culbin (or *Cowbin*) stood on a peninsula in the middle of the coastal area until a great storm in 1694 blew most of it away. The reason a once-productive estate had crumbled so quickly was that generations of gatherers had removed the marram grass that grew wild on the dunes and used it for thatching and for weaving baskets and mats—or so the Scottish Parliament assumed when it subsequently passed an act prohibiting the harvesting of plants whose roots anchored coastal sands.[56]

For the next 230 years, most of Culbin remained a constantly shifting waste; but, on the inner edge of its eastern side, a Mr. Grant of Kincorth decided in 1839 to plant pines and several varieties of deciduous trees to shelter his house from the blowing grit. Shortly afterward, a neighbor on Findhorn Bay began planting marram to fix the dunes and prepare for tree planting.

These attempts proving successful, other plantations were made on the Dalvey estate near the village of Kintessack, on the Brodie estate near Bankhead, and on the Moy estate near the river Findham. During the Second World War, the trees that grew on these estates, being sufficiently dense and healthy, were harvested; but, as H. L. Edlin points out, it was obvious by the time the Forestry Commission began acquiring them (between 1921 and 1956) that uncoordinated efforts by a handful of landlords could never hold back the constantly building and drifting mass.[57]

Eventually the commission did manage to turn Culbin Sands into Culbin Forest—one of Britain's most important reclamation projects. This feat seems to have been beyond Victorian or Edwardian will and perhaps capacity. Even so, the nineteenth century did make contributions to reclamation technology. The most significant was the possibility of applying discoveries made by botanists and biologists. Among the first to do so was Lord Montagu of Beaulieu, whose training as a steam engineer and passion for internal combustion engines made him, like the third duke of Sutherland, an uncommon aristocrat. He described to the Royal Commission how his experiments with imported rice grass, which spread and propagated under water, had made dry land out of the mud flats of Southampton Water. On reading reports of this testimony, J. M. Wood, the Holkham agent, asked to be sent a hamper of the grass and set about planting the species along the muddy sections of the estate coastline.[58] Thus, in the decade before the guns of August sounded in 1914, there were signs that some subjects of the kingdom of the shore might be working out peaceful and "natural" reclamation methods.

But in 1949, hostilities intensified between the two rivals on the edge of Southampton Water. Esso decided to expand its refinery site at Fawley, partly on land reclaimed from the nearby salt marsh. Soon the new supertankers began bringing in Near East crude. These huge ships needed room to maneuver. Facilities had to be constructed nearby to store the quantities of off-loaded oil, and later, as the fashion for enormous carriers spread, to store chemicals, ores, coal, and grain. Industries and power stations gathered nearby to use or process what was being imported and stockpiled. So dredges set to work bringing up muck from harbor floors and depositing it along the soft estuary shores. Wetlands retreated at Southampton and at other harbors as ports around the world were expanded or created specifically to serve the new transport technology. This "gigantism" prevailed on the coastline until the mid-1970s, when Britain and other advanced industrial countries began scaling down heavy industry and when environmental damage reports began reaching the public through the media.[59]

What is left of Britain's coastal wetland, its "last commons," now seems reasonably safe from that line of assault. But new technologies aimed at harnessing or controlling tidal energy along with continuing recreational demands on coastlines make it probable that any truce will be fragile.[60] In the meantime, environmentally conscious people search for less bellicose language to describe border tensions between land and sea and labor to convince policy makers that firm soil does not necessarily "win" when it manages to wrest store from the wat'ry main.

Conclusion

An England motor mad will destroy faster than an England
steam-mill mad or an England railway mad.

J. L. Hammond,
The Growth of Common Enjoyment, *1933*

In the late 1960s and early 1970s, when the modern environmental movement was beginning to attract the attention of a wide spectrum of people,
the American anthropologist Roy Rappaport published the results of his
investigations into the ecosystem of the Tsembaga, a self-contained tribal
society living in the central highlands of New Guinea. The two hundred
or so people of this community engaged in subsistence farming, using
simple tools. Rappaport noted that everyone was intimately attuned to
natural process since the whole community shared in the labor of "swid-
dening." This was an ancient agricultural practice involving the clearing
of spaces in the tropical forest's secondary growth, planting an intricate
intermingling of the many species and varieties of plants required to supply what the culture deemed necessary, then moving on after one or two
harvests to another place and allowing the forest to restore itself—until
the next visitation, perhaps twenty-five years later. Immediate experience
taught the utility of preserving seedlings that sprouted in the clearings.
Workers seemed to have recognized that these tiny trees, although competitors with the crop plants, promised the forest's eventual return once
farming activities ceased, thus ensuring the thin soil's future productivity. As these seedlings became saplings, they made the weeding more laborious and encouraged farmers to move on before they had an opportunity seriously to deplete the soil. The economic organization was simple,
but the ecosystem was highly complex. Rituals, especially those involving
the periodic sacrificial slaughter of pigs, also acted as restraints on over-

use of the land and helped to maintain what Rappaport believed to be a self-correcting or homeostatic social and ecological system. In this tropical forest, still remote from advanced or even advancing industrial societies, people successfully extracted a healthy living from the land without exhausting the reservoir of energy in the local biomass.[1]

According to Rappaport's model, the great historical discontinuity between this way of working and relating to nature and the methods and attitudes of modern industrial societies occurred when entrepreneurs tapped and widely applied the reserves of energy in fossil fuels. This power source freed machines from dependency on the inconstant forces of wind, stream, and muscle. Steam provided high-speed transport and communications to link localities with distant markets; in time, petroleum provided faster and more flexible services as well as abundant supplies of synthetics for managing plant growth. As steam or hydraulic turbines, electric motors, and internal combustion engines replaced conventional steam machinery, the process of specialization in production and management advanced further, and local ecosystems became increasingly simplified and responsive to complex and highly organized world markets. Inexorably, material goods and information flowed from less to more highly organized systems. Formerly self-contained ecosystems began to lose their normal self-corrective capacities: monoculture, with its artificial additives, endangered or eliminated one species after another and degraded the soil to the point where its productivity and stability came to depend on importations from outside.

Increase in the scale and complexity of technological systems encouraged further increases; these increases and the diffusion of technology to new areas encouraged centralization of management; this centralized management encouraged the development of implements and techniques whose performances were predictable and therefore responsive to central management. People came to associate this process, and the steady increase in energy consumption that accompanied it, with progress and the good life. At the same time, many of them felt a growing sense of anxiety about losing personal or local autonomy. They began to suspect that the forward march of material civilization was leading to future environmental disaster.

Reviewers immediately criticized Rappaport's functionalism, with its supposedly untestable "Panglossian" assumption that, in nonindustrial societies, every institution, ritual, and method worked to ensure harmony between individuals and groups and between human beings and nature. These commentators questioned the implied message that, in civilizations where muscle and energy from plants got the work done, simple tools and agricultural methods were effective restraints on tendencies to waste or deplete. George Perkins Marsh, among others, had demonstrated how ancient peoples, similarly equipped, had managed to turn forests into deserts.

Also, as time went on, ecologists began to raise doubts about the equilibrium thesis on which Rappaport had relied. This model, critics pointed out, assumed, as Marsh had assumed, that an ecosystem progresses in a series of stages, each one more complex, until it reaches, at climax, a more or less homeostatic maturity. The time had come, they thought, to move on to a more flexible, dynamic, and open-ended theory that made provision for catastrophe, continuing conflict, even chaos.[2]

But these reservations have not destroyed the model's usefulness in providing a rough map for the changes Britain's physical environment underwent during the Victorian and Edwardian eras. Some of the cases already examined seem to fit important features of the framework closely, none more than the Fenland farmers who felt themselves forced by circumstances to abandon mixed farming and their reliance on manures and claying to stabilize and fertilize their light soil. They surrendered their right to decide what, where, and how much to plant and when to harvest to sugar conglomerates, corporations highly responsive to long-range, rapid transport technology and communications networks and to world commodity prices and financial institutions.

In doing so, these Fenland farmers lost much of their autonomy and, when the late winter and early spring winds swept across the level land, lost tons of their topsoil as well. Specialization made crops more vulnerable to infestation, and heavy treatments of artificial fertilizers stimulated weed growth. Into the farm flowed energy, translated into transport and processing machinery and into chemical herbicides, pesticides, and fertilizers. Energy then flowed out again, converted into commodities. These commodities went to the controlling corporation and eventually to the complex international organization the corporation responded to. In these and other ways the often unexpected effects of the "Green Revolution" in post–Second World War Asia had already been anticipated.

The Scottish Highlands went through much the same evolution. A sheep-grazing monoculture extracted nutrients from a meager store and sent them south to become cloth, tallow, chops, joints, and stews. Similarly, the advent of coastal steam service between London and Aberdeen in the mid-1820s and the arrival of the railway at midcentury motivated farmers and landowners of that region to concentrate almost exclusively

on fattening cattle for shipment to Spitalfields and later to the Caledonian Market.[3] Live meat left the Aberdeen region on steamship and train
in exchange for oil cake and soil enrichers, many of these coming from
great distances. Similar transformations were under way elsewhere along
the new lines of communication. As early as 1838, steamboats were in the
process of turning Mount's Bay into "the great spring-garden, not merely
of Cornwall, but of all England."[4] Although the simplification of the ecosystem that resulted from this concentration on grazing did not have the
same dramatic consequences as the shift to sugar beet monoculture in
some Fenland regions, many of the characteristic forms of what Rappaport calls "ecological imperialism" became evident.

The colonization of the country by the city advanced on all fronts. To
serve the interests of remote urban areas, biologically complex lakes became biologically more simplified urban reservoirs. Railway connections
between large cities and seaside resorts intensified pressures on local environments, making those localities highly dependent on rail services and
on changes in fashion and style of living among urbanites. Among those
who responded to these changes were resort promoters who began to
provide purposely built recreation facilities. Having done so, investors
in these facilities and in coastal building lots found themselves engaged
in an escalating battle with the sea. That battle proving to be expensive,
local authorities appealed for outside subsidy and a measure of outside
control.

Being the center of a world trade network, London was able to transform local environments in far-off places. Free trade policies and improved communications changed the character of foreign and domestic
lands and landscapes. New Brunswick forests were ravaged to supply
British sawmills. Fields and agricultural practices in North America and
elsewhere were also affected. "The ecological burden of English seed-
eating," writes Colin Duncan, "shifted its place of impact to the prairies
of the new world where rapacious soil-miners ripped open pristine
grasslands."[5]

At least some of the ecological impact of British power and metal production was felt at home. Until 1913 the amount of coal mined continued
to increase, at least half of it, by that date, going abroad. Miners and iron
smelters stripped away most of the plant and animal life in the Black
Country in order to exploit the reserves of energy underneath the ground
and turn it into steam, machines, tracks, and implements. Parts of Cheshire subsided so that chemical manufacturers could make alkali for city
merchants to process into cleansers for export and so that distant cot-

ton factories could manufacture shirts and underwear for sale on the world market. All of these operations could be understood as energy transfers from local to distant systems. The turning of fossil fuels into steam power facilitated these transfers. The effect was to degrade local environments and make them vulnerable to remote interests, policies, and events, while at the same time decreasing the diversity of local species and enterprises.

Nevertheless, it would be a mistake to exaggerate the transforming capacities of a technology that depended on coal and steam for much of its energy. Potent though steam machinery was in freeing exploiters from constraints on their ability to turn all phenomena into means and instruments of production, its inherent limitations curbed some of the forces it liberated. Engines that converted heat from coal directly into work had significantly less capacity to "assault" landscapes than turbine electrical generators, electric motors, or internal combustion engines. What has been claimed in the preceding chapters is that the steam era had its own dynamics.

In no place was this more apparent than in the country once described by a French observer as "un énorme tas de charbon et de fer entouré d'eau" (an enormous heap of coal and iron surrounded by water). Enthusiasts hailed the advent of the steam engine that needed no rest and was unaffected by irregularities of climate, wind velocity, and water volume. Here and there, entrepreneurs attempted to adjust methods and even topography to what seemed to them steam's infinite potential, only to discover that the resulting increased productivity came at a prohibitive cost. Agriculture, mining, and quarrying continued to rely heavily on hand tools. Those sectors as well as short-haul transport used more and more horse energy almost to the end of the century. Thus continuity could be found in most spaces and enterprises: horse-drawn barrow runs working in tandem with steam shovels, water balances lifting cut stone to the surface while steam engines pumped water from the quarry floor, horse-drawn wagons and carts contending with electrified tramcars for street space. These factors placed a limit on the extent to which the various ecosystems could be simplified, made dependent on inputs from distant places, and deprived of their self-regulating agencies. Mixed farming, rotational planting courses, the central importance of organic fertilizers, and the absence of cheap and effective herbicides and pesticides tended to keep wildlife comparatively abundant in heath, field, and hedgerow.

Reservations also need to be made about Rappaport's assumption that the "principal values" of industrial societies have been complimentary and unchanging. He contrasted the modern, dysfunctional, "positive feedback" mechanisms—belief systems that encourage innovation and exploitation—to the functional "negative feedback"—belief systems that discourage innovation and limit exploitation—found among the Tsembaga. Whether or not the "prevailing values" of modern industrial and industrializing societies are all as maladaptive as Rappaport claimed they were is a difficult question, beyond the scope of this study. But it does seem obvious that the various values usually found in industrial societies are not of a piece but are frequently contradictory and difficult to reconcile. In Victorian and Edwardian Britain, this was certainly the case. If we shift attention from present preoccupations to those of a century or a century and a half ago, and if we make an adjustment so that the camera's setting is somewhere between infinity and close up, we notice in the viewfinder a culture where "positive and negative feedback" processes contend and where no one value can be selected out as the "prevailing one."

During the so-called age of improvement, philosophers, essayists, and satirists battered away steadily at the improving impulse and its utilitarian premises. Pugin offered Gothic Revival architecture as a polemic against utilitarianism. Ruskin wanted architecture to assert the need to rediscover "wholeness of being." "Old English" and "Queen Anne" architects sought to embody in the structure and decoration of their buildings criticism of mechanization and its tendency to eliminate crafts and organic references. The Arts and Crafts movement carried this critique inside the home in the form of furniture, ornamental glass, wallpaper, fabric, and silverware. Commenting on these attempts to give physical shape to conservationist and preservationist values, Martin Wiener noted that, "in the world's first industrial nation, industrialism did not seem quite at home." That nation, he added, may have "started mankind on the 'Great Ascent'" but, about half way along on that upward course, it came to view economic growth "with suspicion and dislike." He thought that resistance to mechanization and the "aspirations to gentility" that lay behind so much antimachine sentiment helped explain why, in the later Victorian and the Edwardian years, "finance prospered while industry struggled."[6]

It would be an oversimplification to conclude that this generic conservatism, by its refusal to honor processors of raw materials and by its capacity to arouse opposition to innovators, always benefited the land. Likewise, it would be a mistake to conclude that steam-age "improvements" invariably lowered landscape values by regimenting the countryside or intruding into it with objects that were jarring and out of scale. But it seems reasonable to argue that, if considered from the perspective of an ecologist or an anthropologist of the Rappaport persuasion, behavior that Victorian "improvers" thought sentimental, romantic, tradition-bound, stupid, superstitious, feckless, arrogant, or obscurantist might be interpreted instead as a valuable cultural restraint on narrowly self-interested and ultimately self-destructive exploitation.

Among these restraints must be counted the widely shared belief that, in spite of its having become the first urban-industrial nation, Britain remained, in spirit, a lush garden or perhaps a romantic moor or heath. This identification of nation with an imagined Arcadia, in the sense of benign wilderness, animated conservationist and preservationist campaigns. These images were in the minds of their leaders when they defended treasured landscapes and did battle against, say, promoters of a tourist railway to the top of Snowdon or railway engineers intent on invading some Lake District valley. Wordsworthian "natural piety," the "sense sublime of something more deeply interfused," stirred hearts throughout the century and enriched the rhetoric of those who challenged the technocratic, anthropocentric assumption that nature was simply measurable matter, an instrument to be dominated and exploited.[7] What made nature poetry in this tradition such an effective former of attitudes, writes Margaret Drabble, was the appeal it made to a primitive animistic view of the world, a feeling that natural things and forces were infused with the Divine and possessed of a life of their own, life in which human beings, as part of nature, could, if prepared and attuned, participate and find relief from the stress brought on by constant getting and spending.[8]

From the later seventeenth century onward, the different but complimentary notion of stewardship had come to form the justifying ideology of the landed elite. According to its code, the good steward accepts that nature is not a resource to be dealt with at will but is the property of its Creator or, in its secular version, Humanity—thought of as those who once lived, are alive, or are yet to be born.[9]

The continued heavy concentration of land and mineral resource ownership in the hands of a landed elite, imbued with this ideal of how they and nature should relate, could also act as a restraint on radical specialization. Eager though so many landlords may have been to cut, dig, trench, and enrich themselves from unearned increments, the ideology they professed restrained some of them from fully accepting an industrial logic that justified stripping resources for short-term profit and leaving the resulting mess for others to deal with. Clergy preached the paternalist credo, "land has its privileges but also its responsibilities," from pulpits of parish churches across the nation; landlords celebrated it at local fêtes and sometimes put it into practice.

As for the privileges—the landscaped gardens, hunting cults, and field sports of the wealthy could be tolerated because free trade and the huge extent of formal and informal empire ensured an abundance of primary products regardless of what estate owners did with their arable soils, woods, or subsurface resources. Although this arrangement may not have promoted species diversity and landscape amenity in the colonies, it did so, or tended to do so, at home.

To assert this is not to deny that these peculiarities of Victorian and Edwardian land use and class arrangements could work against the interests of those who would further political democracy, seek a greater measure of social justice, or promote national efficiency. Modern critics who want to read landscapes as social and political texts tend to ask: what price beauty, variety, amateurism? The picturesque "traditional" landscape has been called the "Great Pastoral Con Trick," a subtle device used by the rich and powerful to disguise and legitimate their appropriation of so much of the land and the resources under it.[10]

In her *Landscape and Ideology,* Ann Bermingham looks out on the eighteenth and early nineteenth century landscape and sees paradox: landowners commissioning Brown and Repton to fashion informal and irregular parks that evoked the communal open fields while engaged, at the same time, in enclosing, privatizing, and dividing up into geometric parcels the working countryside all around. She notes that suburban developers recognized how much the rustic, with its connotations of older communal ways, appealed to middle-class clients who were leaving the city in search of quiet and privacy. Consequently, they built detached or semidetached "villas" in places like Hampstead, Denmark Hill, and Dulwich, screened them with hedges from each other, and then landscaped the whole to evoke those picturesque country parks that the urban bourgeoisie had come to associate with the natural. This "ambiguous signification," this "reversibility of signifier and signified," served, Bermingham thought, to mask and "naturalize" the expropriation of the land by private wealth and the countryside by urban interests.[11]

This is a formidable indictment. But our primary task has not been to attack, defend, or deconstruct any particular set of institutions or social attitudes but instead to ask of a mind-set or action, as Rappaport claims to have done, "How does it work?"—work, in this context, referring to the capacity to sustain ecosystems. When, for example, a property owner refused to cut short the natural life of trees or animals, that refusal could be said to "work" when it acted to preserve the variety and resilience of the natural habitat whether the impulse derived from respect for natural things as having intrinsic worth; vanity, eccentricity, indolence, soft-mindedness; or desire to appear benevolently paternalistic.[12] Similar judgments might be made about house builders who insisted on using indigenous materials and on siting and scaling their structures in conformity to the lay of the land, about farmers who stubbornly resisted advice to simplify their crop regimens by applying artificial fertilizers and using other new technologies, about workers who threatened sabotage when employers tried to introduce machinery requiring them to abandon their hand tools and adopt "unnatural" work rhythms. Such seemingly intransigent behavior, no matter what assessment one might want to make of it, was common enough to be the despair of a great many contemporary reformers and "improvement" enthusiasts.

Negative feedback, whatever the conscious or unconscious motive, was still in plentiful supply. Throughout the period when most of the energy for operating machines came from burning coal, cultural as well as physical restraints acted together to slow the pace of change and allow time to find balances between old ways and new methods. During the era of steam, Emerson's warning that "Things are in the saddle, / And ride mankind," needed to be taken seriously but did not yet need to be taken literally.

Abbreviations

AHR	*Agricultural History Review*
BPP	*British Parliamentary Papers*
EHR	*Economic History Review*
HMSO	Her Majesty's Stationery Office
HT	*History of Technology*
JE	*Journal of Ecology*
JRASE	*Journal of the Royal Agricultural Society of England*
PICE	*Proceedings of the Institution of Civil Engineers*
RC	Royal Commission
SC	Select Committee
THASS	*Transactions of the Highlands and Agricultural Society of Scotland*
TRSAS	*Transactions of the Royal Scottish Arboricultural Society*

Notes

INTRODUCTION

1. Mary Somerville, *Physical Geography,* vol. 1 (London: Murray, 1848), 1.

2. Thomas Carlyle, "Signs of the Times," in *Critical and Miscellaneous Essays,* vol. 1 (1829); included in *Thomas Carlyle's Works,* vol. 15 (London: Chapman and Hall, 1887), 474.

3. Oliver MacDonagh, "The Nineteenth Century Revolution in Government: A Reappraisal," *Historical Journal* 1 (1958): 57.

CHAPTER 1

1. Charles Turner, "Old Ruralities," in *The Collected Sonnets of Charles (Tennyson) Turner,* ed. F. B. Pinion and M. Pinion (Basingstoke: Macmillan, 1988), 168.

2. Jacquetta Hawkes, *A Land* (London: Cresset Press, 1951), 143.

3. Lewis Mumford, *Technics and Civilization* (London: Routledge and Kegan Paul, 1934), 169.

4. Ibid., 154–55. Mumford borrowed the term *paleotechnic* from Patrick Geddes to define an industrial society fueled by coal, powered by steam, and structured by iron.

5. Francis Klingender, *Art and the Industrial Revolution,* ed. and rev. Arthur Elton (Chatham: Adams and MacKay, 1968), 83, 85–86, 141, 153–56; Arthur Elton, "Art and the Industrial Revolution," introductory essay to *Art and the Industrial Revolution* (Manchester City Art Gallery, 1968), 10–12.

6. A theme in Herbert Sussman's *Victorians and the Machine* (Cambridge, Mass.: Harvard University Press, 1968).

7. Quoted in Donald Worster, ed., *The Ends of the Earth* (Cambridge: Cambridge University Press, 1988), 11.

8. P. H. Ditchfield, *Vanishing England* (London: Methuen, 1910), 3–4.

9. Colin Rosser and Christopher Harris, *The Family and Social Change,* abr. ed. (London: Routledge and Kegan Paul, 1983), 32; John Barr, *The Assault on Our Senses* (London: Methuen, 1970), 14. Max Nicholson, *The New Environmental Age* (Cambridge: Cambridge University Press, 1987), 25, writes that Victorian commercial and industrial development was "uncompromising in its materialism and in its pursuit of expansion and progress" and that these forces were so in ascendance that "the tender plant of caring for nature had to be cosseted among the more perceptive minority."

10. Sylvia Crowe, *The Landscape of Power* (London: Architectural Press, 1958), 10, comments that the legacy of dereliction inherited from Victorian industrialists "is nothing compared with the havoc we shall leave to our descendants."

11. Marion Shoard, *The Theft of the Countryside* (London: Temple Smith, 1980), 47.

12. In addition to the work by Marion Shoard, see John Blunden and Graham Turner, *Critical Countryside* (London: BBC, 1985); Nan Fairbrother, *New Lives, New Landscapes* (New York: Knopf, 1970); Michael Allaby, *The Changing Uplands* (Cheltenham: Countryside Commission, 1983).

13. J. H. Clapham, *An Economic History of Modern Britain,* vol. 2, *Free Trade and Steel, 1850–1886* (Cambridge: Cambridge University Press, 1926), 489, 498–518.

14. David Landes, *The Unbound Prometheus* (Cambridge: Cambridge University Press, 1970), 1–3.

15. "Review of the Report of the Agricultural Committee," *Journal of Steam Transport and Husbandry* (December 1833): 1–10.

16. Asa Briggs, *The Power of Steam* (Chicago: University of Chicago Press, 1982), 93.

17. Landes, *Unbound Prometheus,* 290–92. He includes a table, p. 221, indicating that, starting in 1840, when the capacity of all British steam engines in thousands of horsepower was 620, capacity nearly doubled each decade until 1880 and doubled again, to 13,700, by 1896. Stephen Hill, *The Tragedy of Technology* (London: Pluto Press, 1988), 129, thinks it was in the 1850s that industrialism, with the steam engine at its center, became "widely visible" and "penetrated the consciousness of the people": In 1800 there were 490 Watt engines at work; by the 1850s, the number of steam engines had grown to half a million. For a discussion of the difficulty in making accurate estimates, see G. N. von Tunzelmann, "Coal and Steam Power," in *Atlas of Industrializing Britain, 1780–1914,* ed. John Langton and R. J. Morris (London: Methuen, 1986), 74–79.

18. From Turner, *Collected Sonnets,* 81.

19. Joel Mokyr, *The Lever of Riches* (New York: Oxford University Press, 1990), 133–39.

20. Landes, *Unbound Prometheus,* 282, 291.

21. Ian Winship, "The Gas Engine in British Agriculture c. 1870–1925," *HT* 9 (1984): 182–83.

22. Fred Cottrell, *Energy and Society* (New York: McGraw-Hill, 1955), 81–84.

23. Bertrand Gille, *The History of Techniques,* vol. 1 (New York: Gordon and Breach, 1986), 686–88; Briggs, *Power of Steam,* 175; Richard Hills, *Power from Steam* (Cambridge: Cambridge University Press, 1989), 281–92; Witold Rybczynski, *Home* (Harmondsworth: Penguin, 1987), 148–49.

24. Eugene Ferguson, "Toward a Discipline of the History of Technology," *Technology and Culture* 15 (1974): 13–30; Angus Buchanan, "Technology and History," *Social Studies in the Sciences* 5 (1975): 489–99; R. A. Buchanan, "History of Technology in the Teaching of History," *HT* 3 (1978): 13–27; Asa Briggs, "The Imaginative Response of the Victorians to New Technology: The Case of the Railways," in *On the Move,* ed. Chris Wrigley and John Sheperd (London: Hambledon Press, 1991), 58–75.

25. Jeremy Adelman, "The Social Bases of Technical Change: Mechanization of the Wheatlands of Argentina and Canada, 1890–1914," *Comparative Studies in Society and History* 34 (1992): 271–300, shows that controlled land prices and plentiful credit encouraged immigrants to Canadian prairies to form family farms and survive by increasing land productivity through investment in machinery; while immigrants to the Pampas, denied such opportunities, became leaseholders and wage laborers on large estates with no such incentives. Colin Duncan, "Legal Protection for the Soil of England: The Spurious Context of Nineteenth-Century 'Progress'," *Agricultural History* 66 (1992): 75–94, argues that short leases discouraged farmers from investing in off-farm fertilizers and other technologies for "fine-tuning" arable husbandry to local soil conditions, particularly after 1873.

26. Nathan Rosenberg, *Perspectives on Technology* (Cambridge: Cambridge University Press, 1976), 141–210; see also the discussion of determinism in Langdon Winner, *Autonomous Technology,* chapter 2, "Engines of Change" (Cambridge, Mass.: MIT Press, 1977), 44–106.

27. Charles Singer et al., eds., *A History of Technology,* vol. 5 (Oxford: Clarendon, 1958), 625.

28. A subject explored in depth by G. N. von Tunzelmann, *Steam Power and British Industrialization to 1860* (Oxford: Clarendon, 1978); see also A. E. Musson, "Industrial Motive Power in the United Kingdom, 1800–1870," *EHR,* 2d series, 29 (1976): 415–39; Richard Hills, *Power in the Industrial Revolution* (Manchester: Manchester University Press, 1970), 93; Gerald Graham, "The Ascendency of the Sailing Ship, 1850–1885," *EHR* 9 (1956): 74–88.

29. Eugene Ferguson, "Technology and Its Impact on Society," in *Technology and Its Impact on Society,* ed. Sigvard Strandh (Stockholm: Tekniska Museet, 1979), 276.

30. Leo Marx, *The Machine in the Garden* (Cambridge, Mass.: MIT Press, 1964). For a succinct discussion of the theoretical difficulties in distinguishing between the real and the ideal, see Alan R. H. Baker, "Introduction: On Ideology and Landscape," in *Ideology and Landscape in Historical Perspective,* ed. Alan R. H. Baker and Gideon Biger (Cambridge: Cambridge University Press, 1992).

31. This point is developed and illustrated by Robert L. Thayer Jr., "Prag-

matism in Paradise: Technology and the American Landscape," *Landscape* 30 (1990): 1–11.

32. Blunden and Turner, *Critical Countryside,* 18–24.

33. For a lively discussion of the evolution and implications of that ideal, see *Landscape Meanings and Values,* ed. E. Penning-Rowsell and David Lowenthal (London: Allen and Unwin, 1986). Raymond Williams, *The Country and the City* (London: Chatto and Windus, 1973) remains a classic work on the subject.

34. George Perkins Marsh, *Man and Nature,* ed. David Lowenthal (Cambridge, Mass.: Harvard University Press, 1965), 456.

35. Winner, *Autonomous Technology,* 98.

36. In a message included in Clough Williams-Ellis, ed., *Britain and the Beast* (London: Dent, 1937), vii–viii.

37. W. G. Hoskins, *The Making of the English Landscape* (1955; 2d ed., with introduction and commentary by Henry Taylor, London: Hodder and Stoughton, 1988), 183. David Mattless, "One Man's England: W. G. Hoskins and the English Culture of Landscape," *Rural History* 4 (1993): 187–207, discusses Hoskins's hostility toward modernity and his view that history went wrong sometime in the mid–nineteenth century.

38. Foreword to John Lenihan and William Fletcher, eds., *Reclamation* (Glasgow: Blackie, 1976), vii.

39. Colin Duncan, *The Centrality of Agriculture* (Montreal and Kingston: McGill-Queen's University Press, 1996), 54; see also Richard N. Adams, *Paradoxical Harvest* (Cambridge: Cambridge University Press, 1982), 73–74.

40. Shoard, *Theft of the Countryside,* 9.

CHAPTER 2

1. George Godwin, *An Appeal to the Public, on the Subject of Railways* (London: Weale, 1837), 33. Michael Freeman, "Transport," in *Atlas of Industrializing Britain, 1780–1914,* ed. John Langton and R. J. Morris (London: Methuen, 1986), 88, 90, shows that between 1870 and 1900 "the size of the national space" had shrunk by between a quarter and a third.

2. Eric Jones, "The Environment and the Economy," in *The New Cambridge Modern History,* 13 (companion vol.), ed. Peter Burke (Cambridge: Cambridge University Press, 1979), 35–39; Richard Tucker and John Richards, "The Global Economy and Forest Clearances in the Nineteenth Century," in *Environmental History,* ed. Kendall Bailes (Lanham, Md.: University Press of America, 1985), 579–82; see also Ronald Robinson, "Introduction: Railway Imperialism," in *Railway Imperialism,* ed. Clarence Davis and Kenneth Wilburn (New York: Greenwood Press, 1991), 1–3.

3. David K. C. Jones, "Human Occupance and the Physical Environment," in *The Changing Geography of the United Kingdom,* ed. R. J. Johnson and J. C. Doornkamp (London: Methuen, 1982), 329; R. P. C. Morgan, "Soil Erosion in Britain," in *Green Britain or Industrial Wasteland?* ed. Edward Goldsmith and Nicholas Hildyard (Cambridge: Polity Press, 1986).

4. Piers Blaikie and Harold Brookfield, *Land Degradation and Society* (Lon-

don: Methuen, 1987), 101; Richard Haeuber, "Indian Forestry Policy in Two Eras: Continuity or Change?" *Environmental History Review* 17 (1993): 49–76.

5. The theme of Ramachandra Guha's *The Unquiet Woods* (Berkeley and Los Angeles: University of California Press, 1990), 28–60, 194–95; see also essays by J. F. Richards and Michelle McAlpine, by Michael Adas, and by Richard Tucker in *Global Deforestation and the Nineteenth-Century World Economy,* ed. Richard Tucker and John Richards (Durham, N.C.: Duke University Press Policy Studies, 1983).

6. Madhav Gadgil and Ramachandra Guha, *This Fissured Land* (Berkeley and Los Angeles: University of California Press, 1993), 141–45; see also Richard Tucker, "The Depletion of India's Forests under British Imperialism," in *The Ends of the Earth,* ed. Donald Worster (Cambridge: Cambridge University Press, 1988).

7. Sarah Jewitt, "Europe's 'Others'? Forestry Policy and Practices in Colonial and Postcolonial India," *Society and Space* 13 (1995): 67–90.

8. Richard Grove, *Green Imperialism* (Cambridge: Cambridge Press, 1995), 11–12, 380–473; Grove, "Colonial Conservation, Ecological Hegemony and Popular Resistance: Towards a Global Synthesis," in *Imperialism and the Natural World,* ed. John M. MacKenzie (Manchester: Manchester University Press, 1990), 15–38.

9. Raymond Bryant, "From Laissez-Faire to Scientific Forestry," *Forest and Conservation History* 33 (1994): 163, agrees that Brandis's "Minute on Forest Policy of 1855," ushered in the "dawn of scientific forestry" in British India; see also Richard Tucker, "The Forests of the Western Himalayas: The Legacy of British Colonial Administration," *Journal of Forest History* 26 (July 1982): 112–23.

10. William Schlich, "Forestry in the Colonies and in India," *Proceedings of the Royal Colonial Institute* 21 (1889–90): 196–203; Richard Tucker, "Forest Management and Imperial Politics: Thana District, Bombay, 1823–1887," *The Indian Economic and Social History Review* 16 (1979): 273–300.

11. H. J. Perkin, *The Rise of Professional Society: England since 1880* (London: Routledge, 1989).

12. John Ranlett, "'Checking Nature's Desecration': Late Victorian Environmental Organization," *Victorian Studies* 26 (1983): 198, says the founding of the CPS in 1865 was "a turning point in the public perception of society's relationship to nature."

13. P. D. Lowe, "Values and Institutions in the History of British Nature Conservation," in *Conservation in Perspective,* ed. A. Warren and F. B. Goldsmith (London: Wiley, 1983), 330–40.

14. George John Shaw-Lefevre (Lord Eversley), *English Commons and Forests: The Battle During the Last Thirty Years for Public Rights over the Commons and Forests of England and Wales* (London: Cassell, 1894), 23–25.

15. John Cantlie, *Degeneration among Londoners* (London: n.p., 1885), 24

16. Gill Chitty, "'A Great Entail',", in *Ruskin and Environment,* ed. Michael Wheeler (Manchester: Manchester University Press, 1995), 119.

17. George Perkins Marsh, *Man and Nature* (1864), ed. David Lowenthal (Cambridge, Mass.: Harvard University Press, 1965), 36.

18. Ibid., 13, 15–17.

19. Ibid., 108.

20. Marsh, *Man and Nature,* 52. Robert L. Thayer Jr., "Pragmatism in Paradise: Technology and the American Landscape," *Landscape* 30 (1990): 10, uses the phrase "an interconnected functional web of relationships."

21. Ibid., 38.

22. Ibid., 39–40.

23. Ibid., 36.

24. R. Kates, B. Turner, and W. Clark, "The Great Transformation," in *The Earth as Transformed by Human Action,* ed. B. L. Turner (Cambridge: Cambridge University Press, 1990), 3, exaggerate when they claim that *Man and Nature* "was received enthusiastically by academic and lay audiences in North America and Europe."

25. Graeme Wynn, "Pioneers, Politicians and the Conservation of Forests in Early New Zealand," *Journal of Historical Geography* 5 (1979): 171–88; Wynn, "Conservation and Society in Late Nineteenth-Century New Zealand," *The New Zealand Journal of History* 11 (1977): 124–36; Marsh, *Man and Nature,* xxii.

26. J. M. Powell, *Environmental Management in Australia, 1788–1914* (Melbourne: Oxford University Press, 1976), 59–66, 74–76.

27. Marsh, *Man and Nature,* xxii.

28. Richard Lambert (with Paul Pross), *Renewing Nature's Wealth* (Ontario Department of Lands and Forests, 1967), 158.

29. James Russell Lowell, "Marsh's 'Man and Nature'," *North American Review* 99 (1864): 20.

30. Grove, *Green,* 471, n. 287.

31. Marsh, *Man and Nature,* xxii, n. 31.

32. Ibid., xxi.

33. *Athenaeum* no. 1919 (6 August 1864): 176–77; Sir Henry Holland, "Review of 'Man and Nature' by Marsh," *Edinburgh Review* 120 (1864): 464–500.

34. David Lowenthal, *George Perkins Marsh, Versatile Vermonter* (New York: Columbia University Press, 1958), 237–38.

35. Ibid., 93; Lewis Mumford, *The Brown Decades* (New York: Harcourt, Brace, 1931), 72, stated, "Marsh was one of that group of capacious, perceptive minds who were the miracle of American scholarship before the Civil War."

36. The same tone is evident in an article, "The Natural History of Man," that he wrote much earlier for the *Quarterly Review* 86 (1849–50): 1–40, where he sets out to demonstrate that "the various races of mankind" all "derived from one single pair."

37. Holland, "Review of 'Man and Nature,'" 478.

38. Marsh, *Man and Nature,* 279.

39. Ibid., 47, n. 46.

40. Holland, "Review of 'Man and Nature,'" 500.

41. *Athenaeum* no. 1919: 176.

42. William James, in an essay written in 1895, "Is Life Worth Living?" in *Essays on Faith and Morals,* R. B. Perry's selection(New York: Longmans, Green,

1947), 11, commented on the "awful power that neither loves nor hates, but rolls all things together meaninglessly to a common doom."

43. According to Donald Worster, "The Vulnerable Earth: Toward a Planetary History," in *Ends of the Earth*, ed. Worster (Cambridge: Cambridge University Press, 1988), 7–8, Marsh's work marks the point when the tide began to turn against optimism. What Marsh saw, says Worster, "was not a nobler design emerging out of chaos but a violent ravaging of natural harmonies."

44. William Wordsworth, "Sonnet on the Projected Kendal and Windermere Railway," in *The Prose Works of William Wordsworth*, ed. W. J. B. Owen and J. W. Smyser, vol. 3 (Oxford: Clarendon Press, 1974), 339.

45. S. P. Hays, *Conservation and the Gospel of Efficiency* (Cambridge, Mass.: Harvard University Press, 1959), 123–27; see also David Lowenthal, "Conserving Nature and Antiquity," in *Man, Nature and Technology*, ed. Erik Baark and Uno Svedin (London: Macmillan, 1988), 129–30.

46. Ibid., 141; René Dubos, *The Wooing of the Earth* (New York: Scribner's, 1980), 73–74.

47. Kates, Turner, and Clark, "Great Transformation," 3–5.

48. For the effect of this discussion on the period, see Clarence Glacken, "The Ideas of the Habitable World," in *Man's Role in Changing the Face of the Earth*, ed. William Thomas (Chicago: University of Chicago Press, 1956), 80; David K. C. Jones, "Man Moulds the Landscape," *Geographical Magazine* 45 (1973): 575; Eric Brown, "Man Shapes the Earth," *Geographical Journal* 136 (1970): 74–75.

49. Holland, "Review of 'Man and Nature,'" 466. The first volume of Henry Thomas Buckle's *History of Civilization in England* appeared in 1857 and the second in 1861, a year before Buckle's death.

50. Holland, "Review of 'Man and Nature,'" 445–48. The reference is to John Evelyn (1620–1706) whose *Sylva, or a discourse of forest trees*, published exactly 200 years before *Man and Nature*, also made an argument for the crucial importance of forests and reforestation.

51. Ibid., 486.

52. Ibid., 488.

53. George Perkins Marsh, *The Earth as Modified by Human Action* (New York: Scribner, Armstrong, 1874).

54. R. L. Sherlock, *Man as a Geological Agent* (London: Witherby, 1922): an abridged version, entitled *Man's Influence on the Earth*, was published in London by the Home University Library in 1931.

55. Sherlock, *Man as Geological Agent*, p. 86; see also J. N. Jennings, "Man as a Geological Agent," *Australian Journal of Science* 28 (1966): 150.

56. BPP, 3d Report (on Afforestation) of the RC on Coast Erosion, the Reclamation of Tidal Lands, and Afforestation, vol. 14 (1911): xiv.

57. Mumford, *Brown Decades*, 75.

58. Marsh, *Man and Nature*, 53.

59. Ibid.

60. Ibid., 12–15; see also, David Lowenthal, "George Perkins Marsh on the Nature and Purpose of Geography," *Geographical Journal* 126 (1960): 413–17.

61. Kenneth R. Olwig, "Historical Geography and the Society/Nature 'Prob-

lematic': the Perspective of J. F. Schouw, G. P. Marsh, and E. Reclus," *Journal of Historical Geography* 6 (1980): 36–37; Marsh, *Man and Nature,* 13–15.

62. Olwig, "Historical Geography," 37. The quotation is from Marsh's "The Study of Nature," *The Christian Examiner* 68 (1860): 36.

63. John Passmore, *Man's Responsibility for Nature* (New York: Scribner's Sons, 1974), 24, thinks that Marsh's enduring contribution was the insight that interventions never accomplish only what they intend.

64. Marsh, *Man and Nature,* 29. According to David Lowenthal, "Awareness of Human Impacts: Changing Attitudes and Emphases," in *The Earth,* ed. Turner, 129, *Man and Nature* "unleashed no bitter debate" partly because its revolutionary ecological insights rested on a number of premises that most people found comforting. Daniel Botkin, *Discordant Harmonies* (New York: Oxford University Press, 1990), discusses Marsh's mechanical view of natural processes and his theory of equilibrium in light of modern ecological approaches: see especially, pp. 8–9, 13, 32–49, 107–8, 188–92; see also Norman Christensen, "Landscape History and Ecological Change," *Journal of Forest History,* 33 (April 1989): 116–25. Victor Ferkiss, *Nature, Technology, and Society* (New York: New York University Press, 1993), 85, maintains that for all of his concern for the environment, Marsh was a Baconian in that he rejoiced at the possibility of emancipation from nature's power.

65. Worster, ed., *Ends of the Earth,* 302.

66. Robert Ritchie, *The Farm Engineer* (Glasgow: Blackie, 1849), 70–79.

CHAPTER 3

1. T. Bedford Franklin, *Good Pastures* (Cambridge: Cambridge University Press, 1944), 24.

2. Ibid., 25–27.

3. According to L. B. Wrenn, "Cotton Gins and Cottonseed Oil Mills in the New South," *Agricultural History* 68 (1994): 232–33, the processing of cottonseed oil on a commercial scale began in New Orleans in 1855. By 1879 there were 45 cottonseed mills in the Mississippi Valley. At the industry's peak in 1914, the number had grown to 882.

4. T. Bedford Franklin, *A History of Agriculture* (London: Bell and Sons, 1948), 160.

5. F. M. L. Thompson, "The Second Agricultural Revolution, 1815–1880," *EHR,* 2d series, 21 (1968): 63–65.

6. Ibid., 67–68, 75. According to James Johnston, *Contributions to Scientific Agriculture* (Edinburgh: Blackwood, 1849), 3–5, the Agricultural Chemistry Association of Scotland began to influence enlightened Scottish farmers as early as 1842.

7. Roy Brigden, *Victorian Farms* (Marlborough: Crowood Press, 1986), 196–206; John Sheail, "Elements of Sustainable Agriculture: The UK Experience, 1840–1940," *AHR* 43 (1995): 178–92.

8. Brigden, *Victorian Farms,* 70; Richard Grove, "Coprolite Mining in Cambridgeshire," *AHR* 24 (1976): 136–43; Joan Thirsk, "Suffolk Farming in the Nineteenth Century," in *Suffolk Farming in the Nineteenth Century,* ed. J. Thirsk

and J. Imray (Ipswich: Suffolk Record Society, 1958), 24. Philip Bagwell, *The Transport Revolution* (London: Routledge, 1988), 108, notes that Britain imported 1,700 tons of guano in 1841 and 200,000 tons in 1847, when the extent of the railway system had grown to 4,000 miles.

9. Jonathan Brown and H. A. Beecham, "Arable Farming," in *The Agrarian History of England and Wales*, vol. 6, ed. G. E. Mingay (Cambridge: Cambridge University Press, 1989), 278–81; Thompson, "Second Agricultural Revolution," 68–70; *Journal of the Board of Agriculture* 13 (1906–7): 67–72; B. A. Holderness, "Agriculture and Industrialization in the Victorian Economy," in *The Victorian Countryside*, vol. 1, ed. G. E. Mingay (London: Routledge and Kegan Paul, 1981), 191–95; F. Falkner, *The Muck Manual* (London: Murray, 1843), 39, 95. According to Barbara Kerr, *Bound to the Soil* (London: Baker, 1968), 52, Dorset farmers also dug up ant hills, mixed this soil with lime, and applied it to their fields.

10. See, for example, James Archibald Cambell, "Report on the Application of Sewage," *THASS* 1 (1866): 1–20. John J. Mechi used a "hose and pipe" system on his farm; see Mechi, "The Sewage of Towns as It Affects British Agriculture," *Farmer's Magazine*, 3d series, 17 (1860): 254–55. For a modern discussion, see Nicholas Goddard, "'A Mine of Wealth'? The Victorians and the Agricultural Value of Sewage," *Journal of Historical Geography* 22 (1996): 274–90.

11. Barrow Wall, "The Agriculture of Pembrokeshire," *JRASE*, 2d series, 23 (1887): 82–94.

12. Augustus Voelcker, "On the Commercial Value of Artificial Manures," *JRASE* 23 (1862): 277–78.

13. E. L. Jones, *Agriculture and the Industrial Revolution* (Oxford: Blackwell, 1974), 191–99.

14. Rowland Prothero [Lord Ernle], *English Farming Past and Present* (London: Longmans, 1912), 370.

15. Paul A. David, "The Landscape and the Machine: Technical Interrelatedness, Land Tenure and the Mechanization of the Corn Harvest in Victorian Britain," in *Essays on a Mature Economy: Britain after 1840*, ed. Donald McCloskey (Princeton: Princeton University Press, 1971), 145–214. Mark Overton, "Agriculture," in *Atlas of Industrializing Britain, 1780–1914*, ed. John Langton and R. J. Morris (London: Methuen, 1986), 36, estimates that between 1840 and 1900, output per worker rose by about seventy percent, some of this gain due to the use of steam-powered threshing machines but also the result of improvements in plows and horse-pulled machinery.

16. H. V. Massingham, introduction to H. E. Bates et al., *The English Countryside* (London: Batsford, 1939), 4–8.

17. Robert Allen, "Agriculture and the Industrial Revolution," in *The Economic History of Britain Since 1700*, 2d ed., vol. 1, ed. Roderick Floud and Donald McCloskey (Cambridge: Cambridge University Press, 1994), 114.

18. C. K. Harley, "Skilled Labour and the Choice of Technique in Edwardian Industry," *Explorations in Economic History* 11 (1974): 391–414.

19. Norman Gash, *Aristocracy and People* (Cambridge, Mass.: Harvard University Press, 1979), 321.

20. J. R. Walton, "A Study in the Diffusion of Agricultural Machinery in the

Nineteenth Century," Research Paper no. 5, School of Geography, Oxford (1973), 8, includes a chart showing adoption curves for various implements between 1820 and 1880.

21. E. J. Collins, "The Age of Machinery," in *Victorian Countryside,* vol. 1, ed. Mingay, 211–12.

22. David H. Morgan, *Harvesters and Harvesting, 1840–1900* (London: Croom Helm, 1982), 15–19.

23. Hugh Prince, "Victorian Rural Landscapes," in *Victorian Countryside,* vol. 1, ed. Mingay, 18; W. Harwood Long, "The Development of Mechanization in English Farming," *AHR* 11 (1963): 15–26.

24. Ian Carter, *Farmlife in Northeast Scotland, 1840–1914* (Edinburgh: Donald, 1979), 88–90.

25. Prothero [Ernle], *English Farming,* 372.

26. E. J. Collins, "The Diffusion of the Threshing Machine in Britain, 1790–1880," *Tools and Tillage* 2 (1972): 19–20; John Weller, *The History of the Farmstead* (London: Faber and Faber, 1982), 156.

27. Lord Willoughby de Eresby, *Ploughing by Steam* (London: Ridgway, 1850). His California plow and apparatus required seven men to operate and one man and a horse to haul coal and water for the engine.

28. Clark C. Spence, *God Speed the Plow* (Urbana, Ill.: University of Illinois Press, 1960), 105–34; David Grigg, *English Agriculture* (Oxford: Blackwell, 1989), 149–66; Brigden, *Victorian Farms,* 153–58; Bagwell, *Transport Revolution,* 131–32.

29. Jonathan Brown and H. A. Beecham, "Implements and Machines," in *Agrarian History,* vol. 6, ed. Mingay, 307.

30. T. Barker, "The Transport Revolution from 1770 in Retrospect," in *On the Move,* ed. Chris Wrigley and John Sheperd (London: Hambledon Press, 1991), 5–7.

31. Richard Moore-Colyer, "Aspects of Horse Breeding and the Supply of Horses in Victorian Britain," *AHR* 43 (1955): 47, 58.

32. Grigg, *English Agriculture,* 150; F. M. L. Thompson, "Nineteenth Century Horse Sense," *EHR,* 2d series, 29 (1976): 60–79; "Basic Slag," *Journal of the Board of Agriculture* 13 (April 1906–March 1907): 347.

33. J. A. Scott Watson and May Hobbs, *Great Farmers* (London: Selwyn & Blount, 1937), 90–100.

34. John J. Mechi, *A Lecture on British Agriculture* (London: Longmans, 1852), 15.

35. Ibid., 14.

36. John J. Mechi, *How I Make Farming Pay* (London: 1875), 5.

37. Ibid.

38. Mechi, *Lecture on British Agriculture,* 25.

39. Ibid., 27–28.

40. John J. Mechi, *A Series of Letters on Agricultural Improvement* (London: Longmans, 1845), introduction.

41. Léonce de Lavergne [Guilhaud], *The Rural Economy of England, Scotland, and Ireland,* trans. "A Scottish Farmer" (Edinburgh: Blackwood, 1855),

221–23; see also Stuart Macdonald, "Model Farms," in *Victorian Countryside,* vol. 1, ed. Mingay, 220–22.

42. H. Rider Haggard, *Rural England,* vol. 1 (London: Longmans, 1902), 528.

43. John Prout, *Profitable Clay Farming under a Just System of Tenant Right,* 3d ed. (London: Stanford, 1881), 7–36, 81. A second generation of the Prout-Voelcker team, W. A. Prout and John Voelcker, "Continuous corn growing in its practical and chemical aspects," *JRASE* 66 (1905): 47–51, reported that in 1905, the soil showed a net gain in phosphoric acid and potash and no loss of nitrogen, but it did lose some of its vegetable matter.

44. Prout, *Profitable Clay Farming,* 85–89.

45. Prout, who seems to have been far more concerned about the feasibility of using technology than Mechi, eventually sold his steam tackle and hired contractors to do the steam cultivating; see W. A. Prout and John Voelcker, "Continuous Corn Growing," 39.

46. According to E. J. Collins, "Harvest Technology and Labour Supply in Britain, 1790–1870," *EHR* 22 (1969): 453–73, improved hand tools, not mechanization, allowed a shrinking labor force to bring in harvests with increasing speed and efficiency; but see also J. A. Perkins, "Harvest Technology and Labour Supply in Lincolnshire and the East Riding of Yorkshire, 1750–1850," *Tools and Tillage* 3 (1976–1977): 47–58, 125–35. According to Jonathan Brown, *Agriculture in England* (Manchester: Manchester University Press, 1987), 25–26, mostly horse-drawn machines harvested twenty-five percent of the English corn crop in 1871 and eighty percent in 1900.

47. Christabel Orwin, *Progress in English Farming Systems* (Oxford: Clarendon, 1930), iii—"A Specialist in Arable Farming," 7–24, and iv—"Another Departure in Plough Farming," 5, 14–16.

48. According to David Grigg, "Farm Size in England and Wales, from Early Victorian Times to the Present," *AHR* 35 (1987): 188, there was a reversal in this trend in the 1880s. Robert Allen, "Labor Productivity and Farm Size in English Agriculture before Mechanization: Reply to Clark," *Explorations in Economic History* 28 (1991): 478–92, argues that from the early eighteenth century to the early nineteenth the average open-field farm of the south Midlands grew from 65 to 145 acres and that this increase "reduced agricultural employment and boosted output per worker to record levels."

49. Prince, "Victorian Rural Landscapes," 18, 21.

50. Ibid., 7.

51. Lavergne, *Rural,* 2–14. Why British agriculture should have been more innovative is a question Lavergne avoids. For a recent (revisionist) analysis, see Colin Duncan, *The Centrality of Agriculture* (Montreal and Kingston: McGill-Queen's University Press, 1996), 55–80.

52. J. A. Scott Watson, "English Agriculture in 1850–51," *JRASE* 111 (1950): 9–24; James Caird, *English Agriculture in 1850–51* (1852; 2d ed., New York: Kelly Reprints, 1967).

53. David Howell, "Farming in South-East Wales, 1840–1880," in *Modern South Wales: Essays in Economic History,* ed. Colin Baber and L. J. Williams (Cardiff: University of Wales Press, 1986), 82–95.

54. J. Geraint Jenkins, "Technological Improvement and Social Change in South Cardiganshire," *AHR* 13 (1965): 94–103.

55. Malcolm Gray, "The Regions and Their Issues: Scotland," in *Victorian Countryside*, vol. 1, ed. Mingay, 82–84; J. A. Symon, *Scottish Farming* (Edinburgh: Oliver and Boyd, 1959), 178–80.

56. E. L. Jones, *The Development of English Agriculture, 1815–1873* (London: Macmillan, 1968), 21.

57. The theme of two articles by Albert Pell, "The Making of the Land in England: A Retrospect," *JRASE*, 2d series, 23 (1887): 355–74, and "The Making of the Land of England: A Second Retrospect," *JRASE*, 3d series, 10 (1899): 136–41.

58. F. M. L. Thompson, *English Landed Society in the Nineteenth Century* (London: Routledge and Kegan Paul, 1963), 245–56; Thompson, "Free Trade and the Land," in *Victorian Countryside*, vol. 1, ed. Mingay, 109; J. V. Beckett, *The East Midlands from A.D. 1000* (Harlow: Longman, 1988), 207–8; P. J. Perry, *British Farming in the Great Depression, 1870–1914* (Newton Abbot: David and Charles, 1974), 19–20, 65–66, 123–25, 142–45; J. D. Chambers and G. E. Mingay, *The Agricultural Revolution, 1750–1880* (London: Batsford, 1966), 167–68; Jones, *Development,* 30; David Cannadine, *Aspects of Aristocracy* (New Haven: Yale University Press, 1994), 47–48; Richard N. Adams, *Paradoxical Harvest* (Cambridge: Cambridge University Press, 1982), 73–74.

59. J. L. van Zanden, "The First Green Revolution: the Growth of Production and Productivity in European Agriculture, 1870–1914," *EHR* 44 (1991): 215–39; Brown, *Agriculture,* 55–56.

60. Prothero [Ernle], *English Farming,* 380, 384.

61. T. W. Fletcher, "The Great Depression of English Agriculture, 1873–1896," *EHR,* 2d series, 13 (1960–1961): 417–32; Fletcher, "Lancashire Livestock Farming during the Great Depression," *AHR* 9 (1961): 17–42.

62. J. T. Coppock, "The Changing Face of England: 1850 circa 1900," in *A New Historical Geography of England,* ed. H. C. Darby (Cambridge: Cambridge University Press, 1973), 615–18.

63. Gray, "Regions and Their Issues," in *Victorian Countryside,* vol. 1, ed. Mingay, 83, 90–92.

64. Carter, *Farmlife in Northeast Scotland,* 76–85.

65. David Howell, *Land and People in Nineteenth-Century Wales* (London: Routledge and Kegan Paul, 1977), 2–18.

66. Peter Hall, "England circa 1900," in *New Historical Geography,* ed. Darby, 691–92. Overton, "Agriculture," 48, notes that statistics show that between 1873 and 1911, the area devoted to market gardens grew by an "astonishing" 145 percent—probably, he adds, an underestimate.

67. Ibid., 690–94; William Bear, "Flower and Fruit Farming in England," parts 1 and 2, *JRASE,* 3d series, 9 (1898): 286–316, 512–50, and part 3, *JRASE* 10 (1899): 267–313; E. A. Pratt, *The Transition in Agriculture* (London: Murray, 1906), 8–228; Linda Crust, "William Paddison: Marsh Farmer and Survivor of the Agricultural Depression, 1873–96," *AHR* 43 (1995): 193–204.

68. Fletcher, "Great Depression," 432.

69. E. J. Collins, "Agriculture and Conservation in England: An Historical

Overview, 1880–1939," *JRASE* 146 (1985): 38, 44–45; Prince, "Victorian Rural Landscapes," 24.

70. Muriel Arbor, "Dust-Storms in the Fenland Round Ely," *Geography* 31 (1946): 23–26.

71. H. C. Darby, *The Draining of the Fens*, 2d ed. (Cambridge: Cambridge University Press, 1956), 178.

72. Ibid., 225.

73. Darby, *Draining of the Fens*, 229–31; the photograph is opposite p. 245.

74. Oliver Rackham, *The History of the Countryside* (London: Dent, 1986), 379; Michael Weale, ed., *Environmental Issues*, 3d ed. (Ely: Ely Resources Centre, 1974), 24.

75. Although the definition of *marl* was never precise, the word was usually applied to clay that had a high calcareous content: see, W. M. Mathew, "Marling in British Agriculture: A Case of Partial Identity," *AHR* 41 (1993): 97–103.

76. J. A. Clarke, *Fen Sketches* (1852), 244–45, cited in Darby, *Draining of the Fens*, 239.

77. Mathew, "Marling in British Agriculture," 106–9.

78. Christabel Orwin and Edith Whetham, *History of British Agriculture, 1846–1914* (London: Longmans Green, 1964), 272, 352–53; Grigg, *English Agriculture*, 203–4.

79. Mathew, "Marling in British Agriculture," 109–10.

80. Arbor, "Dust-Storms in the Fenland," 25–26; A. D. Hall, "The Growth of Sugar Beets," *Journal of the Board of Agriculture* 11 (1904–5): 577–81; Sidney Rogerson, *Both Sides of the Road* (London: Collins, 1949), 93–97.

81. Franklin, *Good Pastures*, 68–70.

CHAPTER 4

1. George Perkins Marsh, *Man and Nature*, ed. David Lowenthal (Cambridge, Mass.: Harvard University Press, 1965), 13.

2. Ibid., 38

3. Robin Atthill, *Old Mendip* (London: David and Charles, 1964), 48–53.

4. John Billingsley, *A General View of the Agriculture of Somerset* (London: W. Smith, 1797), 34–61.

5. Ibid., 83.

6. Ibid., 45.

7. John Watson, "On Reclaiming Heath Land," *JRASE* 6 (1845): 79.

8. Michael Williams, "The Enclosure and Reclamation of the Mendip Hills, 1770–1870," *AHR* 19 (1971): 65–81.

9. Thomas Dyke Acland, "On the Farming of Somersetshire," *JRASE* 11 (1850): 727–29; see also Acland, *The Farming of Somersetshire* (London: Murray, 1851), 9–15.

10. W. G. Hall, ed., *Man and the Mendips* (Mendip Society, 1971), 8, 37–44.

11. *Hansard's Parliamentary Debates*, 4th series, 2 (1892): 101.

12. Roy Millward and Adrian Robinson, *Upland Britain* (Newton Abbot: David and Charles, 1980), 136–45.

13. Robert Dodgshon, "The Origins of Traditional Field Systems," in *The Making of the Scottish Countryside,* ed. Martin Parry and T. R. Slater (London: Croom Helm, 1980), 76–81, and Ian Whyte and Kathleen Whyte, *The Changing Scottish Landscape* (London: Routledge, 1991), 55–58, give clear presentations of this model.

14. J. M. Linsay, "Forestry and Agriculture in the Scottish Highlands, 1700–1850: A Problem in Estate Management," *AHR* 25 (1977): 25; R. Alun Roberts, "Ecology of Human Occupation and Land Use in Snowdonia," *JE* 47 (1959): 317–23.

15. Albert Bil, "Transhumance Economy, Setting and Settlement in Highland Perthshire," *Scottish Geographical Magazine* 105 (1989): 158–67.

16. R. V. Birnie and P. D. Hulme, "Overgrazing of Peatland Vegetation in Scotland," *Scottish Geographical Magazine* 106 (1990): 28–36; S. A. Grant, L. Torvell, H. K. Smith, D. E. Suckling, T. D. Forbes, and J. Hodgson, "Comparative Studies of Diet Selection by Sheep and Cattle: Blanket Bog and Heather Moor," *JE* 75 (1987): 947–60; P. Anderson and D. W. Yalden, "Increased Sheep Numbers and the Loss of Heather Moorland in the Peak District, England," *Biological Conservation* 20 (1981): 195–213; C. H. Gimingham, *Ecology of Heathlands* (London: Chapman and Hall, 1972), 171; Gimingham, *An Introduction to Heathland Ecology* (Edinburgh: Oliver and Boyd, 1975), 82–84.

17. R. Evans, "Erosion in England and Wales—The Present Key to the Past," in *Past and Present Soil Erosion,* ed. Martin Bell and John Boardman (Oxford: Oxbow Books, 1992), 53–54; Margaret Bower, "The Cause of Erosion in Blanket Peat Bogs," *Scottish Geographical Magazine* 78 (1962): 33–43. J. Geikie, the leading Victorian authority on the subject, attributed moorland erosion to climate, as the title of his article indicates: "On the buried forests and peat deposits of Scotland and changes in climate which they indicate," *Transactions of the Royal Society, Edinburgh* 24 (1866): 363–84.

18. Richard Muir and Nina Muir, *Fields* (London: Macmillan, 1989), 106.

19. Robert Dodgshon, "Ecological Basis of Highland Peasant Farming," in *The Cultural Landscape: Past, Present, and Future,* ed. Hilary Birks, H. J. Birks, Peter Kaland, and Dagfinn Moe (Cambridge: Cambridge University Press, 1988), 140–50.

20. David Turnock, "North Morar: The Improving Movement on a West Highland Estate," *Scottish Geographical Magazine* 85 (1969): 17–30; T. C. Smout, *A History of the Scottish People, 1560–1830* (London: Collins, 1969), 349–51.

21. A conclusion E. Wyllie Fenton came to in "The Influence of Sheep on the Vegetation of Hill Grazings in Scotland," *JE* 25 (1937): 429.

22. Hugh Miller, *Sutherland as it Was and Is or, How a County May be Ruined* (Edinburgh: Johnstone, 1843), 6.

23. Robert Dodgshon, "The Economy of Sheep Farming in the Southern Upland during the Age of Improvement, 1750–1833," *EHR* 29 (1976): 555–56.

24. *BPP,* RC on Agriculture, 17 (1881): q. 37, 697.

25. James Hunter, "Sheep and Deer: Highland Sheep Farming, 1850–1900," *Northern Scotland* 1 (1973): 199–201.

26. Gimingham, *Ecology of Heathlands*, 178–80.

27. A. C. Imeson, "Heather Burning and Soil Erosion on the North Yorkshire Moors," *Journal of Applied Ecology* 8 (1971): 537–42; Oliver Rackham, *The History of the Countryside* (London: Dent, 1986), 320–22.

28. Gimingham, *Introduction to Heathland Ecology*, 10–12, 100.

29. George Malcolm and Aymer Maxwell, *Grouse and Grouse Moors* (London: Black, 1910), 62–63; R. N. Millman, *The Making of the Scottish Landscape* (London: Batsford, 1975), 134.

30. The military language is borrowed from Alex Watt, "Bracken Versus Heather, A Study in Plant Sociology," *JE* 43 (1955): 490–506.

31. Marjorie Sykes, "Bracken: Friend or Foe?" *Ecologist* 17 (1987): 241–42.

32. Millman, *Making of the Scottish Landscape*, 134; Hunter, "Sheep and Deer," 203–5.

33. Rackham, *History of the Countryside*, 319.

34. Charles Gay Roberts, "Sutherland Reclamation," *JRASE* 15 (1879): 444.

35. Ibid., 444–48.

36. James Macdonald, "On the Agriculture of the County of Sutherland," *THASS*, 4th series, 12 (1880): 76–85; P. T. Wheeler, "Land Ownership and the Crofting System in Sutherland since 1800," *AHR* 14 (1966): 46.

37. Macdonald, "Agriculture of the County of Sutherland," 28.

38. Eric Richards, "An Anatomy of the Sutherland Fortune: Income, Consumption, Investments and Returns, 1780–1880," *Business History* 21 (1979): 70.

39. Charles Kindleberger, *Economic Growth in France and Britain, 1851–1950* (Cambridge, Mass.: Harvard University Press, 1964), 155.

40. C. S. Orwin, *The Reclamation of Exmoor Forest* (London: Oxford University Press, 1929), 34–39.

41. Colin Tyler and John Haining, *Ploughing by Steam* (Bath: Ashgrove Press, 1985), 94–98.

42. Michael Lane, *The Story of the Steam Plough Works* (London: Northgate Publishing, 1980), 93.

43. Tyler and Haining, *Ploughing by Steam*, 273–75; "Steam Cultivation," *Engineering* 18 (July 1874): 94–95.

44. Roberts, "Sutherland Reclamation," 409.

45. John Prebble, *The Highland Clearances* (Harmondsworth: Penguin, 1969), 65–68.

46. Macdonald, "Agriculture of the County of Sutherland," 47.

47. George Malcolm, *Deer Forests* (Edinburgh: Douglas, 1890), 21–22.

48. Roberts, "Sutherland Reclamation," 486–87.

49. Willie Orr, *Deer Forests, Landlords, and Crofters* (Edinburgh: John Donald, 1982), 31.

50. Ibid., appendix vii, 191–210.

51. L. Dudley Stamp, *The Land of Britain: Its Use and Misuse.* (London: Longmans, Green, 1948), 165.

52. Thomas Johnston, quoted in *Forbidden Land*, by Tom Stephenson (Manchester: Manchester University Press, 1989), 119. F. M. L. Thompson, *The Rise*

of Respectable Society (London: Fontana, 1988), 268, points out that "the vast majority of deer forests were still owned by the aristocracy at the end of the century," and that most of those aristocrats were Scots.

53. James Winter, *Robert Lowe* (Toronto: University of Toronto Press, 1976), 61–63.

54. Malcolm and Maxwell, *Grouse and Grouse Moors,* 23, 36.

55. See, for example, Philip Gaskell, *Morvern Transformed* (Cambridge: Cambridge University Press, 1968), 109; Hunter, "Sheep and Deer," 213–14; H. L. Wallace, J. E. Good, and T. G. Williams, "The Effects of Afforestation on Upland Plant Communities: An Application of the British National Vegetation Classification," *Journal of Applied Ecology* 29 (1992): 180–94.

56. Orr, *Deer Forests,* 37–44; Stephenson, *Forbidden Land,* 124–27.

57. Anthony Trollope, *The Duke's Children* (1880, reprint, London: Oxford University Press, 1954), 301.

58. *Hansard's Parliamentary Debates,* 4th series, 2 (1892): 93–111.

59. Ibid., 116–17.

60. Stephenson, *Forbidden Land,* 120–41.

61. T. Bedford Franklin, *A History of Scottish Farming* (London: Nelson and Sons, 1952), 169.

62. Léonce de Lavergne [Guilhaud], *The Rural Economy of England, Scotland, and Ireland,* trans. "A Scottish Farmer" (Edinburgh: Blackwood, 1855), 338–39.

63. Marion Shoard, *This Land Is Our Land* (London: Paladin, 1987), 288–89.

64. Howard Hills, *Freedom to Roam* (Ashbourne: Moorland Publishing, 1980), 44–48. Allaby, *Changing,* 66–67, states: "Grouse shooting is by far the most potent force for the maintenance of extensive tracts of heather moorland."

65. Shoard, *This Land Is Our Land,* 269.

66. Orr, *Deer Forests,* 146.

67. Hunter, "Sheep and Deer," 220–22.

68. John Stirling-Maxwell, "Forestry in the Economic Development of Scotland," *TRSAS* 27 (1913): 161–71.

69. Linsay, "Forestry and Agriculture in the Scottish Highlands," 35.

70. Orr, *Deer Forests,* 83.

71. Turnock, "North Morar."

72. Millward and Robinson, *Upland Britain,* 49.

73. *Builder* 35 (1877): 21.

74. Rackham, *History of the Countryside,* 318.

75. The *Independent* (10 March 1995), 11.

CHAPTER 5

1. Chandos Bruce [Marquess of Ailesbury], *A History of Savernake Forest* (Devizes: Charles Woodward, 1962), 82.

2. Ibid., 83–86.

3. Stephen Daniels, "The Political Iconography of Woodland in Later Geor-

gian England," in *The Iconography of Landscape,* ed. Denis Cosgrove and Stephen Daniels (Cambridge: Cambridge University Press, 1988), 45.

4. Bruce, *History of Savernake Forest,* 86.

5. Ibid., 87–92; Peggy Walvin, *Savernake Forest* (Cheltenham: privately printed, 1976), 35–36.

6. Chandos Bruce [Marquess of Ailesbury], *The Wardens of Savernake Forest* (London: Routledge and Kegan Paul, 1949), 301–2.

7. Bruce, *History of Savernake Forest,* 92.

8. Ibid.; Bruce, *Wardens of Savernake Forest,* 315–29.

9. Bruce, *Wardens of Savernake Forest,* 334.

10. Bruce, *History of Savernake Forest,* 94–96; Walvin, *Savernake Forest,* 39.

11. A coppice is a wood where mainly broad-leaved trees grow out of the stumps or "stools" left from previous cuttings. Standards are trees intended for timber and allowed to grow to maturity, planted within a coppice.

12. F. T. Evans, "Wood Since the Industrial Revolution: A Strategic Retreat?" *HT* 7 (1982): 47, points out that armored ships until the 1890s usually had hardwood planks behind the armor.

13. Victorians did not always make this distinction between the terms *arboriculture* and *silviculture* (then usually spelled *sylviculture*); some tended to use *arboriculture* for any systematic forestry aimed at maximizing utility, whether or not the plantation was conceived of as a collection of individual trees or an abstract unit. However, when comparing continental practices with their own, they usually had this distinction in mind.

14. Roger Miles, *Forestry in the English Landscape* (London: Faber and Faber, 1967), 42.

15. Reprinted in *TRSAS* 22 (1909): 97–103.

16. A. C. Forbes, *English Estate Forestry* (London: Arnold, 1904), 30. Evans, "Wood," 40, notes that, according to a Forestry Commission census in 1924, fewer than half of Britain's three million acres of woodland were reasonably productive, and 27 percent produced nothing.

17. John Croumbie Brown, *Modern Forest Economy* (Edinburgh: Oliver and Boyd, 1884), 1–2; Richard Grove, "Origins of Western Environmentalism," *Scientific American* 267 (July 1992): 46, comments on Brown's career.

18. James Brown, *The Forester* (Edinburgh: Blackwood and Sons, 1847; 2d ed., 1851); subsequent page references are to the 2d ed.

19. Ibid., 10.

20. Ibid., 6–11.

21. John Simpson, *The New Forestry* (Sheffield: Pawson and Brailsford, 1900), 7–13, thought that there was no chance that British forestry could be put on a rational basis unless the conflict between silviculture and game preserving could be resolved.

22. H. L. Edlin, *Trees, Woods, and Man,* 3d revised ed. (London: Collins, 1970), 120–21; Miles, *Forestry in the English Landscape,* 47; Eoin Neeson, *A History of Irish Forestry* (Dublin: Lilliput Press, 1991), 139; William Addison, *Portrait of Epping Forest* (London: Hale, 1977), 43; N. D. G. James, *A History of English Forestry* (Oxford: Blackwell, 1981), 190–91; William Linnard,

Welsh Woods and Forests: History and Utilization (Cardiff: National Museum of Wales, 1982), 141, 145; Colin Tubbs, *The New Forest: An Ecological History* (Newton Abbot: David and Charles, 1968), 193–96.

23. Forbes, *English Estate Forestry,* 35.

24. John Simpson, *British Woods and their Owners* (Sheffield: Pawson and Brailsford, 1909), 11, 32.

25. A. C. Forbes, "Is British Forestry Progressive?" *TRSAS* 15 (1898): 44–45.

26. James, *History of English Forestry,* 176–77.

27. Brown, *Forester,* 1–3.

28. Madhav Gadgil and Ramachandra Guha, *This Fissured Land* (Berkeley and Los Angeles: University of California Press, 1993), 118–19.

29. R. W. Phipps, "Across the Watershed of Eastern Ontario" [from a section of his "Report on Forestry," 1884], *Journal of Forest History* (9 October 1965): 4–8. Robert Bell, "The Forests of Canada," *British Association for the Advancement of Science* 54 (1884): 856–60, described the explosive effect ("almost incredible") of fire where gummy tops of conifers were left to accumulate and dry out; see also George Perkins Marsh, *Man and Nature,* ed. David Lowenthal (Cambridge, Mass.: Harvard University Press, 1965), 233–35.

30. Three works focus on the impact of resource exploitation on New Brunswick's political, social, and economic institutions: Graeme Wynn, *Timber Colony, A Historical Geography of Early Nineteenth Century New Brunswick* (Toronto: University of Toronto Press, 1981); Arthur Lower, *Great Britain's Woodyard: British North America and the Timber Trade, 1763–1867* (Montreal and Kingston: McGill-Queen's University Press, 1973); R. Peter Gillis and Thomas Roach, *Lost Initiatives* (New York: Greenwood Press, 1986). For the ecological effects of resource exploitation on the eastern United States, see William Cronon's pioneering work, *Changes in the Land: Indians, Colonists, and the Ecology of New England* (New York: Hill and Wang, 1983), including the bibliographical essay, and Jamie Eves, "Shrunk to a Comparative Rivulet: Deforestation, Stream Flow, and Rural Milling in Nineteenth Century Maine," *Technology and Culture* 33 (1992):38–65. Alfred Crosby, *Ecological Imperialism* (Cambridge: Cambridge University Press, 1986), provides a broad survey of the effects of European biological imperialism from 900–1900; see also the articles in Richard Tucker and John Richards, eds., *Global Deforestation and the Nineteenth-Century World Economy* (Durham, N.C.: Duke University Press Policy Studies, 1983).

31. Barrie Trinder, ed., *Industrial Archaeology* (Oxford: Blackwell, 1992), 668.

32. Richard C. Davis, ed., *Encyclopedia of American Forest and Conservation History,* vol. 1 (New York: Macmillan, 1983), 350–61; Peter Rutledge, "Steam Power for Loggers," *Journal of Forest History* 14 (April 1970): 18–29; Ken Drushka, *Working in the Woods* (Madeira Park, B.C.: Harbour Publishing, 1992), 61–73.

33. Miles, *Forestry in the English Landscape,* 59.

34. Or so Lord Lovat, Chairman of the Forestry Commission, maintained: *Times* (8 July 1920), 11.

35. Christopher Hussey, *The Picturesque* (London: Putnam's Sons, 1927), 36, 141.

36. John Ruskin, "The Poetry of Architecture," (1837–38), in *The Works of John Ruskin*, vol. 1, ed. E. T. Cook and Alexander Wedderburn (London: Allen, 1903), 102–3.

37. *Times* (17 September 1920), 9.

38. Daniels, "Political," 51; anyone familiar with Daniels's work will notice how much this section owes to his discussion of woodland as political iconography.

39. John Grigor, *Arboriculture*, 2d ed. (Edinburgh: Oliphant, Anderson and Ferrier, 1881), 208–10; Edlin, *Trees Woods, and Man*, 119; Mark Anderson, *A History of Scottish Forestry*, vol. 1 (London: Nelson, 1967), 585–94; A. C. O'Dell and K. Walton, *The Highlands and Islands of Scotland* (Edinburgh: Nelson, 1962), 148–49; R. N. Millman, *The Making of the Scottish Landscape* (London: Batsford, 1975), 142–44.

40. L. Dudley Stamp, *Man and the Land* (London: Collins, 1955), 193.

41. Simon Schama, *Landscape and Memory* (Toronto: Random House, 1995), 56.

42. Robert Pogue Harrison, *Forests: The Shadow of Civilization* (Chicago: University of Chicago Press, 1992), 93; see also Schama, *Landscape and Memory*, chapter 3, "The Liberties of the Greenwood."

43. R. Cole Harris, P. Roulston and C. D. Freitas, "The Settlement of Mono Township," *Canadian Geographer* 14 (1975): 1–17.

44. George Rolleston, "The Modification of the External Aspects of Organic Nature Produced by Man's Interference," *Journal of the Royal Geographical Society* 49 (1879): 336.

45. Ibid., 320–33, 391–92.

46. See for example, "Afforestation of Waste Lands in Denmark, Holland, France, and Germany," *TRSAS* 22 (1909): 207–211.

47. Quoted in Neeson, *History of Irish Forestry*, 112; Peter Anderson Graham, *Reclaiming the Waste* (London: Country Life, 1916), 120–21; see also the comment of William Schlich, *BPP*, Coast Erosion and Afforestation, 2d Report (on Afforestation) of the RC on Coast Erosion, and the Reclamation of Tidal Lands, and Afforestation, 14 (1909): q. 19112. [Sometimes the s is added to Knockboy, sometimes not.]

48. Sheila Pim, *The Wood and the Trees* (Kilkenny: Boethius Press, 1984), 135–36; Neeson, *History of Irish Forestry*, 110–14, 119–21.

49. Testimony of J. P. Pye, *BPP*, Report of Departmental Committee on Irish Forestry 23 (1908): qq. 1771–1810.

50. Ibid., q. 1771.

51. T. Summerbell, *Afforestation: The Unemployed and the Land* (London: I. L. P. Publication, 1908), 3–13.

52. "Afforestation Conference in London," *Quarterly Journal of Forestry* 1 (1907): 373–74.

53. *BPP*, RC on Coast Erosion, 14 (1909); Miles, *Forestry in the English Landscape*, 50–51.

54. Miles, *Forestry in the English Landscape*, 138–41.

55. Ibid., 61; Tubbs, *New Forest*, 86–87.

56. Miles, *Forestry in the English Landscape*, 72.

57. C. E. M. Joad, *The Untutored Townsman's Invasion of the Country* (London: Faber and Faber, 1945), 136–37.

58. Nan Fairbrother, *New Lives, New Landscapes* (New York: Knopf, 1970), 23, 122–27, 232, 250, 335–36.

59. Oliver Rackham, *Trees and Woodlands in the British Landscape*, rev. ed. (London: Dent, 1990), 104–5, 190–92; M. E. D. Poore, "Agriculture, Forestry and the Future of the Landscape," in *The English Landscape*, ed. S. R. Woodell (Oxford: Oxford University Press, 1985), 191–201.

60. D. O. Baylis, "Recreational Potential of Welsh Forests," in *Environmental Aspects of Plantation Forestry in Wales*, ed. J. E. Good (Grange-Over-Sands, Cumbria: Institute of Terrestrial Ecology, 1987), 52.

61. Robert Arvill, *Man and Environment*, 3d ed. (Harmondsworth: Penguin, 1973), 56.

62. Literature on this subject is steadily expanding; the following is only a sample: essays in Good, ed., *Environmental Aspects of Plantation Forestry;* essays, especially those by S. J. Essex and T. G. Williams, C. Watkins, G. F. Peterken, C. Lavers and R. Haines-Young, N. Allott, M. Brennen, P. Mills, and A. Eacrett in *Ecological Effects of Afforestation,* ed. Charles Watkins (Wallingford: C. A. B. International, 1993); H. L. Wallace, J. E. Good, and T. G. Williams, "The Effects of Afforestation on Upland Plant Communities: An Application of the British National Vegetation Classification." *Journal of Applied Ecology* 29 (1992): 180–94; Charles Watkins, *Nature Conservation and the New Lowland Forests* (Peterborough: Nature Conservancy Council, 1991).

63. Aldo Leopold, *A Sand County Almanac* (1949; reprint, New York: Ballentine Books, 1970), 240.

CHAPTER 6

1. Cuthbert Johnson, *The Advantages of Railways to Agriculture,* 2d ed. (London: Simpkin and Marshall, 1837), 4–5, 9; see also the Reverend Dionysius Lardner, *The Steam Engine,* 5th ed. (London: John Talor, 1836), 171–77.

2. P. J. Ransom, *The Victorian Railway and How It Evolved* (London: Heinemann, 1990), 63–64. A gradient of 1 in 330 means 1 foot of change in incline or decline in 330 horizontal feet. Even at the time, locomotives were capable of far more than this.

3. Francis Whitshaw, *The Railways of Great Britain,* 2d ed. (1842; reprint, New York: Kelley, 1969), 224.

4. Francis Bond Head, *Stokers and Pokers or the London and North-West Railway* (1849; reprint, London: Cass, 1968), 15.

5. John Francis, *A History of the English Railway* (1851; reprint, New York: Kelley, 1968), 173–75.

6. Ibid., 187.

7. See "Investigator," *Remarks on Proposed Railways* (London: Roake and Varty, 1831), 81–84; *Meeting of Proprietors and Occupiers of Houses and*

Lands, and other Persons Interested in Property and Estates Between Padding-ton and Leighton (Hemel Hempstead, 1831); *Meeting of the proprietors and oc-cupiers of lands in the County of Northampton,* (1831), 4.

8. R. Cort, *Rail-Road Impositions Detected,* 2d ed. (London: n.p., 1834), vi, 55, 87. Barham Livius, *Letter on Steam Power on Canals* (London: Hatchard, 1842), regretted that innovations aimed at adapting steam power to canal boats and lessening the effect of the speed of such boats on canal banks were not be-ing followed up. An engineer, William Bridges Adams, *Road Progress and Steam Farming* (London: Luxford, 1850), hoped that future railways would be light and their tracks would be laid at the side of existing roads, improved for the pur-pose by leveling.

9. William Wordsworth, "To the Editor of the Morning Post," in *The Prose Works of William Wordsworth,* vol. 3, ed. W. J. Owen and J. W. Smyser (Ox-ford: Clarendon Press, 1974), 352–53. J. Peace, *Descant upon Railroads* (Lon-don: John Bohn, 1842), 11, lamented the banishment of "remoteness": "Imagi-nation is murdered, and her province seized upon by an ugly monster that with horrid magic hurries me 'This moment to Brystowe, the next to Carlisle.' "

10. John Ruskin, "The Extension of Railways in the Lake District," in *The Works of John Ruskin,* vol. 34, ed. E. T. Cook and Alexander Wedderburn (Lon-don: Allen, 1908), 137, 141.

11. *BPP,* Lords Committee, The Bill entitled "An Act for making a Railway from London to Birmingham" (London: 1831–32).

12. These details were not informed by anything more than the most rudi-mentary grasp of structural theory or soil mechanics: see J. P. M. Pannell, *An Illustrated History of Civil Engineering* (London: Thames and Hudson, 1964), 112. "A Resident Assistant Engineer," *A Practical Inquiry into Laws of Excava-tion and Embankment on Railways* (London: Saunders and Otley, 1840), re-marks on the discrepancies in the testimony of celebrated engineers about large cuttings and embankments. "The subject," he wrote, (p. 15.) "is entirely new."

13. *An Account of the Proceedings of the Great Western Railway Company* (London: Smith & Ebbs, 1834), 42.

14. Whitshaw, *Railways of Great Britain,* 224; Frederick Williams, *Our Iron Roads* (1852: reprint, London: Cass, 1968), 113–14.

15. *BPP,* Lords Committee, Minutes of Evidence (1831–32), 135.

16. R. L. Sherlock, *Man as a Geological Agent* (London: Witherby, 1922), 81.

17. Thomas Roscoe, *The London and Birmingham Railway* (London: Tilt, 1839), 91–95; Peter Lecount, *The History of the Railway connecting London and Birmingham* (London: Simpkin and Marshall, 1839), 40–44; John Bourne, *Historical and Descriptive Accounts of the Origin, General Execution, and Char-acteristics of the London and Birmingham Railway* (London: Bourne, 1839); J. C. Jeaffreson, *The Life of Robert Stephenson,* vol. 1 (London: Longman, 1864), 191–95; Samuel Smiles, *Lives of the Engineers,* vol. 3 (1862; reprint, Newton Abbot: David and Charles, 1968), 312–314; Edward Osborne, *Osborne's Lon-don and Birmingham Railway Guide* (Birmingham: Simpkin and Marshall, 1840), 150–53. Robert Stephenson's plan for the underpinnings of the Blis-worth cutting are included in S. C. Brees, *Railway Practice,* vol. 1 (London: John Williams Library of Science and Art, 1837).

18. Roscoe, *London and Birmingham Railway,* 96.; see also the photograph in Robin Glasscock, ed., *Historic Landscapes of Britain from the Air* (Cambridge: Cambridge University Press, 1992), 208.

19. Subcontractors for excavating the line for the London and Birmingham were required to spread one or two feet of topsoil on embankment walls and sow them with rye and clover: see Brees, *Railway Practice,* 5, 20.

20. Williams, *Our Iron Roads,* 137.

21. Osborne, *Osborne's Railway Guide,* 10.

22. Ibid., i, 150–54.

23. Wolfgang Schivelbusch, *The Railway Journey,* trans. Anselm Hollo (Oxford: Blackwell, 1980), 25.

24. Ibid., 57–72; see also Nicholas Faith, *The World the Railways Made* (London: Bodley Head, 1990), 35–57.

25. Arthur Freeling, *The Railway Companion, From London to Birmingham, Liverpool, and Manchester* (London: Whittaker, 1837), 19; James Scott Walker, *An Accurate Description of the Liverpool and Manchester Railway* (Liverpool: Cannell, 1830), 31; James Drake, *Road Book* (London: Hayward & Moore, 1839), 16–17; Hudson Scott, *Scott's Railway Companion* (Newcastle: H. Scott, 1857), 8; Frederick McDermott, *The Life and Works of Joseph Firbank* (London: Longman, 1887), 106.

26. F. R. Conder, *Personal Recollections of English Engineers* (London: Hodder and Stoughton, 1868), 71–72, 107–11.

27. Ibid., 211–13; see also *Railroadiana or a New History of England* (London: Simpkin and Marshall, 1838), vi–vii.

28. Thomas Hughes, *Tom Brown's School Days* (London: Macmillan, 1888), 5–7.

29. Terry Coleman, *The Railway Navvies* (Harmondsworth: Pelican, 1968), 45–47.

30. James Day, *A Practical Treatise on the Construction and Formation of Railways* (London: Weale, 1839), 58–59. Ian Kerr, *Building the Railways of the Raj, 1850–1900* (Delhi: Oxford University Press, 1995), 174–76, shows why the refusal of Indian laborers to cart away earth in wheelbarrows instead of in baskets on their heads was, from their point of view, perfectly rational.

31. *Builder* 4 (1846): 142.

32. Samuel Stueland, "The Otis Steam Excavator," *Technology and Culture* 35 (1994): 571–74.

33. Charles Douglas Fox, "Description of the Excavating Machine, or Steam Navvy, with the Results of its Use, on the West Lancashire Railway," *PICE* 52 (1878): 250–56; Messrs. Rushton and Co., "Remarks on Steam-excavating Apparatus, and its Results and Uses," *PICE* 52 (1878):266–69. According to Philip Bagwell, *The Transport Revolution* (London: Routledge, 1988), 93, mechanical earthmovers were used in the 1890s to help build the Great Central, the last main line railway.

34. W. Burnett Tracy, "The Manchester Ship Canal," *Journal of the Manchester Geographical Society* 12 (1896): 211–12.

35. "Manchester Ship Canal," *Engineering* 57 (26 January 1894): 130.

36. Ian Harford, *Manchester and Its Ship Canal Movement* (Staffordshire: Keele University Press, 1994).

37. Arthur Redford, *The History of Local Government in Manchester*, vol. 2 (London: Longmans Green, 1940), 378–80; Arthur Jacob, "The Conservancy of Rivers: The Valley of the Irwell" *PICE* 67 (1882): 237–45.

38. Anthony Wohl, *Endangered Lives* (Cambridge, Mass.: Harvard University Press, 1983), 234–35.

39. Redford, *Local Government in Manchester*, 380, 385–86.

40. Bosdin Leech, *History of the Manchester Ship Canal*, vol. 2 (Manchester: Sherratt and Hughes, 1907), 21.

41. Wohl, *Endangered Lives*, 238.

42. Writes Robert Burgess, "In Search of a Paradigm," in *Ecosystem Rehabilitation*, vol. 2 (The Hague: Academic Publishing, 1992), 38, "we find in 1990 those who still believe that the highest and best use of a river is to carry away the wastes of human society."

43. Wohl, *Endangered Lives*, 238.

44. Testimony of Thomas Foster, the Trafford Estate representative and W. H. Watson before a House of Commons committee in 1883; reported in Leech, *Ship Canal*, vol. 1, 161.

45. See Sherlock, *Man as a Geological Agent*, 295.

46. Ibid., 175–76, 241.

47. V. Williams, *The Manchester Guardian Weekly* (May 8, 1994), 23.

48. L. F. Vernon-Harcourt, *A Treatise on Rivers and Canals*, 2 vols. (Oxford: Clarendon Press, 1882), and W. H. Wheeler, *Tidal Rivers* (London: Longmans, Green, 1893).

49. Vernon-Harcourt, *Rivers and Canals*, vol. 1, 1–5.

50. H. Yule Oldham, "The Manchester Ship Canal," *Geographical Journal* 3 (1894): 491.

51. Leech, *Ship Canal*, vol. 2, 22.

52. Ibid.

53. David Owen, *The Manchester Ship Canal* (Manchester: Manchester University Press, 1983), 18–25.

54. Vernon-Harcourt, *Rivers and Canals*, 263–65; Wheeler, *Tidal Rivers*, 197.

55. William Forwood, *Recollections of a Busy Life* (Liverpool: Young and Sons, 1910), 107–8.

56. Wheeler, *Tidal Rivers*, 374–76.

57. Leech, *Ship Canal*, vol. 1, 284.

58. *Hansard's Parliamentary Debates*, 3d series, 289 (1884): 1386–87.

59. *Engineering* 57 (26 January 1894): 98.

60. Leech, *Ship Canal*, vol. 2, 35.

61. H. L. Saeijs, *Changing Estuaries* (The Hague: Government Publications Office, 1982), 17, 27; L. Eugene Cronin, "The Role of Man in Estuarine Processes," in *Man's Impact on the Environment*, ed. Thomas Detwyler (New York: McGraw-Hill, 1971), 266–94.

CHAPTER 7

1. R. L. Sherlock, *Man as a Geological Agent* (London: Witherby, 1922), 21, 14–15, 324–28.

2. Ibid., 35–38.

3. According to John Barr, *Derelict Britain* (Harmondsworth: Penguin, 1969), 48, there were at the date of publication about 30,000 badly pitted acres in England and Wales.

4. Ibid., 53–54.

5. Reprinted in *Life in Cornwall in the Late Nineteenth Century,* ed. R. M. Barton (Truro: Barton, 1972), 45.

6. A. C. Todd and Peter Laws, *The Industrial Archaeology of Cornwall* (Newton Abbot: David and Charles, 1972), 160.

7. Raphael Samuel, "Mineral Workers," in *Miners, Quarrymen and Saltworkers,* ed. Raphael Samuel (London: Routledge and Kegan Paul, 1977), 5, 11–12; Barrie Trinder, *The Making of the Industrial Landscape* (London: Dent, 1982), 241.

8. *Penny Magazine* 246 (1835): 47; 260 (1836): 158; testimony of Thomas Tancred before the Midland Mining Commission, *BPP* 13 (1843): iv–v, quoted in Michael Reed, *The Landscape of Britain* (London: Routledge, 1990) 322, who calls that part of South Staffordshire one of the most "desolate and dehumanized industrial landscapes in Britain."

9. "Great Landslip at Dunkirk," *Northwich and Knutsford Guardian* (11 December 1880), 4; Albert Calvert, *Salt and the Salt Industry* (London: Pitman, 1919), 104, 113–15; K. L. Wallwork, "Subsidence in the Mid-Cheshire Industrial Area," *Geographical Journal* 122 (1956): 48; Sherlock, *Man as a Geological Agent,* 150; *Chambers Journal,* 5th series, 5 (1888): 750, 758–60; *Builder* 39 (1880 ii): 715–16; *Illustrated London News* 78 (1881): 11–12, describes the subsidence and supplies illustrations; Joseph Dickson, Inspector of Mines, noted in a report to the home secretary in 1873, *BPP,* Report on Landslips in Salt Districts, 53 (1873): 593, that in or about 1533 a treed hill had sunk and turned into a pond.

10. "Great Landslip," *Northwich and Knutsford Guardian* (11 December 1880), 4.

11. T. W. Freeman, H. B. Rodgers, and R. H. Kinvig, *Lancashire, Cheshire, and the Isle of Man* (London: Nelson, 1966), 175.

12. Sherlock, *Man as a Geological Agent,* 146–50.

13. Wallwork, "Subsidence in Mid-Cheshire," 46–50; F. G. Bell, "Salt and Subsidence in Cheshire, England," *Engineering Geology* 9 (1975): 240–44; *BPP,* Report on Landslips, 644.

14. *BPP,* Report on Landslips, 594.

15. Sherlock, *Man as a Geological Agent,* 149–50.

16. *BPP,* SC on Brine Pumping, 11 (1890–91): 235, 275.

17. *BPP,* Report on Landslips, 295.

18. Ibid., 644–47. William Stanley Jevons had caught the attention of politicians and the informed public with his warning about the depletion of Britain's coal supply when he published *The Coal Question* in 1865. See G. N. Von Tun-

zelmann, "Exhaustibility of British Coal in Long-Run Perspective," in *Human Impact on the Environment: Ancient Roots, Current Challenges,* ed. Judith Jacobsen and John Firor (Boulder, Colo.: West View Press, 1992).

19. The Leblanc process decomposes salt (sodium chloride) with sulfuric acid; the Solvay process decomposes ammonium bicarbonate and sodium chloride (in the form of brine) together as a first step.

20. Brian Didsbury, "Cheshire Saltworkers," in *Miners,* ed. Samuel, 180–84.

21. Calvert, *Salt and the Salt Industry,* 120.

22. Ibid., 121; Bell, "Salt and Subsidence," 246.

23. Bell, "Salt and Subsidence," 246–47. As L. Dudley Stamp warned in *The Land of Britain: Its Use and Misuse* (London: Longmans, Green 1948), 235, this solution is not necessarily a total and permanent one.

24. K. L. Wallwork, "Some Problems of Subsidence and Land Use in the Mid-Cheshire Industrial Area," *Geographical Journal* 126 (1960): 195–98; Freeman, Rodgers, and Kinvig, *Lancashire,* 175.

25. See Raymond Gemmell, *Colonization of Industrial Wasteland* (London: Arnold, 1977), 11, and D. W. F. Hardie, *A History of the Chemical Industry in Widnes* (Birmingham: I.C.I., 1950), 127.

26. Sherlock, *Man as a Geological Agent,* 14–15.

27. Ibid., 15–16, 151–52.

28. This is not to suggest that the problem has disappeared: see Ian Douglas, "Geomorphology and Urban Development in the Manchester Area," in *The Geomorphology of North-West England,* ed. R. H. Johnson (Manchester: Manchester University Press, 1985), 347–52, and Howard Humphries et al., *Subsidence in Norwich* (HMSO, 1993).

29. See especially A. E. Musson, "Industrial Motive Power in the United Kingdom, 1800–1870," *EHR,* 2d series, 29 (1976): 415–39. According to Todd and Laws, *Cornwall,* 13, there were still 300 water-powered mills operating in Cornwall in 1880.

30. W. J. Reader, *Imperial Chemical Industries: A History,* vol. 1 (London: Oxford University Press, 1970), 11–30; Ian McNeil, ed., *An Encyclopaedia of the History of Technology* (London: Routledge, 1990), 223, 470–72. Samuel, "Mineral Workers," 42, mentions that two steam ("Goliath") cranes were used in 1875 at a sandstone quarry near Bradford.

31. *BPP,* Report of the Departmental Committee upon Merionethshire Slate Mines, 35 (1895): 435.

32. Henry Tomkins, *The Pavements of London* (London: n.p., 1874), 3–16; James Winter, *London's Teeming Streets, 1830–1914* (London: Routledge, 1993), 36–40, 118–34; H. Hamilton, "The Granite Industry," in *Further Studies in Industrial Organization,* ed. M. P. Fogarty (London: Methuen, 1948), 181–82.

33. Alexander Mackie, *Aberdeenshire* (Cambridge: Cambridge University Press, 1911), 87

34. An aerial photograph is reproduced in Robert Smith, *City of Granite* (Edinburgh: John Donald, 1989), 41. "Muckle" means huge here. Aberdeen natives are noted for their respect for the adage, "Many a little makes a mickle, and many a mickle makes a muckle."

35. William Diack, *Rise and Progress of the Granite Industry in Aberdeen* (Aberdeen: Institute of Quarrying, 1950), 32.

36. Ibid., 31.

37. Ibid., 45.

38. T. Donnelly, "The Rubislaw Granite Quarries, 1750–1939," *Industrial Archaeology* 11 (1974): 226–27, 231. In *Engineering* 21 (1876): 267, there is an engraving of an American-made Steam Stone Cutter, displayed at the Philadelphia Exposition, which needed to be moved to the quarry face on rails.

39. Jacquetta Hawkes, *A Land* (London: Cresset Press, 1951), 109–10.

40. Hamilton, "Granite Industry," in *Further Studies,* ed. Fogarty, 182–83, 188.

41. Judd Alexander, *In Defense of Garbage* (Westport, Conn.: Praeger, 1993), 5–10, 154.

42. N. J. Coppin and A. D. Bradshaw, *Quarry Reclamation* (London: Mining Journal Books, 1982), 12–15.

43. Barr, *Derelict Britain,* 57–58. John Blunden and Graham Turner, *Critical Countryside* (London: BBC, 1985), 88, comment on the paradox that disused industrial workings and quarries "now provide inviting habitats for many plants and animals ousted from their more traditional rural haunts"; see also Lyndis Cole, "Urban Nature Conservation," in *Conservation in Perspective,* ed. A. Warren and F. B. Goldsmith (Chichester: Wiley, 1983), 273.

44. Dov Nir, *Man, A Geomorphological Agent* (Jerusalem: Keter, 1983), 73; T. U. Hartwright, "Development of Gravel-Pit Lakes for Leisure Purposes," in *Minerals and the Environment,* ed. M. J. Jones (Institution of Mining and Metallurgy, 1975), 333–34.

45. J. G. Kohl, *England and Wales* (1844; reprint, New York: Kelly, 1968), 61.

46. J. E. Cairnes, "Co-operation in the Slate Quarries of North Wales," *Macmillan's Magazine* 11 (1864): 182.

47. Trevor Thomas, "Wales: Land, Mines, and Quarries," *Geographical Review* 46 (1956): 80. Peter Lund Simmonds, *Waste Products and Undeveloped Substances,* 3d ed. (London: Hardwicke and Bogue, 1876), 420, noted that a French patent had been taken out for pulverizing slate refuse to make artificial stone.

48. Stamp, *Land of Britain,* 236.

49. Sherlock, *Man as a Geological Agent,* 52.

50. Cairnes, "Co-operation in the Slate Quarries," 182–83.

51. D C. Davies, *A Treatise on Slate and Slate Quarrying* (London: Crosby Lockwood, 1878), 25, 158, 165–67.

52. E. M. Bridges, *Surveying Derelict Land* (Oxford: Clarenden, 1987), 34.

53. M. J. Lewis, ed., *The Slate Quarries of North Wales in 1873* (Plas Tan-y-Bwlch: n.p., 1987), 19.

54. John Burnett, *A Social History of Housing, 1815–1970* (London: Methuen, 1983), 27, makes the point that this substitution of brick and slate for vernacular materials brought monotony and uniformity to towns and cities but also tended to make houses warmer, dryer, and healthier.

55. Merfyn Jones, "Y Chwarelwyr: The Slate of Quarrymen of North Wales," in *Miners,* ed. Samuel, 102.

56. Lewis, *Slate Quarries of North Wales*, 88–89.

57. Jean Lindsay, *A History of the North Wales Slate Industry* (Newton Abbot: David and Charles, 1974), 106.

58. Thomas, "Wales," 70; Lindsay, *History*, 92.

59. Lindsay, *History*, 157.

60. Davies, *Treatise on Slate*, 127.

61. Francis Klingender, *Art and the Industrial Revolution*, ed. and rev. Arthur Elton (Chatham: Adams and MacKay, 1968), 95, reproduces Crane's dramatic lithograph with commentary.

62. Penrhyn quarrymen testified that often the tramway tracks were not set well back from the gallery edge, as the picture suggests, but could be so close to the edge that stones sometimes fell off the wagons and injured workers below: *BPP*, SC Minutes of Evidence, Committee of Inquiry on Stone, Limestone, Slate and Clay Quarrying, 73 (1893–94): 57.

CHAPTER 8

1. George Head, *A Home Tour through the Manufacturing Districts in the Summer of 1835*, new edition (London: Murray 1836), 131–32.

2. Charles Dickens, *The Old Curiosity Shop* (1841; reprint, Oxford: Oxford University Press, 1987), 335.

3. Roy MacLeod, "Government and Resource Conservation, 1860–1886," *Journal of British Studies* 7 (1968): 115–50; MacLeod, "The Alkali Acts Administration, 1863–1864," *Victorian Studies* 9 (1965–66): 86–112; Carlos Flick, "The Movement for Smoke Abatement in Nineteenth Century Britain," *Technology and Culture* 21 (1980): 29–50; P. Brimblecombe and C. Bowler, "Air Pollution in York, 1850–1900," in *The Silent Countdown*, ed. P. Brimblecombe and C. Pfister (Berlin: Springer, 1990); E. Ashby and M. Anderson, *The Politics of Clean Air* (Oxford: Clarendon, 1981); Anthony Wohl, *Endangered Lives* (Cambridge, Mass.: Harvard University Press, 1983), 220–31, 246–53.

4. Elizabeth Gaskell, *North and South* (1854–55; reprint, Harmondsworth: Penguin Books, 1970).

5. A. J. Taylor, "Coal," in *Victoria History of the Counties of England, A History of the County of Stafford*, vol. 2, ed. M. W. Greenslade and J. G. Jenkins (London: Institute of Historical Research, London University, 1967), 98–99. For a detailed description of how mining was organized in the Victorian Black Country, see *BPP*, First Report of the Midland Mining Commission, 13 (1843).

6. *Herne Bay Argus* (20 September 1890), 3; "Basic Slag for Poor Pastures," *Journal of the Board of Agriculture* 11 (1904–5): 414–15; *Journal of the Board of Agriculture* 13 (1906–7): 549–53; Frederick Hackwood, *Olden Wednesbury* (Wednesbury: Ryder and Son, 1899), 33; The Chevalier C. de Schwarz, "Slag Cement," *Engineering* 75 (1903): 671–72.

7. E. G. Attwood and H. G. Evans, *The Economics of Hill Farming* (Cardiff: University of Wales Press, 1961), 181.

8. Dov Nir, *Man, A Geomorphological Agent* (Jerusalem: Keter, 1983), 71–72.

9. Peter Lund Simmonds, *Waste Products and Undeveloped Substances,* 3d. ed. (London: Hardwicke and Bogue, 1876), 460–61.

10. *BPP,* Midland Mining Commission, 13 (1843): 69.

11. Dick Wilson's comment on a paper given by Hal Moggridge, "The Delights and Problems of Practice," in *Landscape Meanings and Values,* ed. E. Penning-Rowsell and David Lowenthal (London: Allen and Unwin, 1986), 113.

12. Trevor Raybould, "Aristocratic Landowners and the Industrial Revolution: The Black Country Experience, 1760–1840," *Midland History* 9 (1984): 59–86; Raybould, "Lord Dudley and the Making of the Black Country," *Blackcountryman* 3 (1970): 53–58; Taylor, "Coal," 95–96.

13. S. Leonard Bastin, "Tree-Planting in the Black Country," *JRASE* 75 (1914): 71.

14. Ibid.

15. Eric Tonks, *The Ironstone Quarries of the Midlands,* Part 1, "Introduction" (Cheltenham: Runpost Publishing, 1988), 31–99, 116–32.

16. R. W. B. Newton, "Afforestation of Unrestored Land," *Quarterly Journal of Forestry* 65 (1951): 38–41. The Boughton Head Forester, R. I. Daykin, reports that, since the 1930s, the husbandry of these plantations has won several national competitions.

17. René Dubos, *The Resilience of Ecosystems* (Boulder, Colo.: Colorado Associated University Press, 1978), 3.

18. Roy Millward and Adrian Robinson, *The South-West Peninsula* (London: Macmillan, 1971), 102.

19. Augustine Henry, *Forests Woods and Trees in Relation to Hygiene* (London: Constable, 1919), 68–69; also described by P. Murray Thompson, "The Utilisation of Disused Pit-banks," *TRSAS* 27 (1913): 30–33.

20. See, for example, the note from A. Neil to Prof. Fisher and the letter from W. Schlich to Douglas Thring, Boughton Estate Papers (28 April 1909).

21. Henry, *Forests Woods and Trees,* 67; see also Peter Anderson Graham, *Reclaiming the Waste* (London: Country Life, 1916), 142–47.

22. Bastin, "Tree-Planting in the Black Country," 73; M. Guidi, N. Piussi, and P. Piussi, "The Influence of Old Rural Land-Management Practices," in *Ecological Effects of Afforestation,* ed. Charles Watkins (Wallingford: C. A. B. International, 1993), 60–62.

23. According to J. V. Thirgood, "Approaches to Land Reclamation in Britain and North America," in *Environmental Management of Mineral Wastes,* ed. Gordon Goodman and Michael Chadwick (Alphen aan den Rijn: Sijhoft, Noordhoff, 1978), 7, leveling and building had reduced this area to 8,000 acres by 1945.

24. Bastin, "Tree-Planting in the Black Country," 71. W. K. Gale, *The Black Country Iron Industry* (London: Iron and Steel Institute, 1966), 1–3, discusses problems of defining "Black Country" and offers this one: "that part of South Staffordshire and North Worcestershire in which the iron trade was carried on between the years 1750 and 1900."

25. *Birmingham Daily Mail,* "Beautifying the Black Country" (23 August 1884), 2.

26. Quoted in Glenn Watson, ed., *Recycling Disused Industrial Land in the Black Country* (Oxford: Oxford Polytechnic, Dept. of Town Planning, 1987), iv.

27. *Birmingham Daily Mail,* "Swallowed by Earth" (14 December 1903), 2.

28. Report of Thomas Tancred, *BPP,* Midland Mining Commission, 13 (1843): iv; referred to in Michael Reed, *The Landscape of Britain* (London: Routledge, 1990), 322.

29. Elihu Burritt, *Walks in the Black Country and Its Green Borderland* (1868; reprint, Kineton, Gloucestershire: Roundwood Press, 1976), 1–3, 97.

30. Ibid., 87–88, 103–4.

31. Ibid., 97.

32. *Birmingham Daily Mail* (23 August 1884), 2.

33. Ibid., (24 January 1903), 2; *Wednesbury, Faces, Places, and Industries* (Wednesbury: Ryder and Son, 1897), 2, 24, 36; Hackwood, *Olden Wednesbury,* 32–33.

34. Frederick Hackwood, *Odd Chapters in the History of Wednesbury* (Wednesbury: n.p., 1919), 65; M. J. Wise, "The Midland Reafforestation Association, 1903–1924, and the Reclamation of Derelict Land in the Black Country," *Journal of the Institute of Landscape Architects* 57 (1962): 15.

35. *Birmingham Daily Mail,* "Black Country Trees" (22 January 1903), 2.

36. Quoted by Charles Bradlaugh, "Compulsory Cultivation of Land," [1887], in *A Selection of the Political Pamphlets of Charles Bradlaugh,* ed. John Saville (New York: Kelley, 1970), 19.

37. *Hansard's Parliamentary Debates,* 3d series, 316 (1887): 1510–11; Bradlaugh, "Compulsory Cultivation of Land," 4, 18–21; *Birmingham Daily Mail,* "Letter from F. W. H." (24 January 1903), 2; Hackwood, *Olden Wednesbury,* 34.

38. See, for example, the leading article in the *Times* (2 July 1887), 11.

39. The Black Country was blighted in the sense that the land surface was denuded and littered early in the nineteenth century. When it became a derelict area is more difficult to fix. By the 1850s some of the coal areas were exhausted. Ten years later much of the coal, ironstone, and limestone was being imported. By 1913 the number of blast furnaces in operation had declined from some 200 to 21. Therefore 1900 seems to be an acceptable date. See Gale, *Black Country,* 115–19.

40. Kenneth Olwig, *Nature's Ideological Landscape* (London: Allen and Unwin, 1984), 57–58.

41. Ibid., 64–79.

42. A. P. Grenfell, "Recent Progress in Afforestation," *Quarterly Journal of Forestry* 3 (1909): 26; Wise, "Midland Reafforestation Association," 15.

43. Grenfell, "Recent Progress in Afforestation," 26.

44. Ibid., 26–30; Bastin, "Tree-Planting in the Black Country," 70–75; testimony of P. E. Martineau, *BPP,* 2d Report (on Afforestation) of the RC on Coast Erosion, and the Reclamation of Tidal Lands, and Afforestation, 14 (1909): qq. 18840–927.

45. P. E. Martineau, "The Planting of Pit Mounds," *Report of the British Association for the Advancement of Science* 86 (1916): 494–95.

46. Ibid., 31. R. L. Sherlock, *Man as a Geological Agent* (London: Witherby, 1922), 318, mentions East Park, Wolverhampton, where municipal authorities fashioned a bowling green out of old slag heaps.

47. *Engineering* 110 (1920): 190.

48. E. D. Till, "The Arbor Day Movement," *Pearson's Magazine* 17 (1904): 203–9.

49. Henry, *Forests Woods and Trees,* 63–64, summarizes Teague's report and includes a photograph of the project.

50. Ibid., 65.

51. For a discussion of modern reclamation problems and proposals in the Black Country, see Watson, ed., *Recycling Disused Industrial Land.*

52. For an account of the background of the project and its aims and activities during the 1960s, see John Barr, *Derelict Britain* (Harmondsworth: Pelican, 1969), 79–156; see also K. J. Hilton, ed., *The Lower Swansea Valley Project* (London: Longmans, 1967) and the *Lower Swansea Valley Project, Study Reports* (Swansea: University College, 1966).

53. R. Weston, R. Gadgil, B. R. Salter, and G. T. Goodman, "Problems of Revegetation in the Lower Swansea Valley: An Area of Extensive Industrial Dereliction," in *Ecology and the Industrial Society,* ed. Gordon Goodman, R. W. Edwards, and J. M. Lambert (New York: Wiley, 1965), 297.

54. Colin Baber and Jeffrey Dessant, "Modern Glamorgan," in *Glamorgan County History,* vol. 5, "Industrial Glamorgan," ed. Arthur John and Glanmor Williams (Cardiff: Glamorgan County Historical Trust, University of Wales Press, 1980), 630.

55. A phrase used by Geoffrey Grigson, "Meanings of Landscape," quoted in John Peake, "The Industrial Heritage of Britain," *Town and Country Planning* 26 (1958): 199.

56. Barr, *Derelict Britain,* 79.

57. Stephen J. Lavender, *New Land for Old* (Bristol: Adam Hilger, 1981), 5–6; K. J. Hilton, "Restoring an Industrial Desert," *Geographical Magazine* 37 (1964): 373.

58. Charles Frederick Cliffe, *The Book of South Wales* (London: Hamilton, Adams, 1847), 155.

59. Ibid.

60. Quoted in Lavender, *New Land for Old,* 47, who gives a summary of some of the points made by defendants and plaintiffs in "The Cooper Smoke Trial," as reported in the *Cambrian* (16 March 1833).

61. R. O. Roberts, "The Smelting of Non-Ferrous Metals since 1750," in *Glamorgan County History,* vol. 5, "Industrial Glamorgan," ed. Arthur John and Glanmor Williams (Cardiff: Glamorgan County Historical Trust, University of Wales Press, 1980), 71–72.

62. Ibid.; Lavender, *New Land for Old,* 48–49.

63. Hilton, "Restoring an Industrial Desert," 373.

64. Michael Chishom and Jeremy Howells, "Derelict Land in Great Britain," in *Dealing with Dereliction,* ed. Rosemary Bromley and Graham Humphrys (Swansea: University College of Swansea, 1979), 17; E. M. Bridges, *Surveying Derelict Land* (Oxford: Clarendon Press, 1987), 109.

65. B. R. Salter, "Afforestation of the Lower Swansea Valley," in *Lower Swansea Valley Project,* 1.

66. George Bell, *Floreat Swansea* (Swansea City Council pamphlets, 1912), reprinted in full in Hilton, ed., *Lower Swansea Valley,* 44–46.

67. Ibid., 87.

68. Stephen J. Lavender, "Community Involvement: The Work of the Conservator," in *Dealing,* ed. Bromley and Humphrys, 153–59; see also J. R. Oxenham, *Reclaiming Derelict Land* (London: Faber and Faber, 1966), 177–92.

69. Ruth Gadgil, "Plant Ecology of the Lower Swansea Valley," Study Report 10, *Lower Swansea Valley Project,* 97–102.

CHAPTER 9

1. F. M. L. Thompson's provocative essay, "Towns, Industry, and the Victorian Landscape," appears in *The English Landscape,* ed. S. R. J. Woodell (Oxford: Oxford University Press, 1985).

2. Ibid., 180–82. In *Land Use and Living Spaces* (London: Methuen, 1981), 15, 45–47, Robin Best's estimate of urban land use in 1901 for England and Wales is four times higher than Thompson's; however, since Best includes villages, isolated dwellings, farmsteads, and all land used for transportation under that category, the disparity is far less than it may seem. Like Thompson, Best believes that, considering the great population increase from the later eighteenth century, "the areal extension of towns was still not very substantial."

3. Best, *Land Use,* 46; John Blunden and Graham Turner, *Critical Countryside* (London: BBC, 1985), 24.

4. C. R. Bryant, L. H. Russwurm, and A. G. McLellan, *The City's Countryside* (London: Longman, 1982), 5–16, 35–36; Robin Pryor, "Defining the Rural-Urban Fringe," *Social Forces* 47 (1968): 202–15.

5. Peter Hall, H. Gracey, R. Drewett, and R. Thomas, *The Containment of Urban England,* vol. 1 (London: Allen and Unwin, 1973), 570.

6. Roy Brigden, *Victorian Farms* (Marlborough: Crowood Press, 1986), 219–27; F. Beavington, "The Development of Market Gardening in Bedfordshire, 1799–1939," *AHR* 23 (1975): 31–40.

7. Nathan Rosenberg, *Perspectives on Technology* (Cambridge: Cambridge University Press, 1976), 236; Michael Chisholm, *Rural Settlement and Land Use,* 3d ed. (London: Hutchinson, 1979), 155.

8. John Sheail, "Underground Water Abstraction: Indirect Effects of Urbanization on the Countryside," *Journal of Historical Geography* 8 (1982): 395–408.

9. It does not necessarily follow that efforts to improve water supply and quality did, in fact, reduce the incidence of typhoid and cholera. See J. A. Hassan, "The Growth and Impact of the British Water Industry in the Nineteenth Century," *EHR* 38 (1985): 543–44.

10. Robert Thom, *Report on Supplying Glasgow with Water* (Glasgow: Edward Khull, 1837), 9. T. H. P. Veal, *The Disposal of Sewage* (New York: D. Van Nostrand, 1928), 4–5, notes that the 1861 report of the Committee on Sewage Disposal warned that river pollution from towns relying on middens and cesspools was almost as bad as from towns making use of water carriage systems to flush away sewage.

11. Thomas Duncan, "Description of the Liverpool Corporation Water-works," *PICE* 12 (1853): 460.

12. Manchester City Council, *A Record of Municipal Activity,* ed. Matthew Anderson (1926), 172.

13. Ibid., 173; John Frederic La Trobe Bateman, *History and Description of the Manchester Waterworks* (Manchester: T. J. Day, 1884), 3–20; see also Bateman's "Description of the Manchester Waterworks," *Engineering* 4 (1867): 237, 240–42.

14. For an analysis of the shortcomings of private water ventures, see Hassan, "Growth of British Water Industry," 544–47.

15. Francois Vigier, *Change and Apathy* (Cambridge, Mass.: MIT Press, 1970), 125.

16. Bateman, *Manchester Waterworks,* 42–59. There were mill owners downstream on the Ethrow; and, supported by a railway company with water development plans of its own, they campaigned against the measure in Parliament, see pp. 67–71; textile manufacturers in the city had much to gain by municipalization and were generally behind it.

17. *BPP,* RC on Water Supply 33 (1869): 593, q. 7325.

18. Ibid., 27. Bateman gives credit here to the earlier work in Scotland of Robert Thom and his reports on works to supply water to Greenock and Edinburgh, *A Brief Account of the Shaws Water Scheme* (Greenock: Columbian Press, 1829).

19. In *Report to Sir Michael Shaw Stewart on Supplying Greenock with Water* [published together with *A Brief Account of the Shaws Water Scheme*] (Greenock: Columbian Press, 1829), 49, Robert Thom did point out that an advantage of building a reservoir and aqueduct was that water-driven industry would thereby be served and, as a consequence, "no steam-engines, vomiting forth smoke, and polluting the earth and air for miles around" would be needed.

20. Bateman, *Manchester Waterworks,* 165–66.

21. Ibid., 114–31, 165–67; G. M. Binnie, *Early Victorian Water Engineers* (London: Telford, 1981), 173–83. According to Arthur Redford, *The History of Local Government in Manchester,* vol. 2 (London: Longmans, Green, 1940), 199–203, it was not until 1866 that supplies from Longdendale could be relied on during flood seasons.

22. R. Rawlinson et al., "Discussion on River Outlets," *PICE* 59 (1879): 66–67; Binnie, *Early Victorial Water Engineers,* 62–67.

23. "The Holmfirth Catastrophe," *Annual Register* (1852): 17, 478–81.

24. In the discussion following George Henry Hill's "The Thirlmere Works for the Water Supply of Manchester," *PICE* 76 (1896): 69–70, it was noted that the first masonry-faced concrete reservoir dam was constructed at Abbystead, near Lancaster, in 1876. An article on the masonry and concrete Vyrnwy Dam at Liverpool's reservoir, "The Vyrnwy Dam," *Engineer* (4 June 1886): 439, commented on Britain's continued backwardness in this type of construction.

25. G. M. Binnie, *Early Dam Builders in Britain* (London: Telford, 1987), 138–42, 161.

26. L. F. Vernon-Harcourt, *A Treatise on Rivers and Canals,* vol. 1 (Oxford: Clarendon Press, 1882), 139.

27. *BPP,* RC on Water Supply 33 (1869): 219, q. 1350.

28. Ibid., q. 1349.

29. The account of the disaster is taken from Samuel Harrison, *A Complete History of the Great Flood at Sheffield* (London: Harrison, 1864), and from "Disastrous Inundation at Sheffield," *Annual Register* (1864): 30-39.

30. *BPP,* RC on Water Supply 33 (1869): 410, q. 3940.

31. Rawlinson, "Discussion on River Outlets," 57.

32. This was the finding of Rawlinson's committee. Bateman, who had been criticized for using cast-iron pipes, disagreed, arguing that the cause of the dam's failure was a landslip under the east side of the embankment (*Builder* 22 [1864]: 530; see also Binnie, *Early Victorian Water Engineers,* 264-77).

33. Harrison, *Complete History of the Great Flood,* 23.

34. Ibid., 11-92.

35. Ibid., 156-59.

36. *Builder* 22 (1864): 335. Emphasis is in the original.

37. Bateman, *Manchester Waterworks,* 208-9, 215-18. In his guidebook *Highways and Byways in the Lake District* (London: Macmillan, 1903), 244, A. G. Bradley informed tourists that they would find a good road on Thirlmere's western shore where once only an old packhorse trail had existed: "an innovation which no one will quarrel with."

38. Manchester City Council, *Record of Municipal Activity* (Manchester: 1926), 176.

39. Ibid., 216.

40. Edmund Hodge, *Enjoying the Lakes* (Edinburgh: Oliver and Boyd, 1957), 139.

41. Manchester City Council, *Record of Municipal Activity* (1925), 29.

42. William Wordsworth, "Kendal and Windermere Railway," *The Prose Works of William Wordsworth,* vol. 3, ed. W. J. Owen and J. W. Smyser (Oxford: Clarendon Press, 1972), 339.

43. *BPP,* RC on Water Supply 33 (1869): 21, 26, 163, qq. 300, 378, 382-83. John Bateman described his proposal in *On the Supply of Water to London from the Sources of the River Severn* (Westminster: Vacher and Sons, 1865).

44. William Wordsworth, "Sonnet on the Projected Kendal and Windermere Railway," in *The Prose Works of William Wordsworth,* vol. 3, ed. W. J. Owen and J. W. Smyser (Oxford: Clarendon Press, 1974), 339.

45. Helen Viljoen, ed., *The Brantwood Diary of John Ruskin* (New Haven: Yale University Press, 1971), 607.

46. Robert Somervell, *Water for Manchester from Thirlmere* (London: Simpkins and Marshall, 1877).

47. D. Somervell and D. Somervell, eds., *Robert Somervell* (London: Faber and Faber, 1935), 50-51.

48. Ibid., 52-56.

49. *Manchester Guardian* (14 September and 31 October 1877).

50. "Manchester and the Meres," *Spectator* (8 September 1877): 1118-19.

51. Ibid., 162.

52. John Ruskin, "Fors Clavigera," vol. 7, in *The Works of John Ruskin,* vol. 29, ed. E. T. Cook and Alexander Wedderburn (London: George Allen, 1907),

224–26; see also Keith Hanley, "The Discourse of Natural Beauty," in *Ruskin and Environment,* ed. Michael Wheeler (Manchester: Manchester University Press, 1995), 23–25, and "In Wordsworth's Shadow: Ruskin and Neo-Romantic Ecologies," in *Influence and Resistance in Nineteenth-Century English Poetry,* ed. G. K. Blank and M. K. Louis (Basingstoke: Macmillan, 1993), 227–31.

53. *Punch* 70 (5 February 1876): 34; the poem is called "Lady of the Lake Loquitur."

54. *Times* (20 October 1877): 11.

55. Ibid., 9.

56. Ibid.

57. *Times* (15 December 1877): 4.

58. Ibid.; see also Hodge, *Enjoying the Lakes,* 142–43.

59. *Times* (18 December 1877): 6.

60. Ibid. For a modern discussion about how restoration destroys continuity with the past, see Robert Elliot, "Faking Nature," *Inquiry* 25 (1982): 81–93.

61. *BPP,* SC on the Manchester Corporation Water Bill, Report 16 (1878): 61–63.

62. *Times* (23 March 1878): 11.

63. Tom Stephenson, *Forbidden Land* (Manchester: Manchester University Press, 1989), 101–2, notes that Manchester and other cities receiving water from Longdendale had leased the catchment area to grouse shooters and closed it to ramblers.

64. Cook and Wedderburn, eds., *Works of John Ruskin,* vol. 34, 568.

65. From "Praeterita," vol. 3, in *Works of John Ruskin,* vol. 35, ed. Cook and Wedderburn, 553.

66. Ibid., vol. 22, 70; the passage is from the appendix to "Adriadne Florentina" [1873–76] and "The Extension of Railways in the Lake District," ibid., vol. 34, 137.

67. In "Fors," vol. 8 (April 1877), in *Works of John Ruskin,* vol. 29, ed. Cook and Wedderburn, 95, Ruskin accuses the bishop of "running after the error of Balaam for reward"; see also Ruskin's article in the *Contemporary Review* (February 1877), in *Works of John Ruskin,* vol. 34, ed. Cook and Wedderburn, vol. 29, 401–25.

68. Ibid., vol. 19, lv–lvii; vol. 29, 333; "Fors," vol. viii (January 1878); Hodge, *Enjoying the Lakes,* 139–40.

69. Hodge, *Enjoying the Lakes,* 140.

70. Hill, "Thirlmere Works," 107–8. But Hill notes in "The Manchester Water Works," *Engineering* 52 (1891): 435, that because the local bluish slatey rock was friable, new red sandstone was brought from Dumfriesshire to dress the dam.

71. Manchester City Council, *Record* (1926), 176; (1927): 178–82.

72. Ibid. (1925), 29.

73. Ibid. (1927), 182–84.

74. Roy Millward and Adrian Robinson, *The Lake District* (London: Eyre and Spottiswood, 1970), 88.

75. Norman Nicholson, *Portrait of the Lakes* (London: Hale, 1963), 122.

76. W. G. Collingwood, *The Lake Counties*, 2d ed. (London: Warne, 1932), 155.

77. B. L. Thompson, *The Lake District and the National Trust* (Kendal: Titus Wilson, 1946), 16.

78. H. D. Rownsley, *Literary Associations of the English Lakes* (Glasgow: James MacLehose and Sons, 1906), 239.

79. Hodge, *Enjoying the Lakes,* 147–57. According to H. A. L. Rice, *Lake Country Portraits* (London: Harville Press, 1967), 131, a friend once said of Rownsley's energy: "It was almost a lust of perpetual motion."

80. Hodge, *Enjoying the Lakes,* 141.

81. Millward and Robinson, *Lake District,* 256.

82. Elizabeth Porter, *Water Management in England and Wales* (Cambridge: Cambridge University Press, 1978), 41–48.

83. Steven Bourassa, *The Aesthetics of Landscape* (London: Belhaven Press, 1991), provides a useful discussion of those conceptual problems and how they are being addressed in our own day.

CHAPTER 10

1. *BPP,* SC on Open Spaces (Metropolis), Report 8 (1865): 58. Testimony before the SC on Public Walks 15 (1833) shows that many Londoners were conscious that this same shrinkage of open space was taking place before the railways arrived: see, for example, the remarks of George Offer who grew up near the Tower, q. 133.

2. The pioneering essays by H. J. Dyos, "Railways and Housing in Victorian London," *Journal of Transport History* 2 (1955): 11–21, 90–100, and "Some Social Costs of Railway Building in London," *Journal of Transport History* 3 (1957): 23–31, were greatly expanded by John Kellett, *The Impact of Railways on Victorian Cities* (London: Routledge and Kegan Paul, 1969), and extended further by Jack Simmons, *The Railway in Town and Country, 1830–1914* (Newton Abbot: David and Charles, 1986). They supply most of the material for this brief summary.

3. Lewis Mumford, "The Natural History of Urbanization," in *Man's Role in Changing the Face of the Earth,* ed. William Thomas (Chicago: University of Chicago Press., 1956).

4. R. L. Sherlock, *Man as a Geological Agent* (London: Witherby, 1922), 157.

5. Mumford, "Natural History," 382. For a more recent discussion of urban geomorphology, see David Nicholson-Lord, *The Greening of the Cities* (London: Routledge and Kegan Paul, 1987), 95–98.

6. W. J. Loftie, *In and Out of London* (London: Society for the Promotion of Christian Knowledge, 1875), 15, 23.

7. Michael Hough, *City Form and Natural Process* (London: Routledge, 1989), 6–12.

8. Martin Wiener, *English Culture and the Decline of the Industrial Spirit, 1850–1980* (Cambridge: Cambridge University Press, 1981) 46–49.

9. John Ruskin, "The Stones of Venice," in *The Works of John Ruskin,* vol. 10, ed. E. T. Cook and Alexander Wedderburn, (London: Allen, 1904), 207.

10. *Fifth Annual Report of the Metropolitan Public Gardens Association* (London: 1887), 39. Annmarie Adams, *Architecture in the Family Way* (Montreal and Kingston: McGill-Queen's University Press, 1996), points out that barrenness was commonly believed to be the result of removing women from contact with nature's fecundity.

11. For a brief review of Pennethorne's plans for Victoria Park and how they worked out in practice and for bibliographical references to Victoria Park history, see James Winter, *London's Teeming Streets* (London: Routledge, 1993), 162–66.

12. Nicholson-Lord, *Greening of the Cities,* 30; see also Galen Cranz, *The Politics of Park Design* (Cambridge, Mass.: MIT Press, 1982), 7–24.

13. Godwin has yet to find a biographer. For comments on his life and work, see Robert Thorne, "Building Bridges," in *Victorian Values,* ed. Gordon Marsden (London: Longman, 1990); Anthony King, "Architectural Journalism and the Profession: The Early Years of George Godwin," *Architectural Review* 19 (1976): 32–53; King, "Another Blow for Life: George Godwin and the Reform of Working Class Housing," *Architectural Review* 136 (1964): 448–52; King, introduction to the 1972 reprint of Godwin's *Town Swamps and Social Bridges* (New York: Leicester University Press, 1972), 7–26; King, "George Godwin and the Art Union of London, 1837–1911," *Victorian Studies* 8 (1964): 101–30; Ruth Richardson, "George Godwin of *The Builder,*" *Visual Resources* 6 (1989): 121–40; Winter, *London's Teeming Streets,* 155–60; see also Ruth Richardson and Robert Thorne, *The Builder Illustrations Index, 1843–1883* (Guildford: Hutton and Rostron, 1994). In *An Appeal to the Public, on the Subject of Railways* (London: Weale, 1837), 30, Godwin wrote about his "delight" in "the amazing power to be gained by the use of steam."

14. George Godwin, *London Shadows* (1854; reprint, New York: Garland, 1985), 32. Most of the essays included appeared earlier in the *Builder* editorial pages, making it possible to attribute, according to style and characteristic devices, other items that came from Godwin's pen and to do so with some degree of confidence.

15. Godwin, *Town Swamps,* 91.

16. Godwin, *London Shadows,* 45. By contrast, Octavia Hill cited "the deeply-rooted habit of dirt and untidiness" as a major impediment to housing improvement; see *Homes of the London Poor* (1878; reprint, London: Cass, 1970), 45.

17. Godwin, *London Shadows,* 72–73.

18. *Builder* 28 (1870): 417.

19. Godwin, *London Shadows,* 70.

20. *Builder* 28 (1870): 417–18; 32 (1874): 211, 305; see also Winter, *London's Teeming Streets,* 156–60.

21. William Robinson, *Gleanings from French Gardens* (London: Warme, 1868); *Builder* 26 (1868): 401–2, gave this book an enthusiastic review.

22. *Builder* 20 (1862): 557. *Builder,* 26 (1868): 619, took credit for saving thirteen plane trees along Piccadilly from attacks by street wideners.

23. *Builder* 20 (1862): 557.

24. Hill, *Homes of the London Poor,* 28–30; see also Martin Gaskell, "Gardens for the Working Class: Victorian Practical Pleasures," *Victorian Studies* 23 (1980): 497–501.

25. The Rev. S. Haddon Parkes, Curate of St. George's, Bloomsbury, deserves to share the credit. For accounts of his flower-growing contests in the courts near Little Coram Street, see his *Flower Shows of Window Plants, for the Working Classes of London* (London: 1862) and his *Window Gardens for the People* (London: Partridge, 1864). The Stoke Newington Chrysanthemum Society was one of the oldest, having been founded in 1846; it changed its name to the National Chrysanthemum Society in 1884: see National Chrysanthemum Society, *Centenary Book, 1846–1946* (Barnet, Hartfordshire: 1946), 9.

26. *Builder* 7 (1849): 525.

27. *Builder* 15 (1857): 625.

28. *Builder* 20 (1862): 604.

29. *Builder* 15 (1857): 625.

30. The term "working man's plant" was used by Alfred Smee of the Bank of England, chairman of the recently formed Metropolitan Amalgamated Chrysanthemum Society, in *The Gardener's Weekly Magazine and Floricultural Cabinet* 5 (1863): 92; Samuel Broome, *Culture of the Chrysanthemum as Preached in the Temple Gardens* (London: 1857), 8.

31. *Builder* 17 (1859): 780–81.

32. Ibid., 780.

33. *Builder* 24 (1866): 664; *Builder* 25 (1867): 665.

34. *Builder* 34 (1876): 852.

35. Gaskell, "Gardens for the Working Class," 485; D. Crouch and C. Ward, *The Allotment* (London: Faber and Faber, 1988), 64–71.

36. Francis George Heath, *The Fern Paradise,* 8th ed. (London: Routledge, 1908), 47. Heath's claims were impressionistic, comparative data being hard to find.

37. Nicholson-Lord, *Greening of the Cities,* 29, comments on how the generic term, *open space,* epitomizes the bureaucratic way of seeing, or not seeing, landscape.

38. London County Council, *London Parks and Open Spaces,* Appendix (London: Hodder and Stoughton, 1924). According to G. Gibbon and R. Bell, *History of the London County Council, 1889–1939* (London, Macmillan, 1939), 502, there were 782 persons to one acre of public open space in the administrative county of London; by 1939 the ratio had dropped to 519.

39. *Builder* 5 (1847): 533, 545, 565.

40. *Lancet* (25 February 1865): 206.

41. Reprinted in *Builder* 32 (1874): 305, 337.

42. John Maidlow, "The Law of Common and Open Space," in *Six Essays on Commons Preservation,* by Henry Peek (London: Sampson, Low, Son, and Marston, 1867), 2.

43. Robert Hunter, "The Preservation of Commons in the Neighborhood of the Metropolis," in *Six Essays,* by Peek, 363, 371; see also Winter, *London's Teeming Streets,* 168–69.

44. Ian Greenfield, *Turf Culture* (London: Leonard Hill, 1962), 144; F. Herbert Bormann, Diana Balmori, and Gordon Geballe, *Redesigning the American Lawn* (New Haven: Yale University Press, 1993), 23, 40; Kenneth Jackson, *The Crabgrass Frontier* (New York: Oxford University Press, 1985), 60–61. Adam Rome, "Building on the Land," *Journal of Urban History* 20 (1994): 418–19, notes that "the first important guide to suburban lawn care" in America appeared in 1870.

45. Hough, *City Form,* 151. According to Wade Graham, "The Grassman," *New Yorker* 72 (August 19, 1996): 35, some sixty percent of municipal water in the western United States now goes to lawn maintenance.

46. Henry Mayhew, *London Labour and the London Poor* (1861–62; reprint, New York: Dover Publications, 1968), vol. 1, 153–54.

47. Ibid., 155.

48. Steen Eiler Rasmussen, *London the Unique City* (1934; reprint, Cambridge, Mass.: MIT Press, 1982), 333–38.

49. Nicholson-Lord, *Greening of the Cities,* 18, uses "resource blindness" to describe the loss of connection between a food item and its roots or its live state.

50. Mayhew, *London Labour,* vol. 2, 73–74.

51. Ibid., vol. 1, 126, 129, 139.

52. Thomas Burke, *The Streets of London* (London: Batsford, 1941), 130; P. J. Waller, *Town, City, and Nation* (Oxford: Oxford University Press, 1983), 52–53.

53. *Builder* 29 (1871): 670–71. Hornsey-Wood House, earlier in the century a tea house with a small lake, was built on what was once a large fen; therefore the name of the park (but probably not the London borough of Finsbury) refers to a geographic past; see Ben Weinreb and Christopher Hibbert, eds., *The London Encyclopaedia* (New York: St. Martin's Press, 1983), 277–78.

54. R. Maybe, *Unofficial Countryside* (New York: Collins, 1973); Nicholson-Lord, *Greening of the Cities,* 38–113; Hough, *City Form;* Michael Hounsome, "Bird Life in the City," in *Nature in Cities,* ed. Ian Laurie (Chichester: Wiley, 1979), 188–93; Lyndis Cole, "Urban Nature Conservation," in *Conservation in Perspective,* ed. A. Warren and F. B. Goldsmith (Chichester: Wiley, 1983), 267–80.

CHAPTER 11

1. Elizabeth Gaskell, *Mary Barton* (1848; reprint London: Panther Books, 1966), 15–17.

2. Quoted in James Walvin, *Beside the Seaside* (London: Penguin, 1978), 40–41.

3. Ibid., 31–33.

4. Hugh Cunningham, *Leisure in the Industrial Revolution* (London: Croom Helm, 1980), 160; John K. Walton, *The English Seaside Resort* (Leicester: Leicester University Press, 1983), 58–59.

5. Thomas Creevey, Creevey to Miss Ord (1837), *The Creevey Papers,* vol. 2, ed. Herbert Maxwell (London: Murray, 1903). Jack Simmons, *The Railway in Town and Country, 1830–1914* (Newton Abbot: David and Charles, 1986), 236,

points out that between 1801 and 1841, the year the railway arrived, Brighton grew from 7,000 to 47,000.

6. James Walvin, *Leisure and Society, 1830–1950* (London: Longman, 1978), 73.

7. Stephen G. Jones, *Workers at Play* (London: Routledge and Kegan Paul, 1986), 2–3; David Rubenstein and Colin Speakman, *Leisure, Transport, and the Countryside*, vol. 277 (Fabian Research Series, 1969).

8. Quoted in S. Margetson, *Leisure and Pleasure in the Nineteenth Century* (London: Cassell, 1969), 82.

9. Ouida [Marie Louise de la Ramée], *Views and Opinions* (London: Methuen, 1895), 333–34.

10. Hugh Shimmin, *Town Life* [1858], passages of which are reprinted in *Low Life and Moral Improvement in Mid-Victorian England*, ed. John Walton K. and A. Wilcox (Leicester: Leicester University Press, 1991), 179–84.

11. Valarius Geist, "A Philosophical Look at Recreational Impact on Wildlands," in *Recreational Impact on Wildlands*, Conference Proceedings (Seattle: U.S. Forest Service, 1978), 1–3, compares these conflicts to "The Tragedy of the Commons" dilemma.

12. Lucy Toulmin Smith, ed., *The Itinerary of John Leland in about the Years, 1536–1539*, vol. 3 (Carbondale, Ill.: S. Illinois University Press, 1964); Leland described the terrain as "horrible with the sighte of bare stones"(p. 121).

13. Quoted by G. A. Lister, "The Coming of the Mountaineer," in *The Mountains of Snowdonia*, ed. Herbert Carr and George Lister (London: Bodley Head, 1925), 62.

14. James Bogle, *Artists in Snowdonia* (Tal-y-bont, Ceredigion: Y Lofta Cyf., 1990), 10.

15. Ibid., 71–72; George Barrow, *Wild Wales* (1862; reprint, London: Murray, 1923), 203–7.

16. David Archer, "Managing Public Pressure on Snowdon," in *The Ecological Impacts of Outdoor Recreation on Mountain Areas in Europe and North America*, ed. N. G. Bayfield and G. C. Barrow (Ambleside, Cumbria: Recreation Ecological Research Group, 1985), 155–60.

17. J. G. Kohl, *England and Wales* (1844; reprint, London: Cass, 1968), 61–69.

18. Barrow, *Wild Wales*, 199.

19. John Ranlett, " 'Checking Nature's Desecration': Late Victorian Environmental Organization," *Victorian Studies* 26 (1983): 203.

20. Barrow, *Wild Wales*, 204.

21. Archer, "Managing Public Pressure," 156, 160; J. Allan Patmore, *Recreation and Resources* (Oxford: Blackwell, 1983), 182–83.

22. For a summary of the kinds of damage recreational uses can inflict, see Martin Speight, *Discussion Papers in Conservation* (London: Trinity College, Dublin, Department of Zoology, 1973), 3–27, and F. B. Goldsmith and R. J. Munton, "The Ecological Effects of Recreation," in *Recreational Geography*, ed. P. Lavery (Newton Abbot: David and Charles, 1974). For an examination of the effects on mountains, see N. G. Bayfield, "Effects of Extended Use of Footpaths in Mountain Areas of Britain," in *Ecological*, ed. Bayfield and Barrow;

R. Thomas, P. Anderson, and E. Radford, "The Ecological Effects of Woodland Recreation," *Quarterly Journal of Forestry* 8 (1994): 225–32.

23. Quoted in R. W. Butler, "Evolution of Tourism in the Scottish Highlands," *Annals of Tourism Research* 12 (1985): 377.

24. Jack Simmons, "The Power of the Railway," in *The Victorian City,* vol. 1, ed. H. J. Dyos and Michael Wolff (London: Routledge and Kegan Paul, 1973), 277–310. H. J. Perkin, "The 'Social Tone' of Victorian Seaside Resorts in the North-West," *Northern History* 11 (1975): 180–94, argues that the local landholding system was the main determinant of social tone; M. Higgins, "Social Tone and Resort Development in North-East England: Victorian Seaside Resorts Around the Mouth of the Tees," *Northern History* 20 (1984): 187–206, agrees but introduces modifications, as does John K. Walton, "Railways and Resort Development in Victorian England: The Case of Silloth," *Northern History* 15 (1979): 191–209.

25. F. M. L. Thompson, "Towns, Industry, and the Victorian Landscape," in *The English Landscape,* ed. S. R. J. Woodell (Oxford: Oxford University Press, 1985), 177; see also John K. Walton and P. R. McGloin, "The Tourist Trade in Victorian Lakeland," *Northern History* 17 (1981): 152–82.

26. P. Lavery, "Resorts and Recreation," in *Recreational,* ed. Lavery, 177–78.

27. J. A. Steers, *The English Coast and the Coast of Wales* (London: Fontana, 1966), 133. As Patmore, *Recreation and Resources,* 34–35, points out, the arrival of the horse tram in the 1870s, the electric tram several decades later, the motor charabanc in the early twentieth century as well as the popularization of bicycle touring from the 1880s and 1890s did begin to open up the country inland from seaside resorts to mostly middle-class tourism.

28. Wesley Dougill, "The British Coast and Its Holiday Resorts," *The Town Planning Review* 16 (1935): 266; Stanley Parker, "British Views of Retirement," *Leisure Studies* 2 (1983): 211–16; Walton, *English Seaside Resort,* 78–79.

29. Kenneth Lindley, *Seaside Architecture* (London: Hugh Evelyn, 1973), 103–18.

30. Francis Coghlan, *The Steam-Packet and Coast Companion* (London: Hughes, 1834), 36–42.

31. J. M. Golby and A. W. Purdue, *The Civilisation of the Crowd* (London: Batsford, 1984), 159; Walton, *English Seaside Resort,* 41.

32. *Herne Bay Argus* (8 March and 20 September 1880).

33. R. Kay Cresswell, "The Geomorphology of a South-west Lancashire Coastline," *Geographical Journal* 90 (1937): 335–36.

34. John Liddle, "Estate Management and Land Reform Politics: The Hesketh and Scarisbrick Families and the Making of Southport, 1842 to 1914," in *Patricians, Power, and Politics in Nineteenth-Century Towns,* ed. David Cannadine (Leicester: Leicester University Press, 1982), 135–52.

35. Francis Bailey, "The Origin and Growth of Southport," *The Town Planning Review* 21 (1950): 302–4.

36. John Travis, *The Rise of the Devon Seaside Resorts, 1750–1900* (Exeter: University of Exeter Press, 1993), 189.

37. George Head, *A Home Tour through the Manufacturing Districts of England in the Summer of 1835,* new ed. (London: Murray, 1836), 42–47.

38. J. S., *A Guide to Southport* (Liverpool: n.p., 1849), 23–32; E. Bland, *Annals of Southport* (Southport: Heywood, 1888); Perkin, "Social Tone," 185–86; Francis Bailey, *A History of Southport* (Southport: Angus Downie, 1955), 76, 123–43, 170, 187–91, 205–18; David Cannadine, *Lords and Landlords: The Aristocracy and the Towns, 1774–1967* (Leicester: Leicester University Press, 1980), 65; *New Illustrated Guide to Southport* (Southport: n.p., 1875), 16–57.

39. Nathaniel Hawthorne, *The English Notebooks,* ed. Randall Stewart (New York: Modern Languages Assn., 1941), 397.

40. Ibid., 397–98, 461; W. H. Wheeler, *The Sea-Coast* (London: Longmans, 1902), 313–14, said that a fresh breeze lifted the sand 5 to 20 feet and a heavy gale, 200 feet.

41. Bailey, "Origin and Growth of Southport," 308–10.

42. E. W. Gilbert, "The Growth of Inland and Seaside Health Resorts in England," *Scottish Geographical Magazine* 55 (1939): opposite p. 20.

43. Edmund Dickson, "The Ribble Estuary," in *Southport* (Southport: Fortune and Chant, 1903), 63–67.

44. Paul Theroux, *The Kingdom by the Sea* (New York: Pocket Books, 1984), 239.

45. W. H. Wheeler, *Tidal Rivers* (London: Longmans, 1893), 384–98; William Ashton, *The Battle of Land and Sea* (Southport: Ashton, 1909), 77–81.

46. Liddle, "Estate Management," 153–54.

47. James Barron, *A History of the Ribble Navigation* (Preston: Guardian Press, 1938), 18–45; Bailey, *History of Southport,* 216–18; Bailey, "Origin and Growth of Southport," 316.

48. *Southport* (Bristol: 1897), 10.

49. Sometimes in recent works the word is spelled *groin.* Most Victorians and Edwardians, perhaps embarrassed by connotations, preferred *groyne.*

50. Ibid., 15; T. W. Freeman, H. B. Rogers, and R. H. Kinvig, *Lancashire, Cheshire and the Isle of Man* (London: Nelson, 1966), 238.

51. Lindley, *Seaside Architecture,* 461; a postcard view of the chute and the flying machine appears on p. 65. An Aunt Sally was a figure of a woman at which players threw missiles, the object being to break the pipe in her mouth and win a prize.

52. Bailey, *History of Southport,* 173.

53. Walvin, *Beside the Seaside,* 164.

54. E. Temple Thurston, *The 'Flower of Gloster'* (London: William and Norgate, 1911), 127.

55. John Lowerson, *Sport and the English Middle Classes, 1870–1914* (Manchester: Manchester University Press, 1993), 128–29.

56. Horatio Gordon Hutchinson, "Golf," in *The Encyclopaedia Britannica,* vol. 12 (Cambridge: Cambridge University Press, 1911), 221.

57. Walton, *English Seaside Resort,* 43, 109, 184–5.

58. H. S. C. Everard, *A History of the Royal and Ancient Golf Club, St. Andrews from 1754–1900* (Edinburgh: Blackwood, 1907), 101–2.

59. John Lowerson and John Myerscough, *Time to Spare in Victorian England* (Hassocks, Sussex: Harvester Press, 1977), 126.

60. Hutchinson, "Golf," 220; Harry Vardon, *The Complete Golfer,* 13th ed. (London: Methuen, 1912), 207.

61. Robert Browning, *A History of Golf* (London: Black, 1955), 141-42; Geoffrey Cornish and Ronald Whitten, *The Golf Course* (Leicester: Windward, 1981), 32; Lowerson, *Sport and the English Middle Classes,* 138, 144. The Natural Environment Research Council, *Amenity Grassland—The Needs for Research,* 19 (1977): 8, estimates that 1,714 golf courses covered some 52,000 hectares of Britain's surface in the year the report was published.

62. Browning, *History of Golf,* 167.

63. H. S. Colt, "Landscape," in *Some Essays on Golf-course Architecture,* by H. S. Colt and C. H. Alison (London: *Country Life,* 1920), 14-15, 51; Colt, "Construction of New Courses," in *The Book of the Links,* ed. Martin Sutton (London: W. H. Smith, 1912), 4, 14.

64. Planning and Development Services Department, District of Surrey, British Columbia, *Golf Courses* (1989): 1-3. Reginald Beale, *Lawns for Sports* (London: Marshal, Hamilton, Kent, 1924), 3, writes that the only practical way to develop an estate today is by running a golf course or other sports ground in connection with it.

65. Hutchinson, "Golf," 220.

66. Colt, "Construction of New Courses," 15.

67. David Cannadine, "Victorian Cities: How Different?" *Social History* 2 (1977): 482.

68. Lowerson, *Sport and the English Middle Classes,* 136.

69. Michael Hough, *City Form and Natural Process* (London: Routledge, 1989), 189.

70. David Rubinstein, "Cycling in the 1890s," *Victorian Studies* 21 (1977): 47-52, 59-61.

71. Helen Walker, "The Popularisation of the Outdoor Movement, 1900-1914," *British Journal of Sports History* 2 (1985): 140-53; David Prynn, "The Clarion Clubs, Rambling, and the Holiday Associations in Britain since the 1890s," *Journal of Contemporary History* 11 (1976): 65-77; Jan Marsh, *Back to the Land: The Pastoral Impulse in England, from 1880 to 1914* (London: Quartet Books, 1982); Gordon Cherry, "Changing Social Attitudes Towards Leisure and the Countryside in Britain, 1890-1990," in *Leisure and the Environment,* ed. Sue Glyptis (London: Belhaven Press, 1993), 23-24; Tom Stephenson, *Forbidden Land* (Manchester: Manchester University Press, 1989), 57-80; Howard Hill, *Freedom to Roam* (Ashbourne: Moorland, 1980), 18-41; Peter Donnelly, "The Paradox of Parks: Politics of Recreational Land Use before and after the Mass Trespasses," *Leisure Studies* 5 (1986): 211-31.

72. Lowerson, *Sport and the English Middle Classes,* 146-47.

73. See, for example, Jon Elchells, "Golf Answers Back," *Landscape Design* 210 (1992): 41-43.

74. Michael Bunce, *The Countryside Ideal* (London: Routledge, 1994), 114-17.

75. Paul Cloke, "The Countryside as a Commodity: New Rural Spaces for

Leisure," in *Leisure*, ed. Glyptis, 56; Daniel Boorstin, "The Lost Art of Travel," chap. 3 in *The Image* (New York: Harper and Row, 1961).

76. Peter Bailey, "'A Mingled Mass of Perfectly Legitimate Pleasures': The Victorian Middle Class and the Problem of Leisure," *Victorian Studies* 21 (1977): 24–25.

CHAPTER 12

1. Henry De la Beche, *A Geological Manual* (London: Treuttel and Würtz, 1831), 70–74.

2. Vernon Harcourt, in a discussion following a paper by Ernest Romney Matthews, "Erosion of the Holderness Coast of Yorkshire," *PICE* 159 (1904): 95–99, credits the reports from a committee of the British Association in the mid-1880s for having awakened the public to the problem.

3. W. H. Wheeler, *The Sea-Coast* (London: Longmans, 1902), v.

4. Ibid., 1–34; J. B. Redman, "The South-East Coast," Report of the Committee of the British Association on the Rate of Erosion of the Sea-coasts of England and Wales, *British Association* 54 (1884): 409.

5. R. L. Sherlock, *Man as a Geological Agent* (London: Witherby, 1922), 240–45; Alfred Carey, "Coast Erosion," *PICE* 159 (1904): 48–50; Matthews, "Erosion of the Holderness Coast," 65–67; testimony of Horace Woodward, *BPP*, RC on Coast Erosion and the Reclamation of Tidal Lands, 1st report, 34 (1907): qq. 3310–12, 3331, of Audrey Strahan, qq. 3541–45, of Richard Hansford Worth, qq. 3971–76, and of George Hambry, qq. 6641–54; Nicholas Everitt, "Fighting the Sea on the East Coast," *East Anglian Daily Times* (26 July 1902): 5, and (28 July 1902): 5.

6. Redman, "South-East Coast," 409.

7. Wheeler, *Sea-Coast*, v, 1–6, 23, 33–34, 307–11. For a detailed account of interventions at Brighton and Hove and their unfortunate results, see "Groynes on Shifting Beaches," *Engineer* (6 August 1886): 113, and Edmund Gilbert, *Brighton, Old Ocean's Bauble* (Hassocks, Sussex: Harvester, 1975), 38–39.

8. "The Contest for the Coast," *Chambers's Journal*, 5th series, 8 (1891): 241–43.

9. Jacquetta Hawkes, *A Land* (London: Cresset Press, 1951), 9.

10. Beckles Willson, *Lost England* (London: George Newnes, 1902), 9–10.

11. From the *Referee*, quoted in *Herne Bay Press* (17 February 1906), 2.

12. Carey, "Coast Erosion," 42–57.

13. Quoted in *Herne Bay Press* (3 February 1906), 2.

14. *BPP*, RC on Coast Erosion 34 (1907): 54, q. 1031, pp. 289–91. Because much of Scotland's coastline consisted of hard rock and was, therefore, considered relatively safe from attack, the commissioners confined most of their investigations to England, Wales, and Ireland.

15. Brian W. Clapp, *An Environmental History of Britain since the Industrial Revolution* (London: Longman, 1994), 101.

16. Barrie Trinder, *The Making of the Industrial Landscape* (London: Dent, 1982), 241.

17. Bertram Blount, "Cement," *Encyclopaedia Britannica*, vol. 5 (1911),

653–59; "Of the Use of Concrete in Marine Construction," *Engineering* 34 (1882): 480–81; A. C. Davis, *Portland Cement* (London: Concrete Publications, 1934), 1–15; J. H. Clapham, *An Economic History of Modern Britain,* vol. 2, *Free Trade and Steel* (Cambridge: CUP, 1926), 44–46.

18. Henry Young and Gilbert Redgrave, "The Manufacture and Testing of Portland Cement," *PICE* 62 (1880): 67–69; Edwin Bernays, "Portland Cement, Concrete, and Some Applications," ibid., 87–88; J. M. Preston, *Industrial Medway* (Rochester: J. M. Preston, 1977), 71–81.

19. L. Erdmenger, "The Cement Question in England," *PICE* 64 (1881): 349–50.

20. Joel Mokyr, "Technological Inertia in Economic History," *Journal of Economic History* 52 (1992): 333.

21. Redman, "South-East Coast," 407.

22. *BPP,* RC on Coast Erosion, 34 (1907): 32, q. 349.

23. Ibid., 27, qq. 223–24.

24. Ibid., testimony of Col. F. J. Day, qq. 87–96. Day's statistics about what was happening to the foreshores were confused by the fact that some measurements were based on normal high-tide lines and others were calculated on the unusually high spring tide lines. The legal definition of a foreshore, according to the final report of the RC on Coast Erosion, 14 (1911): 103, was the portion covered by tides, the landward limit consisting of the line reached by the sea at the medium high tide between the spring and the neap.

25. See testimony of T. H. Pelham, Asst. Sec. of the Board of Trade, *BPP,* RC on Coast Erosion, 34 (1907): 20, qq. 48–52.

26. Walter White, *A Londoner's Walk to the Land's End* (London: Chapman and Hall, 1855), 127–30.

27. Richard Hansford Worth, "Geological Conditions Affecting the Coast-Line from Exmouth to Plymouth," reprinted in the appendix to the report of the RC on Coast Erosion, 34 (1907): pp. 705–8; see also *BPP,* RC on Coast Erosion, the Reclamation of Tidal Lands, and Afforestation, 3d Report (on Afforestation) 14 (1911): 78, point 73.

28. Eugene Ferguson, *Oliver Evans: Inventive Genius of the American Industrial Revolution* (Greenville, Del.: The Hagley Museum, 1980), 39–41. "Oruktor Amphibolos" means "Amiphibious Digger."

29. J. J. Webster, "Dredging Operations and Appliances," *PICE* 89 (1887): 2–32.

30. Richard Hansford Worth, "Hallsands and Start Bay," *Report and Transactions of the Devonshire Association* 36 (1904): 325–28.

31. Eric Bird, *Coasts,* 3d ed. (Oxford: Blackwell, 1984), 83.

32. Ibid., 708.

33. Roy Millward and Adrian Robinson, *The South-West Peninsula* (London: Macmillan, 1971), 158. Sherlock, *Man as a Geological Agent,* 241–43, mentions a number of other places where mining of shingle had particularly deleterious effects: the south coast of the river Wear, thirty-four miles of the Holderness coast, Walton in Essex, Clacton, Scotland's Loch Ryan, Goldspie, Culbin Sands, East Sands near St. Andrews, and Macduff Harbour—in Ireland, several places on the coast of County Antrim.

34. Worth, "Hallsands and Start Bay," part 1, *Transactions* 36 (1904): 302–46; part 2, 41 (1909): 301–8; part 3, 55 (1923): 131–47; see also his testimony before the 1907 commission, vol. 34, 160–62, and A. H. W. Robinson, "The Hydrography of Start Bay and Its Relation to Beach Change at Hallsands," *Geographical Journal* 121 (1961): 63–77.

35. *BPP,* RC on Coast Erosion, 34 (1907): 333–34, qq. 9699–701, 9705–23, 9752–59, 9760–66. In their final report, the commissioners expressed their opinion that the threat to Rhyl had been somewhat exaggerated, *BPP,* RC on Coast Erosion, 14 (1911): 79, 101–2.

36. *Herne Bay Press* (3 February 1906), 4; (10 February 1906), 2; *BPP,* RC on Coast Erosion, the Reclamation of Tidal Lands, and Afforestation, 14 (1909): qq. 11606–84.

37. This and the following references to Ramsey's testimony can be found in *BPP,* RC on Coast Erosion, 34 (1907): 299–306, 726, 786–88.

38. *Herne Bay Press* (14 April 1894), 4.

39. Wheeler, *Sea-Coast,* 294–97. For a clear, brief description of the scouring process, see Andrew Goudie, *The Human Impact on the Natural Environment* (Cambridge, Mass.: MIT Press, 1982), 226–31.

40. *BPP,* RC on Coast Erosion, 34 (1907): 307, q. 8816; 309, q. 8872. Sherlock, *Man as a Geological Agent,* 243–44, lists as places where building defenses led to serious erosion elsewhere: Bridlington, Sheringham, Cromer, Corton near Lowestoft, Hastings, Bexhill, Eastbourne, Brighton, Hove, Blackpool, and Silloth.

41. *BPP,* RC on Coast Erosion, 34 (1907): 299, q. 8514; 301, q. 8560; 302, q. 8615; 304, q. 8706.

42. J. A. Steers, *Coastal Features of England and Wales* (Cambridge: Oleander Press, 1981), 167–68; Sherlock, *Man as a Geological Agent,* 247–48; *BPP,* RC on Coast Erosion, 14 (1911): 19–20, 59.

43. James Oldham, "On Reclaiming Land from Seas and Estuaries," *PICE* 21 (1861–62): 454–65; see also John Wiggins, *The Practice of Embanking Lands from the Sea* (London: Weale, 1852).

44. Wheeler, *Sea-Coast,* 237

45. *BPP,* RC on Coast Erosion, 34 (1907): 21, qq. 81–85.

46. Ibid., 73, qq. 1457, 1460, 1463, 1469–70.

47. H. Jesse Walker, "Man's Impact on Shorelines and Nearshore Environments: A Geomorphological Perspective," *Geoforum* 15 (1984): 398.

48. In 1895 Fanny Talbot gave the just-formed National Trust its first stretch of coastline, Dinas Oleu, four acres of Welsh hillside on the Mawddach Estuary. "I wish to put it into the custody," she said, "of some society that will never vulgarise it or prevent wild Nature from having its own way." "Her thoughts," comments Charlie Pye-Smith, *In Search of Neptune* (London: National Trust, 1990), 9, "were entirely parochial."

49. Geoffrey Clark, "The Coastlands," in H. E. Bates et al., *The English Countryside* (London: Batsford, 1939), 212.

50. Reported in "Changes on the Coasts of the British Isles," *Engineering* 82 (1906): 312–32.

51. Ibid., 104–5, qq. 2184–85.

52. *BPP*, RC on Coast Erosion, 34 (1907): 109, qq. 2296–97.

53. Ibid., 713. The extracts are from *Rural England*, vol. 2 (1902): 467–68.

54. *BPP*, RC on Coast Erosion, 14 (1909): qq. 11965–12115.

55. "Palmerston on Fixing Blowing Sands," *Builder* 3 (1845): 167

56. H. L. Edlin, "The Culbin Sands," in *Reclamation*, ed. John Lenihan and William Fletcher (New York: Academic Press, 1976), 4–7; see also George Bain, *The Culbin Sands or the Story of a Buried Estate* (Nairn: *Nairnshire Telegraph*, 1922); Forestry Commission, *Britain's Forests: Culbin* (HMSO, 1951); W. Mackie, "The Sands and Sandstones of Eastern Moray," *Transactions of the Edinburgh Geological Society* 7 (1899): 148; J. D. Ovington, "The Afforestation of Culbin Sands," *JE* 38 (1950): 303–19; Edward Salisbury, *Downs and Dunes* (London: Bell, 1952); J. A. Steers, *The Sea Coast* (London: Collins, 1953); Steers, *The Coastline of Scotland* (Cambridge: CUP, 1973), 217–20.

57. Edlin, "Culbin Sands," 11.

58. *BPP*, RC on Coast Erosion, 14 (1909): q. 12101.

59. David Pinder and Michael Witherick, "Port Industrialization, Urbanization and Wetland Loss," in *Wetlands*, ed. Michael Williams (Oxford: Basil Blackwell, 1990), 234–66.

60. Charlie Pye-Smith and Chris Rose, *Crisis and Conservation: Conflict in the British Countryside* (Harmondsworth: Penguin, 1984), 111–17; David Mercer, "Recreation and Wetlands: Impacts, Conflict, and Policy Issues," in *Wetlands*, ed. Michael Williams, 267–95.

CONCLUSION

1. Roy Rappaport, *Pigs for the Ancestors* (1968; new, enlarged ed., New Haven: Yale University Press, 1984); Rappaport, "The Flow of Energy in an Agricultural Society," *Scientific American* 225 (1971): 116–32, gives a summary of the book's argument and concludes by contrasting the conservative ways of the Tsembaga and the destructive ways of industrial societies.

2. Rappaport answered his critics in the 1984 edition of *Pigs*, 299–479. For a brief and sympathetic appraisal of the model's strengths and limitations, see Donald Worster, *The Wealth of Nature* (New York: Oxford University Press, 1993), 36–44.

3. Geoffrey Channon, "The Aberdeenshire Beef Trade with London: A Study in Steamship and Railway Competition, 1850–69," *Transport History* 2 (1969): 1–24; C. H. Lee, "Some Aspects of the Coastal Shipping Trade: The Aberdeen Steam Navigation Company, 1835–80," *Journal of Transport History*, new series, 3 (1975): 94–107; see also Sarah Palmer, " 'The Most Indefatigable Activity' The General Steam Navigation Company, 1824–50," *Journal of Transport History*, 3d series, 3 (1982): 1–22.

4. R. Edmonds, "A statistical account of the parish of Madron," *Journal of the Royal Statistical Society* 11 (1838): 207, quoted in Alan Harris, "Changes in the Early Railway Age: 1800–1850," in *A New Historical Geography of England*, ed. A. C. Darby (Cambridge: Cambridge University Press, 1973), 509.

5. Colin Duncan, "Legal Protection for the Soil of England: The Spurious Context of Nineteenth Century 'Progress'," *Agricultural History* 66 (1992): 93.

6. Martin Wiener, *English Culture and the Decline of the Industrial Spirit, 1850–1980* (Cambridge: Cambridge University Press, 1981), xiv, 145.

7. Jonathan Bate, *Romantic Ecology* (London: Routledge, 1991). Stephen Daniels, *Fields of Vision* (Cambridge: Polity Press, 1993), 217–36, demonstrates how Constable's landscapes (or rather the social reconstructions of those landscapes) have been used to promote the cause of rural preservation in this century.

8. Margaret Drabble, *A Writer's Britain* (London: Thames and Hudson, 1979), 161.

9. Especially useful in understanding the presuppositions and implementations of this small "c" conservatism are: John Barrell, *The Idea of Landscape and the Sense of Place: An Approach to the Poetry of John Clare* (Cambridge: Cambridge University Press, 1972); J. C. D. Clark, *English Society, 1688–1832: Ideology, Social Structure, and Political Practice* (Cambridge: Cambridge University Press, 1985); Denis Cosgrove, *Social Formation and Symbolic Landscape* (London: Croom Helm, 1984), 189–222; Nigel Everett, *The Tory View of Landscape* (New Haven: Yale University Press, 1994); Alun Howkins, "J. M. W. Turner at Petworth: Agricultural Improvements and the Politics of Landscape," in *Painting and the Politics of Culture, 1700–1850*, ed. John Barrell (Oxford: Oxford University Press, 1992); David Roberts, *Paternalism in Early Victorian England* (New Brunswick: Rutgers University Press, 1979); F. M. L. Thompson, *English Landed Society in the Nineteenth Century* (London: Routledge and Kegan Paul, 1963).

10. Bate, *Romantic Ecology*, 18, uses the phrase but does not endorse it.

11. Ann Bermingham, *Landscape and Ideology* (Berkeley and Los Angeles: University of California Press, 1986), 9–15, 157–72. The last chapter of Everett, *Tory*, called "The Nature of Toryism," is an attempt to answer this kind of "Marxisant" art history; see also Malcolm Andrews, *The Search for the Picturesque: Landscape Aesthetic and Tourism in Britain, 1760–1800* (Stanford: Stanford University Press, 1989); Cosgrove, *Social;* Carol Fabricant, "The Aesthetics and Politics of Landscape in the Eighteenth Century," in *Studies in Eighteenth-Century British Art and Aesthetic*, ed. Ralph Cohen (Berkeley and Los Angeles: University of California Press, 1985); Gary Harrison, *Wordsworth's Vagrant Muse* (Detroit: Wayne State Press, 1994); Roger Sales, *English Literature in History, 1780–1830: Pastoral and Politics* (London: Hutchinson, 1983); C. E. Searle, "Custom, Class Conflict, and Agrarian Capitalism: The Cumbrian Customary Economy in the Eighteenth Century," *Past and Present* 110 (1986): 106–33; Raymond Williams, *The Country and the City* (London: Chatto and Windus, 1973).

12. Bruce Ferguson, "The Concept of Landscape Health," *Journal of Environmental Management* 40 (1994): 135, gives this definition: "Landscape health is the landscape taking care of itself."

Bibliography

PRIMARY SOURCES

MANUSCRIPTS AND OFFICIAL PAPERS

Boughton Estate Papers.

British Parliamentary Papers. 1831–32. Lords Committee: The Bill entitled An Act for Making a Railway from London to Birmingham. Minutes of Evidence. Vol. 311.

———. 1833. SC on Public Walks. Vol. 15.

———. 1843. First Report of the Midland Mining Commission. Vol. 13.

———. 1865. SC on Open Spaces (Metropolis), Report. Vol. 8.

———. 1869. RC on Water Supply. Vol. 33.

———. 1873. Report on Landslips in Salt Districts. Vol. 53.

———. 1878. SC on the Manchester Corporation Water Bill, Report. Vol. 16.

———. 1878–79. Report of Col. Cox on Landslips in the Salt District to the Local Government Board. Vol. 58.

———. 1881. RC on Agriculture. Vol. 17.

———. 1890–91. SC on Brine Pumping. Vol. 11.

———. 1893–94. Committee of Inquiry on Stone, Limestone, Slate and Clay Quarrying. Vol. 73.

———. 1895. Report of the Departmental Committee upon Merionethshire Slate Mines. Vol. 35.

———. 1902. Report of Committee to the Board of Agriculture. Vol. 20.

———. 1907. First Report of the RC on Coast Erosion and the Reclamation of Tidal Lands. Vol. 34; appendix. Vol. 35.

———. 1908. Report of Departmental Committee on Irish Forestry. Vol. 23.

———. 1909. Second Report (on Afforestation) of the RC on Coast Erosion, the Reclamation of Tidal Lands, and Afforestation. Vol. 14.

————. 1911. Third Report (on Afforestation) of the RC on Coast Erosion, the Reclamation of Tidal Lands, and Afforestation. Vol. 14.

County of Northampton. 1831. *Meeting of the proprietors and occupiers of lands in the County of Northampton.*

Hansard's Parliamentary Debates. 1884. Vol. 289. 3d series.

————. 1887. Vol. 316. 3d series.

————. 1892. Vol. 2. 4th series.

Hemel Hempstead. 1831. *Meeting of Proprietors and Occupiers of Houses and Lands, and other Persons Interested in Property and Estates Between Paddington and Leighton.*

London County Council. 1924. *London Parks and Open Spaces.* London.

Manchester City Council. 1926. *A Record of Municipal Activity.* Edited by Matthew Anderson. Manchester.

District of Surrey, British Columbia, Planning and Development Services Department. 1989. *Golf Courses.*

BOOKS (TO 1918)

An Account of the Proceedings of the Great Western Railway Company. 1834. London.

Acland, Thomas Dyke. 1851. *The Farming of Somersetshire.* London.

Adams, William Bridges. 1850. *Road Progress and Steam Farming.* London.

Ashton, William. 1909. *The Battle of Land and Sea.* Southport.

Barrow, George. 1862. *Wild Wales.* 1923 edition. London.

Bateman, John Frederic La Trobe. 1865. *On the Supply of Water to London from the Sources of the River Severn.* Westminster.

————. 1884. *History and Description of the Manchester Waterworks.* Manchester.

Bell, George. 1912. *Floreat Swansea.* Swansea.

Billingsley, John. 1797. *A General View of the Agriculture of Somerset.* London.

Bland, E. 1888. *Annals of Southport.* Southport.

Bourne, John. 1839. *Historical and Descriptive Accounts of the Origin, General Execution, and Characteristics of the London and Birmingham Railway.* London.

Bradley, A. G. 1903. *Highways and Byways in the Lake District.* London.

Brees, S. C. 1837. *Railway Practice.* 5 vols. London.

British Association. 1903. *Southport.* Southport.

Broome, Samuel. 1857. *Culture of the Chrysanthemum as Preached in the Temple Gardens.* London.

Brown, James. 1847. *The Forester.* Edinburgh.

Brown, John Croumbie. 1884. *Modern Forest Economy.* Edinburgh.

Burritt, Elihu. 1868. *Walks in the Black Country and Its Green Borderland.* 1976 edition. Kineton, Gloucestershire.

Caird, James. 1852. *English Agriculture in 1850–51.* 1967 edition. New York.

Cantlie, John. 1885. *Degeneration Among Londoners.* London.

Carlyle, Thomas. 1829. "Signs of the Times." In *Critical and Miscellaneous Essays.* Vol. 1. Included in *Thomas Carlyle's Works.* 17 vols. 1887. London.

Cliffe, Charles Frederick. 1847. *The Book of South Wales.* London.

Coghlan, Francis. 1834. *The Steam-Packet and Coast Companion.* London.

Conder, F. R. 1868. *Personal Recollections of English Engineers.* London.

Cort, R. 1834. *Rail-Road Impositions Detected.* 2d edition. London.

Creevey, Thomas. 1903. *The Creevey Papers.* Edited by Herbert Maxwell. 2 vols. London.

Davies, D. C. 1878. *A Treatise on Slate and Slate Quarrying.* London.

Day, James. 1839. *A Practical Treatise on the Construction and Formation of Railways.* London.

de Eresby, Willoughby. 1850. *Ploughing by Steam.* London.

De la Beche, Henry. 1831. *A Geological Manual.* London.

Dickens, Charles. 1841. *The Old Curiosity Shop.* 1987 edition. Oxford.

Ditchfield, P. H. 1910. *Vanishing England.* London.

Drake, James. 1839. *Road Book.* London.

Everard, H. S. C. 1907. *A History of the Royal and Ancient Golf Club, St. Andrews from 1754–1900.* Edinburgh.

Falkner, F. 1843. *The Muck Manual.* London.

Fifth Annual Report of the Metropolitan Public Gardens Association. 1887. London.

Forbes, A. C. 1904. *English Estate Forestry.* London.

Francis, John. 1851. *A History of the English Railway.* 1968 edition. New York.

Freeling, Arthur. 1837. *The Railway Companion, from London to Birmingham, Liverpool, and Manchester.* London.

Gaskell, Elizabeth. 1848. *Mary Barton.* 1966 edition. London.

———. 1854–55. *North and South.* 1970 edition. Harmondsworth.

Godwin, George. 1837. *An Appeal to the Public, on the Subject of Railways.* London.

———. 1854. *London Shadows.* 1985 edition. New York.

———. 1859. *Town Swamps and Social Bridges.* 1972 edition. New York.

Graham, Peter Anderson. 1916. *Reclaiming the Waste.* London.

Grigor, John. 1881. *Arboriculture.* 2d edition. Edinburgh.

Hackwood, Frederick. 1899. *Olden Wednesbury.* Wednesbury.

Haggard, H. Rider. 1902. *Rural England.* 2 vols. London.

Harrison, Samuel. 1864. *A Complete History of the Great Flood at Sheffield.* London.

Hawthorne, Nathaniel. 1856. *The English Notebooks.* Edited by Randall Stewart. 1941. New York.

Head, Francis Bond. 1849. *Stokers and Pokers or the London and North-West Railway.* 1968 edition. London.

Head, George. 1836. *A Home Tour through the Manufacturing Districts of England in the Summer of 1835.* London.

Heath, Francis George. 1875. *The Fern Paradise.* 1908 edition. London.

Hill, Octavia. 1878. *Homes of the London Poor.* 1970 edition. London.

Hughes, Thomas. 1857. *Tom Brown's School Days.* 1888 edition. London.

Jeaffreson, J. C. 1864. *The Life of Robert Stephenson.* 2 vols. London.

Jevons, William Stanley. 1865. *The Coal Question.* 1965 edition. New York.

Johnson, Cuthburt. 1837. *The Advantages of Railways to Agriculture*. 2d edition. London.

Johnston, James. 1849. *Contributions to Scientific Agriculture*. Edinburgh.

J. S. 1849. *A Guide to Southport*. Liverpool.

Kohl, J. G. 1844. *England and Wales*. 1968 edition. London.

Lardner, Dionysius. 1836. *The Steam Engine*. 5th edition. London.

Lavergne, Léonce de [Guilhaud]. 1855. *The Rural Economy of England, Scotland, and Ireland*. Edinburgh.

Lecount, Peter. 1839. *The History of the Railway connecting London and Birmingham*. London.

Leech, Bosdin. 1907. *History of the Manchester Ship Canal*. 2 vols. London.

Livius, Barham. 1842. *Letter on Steam Power on Canals*. London.

Loftie, W. J. 1875. *In and Out of London*. London.

McDermott, Frederick. 1887. *The Life and Works of Joseph Firbank*. London.

Mackie, Alexander. 1911. *Aberdeenshire*. Cambridge.

Malcolm, George. 1890. *Deer Forests*. Edinburgh.

Malcolm, George, and Aymer Maxwell. 1910. *Grouse and Grouse Moors*. London.

Marsh, George Perkins. 1864. *Man and Nature*. 1965 edition. Edited by David Lowenthal. Cambridge, Mass.

———. 1874. *The Earth as Modified by Human Action*. New York.

Mayhew, Henry. 1861–62. *London Labour and the London Poor*. 4 vols. 1968 edition. New York.

Mechi, John. 1845. *A Series of Letters on Agricultural Improvement*. London.

———. 1852. *A Lecture on British Agriculture*. London.

———. 1875. *How I Make Farming Pay*. London.

Miller, Hugh. 1843. *Sutherland as it Was and Is or, How a County May be Ruined*. Edinburgh.

New Illustrated Guide to Southport. 1875. Southport.

Osborne, Edward. 1840. *Osborne's London and Birmingham Railway Guide*. Birmingham.

Ouida [Marie Louise de la Ramée]. 1895. *Views and Opinions*. London.

Parkes, S. Haddon. 1862. *Flower Shows of Window Plants, for the Working Classes of London*. London.

———. 1864. *Window Gardens for the People*. London.

Peace, J. 1842. *Descant upon Railroads*. London.

Peek, Henry 1867. *Six Essays on Commons Preservation*. London.

A Practical Inquiry into Laws of Excavation and Embankment on Railways. 1840. London.

Pratt, E. A. 1906. *The Transition in Agriculture*. London.

Prothero, Rowland [Lord Ernle]. 1912. *English Farming Past and Present*. London.

Prout, John. 1881. *Profitable Clay Farming under a Just System of Tenant Right*. 3d edition. London.

Railroadiana or a New History of England. 1838. London.

Remarks on Proposed Railways. 1831. London.

Ritchie, Robert. 1849. *The Farm Engineer*. Glasgow.

Robinson, William. 1868. *Gleanings from French Gardens.* London.

Roscoe, Thomas. 1839. *The London and Birmingham Railway.* London.

Rownsley, H. D. 1906. *Literary Associations of the English Lakes.* Glasgow.

Ruskin, John. 1903–12. *The Works of John Ruskin.* Edited by E. T. Cook and Alexander Wedderburn. 39 vols. London.

Scott, Hudson. 1857. *Scott's Railway Companion.* Newcastle.

Shaw-Lefevre, George John [Lord Eversley]. 1894. *English Commons and Forests: The Battle During the Last Thirty Years for Public Rights over the Commons and Forests of England and Wales.* London.

Shimmin, Hugh. 1858. *Town Life.* Liverpool.

Simmonds, Peter Lund. 1876. *Waste Products and Undeveloped Substances.* 3d edition. London.

Simpson, John. 1900. *The New Forestry.* Sheffield.

———. 1909. *British Woods and Their Owners.* Sheffield.

Smiles, Samuel. 1862. *Lives of the Engineers.* 3 vols. 1968 edition. Newton Abbot.

Somervell, Robert. 1877. *Water for Manchester from Thirlmere.* London.

Somerville, Mary. 1848. *Physical Geography.* 2 vols. London.

Stuart, A. J. 1882. *Extracts from Man and Nature . . . with some Notes on Forests and Rain-fall in Madras.* Madras.

Summerbell, T. 1908. *Afforestation: The Unemployed and the Land.* London.

Sutton, Martin, ed. 1912. *The Book of the Links.* London.

Thom, Robert. 1829. *A Brief Account of the Shaws Water Scheme.* Greenock.

———. 1837. *Report on Supplying Glasgow with Water.* Glasgow.

Thurston, E. Temple. 1911. *The 'Flower of Gloster.'* London.

Tomkins, Henry. 1874. *The Pavements of London.* London.

Trollope, Anthony. 1880. *The Duke's Children.* London.

Vardon, Harry. 1912. *The Complete Golfer.* 13th edition. London.

Vernon-Harcourt, L. F. 1882. *A Treatise on Rivers and Canals.* 2 vols. Oxford.

Walker, James Scott. 1830. *An Accurate Description of the Liverpool and Manchester Railway.* Liverpool.

Wednesbury, Faces, Places, and Industries. 1897. Wednesbury.

Wheeler, W. H. 1893. *Tidal Rivers.* London.

———. 1902. *The Sea-Coast.* London.

White, Walter. 1855. *A Londoner's Walk to the Land's End.* London.

Whitshaw, Francis. 1842. *The Railways of Great Britain.* 1969 edition. New York.

Wiggins, John. 1852. *The Practice of Embanking Lands from the Sea.* London.

Williams, Frederick. 1852. *Our Iron Roads.* 1968 edition. New York.

Willson, Beckles. 1902. *Lost England.* London.

ARTICLES (TO 1918)

Acland, Thomas Dyke. 1850. "On the Farming of Somersetshire." *JRASE* 11: 666–764.

"Afforestation Conference in London." 1907. *Quarterly Journal of Forestry* 1: 373–74.

"Afforestation of Waste lands in Denmark, Holland, France, and Germany." 1909. *TRSAS* 22: 207–11.

"Basic Slag." 1906–7. *Journal of the Board of Agriculture* 13: 549–53.

"Basic Slag for Poor Pastures." 1904–7. *Journal of the Board of Agriculture.* 11: 414–15; 13: 549–53.

Bastin, S. Leonard. 1914. "Tree-Planting in the Black Country." *JRASE* 71: 70–75.

Bateman, John Frederic La Trobe. 1867. "Description of the Manchester Waterworks." *Engineering* 4: 237, 240–42.

Bear, William. 1898–99. "Flower and Fruit Farming in England." *JRASE,* 3d series, 9: 286–313, 512–50; *JRASE* 10: 267–313.

"Beautifying the Black Country." 23 August 1884. *Birmingham Daily Mail:* 2.

Bell, Robert. 1884. "The Forests of Canada." *British Association for the Advancement of Science* 54: 856–60.

Bernays, Edwin. 1880. "Portland Cement, Concrete, and some Applications." *PICE* 62: 87–97.

"Black Country Trees." 22 January 1903. *Birmingham Daily Mail:* 2.

Blount, Bertram. 1911. "Cement." *Encyclopaedia Britannica* 5: 653–59.

Cairnes, J. E. 1864. "Co-operation in the Slate Quarries of North Wales." *Macmillan's Magazine* 11: 181–90.

Cambell, James Archibald. 1866. "Report on the Application of Sewage." *THASS* 1:1–20.

Carey, Alfred. 1904. "Coast Erosion." *PICE* 159: 42–57.

"Changes on the Coasts of the British Isles." 1906. *Engineering* 82: 312–32.

Colt, H. S. 1912. "The Construction of New Courses." In *The Book of the Links.* Edited by Martin Sutton. London.

"The Contest for the Coast." 1891. *Chambers's Journal.* 5th series. 8: 241–43.

de Schwarz, the Chevalier. 1903. "Slag Cement." *Engineering* 75: 671–72.

Dickson, Edmund. 1903. "The Ribble Estuary." In British Association Report: *"Southport."*

"Disastrous Inundation at Sheffield." 1864. *Annual Register.* 30–39.

Duncan, Thomas. 1853. "Description of the Liverpool Corporation Waterworks." *PICE* 12: 460–505.

Edmonds, R. 1838. "A statistical account of the parish of Madron." *Journal of the Royal Statistical Society* 11: 207.

Erdmenger, L. 1881. "The Cement Question in England." *PICE* 64: 349–50.

Everitt, Nicholas. 26 and 28 July 1902. "Fighting the Sea on the East Coast." *East Anglian Daily Times.*

Forbes, A. C. 1898. "Is British Forestry Progressive?" *TRSAS* 15: 44–45.

Fox, Charles Douglas. 1878. "Description of the Excavating Machine, or Steam Navvy, with the Results of Its Use, on the West Lancashire Railway." *PICE* 52: 250–56.

Geikie, J. 1866. "On the buried forests and peat deposits of Scotland and changes in climate which they indicate." *Transactions of the Royal Society, Edinburgh* 24: 363–84.

"Great Landslip at Dunkirk." 11 December 1880. *Northwich and Knutesford Guardian.*

Grenfell, A. P. 1909. "Recent Progress in Afforestation." *Quarterly Journal of Forestry* 3: 21–31.

"Groynes on Shifting Beaches." 6 August 1886. *Engineer,* 113.

Hackwood, Frederick W. 24 January 1903. "Letter from F. W. H." *Birmingham Daily Mail:* 2

Hall, A. D. 1904–5. "The Growth of Sugar Beets." *Journal of the Board of Agriculture* 11: 577–81.

Hill, George Henry. 1891–92. "The Manchester Water Works." *Engineering* 52: 434–38, 495–98, 553–56, 615–17, 677–80, 746–48; 53: 33–35, 102–3, 161.

———. 1896. "The Thirlmere Works for the Water Supply of Manchester." *PICE* 76: 69–70.

Holland, Henry. 1849–50. "The Natural History of Man." *Quarterly Review* 86: 1–40.

———. 1864. Review of 'Man and Nature' by Marsh. *The Edinburgh Review* 120: 464–500.

"The Holmfirth Catastrophe." 1852. *Annual Register.* 17: 478–81.

Hutchinson, Horatio Gordon. 1911. "Golf." *Encyclopaedia Britannica.* Vol. 12. Cambridge.

Jacob, Arthur. 1882. "The Conservancy of Rivers: The Valley of the Irwell." *PICE* 67: 237–45.

"The Lakes and the Railways." 28 October 1876. *Spectator:* 1338–39.

Macdonald, James. 1880. "On the Agriculture of the County of Sutherland." *THASS,* 4th series, 12: 1–90.

Mackie, W. 1899. "The Sands and Sandstones of Eastern Moray." *Transactions of the Edinburgh Geological Society* 7: 148.

"Manchester and the Meres." 8 September 1877. *Spectator.* 1118–19.

Manchester Guardian. 14 September and 31 October 1877. Articles on Thirlmere.

"Manchester Ship Canal." 1894. *Engineering* 57: 97–142.

Martineau, P. E. 1916. "The Planting of Pit Mounds." *Report of the British Association for the Advancement of Science* 86: 494–95.

Matthews, Ernest Romney. 1904. "Erosion of the Holderness Coast of Yorkshire." *PICE* 159: 58–142.

Mechi, John. 1860. "The Sewage of Towns as it Affects British Agriculture." *Farmer's Magazine,* 3d series, 17: 254–55.

"Of the Use of Concrete in Marine Construction." 1882. *Engineering* 34: 480–81.

Oldham, H. Yule. 1894. "The Manchester Ship Canal." *Geographical Journal* 3: 491.

Oldham, James. 1861–1862. "On Reclaiming Land from the Seas and Estuaries." *PICE* 21: 454–65.

"Palmerston on Fixing Blowing Sands." 1845. *Builder* 3: 167.

Peek, Henry. 1867. *Six Essays on Common Preservation.* London.

Pell, Albert. 1887. "The Making of the Land in England: A Retrospect." *JRASE,* 2d series, 23: 355–74.

———. 1899. "The Making of the Land of England: A Second Retrospect." *JRASE,* 3d series, 10: 136–41.

Phipps, R. W. 1884. "Report on Forestry." The section, "Across the Watershed of Eastern Ontario." Reprinted in *Journal of Forest History* 9 October 1965: 2–8.

Prout, W. A., and John Voelcker. 1905. "Continuous Corn Growing in Its Practical and Chemical Aspects." *JRASE* 66: 35–51.

"Quarrying Machinery." 1876. *Engineering* 21: 267, 276.

Rawlinson, R., et al. 1879. "Discussion on River Outlets." *PICE* 59: 66–67.

Redman, J. B. 1884. "The South-East Coast." *British Association* 54: 408–10.

Review of *Man and Nature.* 6 August 1864. *The Athenaeum,* no. 1919: 176–77.

"Review of the Report of the Agricultural Committee." 1833. *Journal of Steam Transport and Husbandry,* 1–10.

Roberts, Charles Gay. 1879. "Sutherland Reclamation." *JRASE* 15: 397–487.

Rolleston, George. 1879. "The Modification of the External Aspects of Organic Nature Produced by Man's Interference." *Journal of the Royal Geographical Society* 49: 320–92.

Sanbourne, Linley. 5 February 1876. "Lady of the Lake Loquitur." *Punch* 70: 34.

Schlich, William. 1889–90. "Forestry in the Colonies and in India." *Proceedings of the Royal Colonial Institute* 21: 187–238.

"Sheffield Reservoir." 1864. *Builder* 22: 333–35, 530.

Smee, Alfred. 1863. Metropolitan Amalgamated Chrysanthemum Society. *The Gardener's Weekly Magazine and Floricultural Cabinet* 5: 93.

"Steam Cultivation." 1874. *Engineering* 18: 94–95.

Stirling-Maxwell, John. 1913. "The Place of Forestry in the Economic Development of Scotland." *TRSAS* 27: 161–71.

"Swallowed by Earth." 14 December 1903. *Birmingham Daily Mail:* 2.

"Thirlmere." 31 October 1877. *Manchester Guardian:* 6.

Thompson, P. Murray. 1913. "The Utilisation of Disused Pit-banks." *TRSAS* 27: 30–33.

Till, E. D. 1904. "The Arbor Day Movement." *Pearson's Magazine* 17: 203–9.

Times. 20 October, 15, 18 December 1877. Articles on Thirlmere.

Tracy, W. Burnett. 1896. "The Manchester Ship Canal." *Journal of the Manchester Geographical Society* 12: 211–12.

Voelcker, Augustus. 1862. "On the Commercial Value of Artificial Manures." *JRASE* 23: 277–86.

"The Vyrnwy Dam." 4 June 1886. *Engineer,* 439.

Wall, Barrow. 1887. "The Agriculture of Pembrokeshire." *JRASE,* 2d series, 23: 70–101.

Watson, John. 1845. "On Reclaiming Heath Land." *JRASE* 6: 79–102.

Webster, J. J. 1887. "Dredging Operations and Appliances." *PICE* 89: 2–32.

Worth, Richard Hansford. 1904. "Hallsands and Start Bay." *Report and Transactions of the Devonshire Association* 36: 300–46.

Young, Henry, and Gilbert Redgrave. 1880. "The Manufacture and Testing of Portland Cement." *PICE* 62: 67–86.

SECONDARY SOURCES

BOOKS (AFTER 1918)

Adams, Annmarie. 1996. *Architecture in the Family Way.* Montreal and Kingston.

Adams, Richard N. 1982. *Paradoxical Harvest.* Cambridge.

Addison, William. 1977. *Portrait of Epping Forest.* London.

Alexander, Judd. 1993. *In Defense of Garbage.* Westport, Conn.

Allaby, Michael. 1983. *The Changing Uplands.* Cheltenham.

Anderson, Mark. 1967. *A History of Scottish Forestry.* 2 vols. London.

Andrews, Malcolm. 1989. *The Search for the Picturesque: Landscape Aesthetic and Tourism in Britain, 1760–1800.* Stanford.

Arvill, Robert. 1973. *Man and Environment.* 3d edition. Harmondsworth.

Ashby, E., and M. Anderson. 1981. *The Politics of Clean Air.* Oxford.

Atthill, Robin. 1964. *Old Mendip.* London.

Attwood, E. G., and H. G. Evans. 1961. *The Economics of Hill Farming.* Cardiff.

Baark, Erik, and Uno Svedlin, eds. 1988. *Man, Nature and Technology.* London.

Baber, Colin, and L. J. Williams, eds. 1986. *Modern South Wales: Essays in Economic History.* Cardiff.

Bagwell, Philip. 1988. *The Transport Revolution.* London.

Bailes, Kendall, ed. 1985. *Environmental History.* Lanham, Md.

Bailey, Francis. 1955. *A History of Southport.* Southport.

Bain, George. 1922. *The Culbin Sands or the Story of a Buried Estate.* Nairn.

Baker, Alan R. H., and Gideon Biger, eds. 1992. *Ideology and Landscape in Historical Perspective.* Cambridge.

Barr, John. 1969. *Derelict Britain.* Harmondsworth.

———. 1970. *The Assault on Our Senses.* London.

Barrell, John. 1972. *The Idea of Landscape and the Sense of Place: An Approach to the Poetry of John Clare.* Cambridge.

———, ed. 1992. *Painting and the Politics of Culture, 1700–1850.* Oxford.

Barron, James. 1938. *A History of the Ribble Navigation.* Preston.

Barton, R. M., ed. 1972. *Life in Cornwall in the Late Nineteenth Century.* Truro.

Bate, Jonathan. 1991. *Romantic Ecology.* London.

Bates, H. E., et al., eds. 1939. *The English Countryside.* London.

Bayfield, N. G., and G. C. Barrow, eds. 1985. The Ecological Impacts of Outdoor Recreation on *Mountain Areas in Europe and North America.* Ambleside, Cumbria.

Beale, Reginald. 1924. *Lawns for Sports.* London.

Beckett, J. V. 1988. *The East Midlands from A.D. 1000.* Harlow.

Bell, Martin, and John Boardman, eds. 1992. *Past and Present Soil Erosion.* Oxford.

Bermingham, Ann. 1986. *Landscape and Ideology.* Berkeley and Los Angeles.

Best, Robin. 1981. *Land Use and Living Spaces.* London.

Binnie, G. M. 1981. *Early Victorian Water Engineers.* London.

———. 1987. *Early Dam Builders in Britain.* London.

Bird, Eric. 1984. *Coasts.* 3d edition. Oxford.

Birks, Hilary, et al., eds. 1988. *The Cultural Landscape: Past, Present, and Future.* Cambridge.

Blaikie, Piers, and Harold Brookfield. 1987. *Land Degradation and Society.* London.

Blank, G. K., and M. K. Louis, eds. 1993. *Influence and Resistance in Nineteenth-Century English Poetry.* Basingstoke

Blunden, John, and Graham Turner. 1985. *Critical Countryside.* London.

Bogle, James. 1990. *Artists in Snowdonia.* Tal-y-bont.

Boorstin, Daniel. 1961. *The Image.* New York.

Bormann, F. Herbert, Diana Balmori, and Gordon Geballe. 1993. *Redesigning the American Lawn.* New Haven.

Botkin, Daniel. 1990. *Discordant Harmonies.* New York.

Bourassa, Steven. 1991. *The Aesthetics of Landscape.* London.

Bridges, E. M. 1987. *Surveying Derelict Land.* Oxford.

Brigden, Roy. 1986. *Victorian Farms.* Marlborough.

Briggs, Asa. 1982. *The Power of Steam.* Chicago.

Brimblecombe, P., and C. Pfister, eds. 1990. *The Silent Countdown.* Berlin.

Bromley, Rosemary, and Graham Humphrys, eds. 1979. *Dealing with Dereliction.* Swansea.

Brown, Jonathan. 1987. *Agriculture in England.* Manchester.

Browning, Robert. 1955. *A History of Golf.* London.

Bruce, Chandos [Marquess of Ailesbury] 1949. *The Wardens of Savernake Forest.* London.

———. 1962. *A History of Savernake Forest.* Devizes.

Bryant, C. R., L. H. Russwurm, and A. G. McLellan. 1982. *The City's Countryside.* London.

Bunce, Michael. 1994. *The Countryside Ideal.* London.

Burgess, Robert. 1992. *In Search of a Paradigm: Ecosystem Rehabilitation.* 2 vols. The Hague.

Burke, Peter, ed. 1979. *The New Cambridge Modern History.* Vol. 13. Companion vol. Cambridge.

Burke, Thomas. 1941. *The Streets of London.* London.

Burnett, John. 1983. *A Social History of Housing, 1815–1970.* London.

Calvert, Albert. 1919. *Salt and the Salt Industry.* London.

Cannadine, David. 1980. *Lords and Landlords: the Aristocracy and the Towns, 1774–1967.* Leicester.

———. 1994. *Aspects of Aristocracy.* New Haven.

———, ed. 1982. *Patricians, Power, and Politics in Nineteenth-Century Towns.* Leicester.

Carr, Herbert, and George Lister, eds. 1925. *The Mountains of Snowdonia.* London.

Carter, Ian. 1979. *Farmlife in Northeast Scotland, 1840–1914.* Edinburgh.

Chambers, J. D., and G. E. Mingay. 1966. *The Agricultural Revolution, 1750–1880.* London.

Chisholm, Michael. 1979. *Rural Settlement and Land Use.* 3d edition. London.

Clapham, J. H. 1926. *An Economic History of Modern Britain.* 2 vols. Cambridge.

Clapp, Brian W. 1994. *An Environmental History of Britain since the Industrial Revolution.* London.

Clark, J. C. D. 1985. *English Society 1688–1832: Ideology, Social Structure, and Political Practice.* Cambridge.

Cohen, Ralph, ed. 1985. *Studies in Eighteenth-Century British Art and Aesthetic.* Berkeley and Los Angeles.

Coleman, Terry. 1968. *The Railway Navvies.* Harmondsworth.

Colt, H. S., and C. H. Alison. 1920. *Some Essays on Golf-course Architecture.* London.

Collingwood, W. G. 1932. *The Lake Counties.* 2d edition. London.

Coppin, N. J., and A. D. Bradshaw. 1982. *Quarry Reclamation.* London.

Cornish, Geoffrey, and Ronald Whitten. 1981. *The Golf Course.* Leicester.

Cosgrove, Denis. 1984. *Social Formation and Symbolic Landscape.* London.

Cosgrove, Denis, and Stephen Daniels, eds. 1988. *The Iconography of Landscape.* Cambridge.

Cottrell, Fred. 1955. *Energy and Society.* New York.

Cranz, Galen. 1982. *The Politics of Park Design.* Cambridge, Mass.

Cronon, William. 1983. *Changes in the Land: Indians, Colonists, and the Ecology of New England.* New York.

Crosby, Alfred. 1986. *Ecological Imperialism.* Cambridge.

Crouch, D., and C. Ward. 1988. *The Allotment.* London.

Crowe, Sylvia. 1958. *The Landscape of Power.* London.

Cunningham, Hugh. 1980. *Leisure in the Industrial Revolution.* London.

Daniels, Stephen. 1993. *Fields of Vision.* Cambridge.

Darby, H. C. 1956. *The Draining of the Fens.* 2d edition. Cambridge.

———, ed. 1973. *A New Historical Geography of England.* Cambridge.

Davis, A. C. 1934. *Portland Cement.* London.

Davis, Clarence, and Kenneth Wilburn, eds. 1991. *Railway Imperialism.* New York.

Davis, Richard C., ed. 1983. *Encyclopedia of American Forest and Conservation History.* 2 vols. New York.

Detwyler, Thomas, ed. 1971. *Man's Impact on the Environment.* New York.

Diack, William. 1950. *Rise and Progress of the Granite Industry in Aberdeen.* Aberdeen.

Drabble, Margaret. 1979. *A Writer's Britain.* London.

Drushka, Ken. 1992. *Working in the Woods.* Madeira Park, B.C.

Dubos, René. 1978. *The Resilience of Ecosystems.* Boulder, Colo.

———. 1980. *The Wooing of the Earth.* New York.

Duncan, Colin. 1996. *The Centrality of Agriculture.* Montreal and Kingston.

Dyos, H. J., and Michael Wolff, eds. 1973. *The Victorian City.* 2 vols. London.

Edlin, H. L. 1956. *Trees, Woods, and Man.* 1970 revised edition. London.

Everett, Nigel. 1994. *The Tory View of Landscape.* New Haven.

Fairbrother, Nan. 1970. *New Lives, New Landscapes.* New York.

Faith, Nicholas. 1990. *The World the Railways Made.* London.

Fedden, Robin. 1968. *The Continuing Purpose.* London.

Ferguson, Eugene. 1980. *Oliver Evans: Inventive Genius of the American Industrial Revolution.* Greenville, Del.

Ferkiss, Victor. 1993. *Nature, Technology, and Society.* New York.

Floud, Roderick, and Donald McCloskey, eds. 1994. *The Economic History of Britain Since 1700.* 2d edition. 2 vols. Cambridge.

Fogarty, M. P., ed. 1948. *Further Studies in Industrial Organization.* London.

Forestry Commission. 1951. *Britain's Forests: Culbin.* HMSO.

Franklin, T. Bedford. 1944. *Good Pastures.* Cambridge.

———. 1948. *A History of Agriculture.* London.

———. 1952. *A History of Scottish Farming.* London.

Freeman, T. W., H. B. Rogers, and R. H. Kinvig. 1966. *Lancashire, Cheshire, and the Isle of Man.* London.

Gadgil, Madhav, and Ramachandra Guha. 1993. *This Fissured Land.* Berkeley and Los Angeles.

Gale, W. K. 1966. *The Black Country Iron Industry.* London.

Gash, Norman. 1979. *Aristocracy and People.* Cambridge, Mass.

Gaskell, Philip. 1968. *Morvern Transformed.* Cambridge.

Gemmell, Raymond. 1977. *Colonization of Industrial Wasteland.* London.

Gibbon, G., and R. Bell. 1939. *History of the London County Council, 1889–1939.* London.

Gilbert, Edmund. 1975. *Brighton, Old Ocean's Bauble.* Hassocks, Sussex.

Gille, Bertrand. 1986. *The History of Techniques.* 2 vols. New York.

Gillis, R. Peter, and Thomas Roach. 1986. *Lost Initiatives.* New York.

Gimingham, C. H. 1972. *Ecology of Heathlands.* London.

———. 1975. *An Introduction to Heathland Ecology.* Edinburgh.

Glasscock, Robin, ed. 1992. *Historic Landscapes of Britain from the Air.* Cambridge.

Glyptis, Sue, ed. 1993. *Leisure and the Environment.* London.

Golby, J. M., and A. W. Purdue. 1984. *The Civilization of the Crowd.* London.

Goldsmith, Edward, and Nicholas Hildyard, eds. 1986. *Green Britain or Industrial Wasteland?* Cambridge.

Good, J. E., ed. 1987. *Environmental Aspects of Plantation Forestry in Wales.* Grange-Over-Sands, Cumbria.

Goodman, Gordon, and Michael Chadwick, eds. 1978. *Environmental Management of Mineral Wastes.* Alphen aan den Rijn.

Goodman, Gordon, R. W. Edwards, and J. M. Lambert, eds. 1965. *Ecology and the Industrial Society.* New York.

Goudie, Andrew. 1982. *The Human Impact on the Natural Environment.* Cambridge, Mass.

Greenfield, Ian. 1962. *Turf Culture.* London.

Greenslade, M. W., and J. G. Jenkins, eds. 1967. *A History of the County of Stafford.* Vol. 2. *Victoria Histories of the Counties of England.* London.

Grigg, David. 1989. *English Agriculture.* Oxford.

Grove, Richard. 1995. *Green Imperialism.* Cambridge.

Guha, Ramachandra. 1990. *The Unquiet Woods.* Berkeley and Los Angeles.

Hackwood, Frederick W. 1919. *Odd Chapters in the History of Wednesbury.* Wednesbury.

Hall, Peter, H. Gracey, R. Drewett, and R. Thomas. 1973. *The Containment of Urban England.* 2 vols. London.

Hall, W. G., ed. 1971. *Man and the Mendips.* Mendip Society.

Hardie, D. W. F. 1950. *A History of the Chemical Industry in Widnes.* Birmingham.

Harford, Ian. 1994. *Manchester and Its Ship Canal Movement.* Staffordshire.

Harrison, Gary. 1994. *Wordsworth's Vagrant Muse.* Detroit.

Harrison, Robert Pogue. 1992. *Forests, The Shadow of Civilization.* Chicago.

Havinden, Michael. 1981. *The Somerset Landscape.* London.

Hawkes, Jacquetta. 1951. *A Land.* London.

Hayes, S. P. 1959. *Conservation and the Gospel of Efficiency.* Cambridge, Mass.

Henry, Augustine. 1919. *Forest, Woods, and Trees in Relation to Hygiene.* London.

Hill, Howard. 1980. *Freedom to Roam.* Ashbourne.

Hill, Stephen. 1988. *The Tragedy of Technology.* London.

Hills, Richard. 1970. *Power in the Industrial Revolution.* Manchester.

———. 1989. *Power from Steam.* Cambridge.

Hilton, K. J., ed. *The Lower Swansea Valley Project.* London.

Hodge, Edmund. 1957. *Enjoying the Lakes.* Edinburgh.

Hoskins, W. G. 1955. *The Making of the English Landscape.* 2d edition, 1988. London.

Howell, David. 1977. *Land and People in Nineteenth-Century Wales.* London.

Hough, Michael. 1989. *City Form and Natural Process.* London.

Humphries, Howard, et al. 1993. *Subsidence in Norwich.* HMSO.

Hussey, Christopher. 1927. *The Picturesque.* London.

Jackson, Kenneth. 1985. *The Crabgrass Frontier.* New York.

Jacobsen, Judith, and John Firor, eds. 1992. *Human Impact on the Environment: Ancient Roots, Current Challenges.* Boulder, Colo.

James, N. D. G. 1981. *A History of English Forestry.* Oxford.

Joad, C. E. M. 1945. *The Untutored Townsman's Invasion of the Country.* London.

John, Arthur, and Glanmor Williams, eds. 1980. *Glamorgan County History.* Vol. 5. Cardiff.

Johnson, R. H., ed. 1985. *The Geomorphology of North-West England.* Manchester.

Johnson, R. J., and J. C. Doornkamp, eds. 1982. *The Changing Geography of the United Kingdom.* London.

Jones, E. L. 1968. *The Development of English Agriculture, 1815–1873.* London.

———. 1974. *Agriculture and the Industrial Revolution.* Oxford.

Jones, M. J., ed. 1975. *Minerals and the Environment.* Institution of Mining and Metallurgy.

Jones, Stephen G. 1986. *Workers at Play.* London.

Kellett, John. 1969. *The Impact of Railways on Victorian Cities.* London.

Kerr, Barbara. 1968. *Bound to the Soil.* London.

Kerr, Ian. 1995. *Building the Railways of the Raj: 1850–1900*. Delhi.

Kimber, Richard, and J. J. Richardson, eds. 1974. *Campaigning for the Environment*. London.

Kindleberger, Charles. 1964. *Economic Growth in France and Britain, 1851–1950*. Cambridge, Mass.

Klingender, Francis. 1968. *Art and the Industrial Revolution*. Edited and revised by Arthur Elton. Chatham.

Lambert, Richard (with Paul Pross) 1967. *Renewing Nature's Wealth*. Ontario.

Landes, David. 1970. *The Unbound Prometheus*. Cambridge.

Lane, Michael. 1980. *The Story of the Steam Plough Works*. London.

Langton, John, and R. J. Morris, eds. 1986. *Atlas of Industrializing Britain, 1780–1914*. London.

Laurie, Ian, ed. 1979. *Nature in Cities*. Chichester.

Lavender, Stephen J. 1981. *New Land for Old*. Bristol.

Lavery, P., ed. 1974. *Recreational Geography*. Newton Abbot

Lee, Laurie. 1959. *Cider With Rosie*. Harmondsworth.

Lenihan, John, and William Fletcher, eds. 1976. *Reclamation*. New York.

Leopold, Aldo. 1949. *A Sand County Almanac*. 1970 edition. New York.

Lewis, M. J., ed. 1987. *The Slate Quarries of North Wales in 1873*. Plas Tan-y-Bwlch.

Lindley, Kenneth. 1973. *Seaside Architecture*. London.

Lindsay, Jean. 1974. *A History of the North Wales Slate Industry*. Newton Abbot.

Linnard, William. 1982. *Welsh Woods and Forests: History and Utilization*. Cardiff.

Lowenthal, David. 1958. *George Perkins Marsh, Versatile Vermonter*. New York.

Lower, Arthur. 1973. *Great Britain's Woodyard: British North America and the Timber Trade, 1763–1867*. Montreal.

Lowerson, John. 1993. *Sport and the English Middle Classes, 1870–1914*. Manchester.

Lowerson, John, and John Myerscough. 1977. *Time to Spare in Victorian England*. Hassocks, Sussex.

Lower Swansea Valley Project, Study Reports. 1966. Swansea.

McCloskey, Donald, ed. 1971. *Essays on a Mature Economy: Britain after 1840*. Princeton.

MacKenzie, John M., ed. 1990. *Imperialism and the Natural World*. Manchester.

McNeil, Ian, ed. 1990. *An Encyclopaedia of the History of Technology*. London.

Manchester Art Gallery. 1968. *Art and the Industrial Revolution*. Manchester.

Margetson, S. 1969. *Leisure and Pleasure in the Nineteenth Century*. London.

Marsden, Gordon, ed. 1990. *Victorian Values*. London.

Marsh, Jan. 1982. *Back to the Land: The Pastoral Impulse in England, from 1880 to 1914*. London.

Marx, Leo. 1964. *The Machine in the Garden*. Cambridge, Mass.

Maybe, R. 1973. *Unofficial Countryside*. New York.

Miles, Roger. 1967. *Forestry in the English Landscape*. London.

Millman, R. N. 1975. *The Making of the Scottish Landscape*. London.

Millward, Roy. 1980. *Upland Britain*. Newton Abbot.

Millward, Roy, and Adrian Robinson. 1970. *The Lake District.* London.
——. 1971. *The South-West Peninsula.* London.
Mingay, G. E., ed. 1981. *The Victorian Countryside.* 2 vols. London.
——, ed. 1989. *The Agrarian History of England and Wales.* Vol. 6. Cambridge.
Mokyr, Joel. 1990. *The Lever of Riches.* New York.
Morgan, David H. 1982. *Harvesters and Harvesting: 1840–1900.* London.
Muir, Robert, and Nina Muir. 1989. *Fields.* London.
Mumford, Lewis. 1931. *The Brown Decades.* New York.
——. 1934. *Technics and Civilization.* London.
National Chrysanthemum Society. 1946. *Centenary Book, 1846–1946.* Barnet, Hertfordshire.
Natural Environment Research Council. 1977. *Amenity Grassland—The Needs for Research,* no. 19. London.
Neeson, Eoin. 1991. *A History of Irish Forestry.* Dublin.
Nicholson, Max. 1987. *The New Environmental Age.* Cambridge.
Nicholson, Norman. 1963. *Portrait of the Lakes.* London.
Nir, Dov. 1983. *Man, a Geomorphological Agent.* Jerusalem.
O'Dell, A., and K. Walton. 1962. *The Highlands and Islands of Scotland.* Edinburgh.
Olwig, Kenneth. 1984. *Nature's Ideological Landscape.* London.
Orr, Willie. 1982. *Deer Forests, Landlords, and Crofters.* Edinburgh.
Orwin, C. S. 1929. *The Reclamation of Exmoor Forest.* London.
——. 1930. *Progress in English Farming Systems.* Oxford.
Orwin, Christabel S., and Edith Whetham. 1964. *History of British Agriculture, 1846–1914.* London.
Owen, David. 1983. *The Manchester Ship Canal.* Manchester.
Owen, W. J., and J. W. Smyser, eds. 1974. *The Prose Works of William Wordsworth.* 3 vols. Oxford.
Oxenham, J. R. 1966. *Reclaiming Derelict Land.* London.
Pannell, J. P. M. 1964. *An Illustrated History of Civil Engineering.* London.
Parry, Martin, and T. R. Slater, eds. 1980. *The Making of the Scottish Countryside.* London.
Passmore, John. 1974. *Man's Responsibility for Nature.* New York.
Patmore, J. Allen. 1983. *Recreation and Resources.* Oxford.
Penning-Rowsell, E., and David Lowenthal, eds. 1986. *Landscape Meanings and Values.* London.
Perkin, Harold J. 1989. *The Rise of Professional Society: England since 1880.* London.
Perry, P. J. 1974. *British Farming in the Great Depression, 1870–1914.* Newton Abbot.
Pim, Sheila. 1984. *The Wood and the Trees.* Kilkenny.
Pinion, F. B., and M. Pinion, eds. 1988. *The Collected Sonnets of Charles (Tennyson) Turner.* Basingstoke.
Porter, Elizabeth. 1978. *Water Management in England and Wales.* Cambridge.
Powell, J. M. 1976. *Environmental Management in Australia, 1788–1914.* Melbourne.

Prebble, John. 1969. *The Highland Clearances*. Harmondsworth.

Preston, J. M. 1977. *Industrial Medway*. Rochester.

Pye-Smith, Charlie. 1990. *In Search of Neptune*. London.

Pye-Smith, Charlie, and Chris Rose. 1984. *Crisis and Conservation: Conflict in the British Countryside*. Harmondsworth.

Rackham, Oliver. 1986. *The History of the Countryside*. London.

———. 1990. *Trees and Woodlands in the British Landscape*. Revised edition. London.

Ransom, P. J. 1990. *The Victorian Railway and How It Evolved*. London.

Rappaport, Roy. 1984. *Pigs for the Ancestors*. New enlarged edition. New Haven.

Rasmussen, Steen Eiler. 1934. *London the Unique City*. 1982 edition. Cambridge, Mass.

Reader, W. J. 1970. *Imperial Chemical Industries: A History*. 2 vols. London.

Redford, Arthur. 1940. *The History of Local Government in Manchester*. 2 vols. London.

Reed, Michael. 1990. *The Landscape of Britain*. London.

Rice, H. A. L. 1967. *Lake Country Portraits*. London.

Richardson, Ruth, and Robert Thorne. 1994. *The Builder Illustrations Index: 1843–1883*. Guildford.

Roberts, David. 1979. *Paternalism in Early Victorian England*. New Brunswick.

Roberts, Robert. 1973. *The Classic Slum*. Harmondsworth.

Rogerson, Sidney. 1949. *Both Sides of the Road*. London.

Rosenberg, Nathan. 1976. *Perspectives on Technology*. Cambridge.

Rosser, Colin, and Christopher Harris. 1983. *The Family and Social Change*. Abridged edition. London.

Rubenstein, David, and Colin Speakman. 1969. *Leisure, Transport, and the Countryside*. Vol. 277. London.

Rybczynski, Witold. 1987. *Home*. Harmondsworth.

Saeijs, H. L. 1982. *Changing Estuaries*. The Hague.

Sales, Roger. 1983. *English Literature in History, 1780–1830: Pastoral and Politics*. London.

Salisbury, Edward. 1952. *Downs and Dunes*. London.

Samuel, Raphael, ed. 1977. *Miners, Quarrymen, and Saltworkers*. London.

Saville, John, ed. 1970. *A Selection of the Political Pamphlets of Charles Bradlaugh*. New York.

Schama, Simon. 1995. *Landscape and Memory*. Toronto.

Schivelbusch, Wolfgang. 1980. *The Railway Journey*. Oxford.

Sherlock, R. L. 1922. *Man as a Geological Agent*. London.

Simmons, Jack. 1986. *The Railway in Town and Country, 1830–1914*. Newton Abbot.

Singer, Charles, et al., eds. 1958. *A History of Technology*. Vol. 5. Oxford.

Shoard, Marian. 1980. *The Theft of the Countryside*. London.

———. 1987. *This Land Is Our Land*. London.

Smith, Lucy Toulmin, ed. 1964. *The Itinerary of John Leland in about the Years, 1536–1539*. 5 vols. Carbondale, Ill.

Smith, Robert. 1989. *City of Granite*. Edinburgh.

Smout, T. C. 1969. *A History of the Scottish People, 1560–1830*. London.
Somervell, D., and D. Somervell, eds. 1935. *Robert Somervell*. London.
Speight, Martin. 1973. *Discussion Papers in Conservation*. London.
Spence, Clark. 1960. *God Speed the Plow*. Urbana, Ill.
Stamp, L. Dudley. 1948. *The Land of Britain: Its Use and Misuse*. London.
———. 1955. *Man and the Land*. London.
Steers, J. A. 1953. *The Sea Coast*. London.
———. 1966. *The English Coast and the Coast of Wales*. London.
———. 1973. *The Coastline of Scotland*. Cambridge.
———. 1981. *Coastal Features of England and Wales*. Cambridge.
Stephenson, Tom. 1989 *Forbidden Land*. Manchester.
Strandh, Sigvard. 1979. *Technology and Its Impact on Society*. Stockholm.
Sussman, Herbert. 1968. *Victorians and the Machine*. Cambridge, Mass.
Symon, J. A. 1959. *Scottish Farming*. Edinburgh.
Theroux, Paul. 1984. *The Kingdom by the Sea*. New York.
Thirsk, Joan, and J. Imray, eds. 1958. *Suffolk Farming in the Nineteenth Century*. Ipswich.
Thomas, William, ed. 1956. *Man's Role in Changing the Face of the Earth*. Chicago.
Thompson, B. L. 1946. *The Lake District and the National Trust*. Kendal.
Thompson, F. M. L. 1963. *English Landed Society in the Nineteenth Century*. London.
———. 1988. *The Rise of Respectable Society*. London.
Todd, A. C., and Peter Laws. 1972. *The Industrial Archaeology of Cornwall*. Newton Abbot.
Tonks, Eric. 1988. *The Ironstone Quarries of the Midlands*. Cheltenham.
Travis, John. 1993. *The Rise of the Devon Seaside Resorts, 1750–1900*. Exeter.
Trinder, Barrie. 1982. *The Making of the Industrial Landscape*. London.
———, ed. 1992. *Industrial Archaeology*. Oxford.
Tubbs, Colin. 1968. *The New Forest: An Ecological History*. Newton Abbot.
Tucker, Richard, and John Richards, eds. 1983. *Global Deforestation and the Nineteenth-Century World Economy*. Durham, N.C.
Turner, B. L., ed. 1990. *The Earth as Transformed by Human Action*. Cambridge.
Tyler, Colin, and John Haining. 1985. *Ploughing by Steam*. Bath.
Veal, T. H. P. 1928. *The Disposal of Sewage*. New York.
Vigier, Francois. 1970. *Change and Apathy*. Cambridge, Mass.
Viljoen, Helen, ed. 1971. *The Brantwood Diary of John Ruskin*. New Haven.
von Tunzelmann, G. N. 1978. *Steam Power and British Industrialization to 1860*. Oxford.
Waller, P. J. 1983. *Town, City, and Nation*. Oxford.
Walton, John K. 1983. *The English Seaside Resort*. Leicester.
Walton, John K., and A. Wilcox, eds. 1991. *Low Life and Moral Improvement in Mid-Victorian England*. Leicester.
Walvin, James. 1978. *Beside the Seaside*. London.
———. 1978. *Leisure and Society, 1830–1950*. London.
Walvin, Peggy. 1976. *Savernake Forest*. Cheltenham.
Warren, A., and F. B. Goldsmith, eds. 1983. *Conservation in Perspective*. London.

Watkins, Charles. 1991. *Nature Conservation and the New Lowland Forests.* Peterborough.
———, ed. 1993. *Ecological Effects of Afforestation.* Wallingford.
Watson, Glenn, ed. 1987. *Recycling Disused Industrial Land in the Black Country.* Oxford.
Watson, J. A. Scott, and May Hobbs. 1937. *Great Farmers.* London.
Weale, Michael, ed. 1974. *Environmental Issues.* 3d edition. Ely.
Weinreb, Ben, and Christopher Hibbert. 1983. *The London Encyclopaedia.* New York.
Weller, John. 1982. *The History of the Farmstead.* London.
Wheeler, Michael, ed. 1995. *Ruskin and Environment.* Manchester.
Whyte, Ian., and Kathleen Whyte. 1991. *The Changing Scottish Landscape.* London.
Wiener, Martin. 1981. *English Culture and the Decline of the Industrial Spirit, 1850–1980.* Cambridge.
Williams, Michael, ed. 1990. *Wetlands.* Oxford.
Williams, Raymond. 1973. *The Country and the City.* London.
Williams-Ellis, Clough, ed. 1937. *Britain and the Beast.* London.
Winner, Langdon. 1977. *Autonomous Technology.* Cambridge, Mass.
Winter, James. 1976. *Robert Lowe.* Toronto.
———. 1993. *London's Teeming Streets.* London.
Wohl, Anthony. 1983. *Endangered Lives.* Cambridge, Mass.
Woodell, S. R. J. ed. 1985. *The English Landscape.* Oxford.
Worster, Donald, ed. 1988. *The Ends of the Earth.* Cambridge.
———. 1993. *The Wealth of Nature.* New York.
Wrigley, Chris, and John Sheperd, eds. 1991. *On the Move.* London.
Wynn, Graeme. 1981. *Timber Colony, A Historical Geography of Early Nineteenth Century New Brunswick.* Toronto.

ARTICLES (AFTER 1918)

Adelman, Jeremy. 1992. "The Social Bases of Technical Change: Mechanization of the Wheatlands of Argentina and Canada, 1890–1914." *Comparative Studies in Society and History* 34: 271–300.
Allen, Robert. 1991. "Labor Productivity and Farm Size in English Agriculture before Mechanization: Reply to Clark." *Explorations in Economic History* 28: 478–92.
Anderson, P., and D. W. Yalden. 1981. "Increased Sheep Numbers and the Loss of Heather Moorland in the Peak District, England." *Biological Conservation* 20: 195–213.
Arbor, Muriel. 1946. "Dust-Storms in the Fenland Round Ely." *Geography* 31: 23–26.
Bailey, Francis. 1950. "The Origin and Growth of Southport." *The Town Planning Review* 21: 299–317.
Bailey, Peter. 1977. "'A Mingled Mass of Perfectly Legitimate Pleasures': The Victorian Middle Class and the Problem of Leisure." *Victorian Studies* 21: 7–28.

Beavington, F. 1975. "The Development of Market Gardening in Bedfordshire, 1799–1939." *AHR* 23: 23–47.

Bell, F. G. 1975. "Salt and Subsidence in Cheshire, England." *Engineering Geology* 9: 240–44.

Bil, Albert. 1989. "Transhumance Economy, Setting, and Settlement in Highland Perthshire." *Scottish Geographical Magazine* 105: 158–67.

Birnie, R. V., and P. D. Hulme. 1990. "Overgrazing of Peatland Vegetation in Scotland." *Scottish Geographical Magazine* 106: 28–36.

Bower, Margaret. 1962. "The Cause of Erosion in Blanket Peat Bogs." *Scottish Geographical Magazine* 78: 33–43.

Brandon, Peter. 1984. "Wealden Nature and the Role of London in Nineteenth-Century Artistic Imagination." *Journal of Historical Geography* 10: 53–74.

Brown, Eric. 1970. "Man Shapes the Earth." *Geographical Journal* 136: 74–85.

Bryant, Raymond. 1994. "From Laissez-Faire to Scientific Forestry." *Forest and Conservation History* 33: 160–70.

Buchanan, Angus. 1975. "Technology and History." *Social Studies in the Sciences* 5: 489–99.

Buchanan, R. A. 1978. "History of Technology in the Teaching of History." *HT* 3: 13–27.

Butler, R. W. 1985. "Evolution of Tourism in the Scottish Highlands." *Annals of Tourism Research* 12: 371–91.

Cannadine, David. 1977. "Victorian Cities: How Different?" *Social History* 2: 457–82.

Channon, Geoffrey. 1969. "The Aberdeenshire Beef Trade with London: A Study in Steamship and Railway Competition, 1850–69." *Transport History* 2: 1–24.

Christensen, Norman. 1989. "Landscape History and Ecological Change." *Journal of Forest History* 33: 116–25.

Collins, E. J. 1969. "Harvest Technology and Labour Supply in Britain, 1790–1870." *EHR* 22: 453–73.

———. 1972. "The Diffusion of the Threshing Machine in Britain, 1790–1880." *Tools and Tillage* 2: 16–32.

———. 1985. "Agriculture and Conservation in England: An Historical Overview, 1880–1939." *JRASE* 146: 38–46.

Cresswell, R. Kay. 1937. "The Geomorphology of a South-west Lancashire Coast-line." *Geographical Journal* 90: 335–49.

Crust, Linda. 1995. "William Paddison: Marsh Farmer and Survivor of the Agricultural Depression, 1873–96." *AHR* 43: 193–204.

Dodgshon, Robert A. 1976. "The Economy of Sheep Farming in the Southern Upland during the Age of Improvement, 1750–1833." *EHR* 29: 551–69.

Donnelly, Peter. 1986. "The Paradox of Parks: Politics of Recreational Land Use before and after Mass Trespasses." *Leisure Studies* 5: 211–31.

Donnelly, T. 1974. "The Rubislaw Granite Quarries, 1750–1939." *Industrial Archaeology* 11: 225–38.

Dougill, Wesley. 1935. "The British Coast and Its Holiday Resorts." *The Town Planning Review* 16: 265–78.

Duncan, Colin. 1992. "Legal Protection for the Soil of England: The Spurious Context of Nineteenth Century 'Progress.'" *Agricultural History* 66: 75–94.

Dyos, H. J. 1955. "Railways and Housing in Victorian London." *Journal of Transport History* 2: 11–21, 90–100.

———. 1957. "Some Social Costs of Railway Building in London." *Journal of Transport History* 3: 23–31.

Elchells, Jon. 1992. "Golf Answers Back." *Landscape Design* 210: 41–43.

Elliot, Robert. 1982. "Faking Nature." *Inquiry* no. 25: 81–93.

Evans, F. T. 1982. "Wood Since the Industrial Revolution: A Strategic Retreat?" *HT* 7: 37–55.

Eves, Jamie. 1992. "Shrunk to a Comparative Rivulet: Deforestation, Stream Flow, and Rural Milling in Nineteenth-Century Maine." *Technology and Culture* 33: 38–65.

Fenton, E. Wyllie. 1937. "The Influence of Sheep on the Vegetation of Hill Grazings in Scotland." *JE* 25: 424–30.

Ferguson, Bruce. 1994. "The Concept of Landscape Health." *Journal of Environmental Management* 40: 129–37.

Ferguson, Eugene. 1974. "Toward a Discipline of the History of Technology." *Technology and Culture* 15: 13–30.

Fletcher, T. W. 1960–61. "The Great Depression of English Agriculture, 1873–1896." *EHR,* 2d series, 13: 417–32.

———. 1961. "Lancashire Livestock Farming during the Great Depression." *AHR* 9: 17–42.

Flick, Carlos. 1980. "The Movement for Smoke Abatement in Nineteenth Century Britain." *Technology and Culture* 21: 29–50.

Gaskell, Martin. 1980. "Gardens for the Working Class: Victorian Practical Pleasures." *Victorian Studies* 23: 497–501.

Geist, Valarius. 1978. "A Philosophical Look at Recreational Impact on Wildlands." In *Recreational Impact on Wildlands.* Seattle.

Gilbert, E. W. 1939. "The Growth of Inland and Seaside Health Resorts in England." *Scottish Geographical Magazine* 55: 6–35.

Goddard, Nicholas. 1996. "'A Mine of Wealth'? The Victorians and the Agricultural Value of Sewage." *Journal of Historical Geography* 22: 274–90.

Graham, Gerald. 1956. "The Ascendency of the Sailing Ship, 1850–1885." *EHR* 9: 74–88.

Graham, Wade. August 19, 1996. "The Grassman." *The New Yorker* 72: 34–37.

Grant, S. A., et al. 1987. "Comparative Studies of Diet Selection by Sheep and Cattle: Blanket Bog and Heather Moor." *JE* 75: 947–60.

Grigg, David. 1987. "Farm Size in England and Wales, from Early Victorian Times to the Present." *AHR* 35: 179–89.

Grove, Richard. 1976. "Coprolite Mining in Cambridgeshire." *AHR* 24: 36–43.

———. 1992. "Origins of Western Environmentalism," *Scientific American* 267: 464–500.

Haeuber, Richard. 1993. "Indian Forest Policy in Two Eras: Continuity or Change?" *Environmental History Review* 17: 49–76.

Harley, C. K. 1974. "Skilled Labour and the Choice of Technique in Edwardian Industry." *Explorations in Economic History* 11: 391–414.

Harris, R. Cole, P. Roulston, and C. D. Freitas. 1975. "The Settlement of Mono Township." *Canadian Geographer* 14: 1–17.

Hassan, J. A. 1985. "The Growth and Impact of the British Water Industry in the Nineteenth Century." *EHR* 38: 531–47.

Higgins, M. 1984. "Social Tone and Resort Development in North-East England: Victorian Seaside Resorts Around the Mouth of the Tees." *Northern History* 20: 187–206.

Hilton, K. J. 1964. "Restoring an Industrial Desert." *Geographical Magazine* 37: 372–83.

Hunter, James. 1973. "Sheep and Deer: Highland Sheep Farming, 1850–1900." *Northern Scotland* 1: 199–222.

Imeson, A. C. 1971. "Heather Burning and Soil Erosion on the North Yorkshire Moors." *Journal of Applied Ecology* 8: 537–42.

Jenkins, J. Geraint. 1965. "Technological Improvement and Social Change in South Cardiganshire." *AHR* 13: 94–103.

Jennings, J. N. 1966. "Man as a Geological Agent." *Australian Journal of Science* 28: 150–56.

Jewitt, Sarah. 1995. "Europe's 'Others'? Forestry Policy and Practices in Colonial and Postcolonial India." *Society and Space* 13: 67–90.

Jones, David K. C. 1973. "Man Moulds the Landscape." *Geographical Magazine* 45: 575–81.

King, Anthony. 1964. "Another Blow for Life: George Godwin and the Reform of Working Class Housing." *Architectural Review* 136: 448–52.

———. 1964. "George Godwin and the Art Union of London, 1837–1911." *Victorian Studies* 8: 101–30.

———. 1976. "Architectural Journalism and the Profession: The Early Years of George Godwin." *Architectural History* 19: 32–53.

Lee, C. H. 1975. "Some Aspects of the Coastal Shipping Trade: The Aberdeen Steam Navigation Company, 1835–1880." *Journal of Transport History*, new series, 3: 94–107.

Linsay, J. M. 1977. "Forestry and Agriculture in the Scottish Highlands, 1700–1850: A Problem in Estate Management." *AHR* 25: 23–36.

Long, W. Harwood. 1963. "The Development of Mechanization in English Farming." *AHR* 11: 15–26.

Lowenthal, David. 1960. "George Perkins Marsh on the Nature and Purpose of Geography." *Geographical Journal* 126: 413–17.

MacDonagh, Oliver. 1958. "The Nineteenth Century Revolution in Government: A Reappraisal." *Historical Journal* 1: 52–67.

MacLeod, Roy. 1965–66. "The Alkali Acts Administration, 1863–64." *Victorian Studies* 9: 86–112.

———. 1968. "Government and Resource Conservation, 1860–1886." *Journal of British Studies* 7: 115–50.

Mathew, W. M. 1993. "Marling in British Agriculture: A Case of Partial Identity." *AHR* 41: 97–110.

Mattless, David. 1993. "One Man's England: W. G. Hoskins and the English Culture of Landscape." *Rural History* 4: 187–207.

Mokyr, Joel. 1992. "Technological Inertia in Economic History." *Journal of Economic History* 52: 325–38.

Moore-Colyer, Richard. 1955. "Aspect of Horse Breeding and the Supply of Horses in Victorian Britain." *AHR* 43: 47–64.

Musson, A. E. 1976. "Industrial Motive Power in the United Kingdom, 1800–1870." *EHR*, 2d series, 29: 415–39.

Newton, R. W. B. 1951. "Afforestation of Unrestored Land." *Quarterly Journal of Forestry* 65: 38–41.

Olwig, Kenneth R. 1980. "Historical Geography and the Society/Nature 'Problematic': The Perspective of J. F. Schouw, G. P. Marsh, and E. Reclus." *Journal of Historical Geography* 6: 29–45.

Ovington, J. D. 1950. "The Afforestation of Culbin Sands." *JE* 38: 303–19.

Palmer, Sarah. 1982. "'The Most Indefatigable Activity' The General Steam Navigation Company, 1824–50." *Journal of Transport History*, 3d series, 3: 1–22.

Parker, Stanley. 1983. "British View of Retirement." *Leisure Studies* 2: 211–16.

Peake, John. 1958. "The Industrial Heritage of Britain." *Town and Country Planning* 26: 198–200.

Perkin, H. J. 1975. "The 'Social Tone' of Victorian Seaside Resorts in the North-West." *Northern History* 11: 180–94.

Perkins, J. A. 1976–77. "Harvest Technology and Labour Supply in Lincolnshire and the East Riding of Yorkshire, 1750–1850." *Tools and Tillage* 3: 47–58, 125–35.

Prynn, David. 1976. "The Clarion Clubs, Rambling, and the Holiday Associations in Britain since the 1890s." *Journal of Contemporary History* 11: 65–77.

Pryor, Robin. 1968. "Defining the Rural-Urban Fringe." *Social Forces.* 47: 202–15.

Ranlett, John. 1983. "'Checking Nature's Desecration': Late Victorian Environmental Organization." *Victorian Studies* 26: 197–222.

Rappaport, Roy. 1971. "The Flow of Energy in an Agricultural Society." *Scientific American* 225: 116–32.

Raybould, Trevor. 1970. "Lord Dudley and the Making of the Black Country." *Blackcountryman* 3: 53–58.

———. 1984. "Aristocratic Landowners and the Industrial Revolution: The Black Country Experience, 1760–1840." *Midland History* 9: 59–86.

Richards, Eric. 1979. "An Anatomy of the Sutherland Fortune: Income, Consumption, Investments, and Returns, 1780–1880." *Business History* 21: 45–78.

Richardson, Ruth. 1989. "George Godwin of the *Builder*." *Visual Resources* 6: 121–40.

Roberts, R. Alun. 1959. "Ecology of Human Occupation and Land Use in Snowdonia." *JE* 47: 317–23.

Robinson, A. H. W. 1961. "The Hydrography of Start Bay and Its Relation to Beach Change at Hallsands." *Geographical Journal* 121: 63–77.

Rome, Adam. 1994. "Building on the Land." *Journal of Urban History* 20: 407–34.

Rubinstein, David. 1977. "Cycling in the 1890s." *Victorian Studies* 21: 47–71.

Rutledge, Peter. 1970. "Steam Power for Loggers." *Journal of Forest History* 14: 18–29.

Searle, C. E. 1986. "Custom, Class Conflict, and Agrarian Capitalism: The Cumbrian Customary Economy in the Eighteenth Century." *Past and Present* 110: 106–33.

Sheail, John. 1982. "Underground Water Abstraction: Indirect Effects of Urbanization on the Countryside." *Journal of Historical Geography* 8: 395–408.

———. 1995. "Elements of Sustainable Agriculture: The UK Experience, 1840–1940." *AHR* 43: 178–92.

Stueland, Samuel. 1994. "The Otis Steam Excavator." *Technology and Culture* 35: 571–74.

Sykes, Marjorie. 1987. "Bracken: Friend or Foe?" *Ecologist* 17: 241–42.

Taylor, A. J. 1967. "Coal." In *Victoria History of the Counties of England: Staffordshire*. Vol. 2. London.

Thayer, Robert L., Jr. 1990. "Pragmatism in Paradise: Technology and the American Landscape." *Landscape* 30: 1–11.

Thomas, R., P. Anderson, and E. Radford. 1994. "The Ecological Effects of Woodland Recreation." *Quarterly Journal of Forestry.* 8: 225–32.

Thomas, Trevor. 1956. "Wales: Land, Mines, and Quarries." *Geographical Review* 46: 59–81.

Thompson, F. M. L. 1968. "The Second Agricultural Revolution, 1815–1880." *EHR,* 2d series, 21: 62–77.

———. 1976. "Nineteenth Century Horse Sense." *EHR,* 2d series, 29: 60–79.

Tucker, Richard P. 1979. "Forest Management and Imperial Politics: Thana District, Bombay, 1823–1887." *The Indian Economic and Social History Review* 26: 112–23.

———. 1982. "The Forests of the Western Himalayas: The Legacy of British Colonial Administration." *Journal of Forest History* 26: 112–23.

Turnock, David. 1969. "North Morar: The Improving Movement on a West Highland Estate." *Scottish Geographical Magazine* 85: 17–30.

van Zanden, J. L. 1991. "The First Green Revolution: The Growth of Production and Productivity in European Agriculture, 1870–1914." *EHR* 44: 215–39.

Walker, Helen. 1985. "The Popularisation of the Outdoor Movement, 1900–1914." *British Journal of Sports History* 2: 140–53.

Walker, H. Jesse. 1984. "Man's Impact on Shorelines and Nearshore Environments." *Geoforum* 15: 395–417.

Wallace, H. L., J. E. Good, and T. G. Williams. 1992. "The Effects of Afforestation on Upland Plant Communities: An Application of the British National Vegetation Classification." *Journal of Applied Ecology* 29: 180–94.

Wallwork, K. L. 1956. "Subsidence in the Mid-Cheshire Industrial Area." *Geographical Journal* 122: 40–53.

———. 1960. "Some Problems of Subsidence and Land Use in the Mid-Cheshire Industrial Area." *Geographical Journal* 126: 191–99.

Walton, John K. 1979. "Railways and Resort Development in Victorian England: The Case of Silloth." *Northern History* 15: 191–209.

Walton, John K., and P. R. McGloin. 1981. "The Tourist Trade in Victorian Lakeland." *Northern History* 17: 152–82.

Walton, J. R. 1973. "A Study in the Diffusion of Agricultural Machinery in the Nineteenth Century." Research Paper no. 5. School of Geography. Oxford.

Watson, J. A. Scott. 1950. "English Agriculture in 1850–51." *JRASE* 111: 9–24.

Watt, Alex. 1955. "Bracken Versus Heather, A Study in Plant Sociology." *JE* 43: 490–506.

Wheeler, P. T. 1966. "Land Ownership and the Crofting System in Sutherland since 1800." *AHR* 14: 45–56.

Williams, Michael. 1971. "The Enclosure and Reclamation of the Mendip Hills, 1770–1870." *AHR* 19: 65–81.

Winship, Ian. 1984. "The Gas Engine in British Agriculture c. 1870–1925." *HT* 9: 181–204.

Wise, M. J. 1962. "The Midland Reafforestation Association, 1903–1924, and the Reclamation of Derelict Land in the Black Country." *Journal of the Institute of Landscape Architects* 57: 13–18.

Wrenn, L. B. 1994. "Cotton Gins and Cottonseed Oil Mills in the New South." *Agricultural History* 68: 232–43.

Wynn, Graeme. 1977. "Conservation and Society in Late Nineteenth-Century New Zealand." *The New Zealand Journal of History* 124–36.

———. 1979. "Pioneers, Politicians, and the Conservation of Forests in Early New Zealand." *Journal of Historical Geography* 5: 171–88.

Index

Abercromby, J. F., 225, 227
Aberdeen, 56, 136–39, 251–52. *See also*
  Quarrying industries
Aberfan disaster, 161
Acland, Thomas Dyke, 64
Adelman, Jeremy, 13–14, 263n.25
Agriculture, 18; Argentinean and Canadian compared, 13, 14, 263n.25; crop
  rotation, 15–16, 44, 53, 56, 59–63;
  dairy farms, 55, 57, 167; draining,
  41, 44–45, 47–48, 50; and ecological systems, 3, 40–41, 57, 59, 61,
  252; feed supplements, 42, 44, 54; in
  Fenlands, 58–60, 251; Great Depression in, 54–58, 81, 156, 232; hedgerows, 4, 7, 10, 41, 45, 52, 54, 63–64,
  83, 103, 112, 253; high farming, 16,
  41, 52–54, 60, 62, 253; horses and
  horse machinery, 13–14, 44–48, 50–
  54, 253; in Ireland, 68, 82; and landscape, 49–50, 52–53, 57, 60–61;
  market gardens, 52, 57, 60, 167–68,
  194, 252; railways and steam power
  in, 13–14, 16–17, 39, 41–42, 44–
  53, 57, 73–76, 82, 104–5, 109; Royal
  Commission on, 54–55; in Scotland,
  53, 55–56; sustainable, 3–4, 18,
  40–41, 52–53, 59–61, 249–51; in
  Wales, 53, 56, 66. *See also* Fertilizers
Ailesbury, Lord. *See* Bruce, Chandos,
  sixth marquess of
Alkali manufacture, 11, 252–53; environmental impacts, 128, 131–34;

Leblanc and Solvay processes, 71,
  131, 132, 285n.19; resistance to, 144
Anderson, Michael, 175–76
Arbor, Muriel, 58
Arbor Day, 159
Arboriculture. *See* Forests/forestry:
  arboriculture and silviculture
Arnold, Matthew, 29
Arnold, Thomas, 110–11
Aspidin, Joseph, 235
Assheton-Smith, Thomas, 140
Atholl, dukes of: James, second duke, 95;
  John, fourth duke, 95
Australia, 28
Automobile and automobilism, 15, 214,
  230; expansion of tourism, 82; at sea-
  side, 216, 220, 230
Ayton, Richard, 218

Bailey, Peter, 230
Baker, T. H., 241
Balfour, Andrew, 23
Balfour, Arthur James, 98–99
Balfour, Professor, 78
Barnett, Henrietta, 199
Barnett, Samuel, 199
Barr, John, 134, 161–62
Barrow, George, 212–13
Bateman, John Frederic La Trobe, 121,
  170–71, 173–78
Baylis, George, 51
Bell, George, 163–64. *See also* Lower
  Swansea Valley: reclamation project

Bermingham, Ann, 256
Besant, Annie, 155
Bicycle. *See* Cycling
Billingsley, John, 63–64
Bilston, 127, 130
Birmingham, 127, 157, 202
Black Country, 6, 17, 113, 126, 252;
    blight in, 152–54, 165; definition
    of, 289n.39; plans for restoration of,
    154–61. *See also* Reclamation, land
Blackpool, 210, 215, 219, 223; shoreline
    of, 233
Blaenau Ffestiniog Quarry, 140–42.
    See also Quarrying industries: slate
    in Wales
Blight, industrial, 3, 17–18, 143–65.
    See also Reclamation, land
Blisworth, 109–10. *See also* Railway
    building
Boer War, 234
Boughton estate, 149–51
Brabazon, Lord and Lady, 199
Bradfield, 173–74
Bradlaugh, Charles, 155–56
Brandis, Dietrich, 23
Bridlington, 233
Briggs, Asa, 11
Brighton, 210, 233
British Columbia, 95
Broome, Samuel, 200, 202
Brown, James, 88–89, 91
Brown, John Croumbie, 88
Brown, Lancelot, 84–85, 94, 225, 256
Bruce, Chandos, sixth marquess of Ailes-
    bury, 85–86, 94, 101
Brudenell, George Frederick, Lord Bruce,
    85
Brudenell, Thomas, Lord Bruce, 84–85,
    94
Brudenell, William, Lord Bruce, 85
Brunner, John, 131. *See also* Alkali
    manufacture
Brunner-Mond, 132. *See also* Imperial
    Chemical Industries (I.C.I.)
Bryce, James, 65, 78, 179, 199
Buccleuch, duke of, as model land re-
    former, 149–51
Buckle, Henry Thomas, 34
Budding, Edwin, 205
Buffon, Georges, 38
Builder, George Parker, 105
Burlington, Lord, 85
Burns, John, 99
Burritt, Elihu, 153–54

Caird, James, 53
Campbell-Bannerman, Henry, 99

Canada, 65, 145; forestry in, 28, 91–93,
    96–97, 100
Canals, 13, 35, 63, 108, 218; building
    of, 107, 109; reservoir dams in, 170,
    172. *See also* Manchester Ship Canal;
    Suez Canal
Carlisle, Bishop of, 179–81
Carlyle, Thomas, 2, 192; defense of
    Thirlmere, 177, 184; on machinery,
    9; and railways, 215; "Signs of the
    Times," 1
Carpenter, Edward, 192
Cement. *See* Concrete
Chesil Bank, 232
Cheverton-Brown, Martin, 241
Chitty, Gill, 26
Churchill, Winston, 177
City: density increases, 6, 144, 189–90,
    202; effect of ecological systems, 3,
    6, 53, 191–92; expansion of, 17,
    166, 167, 291n.2; exploitation of
    countryside resources, 6, 10, 17, 159,
    167–88, 252; green spaces in, 3, 17,
    38, 194–95, 197, 202–8; industrial
    concentration in, 6, 166; natural his-
    tory of, 190–92; physical and moral
    evils of, 25, 38, 189, 192–93, 196–
    97, 210; streets, 135–36, 166–68,
    189–90, 199, 204–5, 252; urbaniza-
    tion of, 166–67, 189, 209. *See also*
    Garden cities; Parks; Water resource
    development
Clacton-on-Sea, 241
Clapham, John, 10
Clarke, J. A., 59
Cleghorn, Hugh, 23, 28
Cliffe, Frederick, on Lower Swansea
    Valley, 162
Coastal erosion: concern about, 21–22,
    231–32, 233–36, 303n.2; defenses
    against, 240–43, 245–47, 252;
    government and, 234–37, 238–48,
    304n.24; natural checks on, 231–
    34, 239–46; Royal Commission on,
    35, 235–37, 243–47; and sand and
    shingle mining, 231, 233–43; at
    seaside resorts, 17, 219–23, 232–33,
    240–43, 252. *See also* Concrete;
    Dredging; Erosion; Reclamation,
    land; Tourism
Cobbett, William, 10
Coke, Thomas, earl of Leicester, 95,
    246–47
Coleman, Terry, 115
Coleridge, Samuel Taylor, 24, 176
Collingwood, W. G., 186–87
Collins, E. J., 45, 57

Colt, H. S., 225, 227
Commons Preservation Society, 24–25,
    178, 183, 204, 227
Communications technology; and agri-
    culture, 4; as domestic conservator, 3;
    effect on food and fiber supplies, 11,
    25; and telegraph, 20. See also Rail-
    ways; Steamboats
Concrete, 11; in dam construction, 172;
    sand and shingle mining for, 233,
    235, 237–40, 242–43; use of port-
    land cement in, 235–36. See also
    Coastal erosion
Conder, Francis Roubiliac, 112–14
Conservation, 17, 120, 254: definition
    of, 5, 32–33; of forests in Australia,
    India, New Zealand, North America,
    and South Africa, 22–23, 28, 88; and
    "improvement," 24; movement to-
    ward, 22–23; during romantic era,
    188. See also Preservation
Constable, John, 206
Cook, Thomas, 214, 225
Corot, Jean-Baptiste-Camille, 206
Cort, Henry, 107
Cort, R., 107
Council for the Preservation of Rural
    England, 187
Countryside. See Landscape
Crane, W., 142
Creevey, Thomas, 210
Cripps, Stafford, 17
Cruikshank, George, 167
Crystal Palace Exposition of 1851, 8,
    235
Culbin Forest, 247
Culbin Sands, 247
Cycling, 187, 214; and golfers, 228–30;
    Touring Club, 228

Dalgas, Enrico, 156–57
Damflask, 174
Dams: construction of, 170–73; and
    Holmfirth disaster, 171–72; and Shef-
    field (Dale Dyke) disaster, 173–74.
    See also Reservoirs; Water resource
    development
Daniels, Stephen, 84–85
Darby, H. C., 58–59
Dartmouth College, 29
Darwin, Charles, 19, 33, 40
David, Paul, 45
Davy, Humphry, 163
Day, James, 115
Deer forests. See under Scottish
    Highlands
De la Beche, Henry, 231–32

Devonport (Plymouth Harbor), 237
Dickens, Charles, 9, 144
Dinorwic Quarry, 140–41. See also
    Quarrying industries: slate in Wales
Disraeli, Benjamin, 9
Dodgshon, Robert, 68
Dolbeer, John, 93
Doncaster, 174
Dover, 233
Drabble, Margaret, 255
Dredging, 231; coastal, 231, 233, 236,
    238–40; development of steam
    dredges, 115–17, 119, 238–39; of
    rivers and estuaries, 221–22, 248
Dubos, René, 150
Dudley, first earl of, as model land re-
    former, 149–50
Duncan, Colin: and British estate farm-
    ing, 18; on export of Britain's "eco-
    logical burden," 252
Dundas, Robert, 88
Dynamite, 135

Eades, James Buchanan, 122
Ecology/ecosystems, 5, 29, 53, 57, 61,
    79–80; awareness of, 27–28, 109,
    133–34, 164, 188; chaos theory in,
    250–51; coastal, 244–45; creation
    of a new, 59, 150, 243–44; as critical
    tool, 36–38, 102–3, 119, 191–92;
    and "ecological imperialism," 3, 81,
    252; and equilibrium theory, 38–39,
    251, 269n.64; forests and, 33, 38, 97;
    game reserves and, 79–80; and grass
    monocultures, 205, 228; "hyper-
    developed," 21; river, 119–20; sheep
    and cattle grazing and, 65–68, 71,
    252; of the Tsembaga, 249–51
Edlin, H. L., 247
Elcho, Lord (later earl of Wemys), 78–79
Eliot, George, 8
Ellice, Edward, 77
Emerson, Ralph Waldo, 257
Empire: and environmental effects, 3,
    20–23, 91–94, 252–56; and free
    trade, 3, 16
Engels, Friedrich, 9
Engineering, 108, 133; popular attitudes
    toward, 104–6, 115, 123–24; and
    science, 120; on urban problems,
    190–91, 193
Environment/environmentalism, 18, 22;
    balance between contending uses,
    3–6, 8, 70, 100–101, 210, 230–34;
    concern of state for, 122–25, 131,
    134, 140–41; consciousness of,
    5–6, 19–20, 23–26, 104–10, 120,

Environment/environmentalism (*cont.*)
    188–89, 248; distinction between
    "environmentalism" and "environ-
    mentalist," 19, 33; as global concept,
    20–21, 35–38, 97; popular environ-
    mentalism, 187; remaking, 105, 123;
    and tourism, 82, 210–14, 230, 252.
    See also Coastal erosion; Ecology/
    ecosystems; Erosion; Landscape; Min-
    ing; Nature
Erdmenger, Dr., 236
Ernle, Lord. *See* Prothero, Rowland
Erosion, 109; as geomorphological agent,
    21–22; soil, 23, 58–59, 67–68, 70,
    93, 107, 109; and tourists, 212–14.
    See also Coastal erosion
Evans, Mr. (of Old Hill), 160
Evans, Oliver, 238
Excavators (earth-movers), 6, 115–17,
    120–21, 123, 150. *See also* Dredging
Exmoor, 73, 82
Eynsford, Kent, 159

Fairbrother, Nan, 101–2
Faraday, Michael, 163
Fawcett, Henry, 24, 199
Fawley, 248
Ferguson, Eugene, 5
Fertilizers, 11, 54, 63, 75, 150, 158; ani-
    mal manure, 41–44, 48, 53, 59, 64,
    168, 251; artificial, 41–44, 51–52,
    251, 253, 257; mineral, 43–44, 59–
    60, 64, 70–72, 105, 125, 146–47,
    235, 251. *See also* Agriculture
Fife, John, 136
Findhorn Bay, 247
Fisher, William Rogers, 151, 185–86
Fleetwood, Peter Hesketh, 219
Fletcher, T. W., 55
Folkstone, 233
Forbes, Arthur, 88–90
Forests/forestry, 252; amateurism and, 5,
    83–84, 86–91; arboriculture and
    silviculture, 15, 80, 87–88, 89–91,
    277n.13; conifers, 3, 16, 81, 90–91,
    94–95, 99–100, 102–3; 167, 185–
    86; and conservation movement, 28;
    Danish, 98; Forestry Commission,
    80–81, 84, 86, 100–101, 247; gov-
    ernment and, 80–81, 97–103; hunt-
    ing and game in, 89–90; in India,
    22–23, 28, 88; in Ireland, 98–99;
    Prussian, 98; machinery in, 93; New
    Forest Act of 1877, 101; in North
    America, 91–93, 96–97; recreational
    uses and, 102–3; reform critique of,
    86–91, 101–2; in Scotland, 77, 80–
    82, 95; and the state, 94, 97–102;
    trees as symbols, 87, 94–97; in up-
    lands, 80–81. *See also* Landscape:
    forests and
Forster, W. E., 183
Forwood, William, 122
Fowler, Robert, 74, 76
Fowler, W. H., 225, 227
Francis, John, 106–7
Franklin, T. Bedford, 40–42, 58, 60–61
Fraser, James, bishop of Manchester,
    178
Freeling, Arthur, 112

Gadgil, Madhav, 91
Garden cities, 163, 192, 219–20. *See
    also* City: green spaces in
Gaskell, Elizabeth, 9, 29, 145, 209
Gibson, Alexander, 23
Gimlingham, C. H., 70
Gladstone, William, 92
Godwin, George: appreciation for urban
    values, 196; attitude toward parks
    and green spaces, 197–99; belief in
    social amelioration through architec-
    ture, 196–97; as editor of *Builder,*
    196; on effects of urban density,
    196–98, 202; on gardening and
    window boxes, 199–203; on rail-
    way time, 20; on uncultivated green
    spaces, 203–4
Golf: boom of 1880s and 1890s, 224;
    suburbanites attracted to, 215, 224–
    25, 227–28, 240
Golf courses, 15, 240; and countryside
    conservation, 229–30; as grass mono-
    cultures, 228; Musselburgh, 225;
    resistance to, 227; St. Andrews, 224–
    25; as social and physical barriers,
    223–24, 230; from utilitarian to pic-
    turesque, 225, 227–28
Gooch, Thomas, 47
Gothic revival, 254
Granite industry. *See* Quarrying indus-
    tries: granite in Scotland
Graves, John, 180
Grazing. *See* Upland grazing
Green revolution, 251
Grosvenor, Robert, 199
Grouse shooting, 77, 79. *See also*
    Forests/forestry: hunting and game in
Grove, Richard, 23
Guha, Ramachandra, 91
Guyot, Arnold Henry, 36

Hackwood, Frederick, 155–56
Haggard, Henry Rider, 246–47

Hallsands, 237–40, 242–43, 245
Harley, C. K., 45
Harrison, Robert, 96
Haussmann, Georges-Eugene, 198
Hawkes, Jacquetta, 7–8
Hawksley, Thomas, 172
Hawthorne, Nathaniel, 220
Head, Francis Bond, 105, 145
Head, George, 143–46, 164–65, 219
Heath Society, 156–57
Heleselkab. See Heath Society
Henry, Augustine, 160
Herne Bay, 245; choice of respectability, 217; development as seaside resort, 215–16; shoreline protection for, 241–43. See also Coastal erosion; Railways: as shapers of seaside resorts
Hesketh, Charles, 218–19
Highland and Agricultural Society, 74
Hill, George Henry, 185
Hill, Miranda, 25; defense of Thirlmere, 178
Hill, Octavia: defense of Thirlmere, 178, 181–82; help in forming Commons Preservation Society, 24; and Kyrle Society, 25; and National Trust, 179; promotion of small gardens and playgrounds, 199; view of nature, 181–82, 188. See also Commons Preservation Society; Preservation: as organized movement
Holderness coast, 233, 243–44
Holland, Henry, 29–30, 32–35; review of Marsh, Man and Nature, 28–35
Holme Fen, 59
Hoskins, W. G., 17
Hough, Michael, 192, 205
Hove, 233
Howlett, C. E., 236–37
Huddersfield, 171
Hughes, Thomas, 114
Hunter, Robert, 24, 178–79, 182, 199, 204
Hutchinson, Horatio, 224–25, 227

Imperial Chemical Industries (I.C.I.), 131–32
Innovation, 18, 24; conservative attitude toward, 14–15, 39, 49, 53, 105–8, 253–57. See also Technology
Insularity, 20–23, 26, 234–35
Ireland, 20; forestry, 96, 98–99; land reclamation, 82, 245; potato growing, 68
Isle of Man, 211
Iveagh, viscount (Edward Cecil Guinness), 85

Jackson, John, 237–39
Joad, C. E. M., 101
Johnson, I. C., 235
Johnson, Samuel, 212
Jones, David, 22
Jones, Eric, 21
Jones, Merfyn, 141
Jones, Robin Huws, 163–64. See also Lower Swansea Valley: reclamation project
Jubb, Joseph, 243
Jutland, 98, 157

Kay-Shuttleworth, James, 210
Kemnay Quarry, 136–37. See also Quarrying industries: granite in Scotland
Kettering, 149
Kindleberger, Charles, 73
Knight, Frederic, 73, 82
Knight, John, 73
Knockboys, 98–99
Kohl, J. G., 213
Kyrle Society, 25

Lake District: Friends of the Lakes, 183; landscape, 2, 110–11, 175–76; projected railways into, 2, 107–8, 255; reservoirs in, 25, 168, 174–88; tourists in, 176, 211, 215
Landes, David, 11
Landscape, 12, 17, 148–49, 213–54; agricultural, 52, 57–58; changing perception of, 24, 26–28, 78–79, 84–85, 111–14; as cityscape, 189–208; contrasts in, 153–54; forests and, 10, 16, 24, 80–81, 83–86, 94, 96, 100–102, 252; industrial, 143–44, 161–62, 165; of parks, 194–96; quarrying and, 16–17, 125–27, 138–40, 142; reservoirs in, 168, 182–83; steam machinery and, 5, 16, 49–50, 253–54; as text, 65, 69, 256; tourism and, 214–15; "traditional" ideal of, 5, 10–12, 16, 52, 83–84, 86, 100–103, 106, 149, 230, 254–56; of United States, 15, 30–31, 153–54; upland grazing and, 65–67, 69; as work of art, 18, 244–45. See also Blight, industrial; City; Preservation; Quarrying industries: effect on environment; Railway building; Railways
Lavergne, Léonce de (Guilhaud), 53, 79
Lawes, John Bennet, 43, 49
Lawns, 15, 194–5, 198, 204–5, 219–20; introduction of mower to, 205; as simple monocultures, 205
Leech, Bosdin, 120–21

Leland, John, 212
Leopold, Aldo, 103
Lincoln, Abraham, 29
Liverpool, 20, 133, 139, 175, 202; and
     Manchester Ship Canal, 117, 120–
     23; and popular leisure industry,
     210–12, 218–19, 221–23
Lloyd George, David, 16
Lodge, Oliver, 157. *See also* Midland
     Reafforestation Association
Loftie, W. J., 192
London, 126, 196, 251; cemeteries, 137;
     gardening in, 199–203; parks, 193–
     95, 198; and popular leisure industry,
     210, 217; search for pure water in,
     169; street improvement in, 135–36,
     198–99; railways and, 135, 190;
     retreat of country from, 205–8; as
     world trade center, 20–21, 252
Lovat, eighteenth earl of, 81–82
Lowell, James Russell, 28
Lower Swansea Valley, 6, 152; dereliction
     in, 161–63; reclamation project, 161,
     163–65. *See also* Blight, industrial;
     Reclamation, land; Waste
Luddism, 15
Lyell, Charles, 28, 124
Lyme Regis, 233

MacDonagh, Oliver, 3
Macdonald, James, 72
Machinery, 95; age of, 1, 12, 13–14, 83,
     124, 253–55, 262n.17; dredges, 117,
     119, 231; excavators (earth-movers),
     6, 115–17, 120–21, 123, 150; farm,
     44–51, 58–59, 72–76, 82; impact on
     nature, 1, 9–10, 13, 15–18, 35, 104–
     11, 143–44; and landscape, 5, 8–10,
     49, 52–53, 101–2; limitations of, 4,
     12–14, 18, 46, 82, 92, 141, 253. *See
     also* Agriculture: railways and steam
     power in; Railway building; Railways;
     Steamboats; Technology
MacIver, Lewis, 123
McLennan, John, 74
Manchester, 20, 120, 167, 202, 209;
     and popular leisure industry, 210,
     218–19, 223; and Thirlmere, 174–
     88; Water Corporation, 25, 169–71,
     176–77, 180, 184–88
Manchester Ship Canal, 115; debate over,
     117–23; digging of, 115–17, 133;
     Ship Canal Bill, 121–23. *See also* Ma-
     chinery: excavators (earth-movers)
Marsh, George Perkins, 53, 97, 103, 134,
     165; belief in progress in nature to-
     ward equilibrium, 32, 39, 251; biog-

raphy of, 29; and forest management,
     33, 38, 119; influence of, 28; on new
     way of perceiving nature and land-
     scape, 26–28, 36–38, 103, 119; re-
     view of *Man and Nature,* 28–35; on
     unexpected consequences of human
     action, 17, 26–28, 251; views on con-
     sequences of deforestation, 119–20
Martin, John, 139
Marx, Leo, 15
Massingham, H. V., 45
Mayhew, Henry: on retreat of the coun-
     try from London, 205–8
Mechi, George, 47–51, 58
Medway Valley, 126
Mendip Hills, 63–65, 67
Metropolitan Public Garden Association,
     193
Middlesborough, 147
Middleton, Hugh, 169
Midland Reafforestation Association,
     157–61
Miles, Roger, 100
Mining, 131, 153–54; impact on envi-
     ronment, 143–46, 252; industrial
     structure of, 146–48. *See also* Quar-
     rying industries; Waste
Mond, Ludwig, 131–32. *See also* Alkali
     manufacture
Montagu, John, Lord Montagu of
     Beaulieu, 248
Morris, William, 9, 179, 192
Morton, Julius Sterling, 159
Mosley, Oswald, 169
Mount-Temple, Lord, 199
Mumford, Lewis: coiner of term "carbo-
     niferous capitalism," 12; on 1851
     Crystal Palace Exhibition, 7; on
     George Perkins Marsh, 36; on study
     of urban geomorphology, 191
Murray, Kenneth, and Strath Tirry proj-
     ect, 73–74

Nash, John, 194
Nasmyth, James, 152
National Sea Defence Association, 241.
     See also Coastal erosion: defenses
     against; Herne Bay
National Trust, 179, 187
Nature, 121, 125–26; George Perkins
     Marsh on, 26–28, 30–32, 36–37,
     62; improvement of, 181–83, 186,
     219–20, 245–46; lost contacts with,
     7–8, 15, 96, 197, 229; mastery over,
     31, 83, 96–97, 104–7, 124–25,
     143–46; Octavia Hill on, 181–82;
     powers of retaliation, 32, 106–7,

145, 172, 174, 221; as remedy for urban ills, 38, 78–79, 192–205, 210; sacred places in, 107–8, 179; stewardship over, 31–32, 178, 255–56; taming of, 119–20, 195–96, 204–8. *See also* Ecology/ecosystems; Environment; Marsh, George Perkins
New Brunswick, 93, 252
New Forest, 102
New Zealand, 28
Nicholson, Norman, 186
Nicholson-Lord, David, 195
Nobel, Alfred, 135
Norfolk Broads, 126
Northwich, Cheshire. *See* Salt industry
Nottingham, 202–3

Olwig, Kenneth Robert, 37
Ontario, 91–92, 96–97
Orr, Willie, 81
Osborne, Edward, 111
Osborne, Frances, 151
Otis, William Smith, 115

Palmerston, Henry John Temple, third viscount, 247
Park, Willie, Jr., 225, 227
Parker, John, 212
Parks, 15; and commons, 204, 206; design and function of, 194–99, 203–4; Finsbury, 208; Regent's, 194, 198; St. James, 198, 207; Victoria Park and urban renewal, 194–95, 198, 203–4
Paxton, Joseph, 222
Peak District National Park, 82
Pennant, Richard, 140
Pennethorne, John, 193–95
Penrhyn Quarries, 140–42. *See also* Quarrying industries: slate in Wales
Perkin, Harold, 24
Pheasant shooting, 79, 90
Phipps, R. W., 91–92
Pinchot, Gifford, 32
Playfair, Lyon, 49, 182
Pollution, 158, 165, 168, 200; from chemical manufacture, 17, 132–34, 162–63; Control of Pollution Act of 1947, 134; Deposit of Poisonous Wastes Act of 1972, 134; Noxious Vapours Commission, 162; of water, 117–19, 168–69, 176. *See also* Lower Swansea Valley: dereliction in; Waste
Poole, 233
Potteries, the, 17, 207
Preservation, 96–99, 229–30, 254; conceptual framework, 106–8, 188; definition of, 5; as organized movement, 25–26, 101, 166, 177–88; railways and, 105; as Romantic conservationism, 188. *See also* Conservation; Environment: consciousness of; Nature
Preston, 221–22
Prince, Hugh, 47, 57
Prothero, Rowland (Lord Ernle), 44, 47, 55
Prout, John, 50–52
Pugin, Augustus Welby, 9, 254

Quarrying industries, 124–26, 147, 252; china clay in Cornwall, 125–26; effect of steam on, 134–35, 141–42, 150; effect on environment, 138–41; granite in Scotland, 135–38, 167; slate in Wales, 16–17, 126, 134–35, 139–42, 167, 213; and tourism, 126, 137–38. *See also* Alkali manufacture; Landscape: quarrying and; Salt industry
Quebec, 91

Rackham, Oliver, 71, 82
Railway building: cuttings and embankments, 105–6, 109, 110–12, 114–15, 280n.2; drainage, 109–10; environmental impacts, 106–12, 189–90; fears about, 105–8
Railway companies: Bristol and London, 109; Great Northern, 168; Great Western, 114, 117; Kendal and Windermere, 2, 107, 176; Liverpool and Manchester, 107, 112; London and Birmingham, 105–6, 108–13, 117, 119; London and North West, 149–50; West Lancashire, 115
Railways: effect on agriculture, 13, 16, 49, 57, 104–5, 109; impact on environments, 8–9, 16, 104–7, 214–16, 252; and lengthening of food chain, 11, 21, 44, 57, 60, 167–68, 251–52; and perception of landscape, 111–14; and popular tourist industry, 6, 12, 211–16, 217, 223–25, 300n.27; and recreation opportunities, 210, 230; and resource blindness, 207; and sense of time, 12, 20, 111–14, 214; as shapers of seaside resorts, 17, 215–16; and urban congestion, 17, 189–90, 295n.1. *See also* City; Communications technology; Machinery; Steam: in manufacturing and transport; Technology
Rambling, 78, 103, 187, 214; and golfing, 228–30; kinship with German Wandervogel movement, 229

Ramsey, Harold, 241, 243
Rappaport, Roy: concept of historical
    change, 250–51; on ecology and en-
    ergy use in Tsembaga society, 249–
    51; model of modernization applied
    to Victorian and Edwardian Britain,
    251–57
Rawlinson, Robert, 173
Reclamation, land, 40–41, 72–76, 98–
    99; coastal, 219, 232, 235, 243–48;
    era of, 161, 164–65; in areas of in-
    dustrial blight, 144–65; landlords
    and, 4–5, 147–51; quarrying and,
    138–39, 140; the state and, 147–
    48, 155–59, 161, 164; structural re-
    straints on, 146–47; support for,
    144–45, 157–61; trees as agents of,
    150–52, 158–61, 185–87, 246–47.
    See also Black Country; Coastal ero-
    sion; Lower Swansea Valley: reclama-
    tion project; Midland Reafforestation
    Association; Waste
Reid, Clement, 245
Rennie, Charles, 137
Repton, Humphry, 256
Reservoirs, 50, 142, 168, 252; Bilbury,
    171–72; Bradfield (Dale Dyke Dam),
    173–74; Gorton, 169–70; in Lake
    District, 25, 168, 174–88; Longden-
    dale Valley, 169–71, 173; proposed
    Howeswater-Thirlmere, 176–77;
    Thirlmere, 177–88; Windermere-
    Ullswater-Howeswater complex, 187–
    88. See also Dams; Landscape: reser-
    voirs in; Water resource development
Restoration. See Reclamation, land
Rhyl, 240, 242–43, 245
Richards, Eric, 73
Richie, Robert, 39
Richmond, duke of, 54–55
Ritter, Karl, 36
Rivers: Clwyd, 240; Dee, 136; Etherow,
    169–70; Humber, 233, 243–44;
    Irwell, 117–19, 121; Lea, 168; Lox-
    ley, 174; Medlock, 169; Mersey, 117–
    23, 218; Miramichi, 93; Mississippi,
    22, 122; natural, 119–20, 245; navi-
    gation, 117–18; Ouse, 243; pollution
    of, 117–19, 168–69, 176; Ribble,
    17, 219, 221–22; Schuylkill, 238;
    Thames, 137, 168–69, 176, 194,
    199, 217, 245; tides and estuaries
    of, 119–23, 248; Trent, 243; Twae,
    162; Weaver, 127–28, 133. See also
    Dredging
Roberts, Charles Gay, 71–72, 76
Robinson, William, 198

Rolleston, George, 97
Roosevelt, Theodore, 32
Roscoe, Thomas, 110
Rosenberg, Nathan, 14
Rownsley, Hardwick, 187, 199; co-
    founder of National Trust, 179; and
    Friends of the Lakes, 183; opposition
    to railway to top of Snowdon, 213
Royal Commission on Afforestation and
    Coast Erosion, 35, 99, 235–37, 241,
    243–46, 248
Rubinstein, David, 228–29
Rubislaw Quarries, 136–39. See also
    Quarrying industries: granite in
    Scotland
Rugby, 110
Ruskin, John, 96, 110, 254; as conserva-
    tionist and preservationist, 25–26,
    183–84; defense of Thirlmere, 176–
    81, 183–84; denunciation of utilitari-
    anism, 108; fear of environmental ef-
    fects of steam machinery, 9, 16; and
    Guild of St. George, 177; negative
    view of cities, 179–80, 192–93; on
    reservoirs, 25, 184; and Ruskinian-
    ism, 177; views on railways, 108

St. Austell, 125–26
St. Helens, 17, 166
Salford, 117–19, 223
Salisbury, third marquess of, 118
Salt industry: environmental impacts of,
    127–31, 147, 252; government inter-
    vention in, 131; and Great Subsidence
    of 1880, 127–29, 133; methods,
    129–30. See also Alkali manufacture
Sanbourne, Linley, 179
Savernake Forest, 84–86, 89, 94, 100–
    101
Scarisbrick, Charles, 218–19
Schama, Simon, 95
Schivelbusch, Wolfgang, 112
Schlich, William, 23, 88, 151. See also
    Forests/forestry: in India
Scott, Margaret, 226
Scottish Highlands, 10, 16, 47, 251; ac-
    cess to, 76–79, 214; and Clearances,
    65, 69, 75; crofter farming in, 62,
    66–68, 77–79, 81–82; deer forests,
    16, 76–82, 155; farming and
    landowning practices, 70–72, 89–90;
    forests, 80–81, 89; traditional sys-
    tems, 65–67. See also Upland grazing
Scottish Lowlands, 53, 55–56
Seaside resorts. See under specific names
Sellar, Patrick, 69
Shaw-Lefevre, George John, 24, 179, 199

Sheffield, and failure of Dale Dyke Dam, 173–74
Sherlock, Robert: on mining and quarrying, 124–25, 133–35, 140; on statistics on urban geomorphology, 191–92
Shimmin, Hugh, 211–12
Shoard, Marion, 79
Silviculture. *See* Forests/forestry: arboriculture and silviculture
Simmonds, Peter, 148
Simmons, Jack, 215
Simpson, John, 90
Slapton Sands, 232
Smirke, Sydney, 200
Snowdon (Snowdonia): slate industry in, 126; as tourist attraction, 212–14; water resources of, 176
Society for the Protection of Ancient Buildings, 24
Somervell, Robert, 177–78, 182
Somerville, Mary, 1–2
South Africa, 88, 91
Southampton Water, 248
Southport, 210; as bastion of respectability, 219, 222–24; evolution of, 217–23; golf at, 224, 228; pier, 223; setting of, 218, 220–21
Spurn Point, 243–44
Stanhope, Philip, 155
Start Bay, 232, 237–40
Steam: in agriculture, 13–14, 16–17, 39, 41–42, 44–53, 57, 73–76, 82, 104–5, 109; dredges, 115–17, 119, 238–39; drill, 141; and electric motor, 141–42; engines, 12–13, 15–16, 50, 262n.17; era, 11–13, 48–49, 83, 123, 165; excavator, 114–17, 123; in forestry, 91, 93, 141; in manufacturing and transport, 1, 3, 8–9, 11–13, 17–18, 20, 34–35, 84, 91, 166, 168, 189–90, 214–17, 251–52; in mining and quarrying, 134–35, 141–42, 150; pump, 58–59, 116, 129–31, 134, 141–42, 231, 253. *See also* Railways; Steamboats; Technology
Steamboats, 13, 16, 251–52; and popular tourism, 210, 212–17, 221, 223
Stephenson, George, 12, 105
Stephenson, Robert, 104–5, 109–10, 113
Stirling-Maxwell, John, 80–81
Stone, Herbert, 157. *See also* Midland Reafforestation Association
Storeham, 233
Stuart, A. J., 28
Subsidence, 59, 134. *See also* Salt industry

Suez Canal, 116
Sugar beet cultivation, 60, 251
Sunk Island, 243–44
Sustainability: land, 40, 61–62; forests, 33, 88
Sutherland, first duke of, 69
Sutherland, second duke of, 75; at Kildonan, 74, 82; love of machinery, 72–76, 82; Strath Tirry experiment, 72–74, 83
Sutherland, third duke of, 248
Sutton, William, 217
Swindon, 114

Taylor, Zachary, 29
Teague, Mr. (of Rowley Regis), 159–60
Technology: continuity in, 15–17, 41–42, 45–47, 115–17, 134–35, 141, 253; custom, culture, and, 14–15, 18, 39, 49, 53, 106–7, 256–57; impact on environments, 133–35, 250, 254; as instrument of reclamation, 34, 144; steam, 12–13, 58–59, 73–76, 83–84, 104, 114–17, 134, 168, 215–16; transforming power of, 2–4, 11–17, 104–5, 253. *See also* Agriculture: railways and steam power in; Communications technology; Forests/forestry; Machinery; Railway building; Steam; Steamboats
Telegraph, 20. *See also* Communications technology
Telford, Thomas, 137
Tennis, 224, 228
Tennyson, Alfred, 7
Theroux, Paul, 221
Thirlmere, 174–88. *See also* Reservoirs; Water resource development
Thirlmere Defence Society, 177–78
Thomas, W. Broderick, 182–83
Thompson, B. L., 187
Thompson, F. M. L., 42–43, 166–67, 215
Tipton, 155
Tourism: and attitudes toward countryside preservation, 210; class and, 210–12, 216–17; contention for land use, 6, 209–10, 230; damaging environmental effects of, 3, 82, 210–14, 230, 252; mass, 82, 211, 230; as popular industry, 210–11, 214; railways and, 6, 12, 215; in upland environments, 9, 82, 214
Towcester, Northamptonshire, 40
Town and Country Planning Act of 1947, 244. *See also* Coastal erosion: government and

Transhumance, 66–67
Transport: from private to public, 104, 214–16. *See also* Communications technology
Trees. *See* Forests/forestry
Tring, 109–10
Trollope, Anthony, 78
Tsembaga, 249–51, 254. *See also* Rappaport, Roy
Turner, Charles (Tennyson), 8; "Greatness of England," 12; and "Old Ruralities," 7
Turner, Joseph Mallord William, 9
Turnock, David, 81–82

Upland grazing, 82, 167; and American cotton famine, 69; contribution to soil depletion of, 63–64, 67–71; and development of commercial sheep economy, 65–71, 77–78; and moor ecosystem, 62–68, 71, 79–80; and overgrazing, 63–64, 67–72; and population increase, 68–69; spread of bracken in, 70–71; and tree farming, 77, 80–82, 102. *See also* Scottish Highlands
Urban reform, 38–39, 189–91, 193–94; and physical and moral evils of the city, 25, 38, 189, 192–93, 196–97, 210. *See also* City; Godwin, George

Vernon-Harcourt, Leveson Francis, 119
Vetch, Captain, 244
Victoria Park. *See under* Parks
Vivian, Henry Hussey, 162–63
Vivian, John, 162
Voelker, Augustus, 50–51
Von Humbolt, Alexander, 21, 36, 38

Walker, James Scott, 112
Wash, the, 235
Waste, 246, 251; animal and human, 118–19, 168–69; disposal of, 9–10, 132–33, 138, 140–41, 144–45, 148; recycling of, 138–39, 144, 146–48, 156, 158; toxic, 139, 146, 151, 158, 161–63, 165

Water resource development: at Howeswater, 175–76, 183, 187–88; landscape and, 174; Manchester and, 169–71, 173–88; role of government in, 169, 172–73; at Thirlmere, 174–88; at Ullswater, 176, 183, 187–88; and urban needs, 159, 168–69, 174–75, 252; at Windermere, 183, 187–88. *See also* Dams; Preservation; Reservoirs; Rivers
Watson, John, 64
Wednesbury, 147, 153, 155
Wells, H. G., 192, 229
Wetlands, 248
Weybridge, 229
Wheeler, W. H.: on sea defenses, 233; on tidal and river systems, 119–20, 232–34
Whistler, James McNeill, 177
Whitaker, William, 245–46
White, Walter, 237
Whittlesea Mere, 73
Wibsey Low Moor, 143–44
Wiener, Martin, 254
Wigan, 218, 223
Wild Birds Protection Act of 1880, 80
Williams, Edward Leader, 118, 122
Williams, Frederick Smeeton, 111
Willson, Beckles, 234
Wilson, Maryon, 206
Winans, William, 78
Windermere, 2, 107–8, 176–77, 183, 187–88
Winner, Langdon, 17
Winnington, Cheshire, 131–32. *See also* Alkali manufacture; Salt industry
Wohl, Anthony, 118
Wolverhampton, 127
Wood, J. M., 246–48
Woods. *See* Forests/forestry
Woodstock, Vermont, 29
Wordsworth, William, 5, 24, 110, 187; contribution to preservation movement, 176–77, 180–81; protest against construction of railway, 2, 107–8, 176, 215, 281n.9; view of nature, 5, 24, 96, 179, 255
Worster, Donald, 39
Worth, Richard Hansford, 238, 240

Compositor: G&S Typesetters
Text: Sabon 10/13
Display: Bodoni Open, Sabon
Printer and binder: BookCrafters, Inc.